J. Holmes,
World Peace Foundation,
1991

The Dynamics of European Integration

The Dynamics of European Integration

edited by
WILLIAM WALLACE

Pinter Publishers, London and New York
for
The Royal Institute of
International Affairs,
London

© Royal Institute of International Affairs, 1990
First published in Great Britain in 1990 by
Pinter Publishers Limited
25 Floral Street, London WC2E 9DS

British Library Cataloguing in Publication Data

A CIP catalogue record for this book is available from the
British Library

ISBN 0-86187-843-4

For enquiries in North America please contact
PO Box 197, Irvington, NY 10533

A CIP catalog record for this book is
available from the Library of Congress

Typeset by Florencetype Ltd, Kewstoke Avon
Printed and bound in Great Britain by Biddles Ltd, Guildford and King's Lynn.

Contents

Part IV Legal and institutional patterns

Contributors

Roberto Aliboni, Istituto Affari Internazionali, Rome
Albert Bressand, Prométhée, Paris
Richard Davy, Freelance writer, Oxford
Renaud Dehousse, European Policy Unit, European University Institute, Florence
Stanley Hoffmann, Harvard University
Robert O. Keohane, Harvard University
Kalypso Nicolaïdis, Prométhée, Paris
Federico Romero, Department of Economic History, London School of Economics
Reinhardt Rummel, Stiftung Wissenschaft und Politik, Ebenhausen
Peter Schmidt, Stiftung Wissenschaft und Politik, Ebenhausen
Philippe de Schoutheete, Belgian Permanent Representative to the European Communities
Margaret Sharp, Science Policy Research Unit, University of Sussex
Carl-Einar Stålvant, Department of Political Science, University of Stockholm
Elke Thiel, Stiftung Wissenschaft und Politik, Ebenhausen
Helen Wallace, Royal Institute of International Affairs
William Wallace, Royal Institute of International Affairs
Joseph H.H. Weiler, University of Michigan and European University Institute, Florence
Wolfgang Wessels, Institut für Europäische Politik, College of Europe, Bruges
Per Magnus Wijkman, Economic Affairs Department, EFTA Secretariat, Geneva
Bruno de Witte, University of Limburg, Maastricht, and European University Institute, Florence

Preface

European integration as a formal political process has now been under way for some forty years. The limited number of policy areas with which the institutions constructed in the late 1940s and 1950s were concerned has expanded: partly as a result of new political initiatives, partly in response to the emergence of new issues of governmental concern, partly out of the pressures of social and economic interdependence and the habits of working together. The number of governments involved has grown, and the intensity of their involvement – to measure from the allocation of ministerial time, the number of national officials drawn in, the attention paid by national parliaments and press – has immensely deepened. Greater complexity, greater diversity, higher intensity: far more difficult, therefore, for the observer to grasp the overall picture, or for the participant to stand back from the pressure of immediate preoccupations and gain a sense of underlying trends.

The postwar evolution of European political, economic and social integration was accompanied by the growth of theories of integration: at once political and academic, serving to explain but often used also to recommend. Many of the leading theorists were Americans – and many of *them* 'new Americans' seeking to apply to the continent they had left the principles they had learned in the new world. The flowering of integration theories in the 1950s and 1960s fed on the optimism and apparently rapid progress of integration in Western Europe. The decline in American interests in European integration and in Western Europe in the course of the 1970s similarly went together. The difficulties West European governments experienced in making institutional progress was taken as a sign less of the increasing complexity of the processes of formal integration than of the collapse both of the political commitment to European integration and of the conceptual framework which had supported it. West European governments seemed to have 'no trumps, no luck, no will', as Stanley Hoffmann put it.

Within Western Europe many within the member governments, and particularly within the Commission, clung to the old assumptions and the old rhetoric, even as they struggled to cope with a changing agenda. 'Political union', as Karl Deutsch had remarked many years before, served as a convenient banner under which to gather forces committed to a diversity of outcomes, from loose confederation to tight federation. Dissatisfaction with the wide gap between declared objectives, and achieved agreements between ambitious rhetoric and hard-negotiated practice, spread a sense of malaise – which was overtaken only in the late 1980s by the gradual realization that informal social and economic integration was carrying West European governments, and the Commission's Internal Market Programme, forward.

The greater the complexity of the processes of European integration, the more important it becomes to rebuild acceptable conceptual frameworks with which to order the mass of information about negotiations in progress, rhetorical demands, specific bargains struck, judicial decisions made, regulations implemented and directives translated into national legislation. Those closely involved cannot stand back from their immediate preoccupations to view the overall picture without implicit – or explicit – assumptions about the underlying dynamics. Those at a distance need an overall framework to grasp in order to interpret the partial reports which they receive. The widespread use of politically charged concepts in the European political debate – federalism, sovereignty, supranationality, integration itself – both makes the task of dispassionate definition more difficult and makes the desirability of rediscovering conceptual common ground more pressing.

This volume represents the outcome of an extended dialogue among over thirty social scientists and policy-makers, from a dozen European countries and from North America, which set out to re-examine the contributions which earlier economic, social and political theories had made to our understanding of the processes of international integration in the light of the trends observable in the 1970s and 1980s. We saw this as a ground-clearing exercise, in which the different approaches and assumptions of political scientists and economists, social and economic historians, social psychologists, lawyers, students of administration and of negotiation and bargaining would be examined and tested against the available evidence. Several of those engaged in this exercise had not previously focused on European integration as such; we deliberately set out to bring in a diversity of expertise, national perspectives and disciplines. As the chapters which follow demonstrate, we have not yet reached any single consensus, let alone evolved an agreed model of the interrelated dimensions of European political, economic and social integration. But in the course of our vigorous discussions over successive drafts we learned a great deal from each other, as the links between the different chapters demonstrate. The dynamics of European integration derive from the interaction of multiple activities, private and public, channelled by a multiplicity of rules and institutions. Any approach to understanding must therefore be in large part a collective enterprise, seeking to compile a comprehensive picture from the unavoidably partial views of each of the participants.

My own conclusions about long-term European trends which came out of this project are set out at greater length in *The Transformation of Western Europe* (RIIA/Pinter, 1990). The main objective of this study was, however, to encourage and provoke a wider debate on the underlying dynamics of European integration, and also to encourage further work on its inadequately explored social, legal, technological and political dimensions. It is the surface phenomena which always attract attention: the unanticipated impetus of the

1992 programme, the dilemmas facing the EFTA governments in the negotiations to define a 'European Economic Space', above all the turning-away of Central and East European societies from the Soviet Union towards Western Europe. It is far harder to discern the underlying trends, even with hindsight. But practical men all have their own implicit assumptions about underlying trends, which guide their conduct of day-to-day policy. It is the task of the analyst to make those assumptions explicit, and to test the concepts which guide policy against the available evidence.

The three working conferences out of which this volume arose took place in Ebenhausen in September 1988, in Brussels in April 1989, and in Florence in September 1989. The Stiftung Wissenschaft und Politik (SWP), the Belgian government and the European University Institute (EUI) were our hosts for these meetings. The Thyssen Foundation provided the core funding for the collective enterprise. Additional funding came from the (British) Economic and Social Research Council, the SWP, the Paul-Henri Spaak Foundation, the Commission of the European Communities and the EUI. Michael Palmer, Mark Blacksall and Martin Böcker also contributed papers, not included in the present volume, to our discussions. Others who took part in one or more of our conferences included Peter Katzenstein, Paul Thibaud, Leon Lindberg, Peter Ludlow, Alan Milward, Michael Palliser, Christian Thune, Martin Brands, Loukas Tsoukalis, Jerome Vignon, Nicole Dewandre, and staff and students of the European University Institute.

I am grateful to Clare Pyatt for providing administrative and organizational support from Chatham House for the project and its succession of working conferences; to Marie Ciechanowska for managing relations with our far-flung contributors as deadlines loomed and revisions came in; to Eileen Power for editing the final manuscript; and as always to Pauline Wickham for her advice and expertise on converting a set of papers into an edited volume.

Reinhardt Rummel helped define the project from our first discussion in 1987, and was my host for a month's stay in Ebenhausen. Philippe de Schoutheete, Albert Bressand, Loukas Tsoukalis, Margaret Sharp and (above all) Helen Wallace contributed advice and criticism in shaping the project, and subsequently provided encouragement and written comments as it proceeded.

The events of the autumn and winter of 1989–90 took place as we were revising our papers for the press. Where necessary, the chapters which follow have been revised to take into account developments up to spring 1990. When long-term trends begin to move with the apparently desperate speed of these months, it might seen rash to commit analyses of integration to paper in any final form. But the magnetic attraction of the core European economy for the countries of Eastern Europe, the pressure for social and cultural contacts, the evident impact of technological change on the economies of socialist Europe, and the real difficulties which the new governments will face in coming to terms with the established habits of behaviour and rules which govern the intense interactions among West European countries give us, on reflection, strengthened confidence in the emphases of our study.

May 1990   WILLIAM WALLACE

1 Introduction: the dynamics of European integration
William Wallace

Europe has changed remarkably in the 45 years since the devastation of 1944–5. Economic recovery has been accompanied by a degree of economic integration among West European countries far beyond that which the protected national economies of the interwar years permitted, or the more open European economy of the nineteenth century witnessed. Social interaction has mushroomed with increasing prosperity and education, through new networks of mass transport and telecommunications. New political structures have been erected, alongside Western Europe's re-established nation-states: to manage European security, coordinate economic development, promote democratic values, encourage social integration and combat the problems of crime, drugs and terrorism which accompany rising cross-border interactions.

One of these structures, the European Community, was constructed with the broader political aim 'to establish the foundations of an ever closer union among the European peoples', even 'to substitute for age-old rivalries the merging of their essential interests; to create, by establishing an economic community, the basis for a broader and deeper community among peoples long divided by bloody conflicts; and to lay the foundations for institutions which will give direction to a destiny henceforward shared'.[1] This was political institution-building as a strategy: to promote economic integration, in the expectation that social integration would accompany it, that the interests and loyalties of elites – at least – would thus be progressively transferred from each nation-state to the broader institutionalized community, which would in turn 'lay the foundations' for an eventual political union. It was a process which implied a beginning and an end: from and beyond the nation-state to the eventual achievement of European union. In the circumstances of the early 1950s, 'considering that world peace [and national survival] can be safeguarded only by creative efforts commensurate with the dangers that threaten it', with Western Europe still heavily dependent on the United States for economic support and military protection, the vision of 'an organized and vital Europe' regaining through union the independence and economic strength which its individual states had lost had a powerful appeal.[2]

1

European union, as envisaged in the 1950s, was limited to Western Europe: economic and political integration under American protection, with active American encouragement, within a framework of rules for international economic interaction laid down under American leadership. The relationship between (Western) European union and Atlantic solidarity was, from the outset, ambiguous and ill-defined. American attitudes ranged from assumptions of European recovery to equal partnership to hopes that a revived Western Europe would allow a progressive reduction in American military commitment. European attitudes ranged from ambitions to achieve full partnership with their American patron and protector to dreams of a Europe free from both the 'superpowers'.[3]

Eastern Europe was on the other side of the 'iron curtain', forcibly integrated into the soviet 'bloc'. Germany, the centre of prewar Europe, was divided between the two: its long-term future another matter for ambiguity, its West European partners repeating their formal commitment to reunification as they worked to lock its Western zones into a West European structure. For the past 40 years, 'Europe' has largely been used as a term for Western Europe: a usage both confirmed and qualified by the reorientation of the countries of 'East Central Europe' towards it at the end of the 1980s, their intellectuals talking of 'rejoining the West', their political leaders of reclaiming their place 'in Europe'.[4]

Those who promoted this broad 'federation de l'Ouest' had originally hoped to encompass within the boundaries of their enterprise all those European countries outside the control of Soviet troops which shared 'le même réflexe de refuser le déclin économique qui conduit à la perte des libertés': the 16 countries which met in Paris in July 1947, under the leadership of Britain and France, to respond to the Marshall 'Plan'.[5] Between 1947 and 1957 that broad community had become the loose outer circle around a more tightly institutionalized core: the countries of the Rhine valley and delta, together with Italy. Nevertheless, the strategy was pursued, in the confident expectation that others would apply to join as the original members moved ahead. The confidence of the strategists of European integration was supported by the growth of intellectual theories of integration, from both economists and political scientists.

Thirty years later, the unilinear assumptions of the early proponents and theorists of European integration have long since given way under the pulls and pushes of Community bargaining. The unification of Europe has achieved no final form. On the contrary, the structure and shape of Europe has become more indeterminate, as the Community itself has expanded, and as the 'European space' – that imprecise phrase so frequently used by policy-makers in the 1980s to describe patterns of economic, industrial, social and educational interaction – has so evidently extended across a wider area: to include the six member states of the European Free Trade Area and the Community's several Mediterranean associates, most of them members with the EC states of the OECD and the Council of Europe. Economic integration has drawn *all* the European member states of OECD together into what must now be described as a regional economy. Social interactions across frontiers within this region have expanded enormously, with little distinction between those within and those outside the EC. Even before the political developments of 1989–90, the impermeability of the East–West boundary – as Chapter 8 describes – had begun to yield to the gravitational pull exerted by Western Europe's economic advances, technical superiority, and social and political appeal, spreading across Eastern Europe with trade, tourism and modern communications: raising the prospect of a far wider European space, its structure and boundaries far more indeterminate.

Political integration has moved forward in fits and starts: from the euphoria of the first confident years after the Treaties of Rome to the deadlock over de Gaulle's challenge to the Commission's supranational pretensions and 'Community method'; from the *relance* of the Hague Summit of 1969, after de Gaulle's departure, the launching of the ambitious project for Economic and Monetary Union, the completion of the Community's budgetary arrangements, and the first enlargement, to the divergent reactions of member governments to the economic and politicial storms which hit Western Europe in 1973–4; from the more tentative initiative of the European Monetary System to the *relance* of the 1980s represented by the '1992' Programme and the Single European Act.

The core EC of 6 has grown, after two rounds of enlargement, to 12. A third round is unavoidable during the 1990s, with a lengthening queue of declared and undeclared candidates shuffling into place. The revival of the seven-nation Western European Union in 1984 (and its expansion to nine in 1989), the emergence of the five-nation Schengen group, the larger memberships of such diverse bodies as the 'Eureka' technology partnership and the anti-drug *Groupe Pompidou*, even the re-emergence of political interest in the Council of Europe as a forum for associating the states of East Central Europe with an integrating Western Europe, suggest a more diffuse network of integration than any imagined by Jean Monnet or Ernst Haas.[6] It is hardly surprising that the political *and* intellectual debates about the dynamics and direction of European integration at the end of the 1980s lack agreed concepts or frames of reference. The speed and diversity of change, the diffuseness of the formal and informal processes under way, are such as to leave widespread disagreement about underlying trends, let alone about their political and economic implications.

The aim of this study has been to lay the foundations for a more informed intellectual debate, by identifying as far as we can recent economic, social, administrative and institutional trends in European integration, and drawing some preliminary conclusions from those we identify. It has brought together some 30 participants, from a range of backgrounds and intellectual disciplines, to consider papers presented at a series of three conferences in 1988–9, the majority of which are published below. We set out our objectives at the outset as:

(1) to map the observable patterns of political, economic and social interaction within Western Europe; taking the centrality of the Community framework as an issue to be investigated rather than an *a priori* reality; and taking the distinction between the West European region and broader Atlantic and global networks as similarly to be explored through examination of the available evidence.

(2) to examine the degree of congruity or non-congruity between the different
    patterns observed, and to draw inferences where possible about the links
    between them.
(3) from this, to examine the role and function of the Community as an
    institutional framework within the overall processes of European inter-
    action; deliberately working from a broad definition of Europe inwards
    rather than from Brussels outwards, to explore how far the Community
    framework 'fits' or shapes underlying patterns of economic, social and
    political relations.
(4) to begin to rebuild the conceptual debate on European integration on the
    foundations provided by the accumulation of evidence on current trends
    and on the relationship between formal and informal integration.

In attempting to 'map' Europe, we have, therefore, come closer to the
approach adopted by Karl Deutsch in the 1950s and 1960s than to any other of
the early economic and political model-builders, with their greater certainty
about the direction of the trends which they were studying.[7] We were
conscious that perspectives on 'Europe' depend not only on the place where the
observer stands but on the features which she is trained to identify. We
therefore brought together a group from several different European countries
and from several different disciplines of social science; and included some
American scholars of international relations, and some whose primary interest
had not previously been in European integration, in order to guard against the
biases which all scholars accumulate about their preferred field of study.

Some of the indicators we would have liked to include proved too difficult to
assemble within the limits of a twelve-month project. There is much more
to be done on the psychological dimension of 'mental maps' of Europe,
discussed further below: the imprecise but symbolically significant issue of
European values, self-identification, inclusion and exclusion. There is more
to be done in tracing the rapidly changing patterns of ownership, production,
management, and industrial collaboration, which are discussed by Albert
Bressand and Kalypso Nicolaïdis in Chapter 2. Nevertheless, we hope that the
reader will come away from this volume with a clearer image of the changing
shape of the European region and of the dynamics of change, on which to build
a more informed analysis of the interaction of political, economic and social
factors in international integration – which has been one of the central issues in
both intellectual and the political debate since the emergence of a West
European region in the aftermath of World War II.

As the study proceeded, the relationship between an increasingly integrated
West European region and the other half of Europe began to change,
increasingly rapidly in the autumn and winter of 1989-90. These unanticipated
political developments have not, we concluded, undermined the approach of
this study; indeed, they have in many ways confirmed it. What emerges from
the chapters which follow is the centrality of Germany within Europe, and the
centrality of Western Europe in Europe as a whole: not only in terms of the
European economy, but also in terms of social interchange, security policy,
technological developement, and links with third countries. Western Europe *is*
core Europe; Eastern Europe is regaining its place as part of its periphery.

The structure and dynamics of European integration in the 1990s will be profoundly affected by the reintegration of these excluded countries into the European order which has developed since the 1950s. But the very strength and intensity of the rules, economic links and patterns of social and political interaction which are outlined in the chapters which follow suggest that the continuities will be stronger than the discontinuities, and that the best guide to likely evolution in the 1990s may be provided by an understanding of the forces which have pushed Western Europe together, and which are now pulling Eastern Europe towards it.[8]

The transformation of postwar Europe

The postwar Western Europe for which American and European policy-makers designed the original structures of Atlantic and European cooperation was one in which iron and steel occupied the commanding heights of the industrial economy; in which the railways were the key to inland transport, and river and coastal traffic the key to trade; and in which agriculture employed a quarter or more of the working population in all but a few countries. Until the social disruption caused by the war, only a tiny minority of the population of European countries had ever travelled beyond their national boundaries. Military service, forced labour, deportation, had taken millions of people, unwillingly, for the first time outside their familiar local worlds. International mass communication had begun with the propaganda radio broadcasts of the axis powers in the 1930s, and the BBC's wartime response.

Armed conflict was succeeded by armed confrontation and the perceived threat of internal subversion. The governments of Western Europe drew together in the hope of American protection and aid and in the face of a clear and present danger from the external and internal Communist threats. Torn between their determinedly national frames of reference and their awareness that Europe's nation-states had failed separately to provide either security or prosperity, those who had most directly experienced the destruction of the war argued for an alternative focus of authority and loyalty, while those who had escaped the worst accepted the need for new structures for international cooperation alongside the nation-state.

Nearly half a century later, their children have grown up into a different Europe and a different world. Electronics has displaced the old 'heavy' industries as the key to industrial advance. Telecommunications now carry much of the traffic of financial and service trade, air transport a rising proportion of personal travel. The European economies of the 1960s, relatively autonomous and responsive to the instruments of national economic management, have given way to a regional European economy, in which governments both inside and outside the EC have painfully discovered the limits of autonomous action. The institutional frameworks of the EC and OECD have set the context for the growth of this highly integrated European economy. But it has also been shaped by innovations in production processes and management practices, which have enabled companies to manufacture and market on a continental scale; and by improvements in communications, most crucially through the radical impact of the revolution in telecommunications on corporate structures, on marketing information and techniques, and on financial markets.

Greater prosperity and better communications have also 'shrunk' Western Europe, as elites – and to a lesser extent broader mass publics – have become accustomed to watching each others' television programmes, to crowding through each others' airports, criss-crossing the continent on its connecting motorways, and jostling each other in Europe's summer and winter resorts. As Federico Romero sets out in Chapter 10, the scale of these intra-regional movements, for business, study, and pleasure, is of a qualitatively higher level than a generation ago, and is still increasing. As it adjusts to these flows Europe is acquiring a *lingua franca*, with the advantage – and disadvantage – of sharing that international language not only with North America but with the rest of the world. The positions of French and German as Europe's leading international languages and bearers of its distinctive cultural and intellectual traditions have been challenged, not only in Western Europe but also in Eastern Europe, by the spread of English as the medium for 'European' newspapers and international television and for more and more of the expert and technical material published for an international audience.

The international environment which imposed upon Europe its postwar shape has also shifted very substantially. In retrospect the period between 1955 and 1965 – the years in which the institutions of West European integration took shape – may have been the Indian summer of European centrality in the international system: when economic recovery had been achieved, without any challenge yet visible from East Asia; when Europe's pivotal position in the structure of global security remained unquestioned, while that structure evolved through short-term crises towards a degree of stability; when the relationship between the West European countries and their North American partners thus in effect defined the 'free world', facing a closed socialist bloc, with a defined group of neutral states in between. The apparent certainties and stabilities of that brief period had eroded in the course of the 1970s and 1980s, well before the events of 1989-90 registered their disappearance. In parallel with this shift in Europe's political and security position the rise of the East Asian economies has changed the shape of the global economy, leaving European countries and companies with a more modest share of world manufactures, trade, and services.

The rapidity of this transformation has left us attempting to adapt to new demands, institutions and concepts which were designed for past circumstances. The Treaties of Rome were drafted in the context of theories of economic integration developed in the postwar years, as well as in the expectation that nuclear power would succeed coal as the key source of energy. Different issues have come to preoccupy the agenda of intergovernmental business – many of them directly posed by the consequences of the economic and social transformation we have noted above. Those concerned with the competitiveness of European industry took 'le défi Americain' as their benchmark, not – as in the 1980s – 'le défi Japonais'. The pollution of the Rhine was one of the few environmental issues on the European intergovernmental agenda in the 1950s. The consequences of rising levels of cross-border movement and of highly developed and rapid communications networks have become matters with which European governments are actively engaged, from data protection to financial fraud, from the drugs trade to responses to refugees.

The scale of economic, political and social change since the late 1950s has – we argue – transformed the quality and character of international integration from that which was envisaged by those who constructed the institutions of postwar Europe. One need only recall that at the beginning of the 1960s no direct dialling links between European national telephone networks existed, that most people who travelled across the Atlantic and the North Sea went by ship, and that containers had not yet replaced port labour in handling international trade in goods.[9] Some observers insist that the impact of technological development, in particular of information technology, is sufficiently radical in its consequences to constitute a 'second industrial divide' comparable to that of the nineteenth-century industrial revolution.[10] Others argue more modestly that the decline of American economic dominance and the rise of the 'trading states' of East Asia is creating an international economy which no longer fits the conventional models of liberal economic theory.[11] Theories of economic integration appropriate to the relatively undirected market forces of 30 years ago, based upon the classical trade theory assumptions of comparative advantage, no longer fit the technology- and corporate strategy-driven forces which drive the contemporary international economy; 'the reigning paradigm . . . is embarrassingly at variance with the facts', leaving an 'extraordinary gap between international trade theory and international macro-economics'.[12] That, in turn, leaves us with 'a growing gap between the reality of economic integration and the conceptual and political framework in which we are used to think about it'.[13]

Conceptual and political frameworks, however, are resistant to change, except under the pressure of determined action from central authority or under the bitter experience of political revolution or other social cataclysm. The dominant political concepts remain those of nations and states, of sovereignty and autonomy, in Europe as in the rest of the world – in some ways *more* in Europe than in the rest of the world, since it was in Europe that these concepts developed and became deeply rooted. 'The nation-state is the twin of the industrial society', the product of the technical and economic changes which transformed Europe in the course of the nineteenth century, and of the social consequences of those changes; outmoded – Poul Schlüter has argued – by 'the phasing-in of the information society to replace the industrial culture and industrial technology which have served us so well for almost 200 years'.[14] Some will accept Lothar Späth's admission that 'politicians are determining the rhetoric, but industrialists are determining the reality'.[15] But the experience of the past 30 years suggests that the relationship between political and economic developments is by no means as straightforward as the normative theorists of European integration were arguing in the optimistic years after the signing of the Rome Treaties. Politics follows its *own* logic, not simply those of economics and technology.

The transformation of the global economic and political environment also carries implications for the conceptual framework of European integration. The apparent stability of a region within an American-led alliance and an American-led liberal international economy has given way to a more diverse and uncertain world. For some 'the reality of the closing years of this century is that the world of the democracies is increasingly a world of three centres of power', in need of an 'institutional framework for consultation and coordination among those power centres'.[16] Others see the regional impulse as giving way before the dynamics of a global economy, in which geographical considerations are losing their importance. Informal, politically undirected economic evolution, technological and social change have also had a cumulative impact on the formally stable structures of the global political system and economy. European governments are not unique in having to adjust; political leaders in the United States, the Soviet Union, Japan, even China, are being forced to re-examine their assumptions about the international system and their place within it.

Structures and markets: formal and informal integration

The relationship between politics and economics, between states and markets, has been a matter of intense controversy since the modern world first developed. 'Markets constitute a powerful source of sociopolitical change and produce equally powerful responses as societies attempt to protect themselves against market forces.'[17] Alexander Hamilton argued for a strong central authority in the proposed constitution of the United States as essential to protect American interests against the dominance of the British economy. Karl Marx argued that political and social developments followed economic change, and constructed both a theory of history and a political strategy on that basis. Liberal economists from Adam Smith on have argued that states should interfere as little as possible in the operations of markets, since 'it is the market economy, together with the framework of laws and institutions that enables it to function effectively, which serves to establish order, while *ad hoc* discretionary interferences by governments are a source of disorder.'[18]

Ay, there's the rub: for the framework of laws and institutions does not emerge through the invisible hand which eighteenth-century rationalists believed to govern the markets, but has to be created and maintained. The postwar Western international economy was created and maintained under American leadership, to serve enlightened American security and political interests. Successive initiatives to create a tighter framework of laws and institutions within Western Europe won American support as compatible with these broader interests, while attracting some of their European support precisely because they offered a means of diminishing dependence on American patronage. The ambivalent political objectives which were built into the project of formal European integration from the outset depend partly on divergent views about the liberal and benign, or mercantilist and politicized, nature of international markets and the rules and institutions which order them.

The failure of the theorists of economic and political integration to resolve issues which had vexed generations of theorists before them should thus be put in context. Mitrany, Haas, Lindberg were closer to the idealist than the realist tradition of international relations. But the economists who dominated Atlantic debate on market integration were similarly in the idealist tradition of liberal economics; 'the classic argument for free trade', after all, 'rests on a model of the world in which there is assumed to be perfect competition, absence of market impediments, ample time for markets to adjust, and given technology.'[19] The policy-makers who made the model of an integrated European Community a reality have related to the idealized theory as closely as their trade negotiator colleagues have to *their* conceptual framework: creating, as Helen Wallace observes in Chapter 12, a stable structure for bargaining even as they repeat their commitment to a higher aim. Rhetoric and reality, ideology and practice, intertwine in any discussion of international developments, economic or political.

'There is', Karl Deutsch remarked, 'apt to be confusion about the term "integration".'[20] The working definition adopted here is of the creation and maintenance of intense and diversified patterns of interaction among previously autonomous units. These patterns may be partly economic in character, partly social, partly political: definitions of *political* integration all imply accompanying high levels of economic and social interaction. The question of expectations, of common identity or consciousness, of the emergence of a 'sense of community', is the most contested, because the most difficult to measure. Daniel Frei saw this, alongside social interaction and institutionalized political decision-making, as an essential component of political integration.[21] Karl Deutsch defined integration as 'the attainment, within a territory, of a "sense of community" and of institutions and practices strong enough and widespread enough to assure, for a "long" time, dependable expectations of "peaceful change" among its population'.[22] Frequency of contact, breadth of interactions, were among his measures of the emergence of 'dependable expectations'.

A distinction is drawn here between informal and formal integration. Informal integration consists of those intense patterns of interaction which develop without the impetus of deliberate political decisions, following the dynamics of markets, technology, communications networks, and social change. Formal integration consists of those changes in the framework of rules and regulations which encourage – or inhibit, or redirect – informal flows. Informal integration is a continuous process, a flow: it creeps unawares out of the myriad transactions of private individuals pursuing private interests.[23] Formal integration is discontinuous: it proceeds decision by decision, bargain by bargain, treaty by treaty.

Functionalists and federalists, internationalists and nationalists, have argued at length about the relationship between the two.[24] All accept the importance of formal structures of international rules and intergovernmental collaboration in encouraging or inhibiting informal transactions across national borders. All, equally, accept that informal flows alter the expectations and demands of those who benefit from them, leading to pressures to alter formal structures which stand in the way. The divergence is over the balance between the push of formal institution-building and the pull of informal interaction; and, conversely, over the ability or inability of established formal structures – national governments – to channel and limit informal flows. This divergence, one of the great unanswered and unanswerable questions of theories of integration –

unanswerable because it rests upon different conceptions of human behaviour and values – has direct relevance to policy.

The political strategy which Jean Monnet and the Action Committee for a United States of Europe followed in the 1950s, in relaunching the project of formal European integration after the collapse of the European Defence Community, was one of indirection, of *engrenage*.[25] Establish an institutional framework with limited authority, they planned, and the reorientation of personal links among elites and of economic interests among mass publics which would accompany rising informal flows would in time create political pressures to transform Europe's key institutional structures. The disillusioned report in 1975 from Robert Marjolin – one of Monnet's close associates in the 1950s – that 'experience up to now shows nothing that supports the validity of . . . the idea which has been the basis of the past twenty years of the views of many Europeans, namely that European political unity, particularly in the economic and monetary field, will come about in an almost imperceptible way', pointed back from Monnet's 'functionalist' approach to the formal institution-building 'federalist' approach.[26] 'What may be required', his report went on, 'in order to create the conditions for an economic and monetary union is . . . a radical and almost instantaneous transformation . . . giving rise at a precise point in time to European political institutions.'

Since then, however, the economic and monetary integration of Western Europe – not only of Western Europe institutionalized within the EC but also of OECD Western Europe as a whole – has moved forward a good deal further, with governments adjusting to market- and technology-led developments through successive modest rule changes, reluctantly accepted even by those national governments most determined to defend the principles of national sovereignty. The argument remains, vigorously contested, at the centre of the political debate about the future organization of the European region, as to whether such 'practical' and piecemeal adjustments are sufficient of whether radical institutional transformation is necessary.

It is far easier to agree on the interconnection between deliberate processes of political integration and informal processes of economic and social integration than to establish any clear line of causation between them. The formal structures of Western Europe in the late 1980s do not match the observable patterns of economic flows – nor the less clearly visible patterns of European mental maps, subjective assumptions about identity and community. Sweden and Switzerland are, on most economic and social measures, more clearly part of a Western European region defined by the intensity of its interactions than either Portugal or Greece; yet for reasons of history, national identity and security policy the latter two are full members of a formal Community which the former two have so far resisted joining. Flows of European citizens across national borders have risen far faster than the capacity of European governments to construct new rules to govern their movement. The proliferation of *ad hoc* intergovernmental groupings to cope with the different problems thrown up, and of *ad hoc* cooperation between police and customs agencies, testify to the struggle to catch up. Failure to implement the Treaty of Rome clauses on transport has inhibited but not prevented integration of Europe's transport systems. The pressure of numbers, the consequent build-up of frustration at delays, has already pushed governments into responding in the road transport sector, where the lorry drivers' blocking of frontiers enforced intervention, and is likely to work a similar effect in air transport as flight delays increase public discontent at the inefficiencies of national air control over Europe's cramped and crowded airspace.

There are, we may suggest, two different types of formal integration: the responsive, and the proactive. Much of the detailed work of intergovernmental cooperation can be seen as responsive: recognizing the need to adjust rules to changing economic and social trends, and setting out to amend regulations which were appropriate to the nationally focussed economies and societies of 30–50 years ago but which have been transformed into obstacles by informal developments since then. The arguments for managing such amendments on a European rather than a wider OECD basis are twofold: first, that the greater intensity of interaction within the West European region makes it the 'optimum area' for common rules and political management; and second, that the weight of the US economy (and the complexity of the US political system) makes bargaining over rules within the OECD/GATT system a game in which the USA still holds an undue proportion of the trump cards.

Proactive formal integration has a more deliberate and explicitly political aim: to redirect informal flows into patterns other than those which market forces or social trends might have created. The clearest examples of proactive formal integration within Western Europe in the 1980s, as we would expect, are in the technological field: ranging from the European Space Agency to 'Eureka' and 'Esprit'. Repeated French initiatives since the Fouchet Plan of 1961 to redirect the preferred pattern of cooperation in foreign policy and defence away from an Atlantic to a European framework, first through the creation of European Political Cooperation (EPC) and then through the revival of Western European Union (WEU), have met with resistance from partners reluctant to jeopardize the American commitment; but the evolution of EPC since its establishment, against many sceptical initial expectations, *has* progressively altered European and transatlantic patterns of foreign policy-making.[27] Continuing arguments among West European governments about the detailed implementation of the 1992 programme – most of all about its external implications, about the degree to which it should set boundaries to the benefits of European market integration and about the character of financial and monetary integration – reflect disagreement among the participants about how far these rule-setting exercises should go beyond adjusting to informal trends towards attempting to direct them into different patterns. The Single European Act, that very European compromise between hopes for major institutional reform and fears of national loss of control, was seen by some of its signatories as a practical response to changing circumstances, by others as a deliberate exercise in shifting national policy-making into a tighter European frame; leaving the protagonists to bargain over the direction of its implementation.

The institutional framework within which Western Europe began its post-war recovery was provided most directly by the OEEC, and less directly by the US-led international economic organizations, the IMF and the GATT. The security framework which provided the confidence and stability within which previously antagonistic countries could pursue long-term economic relationships was that of the Atlantic Alliance – 'Europe's American pacifier', as Josef Joffe has unkindly but accurately named it: extending security not only to the European members of NATO but also to the European neutrals, whose security was held in place by the tension between the two alliances.[28] The creation of the ECSC, and much more the creation of the EEC, provided an institutional core to the European region of this Atlantic economic and security community, sufficiently strong to attract other countries towards it, both through association agreements and through applications to join. But that did not *displace* the wider institutional environment. And it is open to argument how far it was idealism and political vision which drove the proponents of a tighter European structure, as against a sober recognition of the underlying dynamics of a reviving European economy in which the German economy would once again emerge as its core: anticipating and adjusting to the geographical advantages which Germany possessed, the skills of its workforce and the potential of its industry, and setting out prudently to build a structure which could contain, and to some extent redirect, the impact of Germany's recovering strength.

Europe, which Europe?

In the optimistic years of the 1960s there was a tendency to equate the concept of Europe with the European Community. Politicians and intellectuals wrote books on 'the European idea'; solemn declarations were made about 'the European identity'; conferences and colloques considered the same theme.[29] Most twisted their definition to fit the current size and shape of the EC. Thus 'Europe' took on a broader identity as additional countries joined the original six. Many of those outside the EC adopted the same terminology; politicians called on their governments to 'join Europe', while others declared themselves vigorously 'anti-European'.[30] In the more fluid international environment of the 1980s alternative Europes re-emerged. 'Europe from Aberdeen to Athens', the Europe of the EC, was complemented by 'Europe from Helsinki to Heraklion': the Europe of the EC plus EFTA, or more broadly of the Council of Europe and European OECD. Broader than that, the shadows of *Mitteleuropa* and of Catholic Christendom were again becoming visible, that 'Europe from Dublin to Lublin' in which both Irish and Poles would find protection against their larger neighbours. Broader still was the image of 'Europe from Vancouver to Vladivostock', the framework of the Conference on Security and Cooperation in Europe: a European northern hemisphere, almost, to which leaders as disparate as Mikhail Gorbachev and Margaret Thatcher have appealed.[31]

There is no single or agreed Europe: different frames of reference, and different explicit or implicit preferences, draw different boundaries. A map of Europe which is based upon its political contours – memberships of alliances and economic organizations – will highlight some features, showing clear boundaries between those inside and those out. Maps based upon geographical contours or on economic or social interaction will highlight other features, with border areas less sharply defined. The contours of cultural Europe are the most passionately disputed, with undertones of religious and political conflicts and of the clash between nationalist tradition and cosmopolitan elites. The Atlanticist concept of 'the free world', sharing the democratic values inherited from the Renaissance, the Enlightenment, and the American and French Revolutions, competes with the concept of a distinctive European society, in which democratic values are blended with a social consensus and concern which – the protagonists argue – the North American culture has rejected.

Part of the problem we face in defining 'Europe' is that for much of the non-European world in the nineteeth-century 'Europeanization' was synonymous with 'modernization': following the examples of Britain, and Germany, and France, acquiring the mixture of technical skills, urban social organization, and 'modern' values needed to compete with these leading countries in a period when they dominated the world. Japanese elites, therefore, dressed in top hats and frock coats, and learned European styles of dancing alongside European methods of chemical and steel production. Kemal Ataturk forbade the wearing of traditional Ottoman dress as part of his drive to transform Turkey into a modern, and therefore European, state. Peter the Great had followed the same path earlier; with the same determination to acquire the skills and social habits needed to compete with the dominant powers of Western Europe, without accepting in full the 'dangerous' political and social doctrines which some European countries had also developed. If Europeanization and modernization were synonymous then, are not 'Americanization' and modernization synonymous now, and for the same reasons of the economic weight and consequent political and cultural influence of dominant powers? The integration of the global economy and of global communications networks is infinitely more highly developed in the 1980s than in the 1900s; and the European region is no longer the centre either of the global economy or of the international political system.

The specificity of the European region is best defined, we argue in this study, not by the claimed uniqueness of history or of ideology, but by the *density* of interactions and the *geographical concentration* of its core countries. The EC of 12 member states occupies a territory 25% the size of the USA, containing a population 140% of the American. Inclusion of the EFTA countries in such a calculation increases marginally the ratio of territory to population, while adding a further 20% to 'Europe's' comparative economic weight. If we accept the definition of 'core Europe' as the countries of the Rhine valley and delta, the geographical concentration and the density of cross-border interactions is even more striking. There is no other grouping of countries which begins to approach such an intensity of interaction; comparisons seem most appropriate with the north-eastern region of the United States, though it may well be that there, too, one has to include Eastern Canada within an integrated economic and social system in which traditional inter-state boundaries are similarly becoming less and less relevant.

But like the north-eastern corner of the North American region, it is easier to discribe Europe's core than its outer limits. The one clear boundary, observable in terms of Karl Deutsch's definition as a marked discontinuity in the flow of economic and social interactions, is between OECD Europe and CMEA Europe. To the West, the North and the South, core Europe shades into less intense interactions with other countries. The gravitational pull of the core European economy has brought the Scandinavian countries into more and more intense relations with it, and has reinforced the dependent relationship of the Mediterranean periphery, with a network of links which ties these countries more tightly to central Europe than to each other. More weakly, across the firm boundaries of the East-West divide, the same process can be observed, pulling the countries of East-central Europe towards the European core. Chapters 7 to 9 explore these border areas of the European region further.

To the West the strength of the North American economy (and society), however, exerts a gravitational pull of its own, offering European governments, companies, elites an alternative network of interactions which has also developed remarkably during the past two decades. And beyond North America there lies East Asia, producing goods which European consumers are increasingly keen to buy, following the trail of American companies in investing in Europe, and holding out to European companies the attraction of strategic alliances and direct investment in the most rapidly growing region of the international economy. From these external developments flow some of the most difficult and value-laden issues which face the governments of core Europe: how far to accept and adjust to these broader informal flows, or rather how far to attempt to regulate and redirect them into other patterns, politically preferred.

The question of boundaries is central to any study of political systems, legal jurisdiction, or economic or social interaction. 'From it all others flow. To draw a boundary around anything is to define, to analyse and reconstruct it, in this case select, indeed adopt, a philosophy of history.'[32] But 'Europe', as we have seen, has never had clear or settled boundaries. Nor, for most of their history, have most of Europe's contemporary states. There were in the Europe of 1989 only ten states with substantially the same boundaries as they had had in 1899 – and that included no state larger than Spain.[33] The fluid geography of Germany, at the centre of almost any definition of Europe, reinforces the point we wish to stress: that the nation-states which constitute Europe are themselves almost all imprecise entities with moveable boundaries. Pomerania, Schleswig-Holstein, Alsace, Silesia, the Trentino, Bohemia, Austria, the German cities in the Slav lands, all testify to the contingency of 'Germany' as a political, even geographical, entity.

So too with Europe, however defined: the observer can identify certain core areas, but not mark out precise or permanent outer limits. The evidence of this study indicates that Germany and its neighbours in the Rhine Valley and across the Alpine passes constitute the contemporary core of Europe, in terms of economic interaction, social interchange and security focus. Historical 'Europes' have largely revolved around the same broadly defined area. The core of eighteenth-century Europe was on most measures to be found in France, then Europe's most populous and wealthy state. The nineteenth-century industrial revolution spread across the continent from Britain into Belgium, the Rhineland, northern France and northern Italy. Part of the ease with which the definition of Europe and of Western Europe was elided in the postwar years, under the forced delimitation imposed by the division of military forces in 1945 (or, by the agreements the three wartime superpowers signed at Yalta), was that

Western Europe included almost all the core territories of political, industrial, financial and cultural Europe of the previous 300 years.

The EEC/ECSC of the Six institutionalized – and strengthened – this core area. The creation of EFTA, the negotiation of a network of association agreements with Mediterranean countries, similarly institutionalized the relations between this political and economic core and its immediate periphery. Expansion of the EC since then has altered the institutional pattern – but, the chapters which follow suggest, not yet reshaped the underlying relationship between core and periphery. Karl Deutsch and his research team concluded from their historical comparisons of the growth of political communities that 'political amalgamation . . . usually turned out to be a nuclear process', in which 'larger, stronger, more politically, administratively, economically and educationally advanced political units were found to form the cores of strength around which in most cases the integrative process developed.'[34] Germany and its immediate neighbours were naturally the focus for the most determined efforts to build a European community to contain national rivalries. It was painfully apparent to France and the Low Countries both that a reviving Germany, even a divided one, would again become a dominant factor in the European economy – and so potentially in European politics – and that they had no alternative but to make the best of their unavoidable entanglement with it. Germany was thus both a negative and a positive factor in the dynamics of European integration: negative, in that fear of the destructive potential of a revived but uncontained Germany was a driving consideration in the minds of the French, Belgian and Dutch politicians as they negotiated the institutional framework for European cooperation; positive, in that as the intensity of such fears subsided the weight of the German economy, the stability of the D-Mark, the competitiveness of German manufactures and capital goods, drew other European countries towards it.

Successful economies, political systems, empires and alliances expand. Unsuccessful ones contract. The same is to be expected of international political communities and regional economies. So, it appears, the West European community has expanded, both formally and informally, its success attracting its neighbours to identify with it. How then should we attempt to measure its spread? Three complementary approaches appear desirable, following the definition of integration proposed by Daniel Frei: through institutional structure and the network of formal bilateral and multilateral ties; through the intensity of significant interactions, economic, social and political; and through the existence of what Deutsch from his studies of national integration called a 'sense of community', of dependable expectations about anticipated behaviour without mutual distrust. The first is the most straightforward. The second is the subject of the majority of contributions to this study. The third is by far the most difficult to measure, however significant in predisposing politicians and publics to cooperate with each other, to share mutual benefits and to accept mutual obligations.

Common interests, common values

Values, loyalties, shared identities are the stuff of political rhetoric, and of intellectual and cultural history. They are, however, the most difficult phenomena for social scientists to study. Economists prefer to exclude them altogether, substituting a model of rational man entirely motivated by calculations of interest. Political scientists and sociologists cannot take this conveniently reductionist way out. Authority, legitimacy, community, all moderate the naked pursuit of power and interest in societies and political systems; the strength or weakness of shared values tipping the scales between solidarity and disintegration when interactions appear to impose more burdens than benefits.[35] The political strategy of *engrenage* rested upon assumptions about the significance of loyalty and of the potential transfer of loyalties from one structure of authority to another. Those who resisted that strategy most vigorously, from de Gaulle to Thatcher, appealed beyond economic interest to the psychic realities of national identity, in order to combat attempts to create an alternative European myth.

Value systems, it should be emphasized, are not static. They are created by shared experience, by learned traditions, by political leadership. Successful policy performance, plus persuasive political rhetoric, builds common identity; unsuccessful performance undermines it. Western Europe's patchwork of national identities and loyalties is not a 'natural' creation; the contingency of Swiss, Dutch, Austrian or West German identity is evident, and the nineteenth-century imposition of British, Italian and Spanish national values and loyalties on their component regions has not totally submerged alternative identities. Postwar initiatives for West European integration rested on a number of explicit values, which their proponents claimed as core European values: plural societies, limited and democratic government, mixed private and public economies. On this foundation was constructed not only the framework of formal institutions which defined Western Europe and the rising tide of informal interaction which this open framework allowed, but also a rhetoric of European identity and community intended to underpin the hard bargaining of economic and political interests with a symbolic 'cement' of shared loyalty and purpose.

Much of this rhetoric was fanciful, particularly in the early years of the political movement for European integration. It presented a 'Sunday clothes interpretation' of European culture, in which 'historiography threatens to become a political pamphlet'.[36] As an attempt to create a new myth, it was a movement of intellectuals, dependent on politicians to propound their preferred interpretation of reality to the mass public – like so many nineteenth-century nationalist movements in their early years. Its failure to capture the imagination of more than a small minority within Western Europe reflected three things. First was its failure to hold the attention of most political leaders within even the core countries of Western Europe – once the first postwar enthusiasms for ideals acquired in the bitter schools of prison camps and exiles had given way before the immediacies of national electoral politics. It also reflected both the lack of the power and authority needed to impose its interpretation on the school books and literature of the different states, and the absence of any sense of grievance or injustice with the status quo comparable with that upon which so many nineteenth-century nationalist movements were built.[37]

For those who saw loyalty to a European entity *replacing* loyalty to seperate nation-states, the basis for full European political integration has not yet been built. For those who saw the strategy of *engrenage* encouraging the development of multiple loyalties, in which the mental maps of European citizens would add an additional dimension to those national and regional loyalties they already possessed, the evidence suggests that 'a sense of solidarity' has developed which clearly approaches Deutsch's definition of a sense of community: but, sadly, there is so far very little evidence.[38]

But here again, deliberate political action has been accompanied by informal private interaction. Human movement, cultural intercommunication, also reshape mental maps: as was, of course, the case during the growth of European nationalisms in the eighteenth and nineteenth centuries. From the creation of the Council of Europe, with its modest cultural exchanges and town-twinning schemes, to the ambitious programmes of Franco–German exchanges, governments have acted on the assumption that increased inter-action under conditions of mutual trust does change attitudes; and the evidence on Franco-German exchanges and their impact supports this.[39] As Chapters 10, 11 and 13 indicate, such interactions on a regular and frequent basis under mutually trusting conditions remain, however, much more a matter for European elites than for the mass publics who travel for tourism alone: raising the prospect of a growing division between cosmopolitan elites and nationalist non-elites across Western Europe. This is an area which we did not explore further within the confines of this study – but one which needs much further exploration.

Values and myths, as we have argued earlier, are significant not only in holding existing political systems together, but also in shaping and reshaping imagined communities. The claim to 'European' status has clear political significance, both to those who claim it and to those who attach the label to others. It sets the context for assumptions about rights and obligations in relations among governments within the region – and also for popular assumptions about anticipated access and mutual behaviour. The contingency of European identity is most evident for states on the periphery of the West European core: as is the political significance – and potential economic benefit – of acceptance as European. Article 237 of the Treaty of Rome states imprecisely that 'Any European state may apply to become a member of the Community'. The definition of a European company; the acceptance of European public and private bodies into organized initiatives to improve 'Europe's' competitive position in high technology; the acceptance of applicant governments into European arrangements for collaboration in security policy, defence, and military procurement, and the acceptability of membership in such arrangements to the national publics concerned; the imposition of standards of expected behaviour in political and civil rights higher than those expected of non-European countries; the definition of the boundaries of a future Europe-wide security system (within 'our common European home'); all these depend upon assumptions about the defining characteristics, not only geographical and economic but also political and cultural, of Europe as an entity.

For countries such as Turkey, or Iceland – or Romania, or the Soviet Union – the claim to be European, and the implications in terms of rights and obligations of asserting that claim, are of major importance. For Austria and Sweden, on the edge of core Europe in so many ways, it has become a matter of intense national debate.[40] For Spain the pressures to join both the European Community and the Western European Union were a mix of economic interests and of determination to reassert Spain's 'role' as a major European country. Here, as in so many other ways, the Swiss present a special case. Confidently situated in the geographic and economic centre of Europe, they do not feel the need to question their European identity, or to accept additional obligations in recognition of it.[41] But perhaps the most passionate in the late 1980s have been those Czech, Hungarian and German intellectuals who set out to revive the concept of 'Central Europe', as the 'Eastern border of the West': claiming to draw the boundaries of 'our' Europe to include the territories of German, Hungarian and Catholic influence, while leaving Orthodox Europe outside.[42] The boundaries of 'our' Europe are in the minds of its inhabitants; the mental maps which move men in Berlin, or in Belgrade, overlap with those which predominate in Belfast or Brest, but they do not coincide.

The definition of Europe in terms of values and shared community is necessarily and unavoidably subjective: the outcome at any moment of political persuasion, cultural development, and popular interaction. It is always easiest to define a community by differentiating it from outgroups: thus, Europe stops where 'Asia' and 'Africa' begin; or where 'Christian' – or Catholic – culture gives way to other creeds; or where the inheritance of the 'Enlightenment' and the 'democractic revolutions' (or of Napoleon and the French Revolution) ceases to be shared. The problem with all of these definitions is how to distinguish European values and identity from those of 'Europe across the Atlantic', which so evidently shares so many of them. There is perhaps an underlying divide on this between European elites – particularly intellectual elites – and mass European publics, with the latter happily absorbing American culture even as the former struggle to construct a distinctive European model. But it is also possible that perceived differences of political outlook – both in foreign policy and in domestic priorities – and of economic interest, as widely spread at mass as at elite level, will in time translate into perceived differences in values between the two sides of the Atlantic as well.

In centralized national political systems such as France and Great Britain, where strong national governments imposed a single identity on subordinate cultures, there is a natural tendency to see the growth of a European identity in terms of the transfer of loyalties, *tout entière*, from one level of authority to another. The realities of communal, ethnic and national identities have in almost all societies been more complex – and confused – than this, with multiple levels of affinity and loyalty. We should expect to observe a particularly confused pattern of loyalties during a period of rapid economic and social change, the reassertion of traditional values paralleling the growth of new.Recognition of a European frame of reference may complement recognition of other frames: Bavarian, for example, as well as German, and even 'free world'. The significant question for students of political change is to measure, as far as is possible, the relative strengths and weaknesses of these multiple loyalties; recognizing that these, too, develop and decay over time.

Patchwork of regimes, or political system?

We are the prisoners of our concepts. Politicians and political scientists in the 1960s assessed the integration of Europe in terms of the most familiar model of a political system which they had: the modern nation-state, with stable patterns of policy-making and sovereign authority, effectively enforced within clearly established boundaries, and encompassing a coherent national society. The diffuse networks of interaction which hold Europe together fall far short of this ideal type. But so, of course, do most states: the arc of national crisis from Belgrade through Sofia and Bucharest to Warsaw and the lands of the Soviet Union illustrates how far many states fall short of the accepted model.

The alternative available model was that of the international system, based upon cautious cooperation in the pursuit of national interests among sovereign states. The Gaullist onslaught on the proponents of European union asserted the reality of this preferred conceptual model. In practice sovereignty was always conditional and relative; the British and French governments, most strongly attached to the principle, have found themselves compromising in sector after sector over the past 30 years.[43] It is more useful to think in terms of a continuum than of a sharp divide, between intergovernmental cooperation among sovereign states and subordination within a supranational political system: a continuum which stretches from limited cooperation based upon separate national interests, through extended cooperation 'in dense policy spaces' within regimes which 'contain norms and principles justified on the basis of values extending beyond self-interest, and regarded as obligatory on moral grounds by governments', to political communities based on relatively stable structures of bargaining, legal authority, and popular acceptance.[44]

Looking back on the hopes and expectations of the 1960s, it is striking how many of the optimistic assumptions about political integration made then would seem commonplace today. Leon Lindberg considered 'the essence of a political community' to be 'the existence of a legitimate system for the resolution of conflict, for the making of authoritative decisions for the group as a whole'; and defined political integration as 'the process whereby political actors in several distinct settings are persuaded to shift their expectations and political activities to a new centre'.[45] Within the EC framework, such system and process were vigorously challenged during the 1960s; but in the 1980s they were becoming an accepted reality, as ministers, officials, interest group representatives, national and European parliamentarians trod the familiar paths of Community bargaining and legitimation.

But neither the domestic nor the international environment of the late 1980s fits so easily into the language and concepts of 20 to 30 years before. The new Europe of 1990 differs radically from the 'New Europe' which enthusiasts for European integration were proclaiming a generation ago.[46] It interacts *far* more intensively, economically and socially; and that interaction is likely to intensify further within the next decade. But the dynamics of such integration are not peculiar to Europe: interaction within national societies and economies, and within the global economy and its associated network of social transactions and communications, has also grown, responding to the same technological and economic changes. What is distinctive about Europe is, first, the concentration of prosperous, educated and skilled populations within such a small geographical area; second, the creation of a relatively stable institutional network for intergovernmental bargaining for the accommodation of shared interests across a very broad agenda; and third, the existence of common traditions of history, culture and political values, to which political leaders and institution-builders can appeal for support in legitimizing the rules they have agreed to implement and the burdens they have agreed to share.[47]

The dynamics of European integration thus depend *both* upon the informal pressures of undirected economic and social forces and on the formal channelling of those forces into particular directions. The structures of NATO and of the OECD set the wider institutional context for these informal flows. The OECD in effect set the outer boundaries of the region, but only because it rested on assumptions about shared political values and shared security – the European neutrals being held in place by the balance which NATO provided – as well as on shared rules of economic behaviour. But the emergence of a more tightly integrated and institutionalized core area has pulled the region more closely together: a gravitational force which has attracted the peripheral countries of the European region towards it.

Successive waves of applications for Community membership, the developing network of miltilateral and bilateral agreements between the EC and other European countries, indicate a pronounced tendency towards convergence of institutionalized bargaining around the Community framework. Confusion between 'Europe' and 'the European Community' may thus gradually resolve itself in a progressive identity between the two, with other non-Community countries concluding, as did Spain, Portugal and Greece on the establishment – or re-establishment – of democratic government, that 'any European state *must* apply to join the European Community'.

A number of discontinuities remain among the network of regimes which make up the broader Europe. The most evident discontinuity in the management of issue areas is the continuing separation of defence and security issues from economic and social ones. This is not, of course, a discontinuity for the countries of the institutionalized core: except for the anomaly of Ireland, all are members of the Atlantic Alliance, all except Greece and Denmark are members of WEU, and all (except perhaps these three countries of the 'inner periphery') appear to accept a strong implicit linkage between defence and security commitments and the other benefits and obligations of European cooperation. But it remains a major issue for such countries as Austria and Sweden, wishing to exclude this crucial area from the diffuse reciprocity of obligations which has become the accepted language of Community bargaining.

The difficulties of drawing any clear or stable boundaries also pose immense problems for the political integration of Europe. The arguments for each new agreement, association, application are difficult to resist, often compelling; the diffusion of European cooperation which results from this spread encourages the growth of inner groups and the dissolution of diffuse reciprocity into a patchwork of specific agreements. The divide between a political system and a network of overlapping regimes must be drawn at the point where the allocation of costs and benefits, real and symbolic, ceases to be made within a common set of institutions with general responsibilities, and is undertaken through a number of separate negotiations following different assumptions and rules. The political debate within Western Europe both about the future internal structure of the EC and about the potential accession of new members at the end of the 1980s revolves around this point.

The rise and decline of political systems – and of regimes – also depends on the capacity of their institutions to cope with the demands placed upon them, to provide mutually acceptable outputs, and to grapple with changes in their environment. The more the central policy-making processes of West European cooperation demonstrate their effectiveness in internal rule-making and external negotiation, the more they will attract hesitant outsiders to accede; the broader the issue-areas they cover, the more outsiders will feel the disadvantages of exclusion. Political values provide a weapon in establishing a claim to inclusion – for a rationale for exclusion. They are available for use – and misuse – in the legitimation of decisions taken and in the building of support for burdens imposed.

Interactions between governments, economies and societies within Western Europe have moved well beyond the traditional model of relations among nation-states. Relations between Western Europe and Eastern Europe, conducted until the end of the 1980s under traditional rules and in conditions of hostility and limited mutual contact, are beginning to experience a similar transformation. The construction of new institutional regimes to manage and direct the expansion of economic and social interactions across the boundary which marked the central European divide will be decisively influenced by the capacity of the core institutional structure of West European cooperation: a structure which is gradually acquiring the stability and the coherence of a political system, under the cumulative impact of internal integration and external challenges.

Notes

1. Preamble to Treaty establishing the European Economic Community, clause one; preamble to Treaty establishing the European Coal and Steel Community, clause five. The stronger language comes from the earlier treaty (signed in April 1951, as against March 1957).
2. Preamble to ECSC Treaty, clause one, clause two.
3. Harold van B. Cleveland, *The Atlantic Idea and its European Rivals* (New York, McGraw-Hill/Council on Foreign Relations, 1966), chapters 5 and 6; Alfred Grosser, *The Western Alliance: Euro-American Relations since 1945* (London, Macmillan, 1978), chapters 4, 6 and 7.
4. William Wallace, *The Transformation of Western Europe* (London; Pinter/RIIA, 1990), chapter 2, explores the overlapping concepts of the West, of Europe and of Western Europe as they have been used in the European political debate.
5. Jean Monnet, *Mémoires* (Paris, Fayard, 1976), pp. 323, 316.

6. Ernst Haas's writings on political integration, most notably *The Uniting of Europe* (Stanford, CA, Stanford University Press, 1958) and *Beyond The Nation State* (Stanford University Press, 1964), did much to set the framework of intellectual expectations about the prospects for European integration on both sides of the Atlantic throughout the 1960s and into the 1970s.

7. Karl Deutsch's most influential contribution in this field was *Political Community and the North Atlantic Area*, with Sidney Burrell and others (Princeton, NJ, Princeton University Press, 1957).

8. This argument is developed further in *The Transformation of Western Europe*, chapter 6.

9. The first STD link in Europe was opened between London and Paris in 1963.

10. See, for one influential American interpretation, M. Piore and C. Sabel, *The Second Industrial Divide: Possibilities for Prosperity* (New York, Basic Books, 1985).

11. See, for example, Robert Gilpin, *The Political Economy of International Relations* (Princeton, NJ, Princeton University Press, 1987). The term 'trading states' is taken from Richard Rosecrance, *The Rise of the Trading State* (New York, Tauris, 1986).

12. Patrick Minford, 'A Labour-based Theory of International Trade', in John Black and Alasdair MacBean, eds, *Causes of Changes in the Structure of International Trade, 1960–85* (London, Macmillan, 1989), pp. 196, 197.

13. Albert Bressand, *1992: the Global Challenge* (Paris: Promethée Perspectives no. 9, 1989), p. 4.

14. Address by Poul Schlüter (then Prime Minister of Denmark) to the American-European Community Association, London, 20 September 1988: a very reflective contribution from a policy-maker, with repeated references to Schumpeter's approach to economic and social change. F.H. Hinsley, in his study of *Sovereignty* (London, Watts; New York, Basic Books, 1966), pp. 214–21, makes the same point about the historical contingency of the nation-state: 'the basic forces producing [the centralized state and the integrated national community] have in each case been those technical and economic changes which have steadily transformed the quality of political and social existence since the beginning of the nineteenth century, and continue to transform it.' (p. 214)

15. Lothar Späth (then Minister-President of Baden-Württemberg), quoted in *Der Spiegel*, no. 31, 1988, p. 32

16. Lawrence Eagleburger, giving testimony to the US Senate Foreign Relations Committee as Deputy Secretary of State designate, 15 March 1989.

17. Robert Gilpin, op. cit., p. 23. For a classic historical overview, see Karl Polanyi, *The Great Transformation: the Political and Economic Origins of our Time* (Boston, Beacon Press, 1957).

18. David Henderson, *Innocence and Design: the Influence of Economic Ideas on Policy* (Oxford, Blackwell, 1986), p. 101.

19. Alan V. Deardorff and Robert M. Stern, 'Current Issues in Trade Policy: an Overview', in Robert M. Stern, (ed), *US Trade Policies in a Changing World Economy* (Boston, MIT Press, 1987), p. 33.

20. Op. cit., p. 2.

21. Daniel Frei, 'Integrationsprozesse: Theoretische Erkenntnisse und Praktische Folgerungen', in Werner Weidenfield, (ed.). *Die Identität Europas* (Bonn, Europa Union, 1985), pp. 113–31.

22. Op. cit., p. 2.

23. Mica Panic labels the same process 'spontaneous integration' in his *National Management of the International Economy* (London, Macmillan, 1988), p. 142.

24. For a brief survey of the extensive literature on functional, neo-functional, federal, and intergovernmental approaches to European integration, see Carole Webb, 'Theoretical Perspectives and Problems', in Helen Wallace et al., *Policy-Making in*

the European Community (Chichester, UK, and New York, Wiley, 1983).

25. Monnet, *op.cit.,* Chapter 16.

26. Report of the Study Group, *Economic and Monetary Union 1980* (Brussels: Commission of the EC, 1975, Vol. 1, p. 5. Marjolin was the chairman of this group; it is probable that the words quoted were drafted by Andrew Shonfield.

27. William Wallace, 'Political Cooperation: Integration through Intergovern-mentalism', chapter 13 in Helen Wallace et al., op.cit.; William Wallace, 'European Defence Cooperation: the reopening debate', *Survival*, May-June 1984; Philippe de Schoutheete, *La Coopération Politique Européene* (Brussels, Labor, second edition 1986).

28. Josef Joffe, 'Europe's American Pacifier', *Foreign Policy*, no. 54, Spring 1984, pp. 64–82.

29. See, out of a *vast* literature in several languages, Lord Gladwyn, *The European Idea* (London, New English Library, 1966). The *Declaration on the European Identity* emerged from lengthy negotiations among diplomats for approval at the Copenhagen Summit in December 1973; characteristically, this unsuccessful attempt at self-definition was a response to the transatlantic challenge of Kissinger's 'Year of Europe'.

30. This habit had not entirely disappeared in the 1980s, as the Scandinavian members of EFTA considered their future relations with the EC. Several of the collaborators within this project were welcomed to a conference in Stockholm in December 1988 with the greeting 'We are very glad to have so many participants from Europe'.

31. Mrs Thatcher's telling reference to 'Europe across the Atlantic' in her Bruges speech of September 1988 stressed the importance of the Atlantic connection; though her extension of 'Europe' to the East included only Poland, Hungary and Czechoslovakia. Mr Gorbachev, in his turn, was reluctant at first to include North America within his definition of a common European home.

32. Fernand Braudel, *The Mediterranean and the Mediterranean World in the Age of Philip II* (New York, Harper and Row, 1972), vol. 1, p. 18.

33. I am grateful for this point and for much else in this section to the paper prepared by Mark Blacksell for this project on 'Images of Europe – the changing spatial context'. France did not include Alsace and Lorraine in 1899, but did include Algeria. Britain still included the whole of Ireland.

34. Deutsch, op. cit., p. 19.

35. 'Support resting on a sense of legitimacy . . . provides a necessary reserve if the system is to weather those frequent storms when the more obvious outputs of the system seem to impose greater hardships than rewards'. David Easton, 'Political Systems', in Roy C. Macridis and Bernard E. Brown, (eds.), *Comparative Politics* (Homewood, IL, Dorsey, 1961), pp. 93–4.

36. Martin Brands, 'Europe halved and united: from a split object to a restored cultural identity?', in A. Rijksbaron et al., (eds.), *Europe from a Cultural Perspective* (The Hague, UPR, 1987), pp. 77, 81. Werner Weidenfield is even sharper about the 'dualism' of the 'European idea', neatly contrasting the 'free' West and the 'unfree' East and thus wiping away the darker side of Western Europe's own history; 'Was ist die Idee Europas?' *Aus Politik und Zeitgeschichte*, June 1984, pp. 5–8.

37. The most evidently available 'grievance' out of which to build a sense of European solidarity in the 1960s and 1970s was anti-Americanism: the argument that Europeans suffered from the American-led structure of the Atlantic system, and must define themselves, therefore, through opposition to the hegemonic power. There are interesting historical parallels here; the roots of American national identity, after all, are to be found in self-conscious opposition to the corruption of 'Europe' and the hegemony of Britain. Elements of anti-Americanism floated through the European debate, from right to left, from Gaullists to Communists.

But the rising prosperity which the American-led international economy delivered throughout the 1960s left little room for passionate campaigns about economic injustice; while governmental awareness, in France as much as elsewhere, of the necessity of maintaining the US security commitment in the face of the continuing weight of Soviet forces held political elites back from resort to this weapon.

38. Miles Hewstone, *Understanding Attitudes to the European Community: A Socio-psychological Study in Four Members States* (Cambridge, UK, Cambridge University Press, 1986), pp. 201–2. Hewstone brings together the theoretical approaches of Kelman and Guetzkow with a small sample survey in depth, and contextual reference to the *Eurobaromètre* data. This paragraph draws heavily on Martin Böckers's paper on 'Mental Maps of Europe' for this project.

39. Of the extensive literature on Franco-German contacts, see Robert Picht, (ed.), *Das Bundnis in Bundnis: Deutsch-Französische Beziehungen im Internationalen Spannungfeld* (Munich, Piper, 1978), and Chapters 4 and 5 (by Caroline Bray) in Roger Morgan and Caroline Bray, (eds.), *Partners and Rivals in Western Europe: Britain, France and Germany* (Aldershot, UK, Gower, 1986).

40. See, for example, Rudolf Kirschläger, 'Auf dem Weg zu einem grösseren Europa', *Europäische Rundschau*, 1/1988.

41. I am grateful to Manfred Scheich, of the Austrian Foreign Ministry, for a succinct statement of the cultural and historical reasons for the different Swiss and Austrian stances to EC membership at the end of the 1980s: 'the Swiss made their nation against Europe; but Austria *was* Europe'.

42. Milan Kundera, 'The Tragedy of Central Europe', *New York Review of Books*, 26 April 1984. See also Karl Schlögel, *Die Mitte Liegt Ostwärts* (Berlin, Corso, 1986), for a survey of the historical and intellectual origins of this reviving image.

43. William Wallace, 'What Price Independence? Sovereignty and interdependence in British Politics', *International Affairs*, Summer 1986, pp. 367–89.

44. The quotations are from Robert O. Keohane, *After Hegemony: Cooperation and Discord in the World Political Economy* (Princeton, NJ, Princeton University Press, 1984), pp. 79, 57.

45. op. cit, pp. vii, 6.

46. See, for example, the many European contributions to Stephen Graubard, (ed.), *A New Europe? A Timely Appraisal,* special edition of *Daedalus,* (journal of the American Academy of Arts and Sciences), Winter 1964.

47. There are, of course, similar resources of history and culture to be activated in other regions: Eastern Asia, Southern Asia, the Arab world, Spanish America. But these are latent, not activated by high levels of interaction across borders under mutually beneficial and relatively stable conditions.

Part I
Economic and technical dynamics

2 Regional integration in a networked world economy
Albert Bressand and Kalypso Nicolaïdis

The current stage of European integration tends to be discussed around the political decisions associated with the Single European Act and notably around the economic measures related to the completion of the 'internal market' as charted in greater detail in the 1985 White Book. Yet, at the time of its signing, the Single Act was perceived almost unanimously as a modest step on the road towards integration. Many of the 279 measures included in the White Book had been on the European agenda for a number of years, while a number of important policies – such as the high technology cooperative research programme and the development of Europe-wide communication networks – also reflected other objectives than the creation of a unified internal market and were not part of the White Book. As for the corporate strategies that are playing a critical role in making '1992' a self-fulfilling prophecy, they have tended to develop, more often than not, in a global rather than a European perspective: the same companies actively 'preparing for 1992' by launching takeover bids across European borders and taking part in EC-sponsored R&D ventures can also be seen acquiring US companies and entering into licensing agreements with Japanese technology suppliers.

Hence the paradox of a very successful rebirth of European economic integration that was not really anticipated by those now claiming credit for it, that has broader and deeper policy roots than usually acknowledged and that fits only partially in the very European framework to which it has given renewed vitality and legitimacy. Understanding this paradox is all the more important as the present level of economic integration and its institutional framework will soon be tested, notably by the watershed changes at work in Eastern Europe and the ever tighter relationships between the EC and EFTA.

In this chapter, we argue that economic dynamics in Europe have changed quite radically since the 1960s and that this has less to do with Europe *per se* than with world-wide changing patterns of economic integration that Europe was institutionally and politically ready to explore before other regions of the world. To support this argument, we investigate the actual links among actors that give integration its substance, and we search for the qualitative changes in the nature of those links that could account for the changed dynamics of

27

European integration. While economic integration in the 1960s could be analysed in the traditional perspective of trade links and of trade-led specialization, integration in the 1980s already reflects the availability and influence of a more diverse and far-reaching set of tools, whether technical ones in the fields of communication and production or strategic ones as illustrated by the role, in corporate development, of external growth and cross-border acquisitions. In particular, and with due definition, the larger part of this chapter will be devoted to substantiating our claim that *networks*, as organizational settings for transnational economic activities, are becoming a critical dimension of global economic interactions among advanced countries and are notably playing an essential role in the changing dynamics of European integration. As defined here, networks include, but are in no way limited to, telecommunication links such as those associated with electronic markets or with Electronic Data Interchange and the development of in-depth links between producers, suppliers and customers. Also included in our definition are the various strategic links – from cooperative R & D to franchising and distribution agreements – whereby corporations can influence and seek to extract value from the web of market and contractual relations on which they depend, as well as the links developing among non-corporate actors – such as universities – to operate on a European rather than national scale.

While it would be premature to describe Europe in the 1980s as already a 'Europe of networks', we see the development of network forms of interaction across borders as an emerging but fast-growing trend, reshaping global as well as regional economic integration. What is specific to the EC context, however, is the fact that interactions are intensifying on the basis of network infrastructures and roles which are increasingly common to the political and economic spheres, as we will explore in the first section. One is then led to contrast the 'Export, Redistribute and Stabilize' (ERS) integration paradigm of the 1960s with the 'Acquire, Distribute and Network' (ADN) paradigm that can be detected behind the momentum of the 1992 programme. The implications for political integration of this change in the nature of economic integration are introduced in the last section, although a full discussion would take us well beyond the limits of the present essay.[1]

One should note that the transformations that we are attempting to describe have their origins in, and have implications for, many other issues than those addressed under the 'regional integration' heading. Deregulation, privatization and the changing role of the state are closely related issues that one could address – as we attempt to do in other settings[2] – as part of the same analysis. Indeed, Euro-believers as we may personally be, it is difficult for our generation to look at regional integration as a topic in itself that one should address under theories of . . . regional integration! As their own proponents make the case, the theories developed in the past for the study of regional integration did not lead them to anticipate the present burst of Euro-activism and actual integration. Insightful as they remain for important aspects of the new dynamics, one may indeed stress, with Keohane and Hoffmann in Chapter 16, that 'what was unpredicted by analysts working with established theories cannot, in general, be adequately explained, *post hoc*, through the use of such theories'. As attempted here through an analysis of network-based integration, one should therefore distinguish between the rain dance of *ex post, ex ante* and *ex cathedra* Euro-pronouncements and the meteorology of change that has brought about this much hoped for, and yet unexpected, rain.

Formal informality and messy formalism

European integration is a multifaceted process which can be approached from many angles. As set out by William Wallace in the introduction, one may identify two broad dimensions of 'integration', namely *formal integration* – rule-making at the political-institutional level – and *informal integration*, which 'consists of those intense patterns of interaction which develop without the intervention of deliberate political decisions, following the dynamics of markets, technology, communication networks and social exchange'.

Social scientists have traditionally explored the interaction between those two dynamics and have come to stress the powerful influence of market dynamics over intergovernmental bargains in fostering European integration in the 1970s and early 1980s. Contrasting with the failure of European political leaders during that period to implement the Monetary and Economic Union endorsed at the 1969 Hague summit as the next institutional step, the signing of the Single European Act in 1985 apparently brings formal integration back to the forefront. But is it still relevant to ask which of the political and economic processes is driving the other?

For our part, we are struck by factors of convergence, over and above mutual influence, between those 'two parallel roads that will merge some day' – in the words of Keohane and Hoffmann. While our focus on networks might, at first sight, be interpreted as a statement regarding the primacy of informal integration, the definition of networks that we use has its roots in an analysis of the increasing capacity of economic factors to set up and manage complex sets of relationships, including the creation of customized rules often rivalling in actual importance the traditional government-centred rule-making process. Networks and networking strategies can then be seen as creating new types of overlaps and synergies among the formal and informal integration processes. Such overlaps and synergies are of special importance for the understanding of the regulatory dimension of cross-border interaction – a pivotal dimension of today's integration – and appear to play an essential part in the changing European integration dynamic.

While we certainly do not see electronic highways or other inter-corporate linkages as the road to the heavens of integration, viewing the European land-scape as a set of interconnected networks of all types does point to patterns of integration that could not have been envisaged in the years of Jean Monnet and Ernst Haas. In particular, it may be that the type of institutions – such as national bureaucracies or the European Commission – that played a central role at the time, while remaining a major force, will have quite a different role to discharge in the future and will do so in a qualitatively different relationship with private actors. While networks, as we see them emerging, are most noticeable for their role in *economic* integration (not a small dimension, anyway, of European integration), their development has major implications for the very concept of integration.

'European integration' is part of a more broadly based reorganization in which local, national, regional and global levels no longer fit into one another on the neat 'Russian dolls' model of the past, but must be apprehended as an integrated whole. The importance for European companies of access to Japanese technology and to the US market – as exporters or, increasingly, as investors and acquirers – implies, for instance, that Europe is not an intermediate level, half way between the nation-state and the open global environment referred to in France as 'le grand large', but rather one dimension in the search for stronger positioning on the global market. By the same token, governments can be expected to react, even if at a later stage than corporations, to the existence of 'short circuits' and to the more complex relationships now developing between the local, national, European and global levels. Indeed, we see common roots behind the process of economic networking analysed here and the development of what Philippe de Schoutheete refers to as the 'Community network'. The networks of cooperation developed by Central Banks in Europe (as well, one should note, as within the global-minded Group of Seven) are, for instance, one of the foundations of the European Monetary System, even if a less visible one than the political agreements that they allow to be implemented. More generally, the types of arrangements called for by the governance of today's advanced societies have much in common with the types of strategies implemented by corporations to access, mobilize and share resources in today's complex, volatile global marketplace. In both cases, formal and informal interactions need to complement each other in increasingly innovative and customized fashions.

Our point, therefore, is not only the well-known observation that certain types of market interactions develop unhindered across and above borders but, also, that the set of rules and the interactions with political authorities that European actors need to take into account are acquiring a European character. Reasons for this broader change, as we see them, have to do both with subterranean changes at work globally and with specific catalytic actions that tend to have an impact in the European community context. An obvious caveat is that such developments are unevenly visible depending on sectors and countries: information technology, 'high tech' as well as a large number of services from air transport to distribution and to financial services offer more striking illustrations of corporate networking and of complex national-European-global interactions than a number of industrial sectors fitted well within the 'common market' trade-centred paradigm as understood in the 1960s. But as services concepts, electronic market links and the search for more efficient organizational approaches permeate even the more traditional sectors, the 'interconnected Europe' described in the latter part of this chapter can be expected to represent an increasing part of the emerging reality.

This chapter leaves open the question, addressed by other contributors, of whether such dynamics can lead to the watershed institutional changes that have tended to be equated with the notion of European integration. Our own view is that such watershed changes may no longer be prerequisites for integration to go beyond the economic dimension. In other words, the new dynamics of *economic* integration at work in Europe provide not only more powerful means to pursue the objectives of European political integration as understood at the time of the Treaty of Rome (and as re-expressed, notably, in the schemes of monetary union at present under consideration), but also make new types of political objectives conceivable and within reach.

The regulatory melting pot

While information technology is the most visible of the various factors accounting for the qualitative changes in economic integration patterns, a related but more fundamental starting point in such an inquiry could be the changing nature of the rules and rule-making processes shaping economic interactions. In the past, all rules tended to be equated with clear-cut legal instruments designed by legislative and executive bodies and enforced by the judiciary, with the power to shape rules seen as the result of a competitive game between governments, political parties, trade unions and organized pressure groups. By contrast, market interactions were perceived as atomistic behaviour taking place within the framework set by the political process, even when they sought to bypass it.

We see this apparently straightforward distribution of roles between actors of the political and market spheres challenged by a threefold evolution: the importance of regulation – 'the regulatory middle ground' – in the political process, the increasingly customized nature of the rules called for by today's advanced economies and the role and relationships of management in contemporary economic interactions.

The regulatory middle ground: Scholars in the field of international political economy have contributed greatly in the last two decades in pointing to the profound impact of private transnational strategies on the outcome of 'high politics'. But the middle field between (to simplify) the power of transnational enterprises on one hand and economic diplomacy on the other is mostly left to technical or sectoral appraisal. Yet, the thrust of international relations, at least among advanced countries, has increasingly to do with complex, technical, sometimes esoteric interactions falling in the broadly defined 'regulatory' domain.[3] In particular, the '1992' programme is only very partially understood in the perspective of 'political' decisions that would then be merely implemented or complemented with regulations as a second-order development. Quite often, the big political decision (such as the priority given to the reduction of capital gains tax and corporate taxes over that of personal income tax) will come in the wake of such esoteric regulations as those covering the definition of monopoly practices, the disclosure rules pertaining to takeovers or the tax treatment of UCITS (Undertakings for Collective Investment in Transferable Securities). The importance of this regulatory dimension has major implications for the relation between formal and informal integration because the process whereby the need for such rules is identified and transformed into actual regulations or self-regulations is, alternatively or concurrently, led by public or private actors. Rather than being a mere technical appendage of the political sphere, *regulation* emerges as a central steering mechanism overlapping with both the political and the economic sphere as traditionally defined and contributing to the blurring of the borders between them.

Regulatory customization: The shift from standardized to customized approaches is now a well-understood feature of the economic scene. What is less often seen is that this move from mass-standardization towards what we label 'mass-customization' also applies to rules and rule-making. Rather than a 'macro' framework in which 'micro' interactions take place, rules now tend to be both generated by actors as an intrinsic part of the routine of economic interactions and also tailored to the specific interactions to which they apply. In other words, formal (rule-making) and informal (value-creating interactions) processes are increasingly intertwined.

Relations management: While establishing and managing relationships between economic actors has always been a precondition of production and transactions, the traditional emphasis on the material dimension of wealth creation and the methodological assumption of 'perfect information' gave to relations management the analytical status of a second-order, logistical function. Production came first, and marketing second. The market came first, and those information links or services needed to make it happen and work came, if at all, second. In today's economy, however, relations tend to come first, before the production of material products and transactions based upon them. In-depth, lasting relations between economic actors increasingly need to be seen as the backbone of wealth creation, while customized and fast-changing products often need to be analysed as *means* for extracting value from such relations rather than *ends* around which relations would revolve. Interdisciplinary cooperation between economists, political scientists, sociologists and other disciplines is more than ever necessary, in keeping with the emergence of relations management as the common foundation of a widening spectrum of real-life interactions.

As a result of these trends, the so-called 'informal' process of integration is no longer really informal as it involves the creation of customized rules and organizations of global relevance, while the 'formal' process of bargaining cannot be equated with political decisions only, but is increasingly shaped by the logic of customized regulatory interactions bringing public and private actors into synergetic relations.

Obviously, there still remains a subset of political interactions that can be looked on as 'high politics' and that is relatively immune to the blurring of borders between formal and informal processes. The creation of a single European currency, not to mention a single army, is not amenable to micro-interactions. Even then, however, the distinction between the 'micro' and 'macro' levels is not quite as tight as it used to be. Market participants have learnt, for instance, to *engineer* their own financial instruments, combining interest rates, currency denomination and regulatory features in ways that do challenge sovereignty prerogatives over currency management.[4]

We are witnessing more than a spillover of intergovernmental cooperation from one sector to another. What we now have on the European scene is *a diffusion of architectural power*, namely the increased involvement of actors in engineering a substantial part of the framework of norms and rules in which their interactions take place, as an intrinsic part of their market interactions. Such a process can hardly be equated with the extension to the regional level of national implementation of 'deregulation' – a vision implicit in Margaret

Thatcher's attitude. This would be contrary to the actual complexity and rule-intensive nature of what is summarily referred to as deregulation, and to the fact that countries have different mixes between public and private regulations and different levels of rule stringencies which are not amenable to competitive pressures.[5]

In the remainder of this chapter, we will therefore attempt to understand how a new dynamics of integration has come about in Europe by focusing on the changing relationship – in many respects the convergence – of the formal rule-making process and of the market-led 'informal' interaction process. We will start from the situation that prevailed in the 1960s, in which these two processes could be clearly separated, and we will ask what changes have gradually eroded this two-tier structure. We will then make the case that these two trends are not specific to Europe but have to do with the changing nature of economic interactions, notably cross-border interactions, away from the simple 'produce and trade' paradigm towards more complex patterns of *joint* value-creation among actors. In this light, we will introduce networks as a key conceptual tool in analysing such processes and their implications for, notably, economic integration.

The historical background

Export, redistribute and stabilize (ERS): The first European paradigm

In the 1960s, informal integration could be equated in a fairly straightforward way with the mobility of people, capital and, more importantly, goods.

Leaving aside the pre-history of what is now called political cooperation, formal integration had three major components. First, even though the Treaty of Rome included a full chapter on services, European economic integration in the 1960s was, first and foremost, about creating a 'Common Market' for goods. Formal interactions therefore revolved in large part around the politics of trade liberalization in the context of a traditional industrial economy. In many respects, the progress made within Europe paralleled, and was made internationally acceptable by, that achieved at the transatlantic and global level in the framework of the GATT Rounds and notably the Kennedy Round.

Common policies complementing the custom union and notably the Common Agricultural Policy (CAP) provided a second, more conflictual layer of interaction that had mostly to do with the socio-political conditions necessary to make this Common Market workable. As illustrated by the 'empty chair' policy of General de Gaulle, the CAP was perceived as a redistributive instrument compensating France and Italy for the special benefits German industry was widely expected to derive from the Common Market. The redistributive mind set of the 1970s coupled with the financial implications of the United Kingdom's entry then elevated *redistribution* as the second explicit pillar of integration, a vision articulated most clearly in the 1978 MacDougall Report.

The 'European snake' and the more stable European Monetary System (EMS) that emerged from its ashes added a third dimension – *stabilization* –

that never fully achieved the status of the other two, yet together they could be seen as the first elements of a higher level of interactions with major systematic implications. Rather than a genuine step towards monetary union and the transfer of sovereignty that it would have implied, what the EMS actually provided was a framework for strengthened intergovernmental cooperation and a degree of protection of intra-European relations (including the CAP and its delicate pricing mechanism) from what French commentators typically describe as the vagaries of world markets.

Hence, by the end of the 1970s, the 'first European integration paradigm' had matured into a hierarchical set of three dimensions that allowed the initial export-led dynamics to survive internal political and external economic challenges:

(1) A free market in goods was clearly the backbone of the system;
(2) *redistributive policies* ranked as a strong conditioning dimension with agriculture, regional policy and social policy as three major channels;
(3) *ad hoc stabilization* of key parameters provided a modicum of shelter from external shocks and took some of the steam out of internal pressures, in a semi-organized (e.g. EMS) or totally improvised (e.g. Monetary Compensatory Amounts; MCAs) fashion.

It was clear, however, that the ERS paradigm had reached its limits, even before the 1992 blueprint was put forward.

Redistribution became less likely to be advocated as an end in itself and was increasingly expected to result from decentralized initiatives. Not only has the 'rebate' of 1984 made EC budgetary implications more acceptable to the UK but, as an 'entrepreneurial culture' spread in Europe, Britain lost its taste for posturing as a 'less prosperous state'. With the partial dismantling of subsidies clearly on many national agendas, it become more difficult to seek political legitimacy for EC subsidies under the name of regional integration. In this respect, Greek over-indulgence in the subsidy game was one of the factors behind decisive moves towards majority voting.

Stabilizing, in spite of the remarkable success of the EMS, came to be understood as calling for more fundamental choices. Major macro-economic misalignments, coexisting with a daily market turnover higher than ever before, implied that an integrated European capital market would spell the end of today's EMS, unless major steps could be taken towards a *common currency*.

Challenges associated with the central trade dynamics are, however, the most critical. *Exporting* is an increasingly complex process, in which such elements as services, standards or electronic data assume increasing importance. More generally, 'trade' has gradually become a narrow concept to describe the type of cross-border interactions now developing among advanced economies and at the heart of European integration.

At the micro level, actors seek to enhance productivity not only in the factory but also on the market. Service- and information-intensive *compacks* (complex packages of goods and services), rather than simple old-fashioned goods, become critical means of extracting value from sales, especially since East Asian countries can hardly be surpassed at the commoditization game.

Hence the key role of *delivery systems*, as shown by the rising share of commercial investment in foreign direct investment, the emphasis on developing, sharing or acquiring distribution channels, and the importance of commercial presence and establishment and of customized approaches to each national, or even local, market. *Financial markets* come to the fore as cross-border M & As (mergers and acquisitions) rival exports as means of increasing market shares. Electronic Data Interchange networks are developing across borders, and temporary movements of individual service-providers are increasing. In short, integration between European economies tends to look more like a web formed by movement of all sorts than just one-way flows of products and payments.

Parallel changes have affected the 'macro' or formal policy agenda, as illustrated by the prominence of services including banking, telecommunications, transport and the professions in the 1992 programme. The EC has also been prominent in the last few years in pushing for multilateral negotiations on services issues in the knowledge that the European countries had become the most important service players worldwide. Although international services transactions are still addressed (out of reverence for the GATT framework) as 'trade' in services, they are qualitatively different from the arm's length market relations associated with trade in goods. In particular, as negotiators are gradually discovering, distinctions between 'exports', 'foreign investment', and 'right of establishment' tend to blur and thus call for integrated approaches.

As a result, while the 'Common Market' of the 1960s focused on what could be called shared consumption opportunities, the corporate and policy emphasis is now clearly moving toward joint wealth-creation processes. We will argue in the next section that the ERS model is gradually giving way to the DNA (Deliver, Network, Acquire) one. First, however, let us turn more systematically to the global context.

The global context

Analysts who write on the nature or impact of the changing character of international economic and industrial integration today usually attempt to increase the readers' awareness of the centrality of one or the other variable: information technologies (including the numerous accounts of the 'computer and communications revolution' along with a stress on information as today's crucial primary resource), management cultures (including the widespread comparison between Japanese, American and European management style and organizational structures), the role of the state and the nature of the social contract (including governments' willingness to coordinate in implementing interventionist measures or the different ways societies allocate property rights and design market relationships), and so on. For our part, we choose a specific focus by considering that *economic growth is increasingly associated with the rise of a specific mode of organizational arrangement between economic actors, namely* networks. Yet our vision is not exclusive but cuts across other approaches: networks are often shaped by *information technologies*, they require new types of *management techniques* and assume that *actors incorporate uncertainty in the contracts* they draw up among themselves. Networks are not a *source* of change – which we would identify as dominant – but the institutional *form* which actors tend to use in order to maximize the profit they may derive from new technologies or the opening of new markets. Highlighting the trend towards a *networked economy* for the twenty-first century would not imply movement beyond the so-called 'information economy' and 'services economy' that observers see as emerging today. Rather, it implies that the trends summarized under these labels are going to develop to their full *organizational logic*, and that we need to understand its implications.

Networks and the expansion of world markets

Evolving patterns of international economic integration are commonly analysed by reference to the way state-led actions and expanding markets affect one another. More extensively, students of international political economy stress numerous external factors affecting and affected by the patterns of market expansion including 'the structure of society, the political framework at the domestic and international levels, and the existing state of scientific theory and technological development'.[6]

At a first level, that of the business press, networks can be seen as one new exogenous variable belonging to the realm of 'technological development' (information technologies) and accelerating the expansion of international markets. That is when, by networks, analysts refer to such phenomena as Electronic Data Interchanges, world-scale information management systems or value added telecommunication services networks implemented by large-scale public or private enterprises. To this extent, networks are meant to contribute to decreased costs and increased speed of international transactions.[7] Global networks are then the tools of global strategies.

At a second level, networks can be seen not only as one more 'external factor' affecting the expansion of markets, but as a means of linking economic actors which cuts across economic transactions, social institutions and political structures: that is, they are themselves forms of markets – be they economic or political – and further, loci of production. This level is paradigmatic rather than descriptive and quantifiable. We may say that 'networks' are not only alternative means of penetrating foreign markets but also the organizational expression of a kind of shift from international division of labour to international integration of labour whereby the location of economic activities around the world and the corresponding distribution of wealth are determined by a logic which may have little to do with geographical features. On what grounds can we make this statement?

Trade theory revisited

Not only Ricardo and Adam Smith but also the drafters of the GATT articles saw trade, unhindered by government intervention, as the means to maximize growth world wide because they believed in *specialization*. The pervasive logic of specialization was based on two assumptions. First, exports and imports of *products* – whether raw materials, finished products or partly manufactured goods – were the major means to transfer economic value internationally. Movements of factors of production (capital, labour) were of secondary importance and tended to reflect the existence of imperfections (notably protectionism) in markets for products. Patterns of trade would hence reflect *country-specific* factor endowments. Secondly, the decentralized process of the market was the best way to allocate resources to particular useage domestically as well as internationally. This process, left to itself, was to determine the optimal mix of activities to be carried out in a given country according to the country's comparative advantage.

Over the last decades, this paradigm has been increasingly challenged and adapted, as analysts and policy-makers have had to grapple with *two major developments* undermining both of the above assumptions.

First, *movements of factors of production have become an essential way for economic actors to secure market shares at the world level*, as shown by the spread of multinational enterprises in the postwar period. As selling goods increasingly requires close contact with local demand, and as services trans-actions become prominent at an international level, foreign direct investment – or temporary migration, for that matter – can no longer be seen only as a second-best solution to circumvent trade barriers, but must be regarded as an all-important way of ensuring the right fit between resources, factors and demand on a global scale.[8] Obviously the logic of specialization through 'free movement' does not extend easily to factors of production as there come to the forefront constraints that were secondary to trade relations and linked to regulatory, monetary or socio-political concerns. More fundamentally, there is no longer doubt that international specialization is determined by the intrinsic characteristics of actors as much as of territories.

Secondly, *technology and intellectual investment (such as R&D, training, corporate culture have become a fundamental driving force behind wealth creation*. Hence, one can no longer think of comparative advantage as given or *static*, but it must be seen instead as created or *dynamic*, with public and private actors investing in shaping and reshaping it. What economists had labelled market *imperfections* (such as learning curves, economics of scale and scope, dynamics of innovation) often look more like the rule than the exception. Actors can manage to secure captive markets (or *rents*) for themselves, implying that the worldwide market forces, if left to themselves, may indeed produce sub-optimal allocation of resources. In this context, government intervention to ensure the location of *strategic industries* on their own territory may theoretically succeed in raising national revenue. Hence, there is no more doubt that, in shaping patterns of specialization and international markets, public and private actors are part of the same strategic games.

From national champions to global corporate alliances

The above analysis was put forward in the early 1980s, by the 'new international economics' school, following on earlier work on oligopolistic behaviour. It is not clear whether such an actualization of the analytical tools of conventional trade theory has ultimately enhanced the legitimacy of interventionist trade policies.[9] More importantly, strategic trade assumptions bring to bear some prominent aspects of economic integration processes: as barriers to trade and investment decrease, states engage in 'profit shifting' as part of their economic prerogatives and/or 'industrial policies'. This applies to European integration dynamics from two angles. First, among European states a 'Common Market' certainly did not imply that leaving specialization to the logic of market forces was an optimal strategy. The prominence of *national champions* was certainly a reflection of intense policy rivalry within Europe throughout the 1960s and 1970s. Secondly, with the rise of optimal scales of production and fixed costs of R&D as well as intensified competition from Japan and the United States in the last decade, European industrial collaboration has served as a means of generating sustainable comparative advantage at a European level. There is indeed wide evidence that through proactive industrial policies at a regional level, the European Community has tried to ensure – more or less successfully – the location within its borders of industries characterized by high rents, notably in the high-tech industries (among many, Airbus, Semiconductors and megachips with 'Jessi', 'HDTV'). Similarly, EC policies with regard to countervailing duties, safeguard actions and other trade-related policies can indeed be discussed (just as may their American counterparts) with reference to these rent-seeking, profit-shifting strategies on the part of European firms and governments. In this light, the 1992 surge can be seen as a direct harnessing by European firms of the EC institutional framework for their global ambitions. To be sure, the theory of trade policy under imperfect competition suggests that predictions about the effect of policies which try to tilt international competition in favour of local firms must be based on specific assessments of market structures in each area under consideration. It follows that European policies will be differentially successful depending on such factors as whether dominant market power is held by EC or non-EC firms or the nature of distortions in a given market.[10]

More broadly, however, the effect of the 1992 project on European firms' global competitiveness is not only a matter of governments efficiently inducing a preferred location of production. Actually, while firms indeed benefit from expanding their 'market share', this does not necessarily imply displacing rivals from domestic or foreign markets or, better, pre-empting their entry into a given market. We also observe that the aim in Europe since the early 1980s has been to multiply extra-European links. Global corporate alliances developed between Europe and the US well before the present wave of intra-European agreements. Indeed, it was the rapid rise in transatlantic corporate agreements[11] that led the Commission and national officials in countries like France to think about ways of encouraging intra-European ties among companies. While their efforts have been quite successful, companies have in fact simply broadened their portfolio of alliances to new European partners without giving up transatlantic or Pacific networking.[12] There is more to this phenomenon than the obvious gap between corporate and government logics.

Joint wealth creation and the new international division of labour

This, we suggest, points to a fruitful avenue for enriching formal models developed under the new international economic school. While strategic trade theory has clearly brought to light the non-static character of endowments in fostering wealth creation, it assumes that profit-sharing and more broad appropriation of wealth is directly correlated with the *location* of production and hence highly sensitive to the behaviour of governments aimed at affecting production *on* the territories under their jurisdiction. Indeed, the international economy cannot but be seen as an intricate web of strategic games. But it is becoming increasingly impossible to consider separately the cards – production processes – and the setting – international markets – of such games. As one includes in the overall analysis revenues raised by firms in ways other than direct control over production, one must also account for cases of profit-sharing rather than all-out profit-shifting. In this light, let us point to three fundamental trends departing from conventional economic assumptions which we feel are not adequately captured by territorially centred approaches.

- *From geographic location to access and integration*: Corporations compete increasingly in terms of the *relative efficiency with which they are able to access, deploy and manage resources on a global scale*. In doing so, they depend increasingly on the capacity to access – or to create – the various types of transnational networks through which cross-border interactions increasingly take place. In other words, country-specific resource endowments lose in relative importance at least among the advanced economies.
- *From economies of scale to mass customization*: All possible implications have not been drawn from the increasingly customized nature of the production process. In a world driven by mass customization, the aim is not to produce more output with the same input but to link buyers and sellers and third parties in such ways as to reduce to a minimum the cost of tailoring products to the buyer's needs. Factors are not available for all actors in a given country in the form of pools of labour, capital and know-how but, rather, are becoming products themselves. In the case of capital, for instance, increasingly efficient and customized techniques are available to turn assets, brand names or managerial capacity into financial resources through securitization, franchising, leveraged buy-outs or any of the dozens of comparable techniques. The importance of customized relations and strategies in mobilizing resources and in defining in what markets actors actually are is an implicit challenge to the Hecksher-Ohlin-Samuelson theorem, as the latter rests on the possibility of distinguishing between factors of production on the one hand and production outputs (goods or services) on the other.
- *From efficient division of labour to co-production of value*: Non-tangible forms of value are now dealt with, nationally and internationally, by increasing productivity. Education and training are as important for the wealth-creation process in the importing side as on the exporting side.[13] Users or customers are instrumental in creating value from what they buy, hence actually becoming *prosumers*. More generally, the arm's length

relationships traditionally associated with market interactions acquire a depth and lasting quality, which mean that the market should not be regarded simply as a set of instantaneous atomistic interactions. Integration (in the narrow sense) complements transaction as a key dimension of market interactions. This leads us to question the neat separation between production (exported) on the one hand and consumption (imported) on the other, which in turn leads us to reconsider what is actually meant by patterns of trade.

The advent of interconnection

The rethinking of international trade issues initiated under the heading – and around the policy agenda – of 'trade in services' brings to light the futility of attempting to draw a line between categories – trade or investment – which do not capture the actual form of international services transactions. It may be more fruitful to think of such activities in terms of combined flows of goods, people, money (as capital) and information (or knowledge), in short G, P, M & I.[14] Actually this categorization in terms of flows may well apply to international transactions as a whole.

As integrated management of G, P, M & I becomes possible *across* countries, actors located in different countries come to be linked in qualitatively new ways. In addition to being interdependent, actors are now increasingly engaged in cross-border joint wealth creation: hence our definition of *interconnection* as a type of relationship between national economies where links between actors across borders allow them to create value jointly instead of simply exchanging it. Patterns of interconnection can then be seen playing a separate role from patterns of interdependence in shaping the global wealth-creation process.

In this light, the trade paradigm behind the European Common Market of the 1960s is becoming far too narrow to account for the type of cross-border interactions behind the emergence, as initiated in the late 1980s, of the 'internal market'. While the 1960s saw economies of scale in the manufacturing sector drive the specialization process at the heart of the Common Market, the late 1980s could be remembered as the time when the interconnection of Europe began to take shape. Not that trade has become unimportant, but actors (notably but not exclusively corporations) can develop a far greater diversity of cross-border relations in their attempts to derive more value, with higher efficiency, from the whole gamut of goods, people, money and information flows. Inter-university links, zero inventory distribution strategies, cooperative R&D, electronic service delivery, competing private standardization fora, cross-sectoral distribution agreements, hostile takeovers and the like are outgrowing the time-honoured concept of trade and calling for upgraded concepts of what free trade and, even more so, economic integration are about.

In practice, interconnection rests on the development of networks across borders. These networks may be said to allow for global customization – that is, mass customization on a global scale. Global data networks play a specific role as they serve to manage the movement of knowledge (as for databases), people (for instance, computer reservation systems), capital (electronic financial networks such as 'Nasdaq' or 'Seaq'), or products (take Hertz for cars) in an integrated worldwide manner. We can see this as the management of 'data images' associated with, and providing a lever on actual flows of G, P, M & I.

As tools for global customization strategies, networks allow for the congruence of the local and the global. Corporations eager to become *global insiders* (as in the 'act locally', think globally' slogan) thrive on the development of increasingly sophisticated networks. Obviously, this will have a direct influence on how relations between agents are structured (or rather restructured) under the assumption explored by scholars of *industrial organization* that to each dominant process of production of value corresponds a mode of organization geared at optimizing such processes. The large-scale corporation appeared in the context of economies-of-scale requirements and Taylorian division of labour. Networks, for their part, are the organizational response to the need to customize on a mass scale and to integrate tasks which may not easily be predefined.

Network properties and European integration

In this light, assessing progress on the way to European integration would reflect the extent to which Europe is a meaningful zone for the definition and conduct of the strategies bringing actors together around joint activities. An 'integrated' Europe would then be one in which actors are able to design, operate and combine the various types of networks (from M&As to electronic networking) that shape and define today's interactions, and to do so with a degree of strategic flexibility and effectiveness comparable to – or maybe higher than – that within national societies.

Such a 'Europe of networks' is in continuity with previous stages of intra-European specialization. The discontinuity has to do with the convergence of this gradual process of economic change and of the political concepts of integration.

The Treaty of Rome states as an explicit goal the free movement of the four constitutive dimensions of economic integration, namely goods, labour, capital and services. In common trade policy parlance, the Single Market initiative consists, for a major part, in extending regional trade liberalization from trade in goods to trade in services, as well as to capital and labour movement.[15] Present developments can be seen in the light of models developed in the late 1970s to explain industrial division of labour within Europe. Specifically, models of intra-industry trade had provided theoretical justification to the counter-intuitive patterns of regional division of labour among countries with similar levels of development: instead of fostering inter-industry specialization according to existing comparative advantages, exchanges within the EC have tended to consist of increasingly similar products.[16] This logic is carried forward in the case of services, whereby the 'intra-industry' trade observed is increasingly 'internal' to the production processes themselves, to the ideal-typical point of consisting of joint production by actors located in two different countries.

From then on, economic integration in the decades to come would therefore define an economic space within which the *exchange* of products is gradually supplanted by the *pooling* of resources which are capable of serving the *differentiated* goals of services providers. Such common resources, which may be seen as accumulated *goodwill* on a transnational scale, we describe as *infrastructures* (a set of physical links) and *infostructures* (a set of regulatory links).

We see 'integration' in Europe developing around the competitive creation and use of such European infostructures and infrastructures. Integration therefore covers two dynamics which are most often analysed separately but which are really two sides of the same coin in our analytical framework. On the one hand, integration describes a *macro-process of convergence* among previously separate national entities. On the other hand, integration describes the *micro-management of wealth creation* among economic actors for whom 'transaction' or 'production' can no longer be envisaged as separate processes. The features of *micro-integration* lead to our reassessment of *macro-integration*. In particular, micro-integration requires actors to interact as co-producers and as market competitors *within* the same structures. Hence, beyond stating that macro-integration thrives both on increased competition and on increased cooperation, we must focus on the development of such structures.

With regard to *infrastructures*, questions would deal with the extent to which European actors can access or develop the type of infrastructures (tailor-made as well as general-purpose ones) called for by today's complexity and depth of interactions. The creation of distribution channels (which, in turn, can be achieved through such strategies as cross-border acquisitions, commercial presence, or electronic delivery systems of the Minitel type) are, for instance, an essential dimension of today's economic interactions. A critical question is whether such delivery systems can be developed on a Europe-wide basis, drawing on as large a gamut of techniques as in the case within a national economy.

With regard to *infostructures*, questions would be asked about legal obstacles facing European actors as they attempt to bring together a number of partners (suppliers, distributors, customers) around a joint value-creating activity. The lack of a European company law is often mentioned as a critical obstacle, although shopping for the appropriate legal framework does introduce key elements of flexibility (like choosing Luxembourg for a financial holding company or the Netherlands for an industrial one). Such questions are not limited to economic issues: the ease with which consortia can be set up to meet defence procurement needs is, for instance, a major dimension of military integration. Similarly, all regulations affecting the movement of people (from police checks to diplomas) have a major impact on the possibility of bringing people of different nationalities into cooperative relationships.

In this light, many of the developments taking place in Europe – whether at the corporate level or in the Commission and intergovernmental process – are related to these twin sets of issues. While 'completing the Common Market' was the initial motto, putting in place the Europe-wide infrastructure and promoting the development of cross-border information is the substance of much of what is going on.

Deliver, network and acquire (DNA): The post-1992 European paradigm

Indeed, far from being a mere addendum to the 1968 'Common Market', the '1992' programme should be seen as the first attempt by a group of countries to deal with the requirements of a networked world economy.

Corporate leaders, notably the members of the *European Roundtable*, played an important role in suggesting the concrete thrust of the new European policies, or what they saw as a pragmatic answer to the increasing cost of doing business in Europe. In doing so, they brought to the forefront, even if implicitly, the agenda of networking. In particular, the blueprint for a European revival, 'Europe 1990', presented in 1984 by Wisse Dekker, Chairman of Phillips, included four key measures of which three – in addition to fiscal matters – had to do with European networks of one type or another: promoting the use of electronic networks to exchange trading information and fulfil trading and customs formalities; promoting standardization at the European level in the fields of electronics and IT to allow for economies of scale and interconnectivity; making the case for Europe-wide telecom services and for the opening up of government procurement in the field of telecom. In the same vein, the European Roundtable has put forward a number of well-researched reports dealing with the 'missing links' in Europe and bringing to light the complex and multifaceted nature of the links necessary for pan-European growth.[17] At a time when zero inventory production means that roads and trucks are no longer just logistical links but part of the production facilities, micro-integration among European business rests on a depth and variety of public and private networks put in place jointly or competitively by public and private actors.

Our ongoing analysis of corporate strategies has led us to put forward a typology of corporate networks (ranging from intra-corporate automation networks to norm-setting 'meta-networks') to account for these diverse links and to identify synergies – as well as significant contradictions – in the present set of EC policies. In particular, many of the critical implications of the 279 'White Paper' liberalization measures and many of the dozen or so programmes currently being discussed or under way at Brussels have to do, explicitly or (more often) implicitly, with the development of European networks of one type or another.

In particular, the development of *corporate networks* (in the sense, notably, of joint ventures, alliances and electronic networking) is the most significant potential outcome of high-technology programmes of the 'Esprit' and 'Eureka' type. What is being subsidized and encouraged is not so much the development of a few additional hi-tech widgets as the setting up of inter-corporate and inter-personal networks on the basis of which more significant, market-driven projects can later develop. In this sense, there is a strong synergy between these technology programmes and the more recent efforts to get European students or teachers to spend time in several national schooling systems ('Erasmus' and 'Comett'). Facilitating cross-border networking is also a fundamental consideration in creating a European Company statute as well as in promoting a number of public and private standardization fora such as 'Spag', 'Odette' or 'Efti'.

Fostering the development of a new generation of network *infrastructures* is at the heart of the 'Race' programme as well as of the European 'Green Book' on telecommunications. It is also a key factor in the approval – not to say active encouragement – given by the Commission to such private projects as the European Payment System and the 'Amadeus' and 'Gallileo' computerized reservation systems. More generally, the focus of *structural policies* at the Community level is changing rapidly from redistribution as a sweetener of trade liberalization towards catalytic networking as a way to promote a self-sustaining integration dynamics. While 'Esprit', 'Eureka', 'Brite', 'Erasmus', 'Science' and other sparklers in the Brussels fireworks display still have limited impact, they are pioneering new policy approaches that give the Commission more of a regulatory function.[18]

More generally, policies developed within the '1992' programme as well as, independently of it, in the high technology field have greatly promoted the density of European networks, both in a proactive and a reactive fashion. Proactively, the Commission has been concerned with fostering Europe-wide infrastructures and networks in fields ranging from telecommunications to R&D. Reactively, it has been adapting its anti-trust approach to deal with cases such as the development of a European Payment System or the setting up of cooperative programmes such as 'Eureka'. In passing, such a perspective leads one to question the alleged primacy of negative integration (removing trade barriers) over positive integration (implementing common policies) in the 1992 process. If trade requires interconnection, supranational rule-making and transterritorial infrastructures, then negative integration is only effective if supported by positive integration.

An implication of these policies and of the consequent qualitative change in the role of the European Commission is that the historical European leaning towards public-private endeavours is entering a new phase. In particular, the shift from harmonization to mutual recognition can be seen as an exercise in combining market forces and intergovernmental initiatives to enhance compatibility among the various European infra- and infostructures. Regulatory competition will be a direct result of mutual recognition and may be enhanced by the expansion of European networks.

Rather than centralized government planning or industrial policies of 'picking winners', this changing mix of public-private networking involves both cooperation and competition. One may take note, for instance, of the growing competition between public and private networks (as in the case of 'Cosine'[19] and 'Euronet' for European Research networks) or among private networks (witness 'Galileo' and 'Amadeus').

The convergence between political and economic networks: which logic?

Integration, therefore, covers two dynamics which are most often analysed separately but which are really two sides of the same coin in our analytical framework. On the one hand, integration describes a *macro-process of convergence* among previously separate national entities. On the other hand, it describes the *micro-management of wealth creation* among economic actors for whom 'transaction' or 'production' can no longer be envisaged as separate processes. The features of *micro-integration* lead to our reassessment of *macro-integration*. In particular, micro-integration requires actors to interact as co-producers and as market competitors *within* the same structures. Hence, the development of such structures by actors themselves is a key aspect of today's integration dynamics. This network perspective, however, leaves open many questions:

- The use of a network model may point alternatively to a set of 'loose' connections between actors involved or to the increasing role of advanced productivity tools, open to *strategic* reconfiguration and influences. Hence, a snapshot of *actual* links may be less relevant to describe the strength of integration than an assessment of *potential* links, obviously a more difficult exercise.
- Networks may require permanent structures, but are also constantly reshaped by the strategies of participants. Hence a type of integration which may not only be in line with 'variable geometry', depending on policy sectors, but also be characterized by more unstable configurations.
- Networks foster both *diffusion* and *exclusion* dynamics. Network external-ities often make expanded membership desirable, yet at the same time, actors may have major interests in excluding others from a given network. Also, whereas networks may have more access points than traditional organizations, it may be hard actually to know when one is out of existing networks. It is therefore not clear in which direction network-based integration will affect the so-called European 'democratic deficit'.

More generally, political and economic networks enhance integration only to the extent that interactions are based on shared resources such as this 'sense of solidarity' which Keohane and Hoffman (in Chapter 16) identify as a main feature of *political networks*. Yet, as these authors point out, there are links which may not create a sense of (political) community but only a propensity to interact within what we may call 'network boundaries'. Network boundaries – which are constantly shifting as a result of strategic choices – may certainly not be equated with regional borders. Actually, such boundaries are strategic rather than territorial objects. Yet the density of network interconnection helps to define an *integrated economic space* even when actors are not pursuing similar objectives.

Hence, the sense that network-led integration appears multi-directional and lacking an identifiable centre. This is the very reason why a network model appears to fit an integration dynamics in which Europeans are actively engaged in reconciling the ideal of *commonality* with the reality of lasting *diversity* among themselves.

Toward a fully fledged Europe of networks?

These ambivalent characteristics of networks as an organizational set-up may indeed by seen by some as implying that the new integration dynamics so obviously at work in Europe will remain limited to the business sphere, with few spillover effects in the political realm.

The other side of ambivalence, however, is that such a limited scenario need not be the only one currently on the cards. Let us conclude, therefore, on a more Euro-optimistc note, with four trends presently at work in Europe and pointing towards a transition from pure 'business networking' to a fully fledged integration dynamics.

First, in the economic sphere itself, cross-border networking in the form of joint ventures, alliances, standardization fora and participation in EC-sponsored cooperative projects has already greatly increased the *political* acceptability of working with – and for – a company of another European nationality. It used to be that Germans would resent working under French bosses, or French under Italian ones. Prejudices such as this North-South implicit hierarchy obviously die hard, but they are clearly and substantially on the decline. Pure products of the French elite school system like Alain Minc are no longer seen as mavericks when working under the likes of Carlo de Benedetti. French financial companies (Victoire and Suez) can actually do what was deemed unthinkable a short while ago – they can acquire the number two German insurance company (Colonia), and then launch hostile takeover attempts at one another without even a word of concern in Germany. Just to put things in perspective, one should remember that only half a decade ago, Cables de Lyon, an affiliate of the French CGE conglomerate, was advised *not* to raise money on the Paris Bourse for Cablesmetal, a leading German wire manufacturer it had acquired, for fear of shedding too much light on the French ownership of that well-established German firm and of losing precious Bundespost contracts. Today, by contrast, the political legitimacy is increasingly there for European companies to network with, to acquire one another and to set up hierarchical structures irrespective of nationality.

Secondly, the principle of *mutual recognition* also has legitimizing implications that reverberate outside its original technical and legal sphere. While learning to develop and discuss national legislation and regulations with an eye on those of the 11 other EC ocuntries, each national government and each national public opinion is gradually educating itself in the behaviour and regulatory norms of the other countries. A socialist government in France no longer surprises anyone by taking it for granted that lower corporate taxes (even if at the expense of higher taxes on earned income) are the European norm. Similarly, when the Peugeot chairman's salary and self-approved pay rise were disclosed in the middle of a strike by low-paid French automobile workers, public discussion did not limit itself to a discussion of wage inequality in France (as would probably have been the case five years ago) but was conducted with explicit references to, notably, German wage structure. More generally, the basic yardsticks and references central to each national political process can be seen to be converging as a result of the increasing interconnection of the legal, regulatory and, of course, business frameworks.

Thirdly, the same networking techniques that have been used as a catalyst of *economic* integration can also be used in other fields. In particular, one should reflect on the potentially far-reaching consequences of the more recent EC programmes aimed at fostering networking among European universities and institutes. While the 'Comett' programme makes it easier for scientists to work in foreign labs, the 'Erasmus' programme aims at exposing each student with more than three years of higher education to the university system of at least one other European country. As a result, the degree of cultural interchange in Europe should substantially increase and universities will have to take a multinational student body as their reference.

Lastly, networks should in no way be defined, as they often are, in negative terms as 'less' than fully fledged institutions. True, part of their strength is that they can operate efficiently well below the degree of institutionalization once taken as a prerequisite by advocates of European integration. But there is nothing in their nature preventing them from evolving towards the traditional types of organization. In fields like monetary integration, the present Europe of networks can very well turn out to be a more hospitable context for the development of a European Federal Reserve System based on gradually institutionalizing patterns of cooperation among national central banks and authorities. Whether this is as critical to the integration of Europe as federalists think is a question on which we, personally, might come up with non-conventional answers. What matters here, in any case, is that networks are not second-best approaches. Rather, they are types of organizations shaped *from within* by actors rather than given *ex ante* as part of a legal or economic system.

In this sense, the Europe of networks may well illustrate the fact that the unit is the individual, so that each European actor (rather than a small group of enlightened political leaders) is now a full participant in the broad and far-reaching process referred to as integration. More architects on the building site may, at first, look confusing as we search for the familiar statelike structures. But, after all, why should one expect the new building to conform to the old blueprints?

Notes

1. For a discussion of implications with regard to monetary union scenarios and to a possible OECD process building on the EC '1992' momentum, see Albert Bressand, 'Beyond Interdependence: 1992 as a Global Challenge', *International Affairs*, January 1990.
2. For a more comprehensive presentation of the network economy concept and some of its policy and corporate implications, see Albert Bressand and Kalypso Nicolaïdis, (eds), *Strategic Trends in Services: An Inquiry into the Global Services Economy* (New York, Harper & Row, 1989); Bressand and Nicolaïdis, 'Les Services au cœur de l'économie relationnelle', in *Revue d'Economie industrielle*, Spring 1988; Bressand, Nicolaïdis and Catherine Distler, 'Vers une économie de réseaux', *Politique industrielle*, Winter 1989; as well as issues 1–10 of *Project Promethée Perspectives*, 1987–9.
3. The English word 'regulation' may sound excessively narrow as it tends to be restricted to technical matters and, in addition, to those aspects of government interventions dealing with externalities in market interactions. By contrast, the French term 'régulation' can cover almost any type of steering of economic and social activities (e.g. 'la régulation par le marché'). We use the word here to cover all rules governing market interactions short of macro-economic steering by governments.

4. To take one small example, at a time when some Latin American countries (e.g. Chile) made debt equity swaps legal while most others (e.g. Argentina) did not, Western banks eager to swap Argentinian debts for equities were nevertheless able to do so by combining 12 or so different swaps, involving the currencies of several third countries thereby transforming some of the fundamental characteristics of the Argentinian Central Bank currency that they held. More generally, the often lamented high ratio of financial to trade transactions (presently in the 50 to 100 range) illustrates not so much the emergence of 'casino society' as the increasing capacity of economic actors *not* to take the legal and political framework as given but to engineer customized frameworks adapted to a specific set of relations and objectives. For a more detailed analysis of 'infocurrencies', see Albert Bressand, 'Currency Chaos – The Newest Strategic Tool', *The International Economy*, vol. 1, no. 1, October–November 1987.

5. For a more detailed analysis of deregulation and re-regulation and their relationship with trade liberalization, see 'Deregulation in the 1990s', *Project Promethée Perspectives* no. 5, March 1988, and *La Déréglementation dans les années 90*, under the direction of Catherine Distler (Paris, Promethée, 1988).

6. Gilpin, *The International Political Economy*, 1988.

7. This is typically the vision of the dual economy theory which attempts to show how the transformation of traditional sectors in to modern sectors has been accelerated by 'advances in communications and transportation, the development of efficient economic institutions, and the reduction of transaction costs'. Ibid.

8. Numerous models of foreign direct investment (FDI) have been developed, based on such factors as analysis of product cycles, risk behaviours, information appropriation strategies and factor substitutability.

9. From the extensive writings on this subject, special mention is due to Paul R. Krugman (ed.), *Strategic Trade Policy and the new International Economics* (Cambridge, MA., MIT Press, 1986). For a critical analysis of the relationship between trade theory, actual trade patterns and the trade policy debate, see notably Jagdish Bhagwati, *Protectionism* (Boston, MIT Press, 1988).

10. This argument is systematically explored in Elhanan Helpman and Paul Krugman, *Trade Policy and Market Structures* (Boston, MIT Press, 1989). The authors stress that in a world of imperfect competition firms base their production strategies on *perceived* marginal revenue (rather than a given price) which itself is affected in a complex manner by expectations related to strategic trade policies.

11. See figures collated by the Italian *Réseau* and *FOR* research groups as well as case studies on transatlantic and intra-European corporate alliances in the telecommunications and electronics fields conducted by Promethée (Paris, 1986).

12. In most cases, so-called 'European' alliances also have a strong US dimension: witness the intimate links between the recent acquisition of Colonia by Victoire and the efforts by Jimmy Goldsmith to divest the US Farmers Insurance Company of its very recent BAT parent.

13. Training Spanish technicians abroad is what the Spanish government now requires from multinational investors rather than financial or material counterparts. Training of Sumitomo employees by Goldman Sachs in New York was the one aspect of a 500 million dollar deal to which the Securities and Exchange Commission objected in a recent ruling.

14. For developments on this point, see notably Geza Feketekuty, *International Trade in Services* (Cambridge, MA., Ballinger, 1988); Kalypso Nicolaïdis, 'Contractors vs Contactors, Towards an Integrated Definition of Trade in Services', Promethée/Unctad working paper, November 1987. The relationship between flows of goods and service flows (in the form, notably, of movements of people) has also been studied as part of the 'tradeability of services issues'. For a discussion of

'splintering' and 'disembodiment' of goods and services, see Jagdish Bhagwati, 'International Trade in Services and its Relevance for Economic Development', in *The Emerging Service Economy*, ed. Orio Giarini for the Services World Forum (Oxford, Pergamon, 1987).

15. Our 'Goods, People, Money, Information' typology focused on actual observable flows rather than on 'policy categories' as implicit in the treaty's fourfold distinction. Services are obviously central to our analysis but, rather than crossing borders, are embodied in tangible products, individuals, capital or knowledge.

16. Explanations as to why such a pattern may develop fall in two broad categories. First, there is the idea that consumer demand for variety within an industry cannot be satisfied thoroughly by national firms, in a context of economies of scale. See, for instance, Avinash Dixit and Joseph Stiglitz, 'Monopolistic Competition and Optimum Product Diversity', *American Economic Review*, no. 67, 1977. See also Kelvin Lancaster, 'Protection and Products Differentiation', in Henryk Kierzkowski, (ed.), *Monopolistic Competition and International Trade* (Oxford, Clarendon, 1984). According to the second category of explanation, firms with no relative cost advantage may find an advantage in capturing foreign markets through initial dumping and sustained economies of scale. See, for instance, James Brander and Paul Krugman, 'A Reciprocal Dumping Model of International Trade', *Journal of International Economics*, no. 15, 1983.

17. See notably, 'The Missing Link', December 1984; 'Keep Europe Mobile', November 1988; and 'Need for Renewing Transport Infrastructure in Europe', March 1989.

18. As the point was made at the Florence Workshop on European Integration (held on 10–12 September 1989), this qualitative change in the nature of the Commission's approach is also seen as a way to overcome the budgetary constraints that had brought traditional policy initiatives to a standstill.

19. In the 'Cosine' case, the Commission took the initiative to bring together leading universities and research centres around an electronic networking project. A number of the participating universities, however, while approving of the cooperation framework, disagreed with the strategic choices of the Commission (i.e. network based on OSI interfaces) and are now going ahead with a competing architecture.

3 Technology and the dynamics of integration
Margaret Sharp

The purpose of this chapter is to examine the role of technology as an integrative factor within Western Europe, broadly throughout the postwar period, but primarily within the last decade. It begins with a discussion of general trends in technology world wide, then focuses on developments in Europe, asking whether these are in any respect different from developments elsewhere. The formal mechanisms being established to encourage technological collaboration within Europe are then discussed, followed by consideration of the informal structures. The concluding section comes back to the central issue – the role of technology within the dynamics of integration.

Global trends

Throughout the history of the industrialized world, technology has advanced by a series of fits and starts, with periods of intense technological activity succeeded by periods of seemingly near stagnation. Part of this pattern reflects broader macro-economic factors, not least the advent of war and its aftermath, and also fashions in the management, or mismanagement, of economic policy. A period of rapid growth usually coincides with an upturn in investment ratios which in turn brings the rapid diffusion of new technologies prevalent at that time. The antithesis is that a period of economic stagnation – the 1920s in Britain, for example – means low investment and little perceived technological advance.

If economic factors influence the pace of technological change, the reverse is also true. Technology itself is observed to have strong cyclical characteristics. There have been periods, such as that of the industrial revolution, when intense technological activity has brought major changes affecting not just what was made and how it was made, but how people lived and worked. Indeed, since the industrial revolution a series of long, 50-year cycles has been observed, associated with major technological changes such as the introduction of the railways, electricity, and the developments in petroleum chemistry in the 1930s. In the wake of the major changes has come a further clustering of

50

associated innovations – better ways of doing things – and this in turn encourages investment and reinforces the cyclical nature of events. When this clustering effect ceases and the new technologies are mature and diffused through the economy, the pace of change slows, growth rates fall, unemployment increases and competitive pressures intensify.

The 50-year periodicity of the long cycle was first measured and noted by the Russian statistician, Kondratieff. The technological explanation for the cycle, however, derives from the work of Joseph Schumpeter, who emphasized the importance of technical change and innovation as a source of dynamism in the capitalist economy.[1] Like other classical economists (Smith, Mill, Ricardo, Marx), Schumpeter developed a unified theory of economic development which, while giving a central role to technology and innovation, linked together organizational, social and managerial changes with the technological. Radical changes in technology, for example the development of the railway engine, had major impact on all aspects of life over a long period.

The resurgence of interest in Schumpeter's ideas came with the slowdown of growth in the world economy in the 1970s and 1980s, and the simultaneous emergence of important new technologies, in particular micro-electronics and information technology.[2] The long boom of the 1950s and 1960s represented, on the one hand, the flowering of the new technologies of that time, particularly those associated with the petrochemical industry – plastics, man-made fibres, detergents, fertilizers – and, on the other, a catching-up on ownership of consumer durables, above all the motor car, which had expanded so fast in America in the 1920s and 1930s. The backlog of investment, created first by the economic mismanagement of the European economies in the interwar period and subsequently by war and its immediate aftermath, helped sustain the long boom through the 1960s and into the 1970s. Its demise coincided, symbolically, with the ending of the period of cheap oil on which both the petrochemical revolution and the motor car were predicated. But the difficulties economic policy-makers encountered in trying to handle simultaneously the inflationary and deflationary impact of the two oil crises did little to smooth the path of technological change. As in the 1930s, the immediate reaction was to attempt to restore the status quo: only in retrospect was it recognized that things would never be quite the same again.

It is difficult to judge how important today's technological changes will be 50 years on. There are those who speak of a second industrial revolution; others who see them as no more, and no less, revolutionary than the petrochemical developments of the 1930s and 1940s. Freeman likens current developments in micro-electronics and information technology to the advent of electricity which over time meant major changes not only in the range of new products available but also in the way in which people worked and their whole lifestyle.[3] Both Freeman and writers such as Piore and Sabel go further and see in current developments a new industrial divide which puts behind us the old Fordist principles of mass production and looks towards a new logic of flexible specialization.[4]

Whatever the view taken about the long-term impact of today's new technologies, few would deny that we are experiencing a period of major technological change. Today's new technologies – micro-electronics, information technology, automation, biotechnology, new materials – are pervasive. All industries are affected, and there is the reinvigoration of the old as well as the development of the new. This has two implications worth noting. First, the growth opportunities are very substantial as a result both of cost reduction and the opening of new markets. Given sound economic management, the inflationary threat of the 1970s is also alleviated because there is an inherent bias in the new technologies towards savings in energy, raw materials and labour which relieves pressures on scarce resources.[5] Secondly, the discontinuity implicit in the technological changes – above all the need for wholesale renewal of equipment and skills – destroys established positions of power and offers opportunities for new entrants. This leads to an active jockeying for position, not only among firms but also in the new geopolitical power structure which is emerging, and in turn to intense competition between old and new players.

In previous cycles, three phases can be identified: the first, when the new technologies emerge but do not diffuse or combine thoroughly; the second, when there is widespread diffusion accompanied by major institutional innovation both to help assimilate new technologies and to mitigate their negative distributional effects; and the third, mature, phase when there is considerable growth but along established trajectories. We appear to be in the second phase. The institutional changes are occurring at various levels. First, in production and distribution, with new approaches, particularly following the Japanese, in the organization of productive activities, such as R&D collaborations, just-in-time techniques, and quality circles. Secondly, in the very processes of technological change as new techniques cut across established boundaries of production organization. 'Cadcam', for example, integrates design with production; biotechnology requires project teams which combine chemists and biologists with information scientists and engineers. Thirdly, changes are taking place in intra- and inter-industry structures where new technologies require industries to redefine core activities and diversify outside traditional areas. Finally, new technologies are demanding changes in regulatory structures with new industries requiring new regulations (for instance, on the use of genetic engineering) and where new technology is making nonsense of existing regulations (as in telecommunications).

Some of these institutional changes are explored in Chapter 2. In essence its authors, like Piore and Sabel, argue that the old Fordist industrial paradigm of mass production and mass competition has now been replaced by a new industrial paradigm of collaboration and cooperation – networking. They see the driving force for integration as the need to work together in networks. The view taken in this chapter will be somewhat different. While acknowledging the existence and growing importance of such collaborative networks, it argues that the driving force behind West European integration has come from fears of technological dependency (and with it, loss of competitiveness) on Japan and the US. The result has been both to foster collaboration within Europe (with some prodding from the Commission) and also to encourage the rationalization and restructuring of European industry to create groupings of a size capable of matching the US and Japanese multinationals.

European trends

Concern about Europe's technological dependence came to the fore in the 1960s with Servan-Schreiber's *Le Défi americain*.[6] At that time the fear was of domination by the US multinationals, particularly IBM. The issue resurfaced in the late 1970s when the very fast advances made by US and Japanese firms in micro-electronics and associated technologies began to impinge upon their European counterparts. By the early 1980s it was widely accepted that a new and more important 'technology gap' existed between Europe and both the US and Japan.

It is worth looking in more detail at this question of the technology gap. Tables 3.1–3.4 derive from work at the Science Policy Research Unit, University of Sussex, by Pari Patel and Keith Pavitt[7] and present a set of statistics which summarize Europe's relative position in technological activities. Tables 3.1 and 3.2 look at R&D statistics, which, although an input rather than an output in relation to technological activities, are the most widely used indicator of such activity. Table 3.1 takes R&D as a proportion of industrial output, looking at both total industrial R&D expenditures and industry-financed expenditures. In Table 3.1 a very different picture emerges if, rather than looking at Western Europe as a whole, the statistics are disaggregated between countries. Two countries, West Germany and Sweden, show a

Table 3.1 Industrial R&D as a proportion of industrial output in some OECD countries, 1967–1985

	Total			Industry financed[a]		
	1967	1975	1985	1967	1975	1985
Japan	0.92	1.28	2.11	0.90	1.26	2.07
USA	2.35	1.84	2.32	1.15	1.18	1.54
France	1.36	1.36	1.78	0.75	0.87	1.24
FRG	1.31	1.65	2.42	1.07	1.30	1.99
Italy	0.43	0.61	0.92	0.41	0.55	0.71
Netherlands	1.45	1.45	1.50	1.31	1.30	1.22
Sweden	1.29	1.64	3.03	0.94	1.48	2.64
UK	2.01	1.72	2.01	1.34	1.08	1.32
W. Europe[b]	1.27	1.35	1.81	0.92	1.00	1.37

[a] Industry-financed R&D excludes that funded by governments which is very important in some defence fields. As a figure it is generally taken to give an indication of industry's commitment to R&D.

[b] Western Europe is defined as the six European countries listed above, plus Belgium, Denmark and Ireland. Total R&D and industrial output for Europe have been calculated by first transforming each country's data into US dollars on the basis of purchasing power parities and then aggregating.

Source: K. Pavitt and P. Patel 'The International Distribution and Determinants of Technological Activity', *Oxford Review of Economic Policy*, vol. 4, No. 4, December 1988. Their figures are based on OECD data.

Table 3.2 Growth rates of industrial R&D compared with growth rates in output, 1967–85 (calculated using 1980 GDP deflator for each country)

	R&D	Output	R&D/Output
Japan	10.0	5.4	5.6
USA	4.6	3.0	1.6
France	5.6	2.8	2.8
FRG	5.8	2.4	3.4
Italy	5.8	2.7	3.1
Netherlands	2.3	2.7	−0.4
Sweden	7.3	1.6	5.7
UK	1.8	1.9	−0.1

Source: OECD.

commitment to R&D which matches the Japanese commitment. France, Italy and the UK are the weaker players. This finding is reinforced by Table 3.2 which looks at growth rates of R&D and output over the period 1967–83. Japan's outstandingly good performance on both scores shows clearly. In Europe, Sweden, West Germany, France and Italy all record major increases in the growth of industrial R&D, and usually also in output. Surprisingly, Sweden (which had topped the R&D league) does not score highly on output growth. Again the poor performance of the UK is notable.

Table 3.3 turns from an input to an output measure of technological activity and looks at patenting in the United States, a good proxy for involvement in mainstream technological activities since any major innovation tends to be patented in the US as well as the home market. There are major differences between industries in the use of patents – they are far more important, for example, in chemicals than in engineering – but these differences tend to hold between countries, and hence patenting does provide a reasonable indication of technological activities both overall and within broad industrial sectors. Table 3.3 looks at the differences in per capita patenting between countries over two five-year periods, 1963–8 and 1980–5. Again the substantial improvement in the Japanese position is noteworthy, as is the significant fall in the US position as leader. As with Tables 3.1 and 3.2, the increasing strength of West Germany and Sweden also stands out.

Table 3.4 breaks down the patent data by industrial sector and looks at the relative position of different countries in different sectors by using an indicator of relative technological advantage, and comparing 1963–8 this time with 1981–6. A number of interesting features emerge from this table:

(1) Western Europe as a whole has a comparative advantage in the chemical and engineering sectors, and does least well in the electrical and electronics sectors;

(2) within Western Europe, West Germany, Sweden and Switzerland have tended to gain advantage in mechanical and electrical engineering sectors

Table 3.3 Trends in per capita patenting in the United States by major OECD countries

Patents per million population

	1963–8	1980–5
Japan	10.40	78.98
USA	236.13	157.88[a]
France	26.64	38.79
FRG	55.32	97.01
Italy	8.15	14.03
Netherlands	36.61	46.89
Sweden	65.30	89.12
Switzerland	140.74	182.34[b]
UK	44.38	40.51
W. Europe[c]	36.71	51.15

[a] The differences in magnitude of per capita patenting between the USA and the other countries are an exaggeration of the differences in innovative activity, as the propensity of US firms to patent in their home country is higher than that of firms from other countries.
[b] Switzerland's high rate of patenting is explained by the concentration of the chemical and pharmaceutical industry in that country.
[c] Western Europe is defined as the seven European countries listed above, plus Belgium, Denmark and Ireland.

Source: As Table 3.1.

(but not electronics) and to lose advantage (though retaining overall comparative advantage) in the chemical sectors. The UK, by contrast, has tended to gain advantage in chemicals but to lose advantage in the mechanical engineering sector and in electronics. Both the UK and France show increasing advantage in the defence sector;

(3) the US has lost advantage in electronics but is still considerably 'better' in this sector than Western Europe. In other sectors its relative position has remained surprisingly stable.

All four tables confirm the considerable and growing technological strength of Japan. Generalization about the position of Western Europe is more difficult, given the variety of trend and pattern of sectoral experience. Two features, however, stand out. First, the dominant position of West Germany: not only does its performance in some sectors match, or even go beyond, that of the Japanese, but it now accounts for more than 40% of all European patenting in the US.[8] Secondly, there is across-the-board weakness among the Europeans in electronics. Both of these factors play an important part in the processes of integration which are discussed next.

Table 3.4 Sectoral patterns of relative advantage in total US patenting for some OECD countries: Revealed Technology Advantage Index[a]

	Chemicals		Mecha	Motor	Raw		Elec.	Electronics[b]	
	Fine	Other	nical	veh.	mater.	Defence	mach.	Cons. goods	Capital
Japan									
1963–8	3.01	1.38	0.77	0.65	0.51	0.35	1.10	1.37	1.80
1981–6	0.87	0.96	0.81	2.08	0.40	0.11	1.11	1.71	1.86
USA									
1963–8	0.89	0.94	1.01	0.95	1.08	0.99	1.01	0.99	1.01
1981–6	0.86	0.98	1.01	0.68	1.21	1.16	1.00	0.92	0.94
France									
1963–8	1.95	0.96	1.02	1.89	0.54	1.10	1.12	1.04	0.80
1981–6	1.45	0.94	0.99	0.80	0.84	1.66	1.08	1.10	0.86
FRG									
1963–8	1.11	1.41	0.96	1.37	0.61	1.03	0.82	1.25	0.88
1981–6	1.17	1.24	1.12	1.48	0.67	1.14	0.90	0.60	0.54
Italy									
1963–8	1.21	1.66	0.95	1.01	0.76	0.78	0.68	0.64	0.36
1981–6	2.23	1.02	1.16	1.15	1.07	0.95	0.69	0.64	0.40
Netherl.									
1963–8	1.72	1.40	0.70	0.17	1.00	0.15	1.16	1.36	2.22
1981–6	0.63	1.05	0.75	0.36	1.69	0.30	1.10	1.44	1.59
Sweden									
1963–8	0.92	0.60	1.20	1.05	1.03	2.35	0.97	0.90	0.57
1981–6	0.59	0.61	1.47	0.75	1.38	2.07	0.95	0.55	0.24
Switzerl.									
1963–8	2.18	1.72	0.89	0.45	0.51	1.44	0.90	0.43	0.48
1981–6	2.02	1.30	1.00	0.44	0.73	1.01	0.98	0.55	0.32
UK									
1963–8	0.88	1.00	1.06	1.55	0.65	1.28	1.04	1.06	1.09
1981–6	2.00	1.00	1.01	0.97	0.86	1.02	0.97	0.89	0.68
W. Europe									
1963–8	1.30	1.24	0.99	1.29	0.66	1.15	0.94	1.05	0.91
1981–6	1.44	1.11	1.08	1.07	0.86	1.18	0.94	0.76	0.62

[a] Revealed Technology Advantage Index is defined as a particular country's share of US patents within a sector divided by that country's share of total US patents. Thus a value of greater than one shows relative strength of a country in a sector and vice versa.

[b] The definition of the sectors is based on an aggregation of three-digit US patent clauses, the precise correspondence being available from the authors.

Source: As Table 3.1

Euro-pessimism and the moves towards integration

The early 1980s, therefore, saw Western Europe confronted, on the one hand, by a foundering of the economic and technological regime which had carried the momentum of growth throughout the postwar period, and, on the other, by the rise of Japan and major changes in the geopolitics of the global economy. Both worked to rekindle a European consciousness and hence to provide a new momentum for West European integration.

As we have seen, Europe's technological performance was in general terms moderately good in relation to the performance of the US and Japan. This was not, however, the perception within Western Europe itself. In particular, the failures in electronics were given high profile. On 31 January 1984, the *Wall Street Journal* carried an article analysing a survey of West European business-men assessing Europe's competence in new technologies and summed up by the headline 'Europe's Technological Erosion Leaves Huge Competitive Gap'.

Europe's businessmen at that time were, indeed, obsessed by developments in electronics. They (rightly) perceived that micro-electronics and its applications in manufacturing and information technology were vital to competitiveness in all industries, but they were deeply pessimistic as to whether Europe was capable of responding to the competitive pressures building up in that industry. Most of the European firms had already pulled out of mainstream semi-conductor production, even with the general recognition that this sector provided the leading edge to the industry.[9] Moreover, in spite of substantial subsidies over many years, neither ICL nor Bull could hold its own against IBM in computers. In telecommunications, long considered a sector where European firms had an edge on other competitors, the Siemens EWS-A fiasco in 1978 had shaken confidence,[10] and it was increasingly clear that, with the next generation of digital switches requiring an R&D expenditure of upwards of $1 billion for a life of uncertain length, Europe could no longer afford the luxury of seven different manufacturers geared largely to national markets. Meanwhile, in consumer electronics, the Japanese, thwarted from exporting by the rapid proliferation of bilateral voluntary export restraints, were steadily increasing their market presence through inward investment, mainly into Britain and West Germany; and in both those countries the indigenous manufacturers were in difficulties.[11]

As if these troubles were not enough, there was a new threat on the horizon. With deregulation in the United States, AT&T had been released from its commitment not to participate in foreign markets, and IBM similarly given the go-ahead to diversify into telecommunications markets. Pressure from US multinationals in the IT sectors, therefore, looked set to increase rather than decrease.

Formal mechanisms for integration

This was the background against which Vicomte Davignon, EC Commissioner for Industry and (after 1982) also for Research and Technology, established his Round Table of Industrialists,[12] gathering together the managing directors of

the 12 largest electronics firms in Europe and confronting them with the state
of their industry and the imminent competitive threat from the US and
Japanese multinationals. Fragmentation of the market among national
champions, he told them, was depriving the industry of the one major
advantage it had over its US and Japanese rivals, namely the European market
of 320 million people; moreover the absolute protection offered by public
purchasing in such important areas as defence and telecommunications meant
too much concentration on lucrative home contracts and insufficient attention
to competitiveness in world markets. With the increasing importance of civilian
markets in electronics, and the advent of satellite and cellular telecommunications, their markets were far from inviolate. Unless they improved performance
they were in great danger of finding themselves 'rolled over' by their American
and Japanese competitors.

Davignon's aim was to establish a Japanese-type consensus programme of
collaborative R&D to be called 'Esprit' (European Strategic Programme for
Research in Information Technology). The Commission had actually been
trying to get such a programme off the ground since the mid-1970s but, until
Davignon's initiative in 1980–81, their pleas had fallen upon deaf ears.[13] His
initial proposals were modest – a pilot scheme in which the 12 companies
could participate for one year to see whether they thought it worthwhile. The
response was favourable and by December 1982 the Commission had the go-
ahead for the pilot phase costing 11.5 million Ecus timed to last through 1983.
This in turn led to the first phase of the full 'Esprit' programme for the years
1984–8 with Community expenditure of 750 million Ecus; this has now been
succeeded by the second phase (1988–92) with expenditure of 1.6 billion Ecus.

Symbolically 'Esprit' has been of far greater importance than either its
expenditure or the specific projects it promoted would imply. There are four
main reasons for this:

(1) It marked a new departure in style for Commission programmes based on
    demand-led projects, where teams of companies and research groups bid
    by project in broadly defined programme areas;
(2) it provided a model for future programmes such as 'Race' (Research in
    Advanced Communications for Europe) and 'Brite' (Basic Research in
    Industrial Technologies for Europe). With 'Esprit' these represent the
    three most important (and most expensive) projects, and all are company-
    led programmes, with tight timetables and monitored schedules;
(3) it has proved to be a turning point in confidence and has helped to bring
    about a reshaping of European industry to meet the challenge coming from
    US and Japanese firms. On the one hand, 'Esprit' has provided a channel
    for cooperation between its European participants that had until now
    been noticeably absent. It has also served as a mechanism for creating
    convergent expectations.[14] For the first time Europe's fragmented elec-
    tronics industry confronted the threat of competition together, and came
    to recognize that in a world of tougher competition, protection and/or
    national champion status had diminishing value. To compete successfully,
    even *within* Europe, they needed to set their sights on global markets and
    global competitiveness;

(4) it has created an important constituency in big business, pressing for the completion of the internal market and the abolition of all remaining internal barriers to trade, such as divergent standards and regulations. Once these firms had discarded their national champion role it was logical that they should begin to look to Europe as their home base and to see the divergent European standards, for example on data transmission, as a major hindrance to effective operation in those markets.

In addition to 'Esprit' and the EC programmes of sponsored collaboration, 'Eureka' has played an important part in helping Western Europen revitalize its technological efforts. 'Eureka' was originally the French alternative to President Reagan's Strategic Defence Initiative (SDI or Star Wars) launched in April 1985. The French government was worried that British and German participation in SDI programmes would further weaken Europe's technological position and suggested 'Eureka' as a civilian alternative to Star Wars, focusing on a number of major civilian technology projects. The British opposed the big project orientation of the French proposals and under their influence 'Eureka' became a much looser collaborative mechanism, aimed at encouraging European firms to collaborate at the near-market end of the R&D spectrum, thus complementing the (initial) emphasis in 'Esprit' on pre-competitive research. From the beginning, 'Eureka' has sought to encourage participation by firms in European countries outside the Community; indeed the British deliberately projected 'Eureka' as an alternative to involvement in the Commission's programme. Unlike the Commission programmes, 'Eureka' offers no direct EC subsidies; instead, any project deemed by the 'Eureka' secretariat to meet 'Eureka' requirements (that is, to be a collaborative R&D project involving firms from at least two participating countries) is eligible for innovation support from the national governments of the countries concerned. 'Eureka's' slim-line secretariat (eight) in Brussels – their task is really to act as registrar of marriages, although on occasion they also play a marriage-broking role – contrasts with the 200-strong DG XIII – the Directorate General responsible for Information and Telecommunications and the present-day successor to the 'Esprit' Task Force.

By mid 1986, the champion of European cooperation, present in one out of every six projects, was the British General Electric Company (GEC), which was one of 'Esprit' 's original 12 Round Table firms (but otherwise better known for its liking of subsidies than for its commitment to European causes). Other firms with high participation in European programmes are Phillips, IRI-Stet, Daimler-AEG, and Thomson, all with involvement in more than 40 projects, while Siemens, CGE, Olivetti, Bull, ICL/STC and the pre-merger ITT are all in the second layer with between 30 and 40 participations. Although some US-based multinationals are involved in various programmes, their presence is seen as token and has been a source of some contention with European-based competitors.[15]

In considering the origin of participants, the dominance of French companies in all programmes stands out. In most programmes, French participants are involved in at least two-thirds of the projects; British and German participation in the 'Esprit' and 'Brite' projects is at a similar level, but considerably lower in

'Eureka'.[16] In 'Eureka', firms and instituitions from smaller European countries have a more marginal role than in the other programmes. In the programmes coordinated by the European Commission the principle of 'juste retour' has had some effect on the degree to which smaller countries participate. In particular, the 'Brite' programme, aimed at helping existing industries to use new technologies, has been more successful in some of the smaller EC countries, but the position of Portugal and Greece is still very weak, largely because of a lack of firms with competence to cooperate. In the case of Greece, the University of Athens is almost the sole participant. Outside the European Community, Sweden and Switzerland have both taken advantage of 'Eureka' to involve themselves in the network of European R&D collaboration, and Austria and Finland also show relatively high participation rates. 'Eureka' has also been an important mechanism for helping to bring companies from the EFTA countries into the fold of other European programmes and has encouraged the Commission to open its programmes to non-EC companies. Note the involvement now of companies such as ASEA, Brown-Boveri and Ericsson in the EC-sponsored programmes.

Firm-to-firm collaborative agreements

The formal mechanisms encouraging collaboration within Europe may have helped to stimulate a network of collaboration, but this has been added to greatly by private collaboration between firms. While the motives underlying 'Esprit' and 'Eureka' have been, at least in part, mercantilist – to promote European technological competence and competitiveness – the motives which have underlain the flowering of firm-to-firm collaboration in the 1980s are more complex and reflect both the underlying uncertainties about technology and the intensification of competition.

Taking a somewhat cynical view, it could be observed that whenever the world economy has encountered a period of great uncertainty associated with the emergence of major new technologies, the gut reaction of industry has been to seek security in the company of others. Hence the trusts of the latter part of the nineteenth century and the cartels of the 1930s. The pressures that impinge on today's world are associated, on the one hand, with the emergence of three major new and pervasive technologies – information technology, biotechnology and new materials technologies – and, on the other, with the expansion of the world trading system to accommodate a large number of new players. These trends combine to create, in almost all markets, intense competition at a global level, which in turn leads the older industrialized countries to seek new markets in which they are insulated from new entrants – hence the push up-market towards higher value-added goods, and the increasing emphasis on research- and technology-intensive activities. The more effort is put into R&D, the faster the pace of technological change, and the higher the cost of keeping up. The intensity of international competition means that new ideas are rapidly picked up and exploited: this is good in so far as it means the rapid diffusion of new ideas, but bad for business in that technological advantage, once gained, is quickly eroded.

These pressures are all interlinked, and they combine, as far as the individual firm is concerned, to make collaboration an obvious route. Collaboration gives the firm:

(1) *access to markets* through cross-licensing and distribution agreements;

(2) *access to technological skills and competences* which they may not have in-house. The pace of change is such that there is often not time to build up in-house teams of experts, particularly since so much knowledge is a matter of learning by doing. The tendency for new technologies to cut across traditional disciplines and to require teams with a wide range of competences also militates in favour of cooperation;

(3) *a means of sharing costs and risks* associated with developing new technologies. Firms are often able to meet the costs, but cannot justify the expenditure because of the very real uncertainties about whether the new technologies will prove feasible either technically or in marketing terms. Sharing costs with others means these risks are spread.

At this juncture it is worth taking a closer look at precisely what is meant by collaboration and at some figures which put developments into perspective. A number of databases of collaborative agreements have been developed.[17] All depend upon combing the press and other published sources for information on agreements and are obviously deficient in so far as many agreements, particularly those involving comparatively little commitment, such as cross-licensing, are not publicized. Nor is publicity given to the dissolution of agreements, or the extent to which agreements or joint ventures culminate in a takeover or merger (which has happened quite frequently). Nevertheless, the figures do provide something of a snapshot of what is happening on collaboration, and for this reason it is worth considering their findings.

The database considered here is that developed at TNO in the Netherlands and has the advantage of covering most of the 1980s but it is concerned

Table 3.5 Number of technological cooperation agreements in information technology and biotechnology

	Before 1970	1970 –75	1976 –79	1980	1981	1982	1983	1984	1985	1986	1987	Total	(%)
Biotechnology	3	5	63	48	55	68	43	55	123	124	108	695	(30.5)
Information technology	12	34	122	68	110	128	161	206	242	252	249	1584	(69.5)
Total	15	39	185	116	165	196	204	261	365	376	357	2279	(100)
(%)	(0.6)	(1.8)	(8.2)	(5.1)	(7.2)	(8.6)	(9.0)	(11.4)	(16.0)	(16.4)	(15.7)	(100)	

Source: J. Hagedoorn and J. Schot, *Cooperation between companies and technological development* (Studiecentrum voor Technologie en Belied, TNO, Delft, 1988).

Table 3.6 Regional distribution of technological cooperation agreements

Regions	Total	Biotechnology	Information technology
W. Europe	352	82	270
	15.4%	11.8%	17.0%
W. Europe-USA	481	117	364
	21.1%	16.8%	23.0%
W. Europe-Japan	104	19	85
	4.6%	2.7%	5.4%
USA	729	316	413
	32.0%	45.5%	26.1%
USA-Japan	388	94	294
	17.0%	13.5%	18.6%
Japan	95	41	54
	4.2%	5.9%	3.4%
Other combinations	130	26	104
	5.7%	3.8%	6.5%
Total	2,279	695	1,584
	100%	100%	100%

Source: J. Hagedoorn and J. Schakenraad, *Strategic Partnering and Technological Cooperation* (MERIT, University of Limburg, 1988).

specifically with information technology and biotechnology.[18] The data relate only to technological cooperation agreements and exclude, therefore, agreements that concern marketing or distribution (but not, of course, agreements that trade market access for technological know-how). The database covers a total of 2,279 agreements, divided approximately one-third/two-thirds between biotechnology and information technology. Table 3.5 sets out the time dimension of agreements. A few date back to the 1970s, but the majority are grouped in the period 1983–7. Table 3.6 sets out the regional distribution of the agreements. The largest number (729, or 32%) are agreements concluded between US firms, the next largest category being agreements concluded between West European firms and the US. To date, agreements between West European firms and Japan lag behind similar agreements between US firms and Japanese firms, but agreements within Western Europe were a not insignificant proportion of the total (15.4%). Unfortunately the regional data are not broken down by time dimension – if they were they would show (as does Table 3.5) a strong push towards intra-European agreements from 1983 onwards.

These figures describe two distinct developments. The first relates to technology. One of the rational reactions to perceptions of the technology gap in the early 1980s has been for European firms to buy-in the process technology they lacked, primarily from outside the Community. Collaborations within the Community have tended to be concerned with new product development. Hence, for example, in 1982–3 Siemens and Phillips combined in what is known as the mega-project to develop, first, a one-megabit chip and subsequently a four-megabit semi-conductor chip. At the same time Siemens

Table 3.7   Community and international mergers (including acquisitions of majority holdings) by companies in the EC

Sector	Community				International			
	1983–4	*1984–5*	*1985–6*	*1986–7*	*1983–4*	*1984–5*	*1985–6*	*1986–7*
Food	2	1	7	11	2	1	2	2
Chem.	13	23	28	27	11	5	6	6
Elec.	2	5	0	6	2	4	3	2
Mech.	3	4	3	8	4	3	7	2
Comp.	0	0	0	0	0	1	0	0
Meta.	0	3	1	4	0	1	2	0
Trans.	3	2	0	6	2	0	4	0
Pap.	1	5	4	7	1	3	5	1
Extra	2	0	3	1	2	0	0	0
Text.	0	0	1	2	0	0	1	0
Cons.	3	1	2	3	1	0	0	3
Other	0	0	3	0	0	0	0	1
Total	29	44	52	75	25	18	30	17

KEY

Food	Food and drink
Chem.	Chemicals, fibres, glass, ceramic wares, rubber
Elec.	Electrical and electronic engineering, office machinery
Mech.	Mechanical and instrument engineering, machine tools
Comp.	Computers and data-processing equipment (in 1983–4 included under mechanical engineering)
Meta.	Production and preliminary processing of metals, metal goods
Trans.	Vehicles and transport equipment
Pap.	Wood, furniture and paper
Extra	Extractive industries
Text.	Textiles, clothing, leather and footwear
Cons.	Construction
Other	Other manufacturing industry

Source: Commission of the European Communities, *Seventeenth Report on Competition* (Luxembourg 1988).

teamed up with Toshiba in order to 'import' the production technology for the project, and admit that without Toshiba's help they would not have achieved their target. The second development has been political. As noted earlier, 'Esprit' broke the ice in respect of collaboration with European partners. The formal collaboration programmes of the Community have led to many more links, formal and informal, being forged between European partners.

There is one further dimension, however, that needs to be explored – that of mergers. Table 3.7 summarizes merger activity in the Community over the course of the period 1983–7. It includes only mergers taking place across country boundaries and excludes the majority of mergers which are with firms within the same country. The two most active areas for both collaborations and mergers have been chemicals and electronics, but the chemicals sector has been far and away the most active in mergers, mainly because companies such as ICI have been seeking to consolidate their position in the speciality chemicals sector. Looking at the table as a whole, perhaps the most interesting feature is the sharp rise in Community mergers in 1986–7 and the relative drop in other international merger activity that year. Again there are a number of factors at work. First, as indicated earlier, collaboration often precedes merger. Hence one of the fruits of more intra-European collaboration is likely to be more intra-European mergers. Secondly, it is reasonable to speculate that the commitment to 1992, which came to the fore in 1985–6 with the Single European Act and the White Paper, also had some effect on this merger activity. Many European companies, unlike the US and Japanese multinational companies, were nationally based and are now hastily seeking to widen their activities across the whole of Europe.

These figures accord well with what we know to be happening on the ground. A number of major mergers have hit the headlines – ASEA-Brown Boveri; Electrolux-Indesit; Nestlé-Rowntree; CGE-ITT; Siemens/GEC-Plessey. In nearly every sector – semiconductors, consumer electronics, telecommunications, heavy electrical equipment, chemicals, pharmaceuticals – we are seeing, both within Europe and within the global framework, a coalescence of activity around large multinational companies. Within Europe, the national champions of yesteryear – Thomson, Olivetti, Siemens, CGE, even GEC – are transforming themselves by a process of collaboration and merger into global players, with research, production and marketing capabilities on a worldwide basis. This, in turn, has resulted in a major rationalization and restructuring of European industry and the creation of firms which are European (or global) rather than national in allegiance. Whether Europe, or the world, has the mechanisms to contain or control the activities of such firms is an important question, but not one for consideration here. Suffice it to register that the processes of cooperation, collaboration and merger have, in the last seven years, brought a marked shift in the degree of integration and concentration in the West European economies.

Conclusions

The previous section has demonstrated how rapidly the fabric of the West European economies is now being woven together through the process of collaboration and merger. 'Being woven together' in fact means being integrated, and the developments discussed in the last section are some of the more obvious and visible signs of the integration that is taking place. However, as William Wallace notes in his introduction, the process of integration is not smooth and continuous, but has proceeded throughout the postwar history of Europe in a series of spurts, followed, it would seem, by a period of adjustment and assimilation – a lull – before another push forward. Another way of looking at it would be to suggest that the process of integration has proceeded through various stages. The first stage involved only aspects of the periphery – the Council of Europe, the Court of Human Rights, the Coal and Steel Community. With the Treaty of Rome it shifted towards the centre, and the rapid growth of internal trade – first among the Six and subsequently among the Twelve of the enlarged Community – bears witness to the degree to which the economies of Member States are becoming interdependent. But trade is about flows of goods and services (primarily goods). One of the notable features of the Community throughout its first 25 years was the vitality of its trade flows and the almost complete absence of movement among factors of production. The Colonna report, for example, lamented the absence of cross-border mergers, regarding these as the sign of a truly consummated union, and this was to be a theme of regret on the part of committed Europeans throughout the 1970s.[19] It was little comfort that the relatively few cross-border mergers that did take place (Dunlop-Pirelli, for example, in tyres, or Hoesch-Hoogovens in steel), proved to be unsuccessful and were unravelled as soon as was feasible.

The new spurt towards integration that is now taking place is marked by the fact that, for the first time, it involves not just trade flows, but substantial movements among factors of production, both capital and labour.[20] This constitutes a significant shift in the process of integration. The question to be answered is what caused this shift. The contention of this chapter is that the main impetus came – and still comes – from technology.

Briefly, the argument is as follows. The 1970s saw the end of the long postwar boom and the beginnings of a period of turbulence from which, by the 1980s, it was clear that the new technologies deriving from micro-electronics – automation, robotics, the information technologies – would rapidly be replacing the technologies of the electro-mechanical era. This technological discontinuity has had major repercussions. Essentially it means that all existing equipment and existing skills are rapidly becoming obsolete and need to be replaced and/or updated. But it has also provided the opportunity for the major Japanese electronics firms to break the established hegemony of the US and enter the world market as major players. This, in turn, has impinged on Europe. First, this entry of Japanese firms enormously intensifies competition. Secondly, Japanese success in breaking US dominance in a number of sectors, including electronics, had led to renewed pressures for protection in the US, and protection not only for manufactured products but also for intellectual property. In other words, whereas throughout the postwar period Europe (and Japan) has had open access to US technology (and it is partly on the basis of this that Europe was able so readily to 'catch up' with the US during this period), Europe was now faced by the possibility of the US closing its doors on this ready source of know-how.

Meanwhile, the relatively slow progress of reequipment and retraining in European firms raised questions over the degree to which they were themselves competitive. There seemed a great danger of being squeezed at both ends of the spectrum of production – at the labour-intensive end by the entry of newly industrialized countries such as South Korea and Taiwan; at the higher value-added end by the escalating R&D costs and the shortening product life of new products. Hence in the early 1980s the era of Euro-pessimism. As we have seen, there was no real need for pessimism. Europe had some sectors of considerable strength (such as chemicals and pharmaceuticals), and some economies, notably West Germany and Sweden, whose performance was in many areas as good as that of Japan. But Euro-pessimism reflected the general feelings of uncertainty and insecurity prevalent at that time.

The 'Esprit' programme was a deliberate attempt to respond to this sense of insecurity. It reflected, it is true, the mood of the moment – joint ventures and other collaborative projects were the fashionable answer to many corporate problems. But there is little doubt that 'Esprit' itself acted as a catalyst to other actions and to encouraging firms to self-help solutions – among them collaborations – as well as government-led action. These moves in turn have paved the way to merger and the wholesale restructuring of European industry that is currently under way. In the process, many European firms have found a new confidence in their own capabilities, and it is this new spirit of confidence that has carried the Single European Act and the commitments for 1992. In other words, 'Esprit' marks not only a new period in technological collaboration, but a new period in European integration.

1990 finds many European firms facing in at least two directions. As the figures on collaborations quoted in the previous section made clear, although intra-European links have been established as never before, so too have what might be called the Triad linkages across the Atlantic and with Japan.[21] To operate successfully as global players, Europe's multinationals must do as other multinationals and establish production and research capabilities around the globe, but particularly in the US and Japan. These remain the countries with the greatest competence in electronics. But the increasing protectionism of the United States (as well as the continuing difficulties of operating in the Japanese market) raises a marker for the future, and provides the rationale for an element of European mercantilism. It is not inconceivable that European firms may, in the future, find that they are 'on their own' – cut off from both Japanese and US sources of technology. It is worth, therefore, hedging bets and backing the European as well as the Triad option.

Notes

1. Schumpeter's theories were expounded in his mammoth work on business cycles (J.A. Schumpeter; *Business Cycles: A Theoretical, Historical and Statistical Analysis of the Capitalist Process* (New York, McGraw Hill, 1939). See also his *Capitalism, Socialism and Democracy* (New York, Harper and Row, 1943).
2. See, in particular, C. Freeman, J. Clark and L.L.G. Soete, *Unemployment and Technical Innovation: A Study of Long Waves in Economic Development* (London, Frances Pinter, 1982) and J.E. Elliot, 'Schumpeter's Theory of Economic Development and Social Change: Exposition and Assessment', *International Journal of Social Economics*, vol. 12, 1984, parts 6 and 7, pp. 6–33.
3. See C. Freeman, 'The Third Kondratieff Wave: Age of Steel, Electrification and Imperialism', paper prepared for international colloquium on 'The Long Waves of the Economic Conjuncture – the Present State of the International Discussion', Vrije Universiteit, Brussels, 12–14 January 1989 (Maastricht: MERIT/Brighton: SPRU, September 1988).
4. M. Piore and C. Sabel, *The Second Industrial Divide: Possibilities of Prosperity* (New York, Basic Books, 1985). See also C. Freeman, *Technology Policy and Performance: Lessons from Japan* (London, Frances Pinter, 1987).
5. The UK is, of course, currently experiencing substantial inflationary pressures, but these derive entirely from internal imbalances and macro-economic mismanagement. For the rest of the world, as a recent GATT report spelled out, the

prospects for growth are good, and forecasts of inflation low. See *Financial Times*, 15 September 1989, 'World markets set for continued rapid expansion'.

6. Jean-Jacques Servan-Schreiber, *Le Défi americain* (London, Hamish Hamilton, 1968).

7. K. Pavitt and P. Patel, 'The International Distribution and Determinants of Technological Activities', *Oxford Review of Economic Policy*, vol. 4, no. 4, December 1988.

8. P. Patel and K. Pavitt, 'Technological Activities in FR Germany and the UK: Differences and Determinants', *National Westminster Quarterly Review*, May 1989, pp. 27–42.

9. M. Sharp, 'European Technology: Does 1992 Matter?', Papers in Science, Technology and Public Policy, No. 19 (Science Policy Research Unit, University of Sussex, 1989).

10. The EWS-A fiasco refers to the first Siemens experiment with a digital telecommunications switching system in 1977–8. The first model it developed for the Bundespost retained an analogue voice transmission system (hence EWS-A) which, by the time it was made public, had been superseded by fully digital systems being developed elsewhere. Siemens rapidly back-tracked and threw resources into developing a fully digital system (EWS-D) which is the backbone of their current very successful range of switching systems. Nevertheless, the Siemens failure to recognize that the product did not match state-of-the-art technology shook West German confidence in their national champion. See G. Dang Nguyen, 'Telecommunications: A Challenge in the Old Order', Chapter 4 in M. Sharp, (ed.), *Europe and the New Technologies* (London, Pinter, 1985).

11. See A. Cawson, P. Holmes, K. Morgan, A. Stevens and D. Webber, *Hostile Brothers: Competition and Closure in the European Electronics Industry* (Oxford, Oxford University Press, forthcoming 1990).

12. Davignon's Round Table consisted of the chief executives of Europe's 12 largest electronic firms: ICL, GEC, Plessey, AEG, Nixdorf, Siemens, Thomson, Bull, CGE, Olivetti, STET and Phillips. Together their output constituted 85% of the output of the European electronics industry. They have continued to play a central role both within Community projects and in the wider collaborations being developed in Europe. Davignon's Round Table of 12 is not to be confused with the wider Gyllenhammer Group of 27, also sometimes known as the Round Table of European Industrialists, which at that time attempted to raise governments' awareness of the need for extensive infrastructure investment in Europe. See M. Sharp and C. Shearman, *European Technological Collaboration*, Chatham House Paper No. 36 (London, Routledge & Kegan Paul, 1987), pp. 49–50.

13. See C. Layton, 'The High Tech Triangle', in Roger Morgan and Caroline Bray, (eds), *Partners and Rivals in Western Europe: Britain, France and Germany* (Aldershot, Gower for the Policy Studies Institute, 1986).

14. The importance of convergent expectations should not be minimized. It is, *par excellence*, the role that MITI performs with Japanese industry, bringing industrialists together, providing them with well-researched information about market trends and technological advances, and encouraging the development of a consensus view as to how best to meet new challenges. Such a process helps to dispel some of the uncertainties that inevitably surround major decisions on new technologies.

15. R. Van Tulde and G. Junne, *European Multinationals in Core Technologies* (Chichester, John Wiley, 1988), p. 277.

16. The high French participation is explained partly by the high level of subsidy offered to firms joining 'Eureka' projects.

17. See, in particular, C.S. Hacklisch, 'International Technical Cooperation in the Semi-conductor Industry: Private Sector Linkages', in H.I. Fusfeld and

R.R. Nelson, (eds), *Technical Cooperation and International Competitiveness* (Proceedings of an International Conference, Lucca, Italy, Centre for Science and Technology Policy, Rensselaer Polytechnic Institute, New York, 1986); J. Hagedoorn and J. Schot, *Cooperation between Companies and Technological Development*, Studiecentrum voor Technologie en Belied, TNO, Delft, 1988; and J. Hagedoorn and J. Schakenraad, *Strategic Partnering and Technological Cooperation* (MERIT, University of Limburg, 1988).

18. See J. Hagedoorn and J. Schot, op. cit. (above, n. 17).

19. See, La Politique Industrielle de la Communauté, (Colonna Report), Commission Memorandum to Council. Com(70)100 Final Commission to the European Community, Brussels, 1970. Also Michael Hodges, 'Industrial Policy: Hard Times or Great Expectations?' in Helen Wallace *et al.*, *Policy-making in the European Community* (Chichester and New York, Wiley, 1983).

20. There is now increasing recruitment of labour, particularly skilled labour and people with professional qualifications, across national boundaries. See *Sunday Times* Business World, 29 October 1989, 'The Rise of the Executive Nomad', pp. 22–3.

21. The concept of the US, Japan and Europe as the Triad, and of the need for multinationals to collaborate between Triad partners rather than within regions was developed by a McKinsey consultant, K. Ohmae, in his book, *Triad Power: The Coming Shape of Global Competition* (London & Basingstoke, Macmillan, 1985).

4 Changing patterns of monetary interdependence
Elke Thiel

Patterns of market interaction have changed considerably during the course of the 1970s and 1980s. The dynamics of market integration have moved from foreign trade to foreign investments. Cross-border production and sales of subsidiaries located abroad have gained weight against foreign trade. The tendency may become even more marked with the deregulation of services and settlement rights. Competition among countries has shifted from trade to overall foreign economic activities, for which the exchange rate is a less important value.[1]

Macro-economic policy conceptions and views on exchange rates have altered as well. When macro-economic policies turned from Keynesianism to monetarism at the end of the 1970s, currency appreciation became a forceful tool in the pursuit of domestic price stability goals. Financial flows are now a major source for the financing of current account deficits. Movements in exchange rates are dominated by capital flows rather than by trade flows. Shifts of capital from one country to another may push exchange rates in a direction unfavourable to the adjustment of trade imbalances.

Monetary interdependence is a worldwide phenomenon. What makes a difference is how countries react to market interdependence. The search for more distinctive patterns of monetary interactions brings into focus the formal or semi-formal framework of institutions, rules and procedures that cause adjustment to external disturbances. Globalization of financial markets has passed Europe by. In the European Community, however, a regional sub-system of formal monetary rules was established in 1979. It is the European Monetary System of pegged exchange rates that distinguishes European cooperation from cooperation pursued within the global monetary system by the Group of Seven.

Rules and procedures provide the formal framework within which market transactions are performed. In this respect, they have an impact on informal flows. Markets have been very ingenious, however, in circumventing formal restrictions, with the present globalization of capital markets as an obvious example. Market forces can also destroy monetary rules when handled inadequately, as happened with the monetary system of Bretton Woods. The

European monetary sub-system has turned out to be more stable than had been anticipated. Adherence to the rules has increasingly shaped domestic policies. As confidence in the system has grown, it has also influenced market expectations and capital flows. Western Europe now looks like an area of closer coherence within a less stable, global monetary system.

The background

Until 1971, monetary interactions among European countries were framed by the global monetary order of Bretton Woods, launched by an Anglo-Saxon initiative in 1944. It was a system of pegged exchange rates, the dollar being the key international currency. The pound sterling was used as a currency of reserve for the sterling area, though the United Kingdom had great difficulty in maintaining that situation.

In the immediate postwar period, European cooperation was aimed at reconstructing the economies and reintegrating them into an open world economy. When the OEEC was founded in 1948, the overall emphasis was on promoting trade liberalization among European countries as a precondition for their integration into the global system of the GATT. In 1950, the European Payment Union (EPU) was established as a multilateral clearing facility for OEEC members' claims and liabilities in foreign transactions. The objective was to facilitate multilateral trade and gradually to implement currency convertibility. This goal was achieved at the end of 1958 by the European Monetary Agreement (EMA), replacing the European Payment Union. With the introduction of convertibility, West European currencies became fully integrated into the dollar area.

Monetary cooperation of the 1960s was global. The IMF was a major actor in promoting credit assistance and also had to approve changes in par values. Because the dollar was the numeraire for all other currencies, it could not change value unilaterally. Adjustment had to come from the other currencies of the dollar-centred system, and realignments thus immediately concerned the US as well.

Cooperation focused particularly on the backing of the reserve currencies of the system, the pound sterling and the dollar. The most important grouping in bringing about rescue operations was the Group of Ten. It was established in 1962, when central bank governors met at the Bank for International Settlements (BIS) in Basle to agree upon actions to stabilize sterling balances (the Basle Agreement). Group of Ten membership formally includes the United States, Canada, the United Kingdom, France, West Germany, Italy, Belgium, the Netherlands, Sweden and Japan. Switzerland also participated before it became a formal member of the Group of Ten in 1984. The BIS provided assistance and the gnomes of Zurich also became important actors in the financing of rescue packages.

The pound sterling was devalued in 1967. In 1971, the United States suspended dollar-gold convertibility and enforced a dollar depreciation. The D-mark emerged as a strong currency and became the currency of reserve second to the dollar when markets built up D-mark balances to diversify dollar reserves, starting in the final years of the Bretton Woods System.

The rules and institutions of the Bretton Woods System provided the monetary order for the Common Market, founded in 1958. The Treaty of Rome leaves macro-economic policy in the domain of national authorities. According to Articles 103–105, however, Member States are obliged to reduce external imbalances, to consider short-term economic and monetary policy with respect to the business cycle and exchange rates a matter of common concern, and to pursue policy coordination. The treaty explicitly provides for the establishment of a consulting Monetary Committee, already in existence in 1958.

In March 1961, the D-mark and the Dutch guilder were revalued upwards. When the Community established a common agricultural policy in the following years, however, currency realignments were to split the Community-wide system of farm prices. A closer coordination of policies thus became even more desirable. In 1964, the Committee of Central Bank Governors was introduced. This came as a belated effort to activate consultations when a rescue operation for the Italian lira had been mounted primarily by American credits and with IMF support, but with no advance notice in Brussels.[2] When the Community later attempted to approach Economic and Monetary Union with the Werner Plan, the institutional equipment for policy coordination was further enlarged by the Economic Policy Committee, introduced in 1974.

In November 1968, the European Community of the Six experienced a major currency crisis, involving the French franc and the D-mark. Both countries declined to adjust parities at this time. The crisis was finally settled by a franc depreciation in August 1969, followed by a D-mark appreciation in October. In the course of events, the Commission launched a new initiative aimed at promoting currency coherence within the Common Market. The Barre Memorandum of February 1969 recommended measures to strengthen and extend economic and monetary policy coordination, including the creation of a mechanism of mutual credit assistance for members experiencing balance-of-payments difficulties. In the same year in December, the Hague summit initiated the Werner Plan for Economic and Monetary Union, submitted in October 1970.

The Werner Plan originally assumed that EMU would be established within the global framework of fixed exchange rates, as provided by the order of Bretton Woods. At the first stage of EMU, margins for currency fluctuations were to be narrowed so that deviation among EC currencies would not exceed currencies' deviation vis-à-vis the dollar, still the numeraire for all other currencies.

The first approach to EMU failed at a time when the end of Bretton Woods made a closer European monetary coherence even more desirable. In March 1971, the Council of Ministers decided to begin with the first stage of EMU. The moment could not have been less auspicious. The global monetary order was about to collapse. The D-mark was subject to large capital flights from the dollar area and was floated freely in May. In August, the dollar-gold convertibility was suspended. In December, the Smithsonian agreement made a last effort to rescue the system. In March 1973, the global system turned to managed floating.

Stage one of the Werner Plan had to be postponed, but started in March 1972 and then involved all members of the Community of Nine. The transition to floating exchange rates in March 1973, however, revealed the differences in economic performances among EC members. While the D-mark was appreciating, other currencies came under downward pressure, in particular the lira and the pound sterling. The United Kingdon, Ireland and Italy left the snake at the very beginning. France tried at first to remain in the system but stepped out later. When the D-mark pulled the snake upwards vis-à-vis the dollar appreciation of the franc was held to be detrimental to French international competitiveness. Countries staying out of the snake also believed that managed floating would give more leeway for domestic demand expansion. The rapid increase of the oil bill, starting in the autumn of 1973, further deepened diversities in economic policies between EC members.

The European snake contracted into a D-mark bloc, formally including the Benelux countries and Denmark as well as Norway and Sweden. Austria and Switzerland informally followed a monetary course that kept their currencies in line with the snake. In 1979, the snake was replaced by the European Monetary System and was thus brought back into the European Community. It then included all members of the Community of Nine, except the United Kingdom, while the Nordic countries left the system.

The European Monetary System can be considered as the European response to the instabilities of the international monetary system. It was triggered by disillusionment with managed floating and the US policy of benign neglect. The overall emphasis was on achieving a zone of monetary stability for Common Market transactions with a view towards making European currencies less vulnerable to disturbances emanating from the dollar. Yet, given large differences in inflation, the reintroduction of pegged exchange rates was widely considered an inadequate response to global interdependence, in particular by German critics. Capital markets would test the system and could easily demolish it. That the system would render European currencies more coherent was scarcely believed at the time.

The EMS-EC relationships

The EMS initiative

The creation of the EMS goes back to the political initiative of the French president, Valery Giscard d'Estaing, and the West German Chancellor, Helmut Schmidt. For France, the emphasis was on restablizing the franc. Bringing the franc back into a system of pegged exchange rates could help to cut past vicious cycles of currency depreciation and high domestic inflation. Italy finally decided to participate for similar reasons, as did Ireland.

At the end of the 1970s, most industrial countries adopted policies to fight high rates of inflation. Accordingly, a strong exchange rate was favoured to support domestic price stability goals. Yet only those countries joining the EMS as a system of pegged exchange rates with the D-mark as the strong currency then committed their anti-inflationary course to formal rules. The

United Kingdom followed an independent track. Like the United States, it looked for gains in price stability from its currency's upwards floating, caused by high interest rate levels and capital imports.

The introduction of the EMS was feasible and the system has been sustainable because economic concepts have become more convergent, starting in the late 1970s. The initial drive to engage in the EMS, however, came from the political sphere. Economic performances in member countries differed enormously when the EMS started. France and Italy were affected by high levels of inflation. Both countries had to fear that their currencies would come under strong downward pressures when pegged with the D-mark. In order to stay in the EMS, they would have to follow a more restrictive monetary course and this could cause too much strain in their inflation-minded domestic economies.

In West Germany, French interest in participating in the European currency system was seen as an opportunity to strengthen the Franco-German relationship and to give new impetus to the European Community. Yet, pegging the D-mark to the French franc and the Italian lira could have put German monetary policy at risk. The commitment of the Bundesbank to support the weaker currencies of the system by intervening in exchange markets would make it more difficult to keep inflation under control. From an economic standpoint, there were thus strong reasons on all sides not to participate in the EMS.

In retrospect, the EMS has worked much better than was anticipated. In the early years, the weakness of the D-mark vis-à-vis the dollar kept EMS currencies together. In France and Italy, EMS membership helped to calm inflation mentalities and could also be used as a scapegoat for unpopular austerity policies.[3] For the Germans, the EMS did not endanger price stability. On the contrary, while strongly supporting the EMS, the Bundesbank also shaped its rules in a way that made the system more resistant to inflation.

The creation of the EMS included elements of bargaining. France had stepped out of the snake twice in the 1970s. By replacing the snake with the EMS, the country could come into the system again without losing face. EMS instruments were framed differently from the snake in order to make participation more acceptable to France. The European Currency Unit (Ecu) was introduced, suggesting a common European currency. The Ecu was also to be used as an indicator for currency divergencies, that should trigger early consultations and adjustment measures. Credit mechanisms were enlarged, and, at the second stage of the EMS, national monetary reserves were to be transferred to the European Monetary Fund. Most of these measures were designed to provide assistance for the weaker currencies in the system. For Italy and Ireland the bargain also included regional compensation.

Yet these specific elements of bargain only played a minor role in the performance of the EMS. What made the EMS a success was a continuous process of learning and common understanding. The watershed year was 1983, when the Mitterrand government turned policy from economic expansion towards a more restrictive course in order to keep the French franc within the EMS. Inflation rates were brought down in the following years and current French price stability is very close to German figures.

Drawing others into the system

The EMS started as a 'two-speed' community. The United Kingdom did not participate in the exchange rate mechanism that pegs currencies together. The whole framework was, however, designed to include all EC members. The EMS works within the institutional framework of the European Community. Regular consultations on economic and monetary issues among all EC members take place at the meetings of the Council of Ministers for Economics and Finance, the Monetary Committee, the Economic Policy Committee and the Committee of Central Bank Governors. The last regularly meets in Basle at the Bank for International Settlements, which also acts as an agent for the settlement of EMS central banks' balances.

Short- and medium-term credit facilities provided by the European Fund for Monetary Cooperation are available to all EC members. These funds were already created in 1971 at the time of the European currency snake and they were expanded in 1979, when the EMS was established. The objective was to provide assistance for members facing balance-of-payment problems, but these funds have never been employed in the more than ten years of the EMS. The Ecu, a basket of EC currencies, included the pound sterling since its creation and the drachma since Greece entered the Community in 1981. The peseta and escudo came into the basket in 1989. All EC members can draw Ecus from the European Fund for Monetary Cooperation by delivering part of their monetary reserves to the Fund.

When the European Summit in Hanover in June 1988 launched a new initiative for an Economic and Monetary Union, all EC members were drawn into the project, although the British were reluctant. All EC central bank governors were members of the Delors Committee, established by the Hanover mandate in order to examine and propose concrete stages leading towards economic and monetary unification. In June 1989, the European Summit in Madrid agreed to start with the first stage of Economic and Monetary Union in July 1990, the date when capital liberalization has to be fully achieved by most EC countries, and all members of the Community are supposed to embark on the process.

Spain had joined the common exchange rate mechanism at the end of the Spanish presidency in the EC. Great Britain, Greece and Portugal are to take part in the course of stage one, although the date for their entry has been left open. The intergovernmental conference, scheduled to convene in December 1990, will bring all EC members together in negotiating a treaty for the subsequent stages of EMU.

EMS rules

The European Monetary System is a system of pegged, but adjustable, exchange rates as opposed to a managed floating system. Currency deviations from the official margins are generally limited to a range of 2.25% in either direction. For Italy, an extended margin of 6% was applied, but the lira was brought into the narrow margin in January 1990, which can also be considered part of the drawing-in process. Since Italy joined the inner circle of the EMS, the 6% margin applies only to Spain.

The system provides a very short-term credit mechanism for the financing of central bank balances occurring from exchange market interventions at the official margins. These interventions are obligatory for all members. The EMS internal exchange rate management has, however, been achieved more frequently by intra-marginal interventions on the part of weak currency countries. Regarding the external exchange rate management, the Bundesbank intervenes primarily in the dollar market, while intra-marginal interventions within the EMS exchange rate combine to keep EMS currencies within the pegged margins.

The accords of Basle and Nyborg in August and September 1987 have therefore extended the use of the very short-term credit mechanism to include intra-marginal interventions as well, although certain restrictions apply regarding the obligation of creditor central banks to accept balance settlements in Ecus. There is, furthermore, no obligation for strong currency central banks to intervene within the margins. This brings about what is called the asymmetry of the system. It implies that the stability-oriented monetary policy of the German Bundesbank has a strong influence in the EMS, and this has sometimes caused other members to complain. Asymmetry is, however, held to be an indispensable element of a monetary system aimed at achieving price stability.[4] As the system now functions, it works towards strengthening the stability-oriented course of the members with the weaker currencies.

Coordination among EMS Central Banks evolved in a rather pragmatic way.[5] Short- and medium-term credit facilities were never used. The EMS functioned more smoothly and private capital flows became a source for the financing of current-account deficits. Since currencies have recently become more coherent, this has also enlarged prospects for a sound 'domestic' European monetary policy instead of having frequent adjustments to currency fluctuations involving the dollar. Although closely linked with global markets, the EMS now seems better prepared to absorb shocks coming from the outside.

Coherence of economic policies

If anything makes the EMS the inner core of West European monetary integration, it has to do with the adherence to the rules of pegged exchange rates. A system of pegged exchange rates is not sustainable unless there is a certain coherence in macro-economic policies and economic fundamentals, namely, monetary policy and inflation, fiscal policy and external balances. The extent to which coherence in these fields has been achieved tells more about the intensity of monetary integration, the sustainability of the system and its strains.

In the early 1970s, the first attempt to achieve a European Economic and Monetary Union failed because national policies of adjustment to international monetary disturbances and rising oil prices had become incompatible. When the EMS was introduced in 1979, conceptions of economic policy had become more congruent. Concern to avoid inflation and currency depreciation similar to the concern which marked the beginning of the EMS was, and still is, however, not confined to the EC Member States which participated in the EMS exchange rate mechanism from the beginning. How do economic performances of the initial EMS 8, therefore, compare with non-EMS 4 countries?

Monetary and fiscal policy

In a system of pegged exchange rates, the scope for an independent domestic monetary policy is very limited. Exchange market interventions and official balance settlements automatically bring about converging monetary policies and inflation rates. In the case of the EMS, coherence of monetary policy has grown, as can be expected in a system of pegged exchange rates. Moreover, inflation rates have converged towards lower levels, indicating a sustained preference for price stability on the part of EMS members. Adjustment to the D-mark as a strong currency has supported or forced this tendency. Inflation rates differed enormously during the first years of the EMS. The difference between the lowest and highest inflation rate was 13.6% in 1980 but then declined to about 4% for 1987–8.

Inflation rates peaked in the years 1980 to 1982 in all EC Member States and steadily decreased from 1983–4 onwards for most countries. In Greece, Portugal and Spain inflation rates moved down only more recently. On a weighted average, the EMS 8 inflation rate was 2.5% in 1987, only half the rate of the non-EMS 4 average, i.e. 5.2%.[6] This was, however, due to the still high (although declining) levels of inflation in Greece and Portugal. For the United Kingdom and for Spain, inflation rates were more or less within the range set by the lowest and highest inflation rates of the EMS currencies in 1987.

Inflationary pressures have increased in all EC countries in 1988–9. For the inner circle of the EMS, i.e. members pegging the exchange rate within the smaller margin, inflation rates were, however, kept on lower levels than in other EC countries. Moreover, those countries' performances in price stability do not differ very much from each other. In the United Kingdom, and also in Italy and Spain, rates of inflation have risen above the EC average.

In a system of pegged exchange rates, the immediate impact of rules is greater on monetary policy than on fiscal policy. If the rules of the system keep monetary policies on a restrictive path, however, this will also restrict options for the financing of public deficits and debts in the medium run.

Most EMS members have made an effort to reduce public deficits and debts in the 1980s, but have not yet reached the same coherence in fiscal policy as in monetary policy. Public deficits are currently highest for Italy (10%), followed by Belgium (6%). Corresponding figures for non-EMS participants are 20% for Greece and 6% for Portugal. Public debts are also high in these countries. Huge fiscal deficits and public debts make it more difficult for countries to pursue a monetary course that keeps their currencies pegged. They are thus a potential source of instability in the EMS exchange rates. Similar progress in budgetary consolidation was achieved by Denmark, France and West Germany, in particular, as well as by the United Kingdom and to a lesser extent by Spain.

Comparing EMS 8 and non-EMS 4 countries, the main difference lies in the way by which adjustment to price stability goals has been brought about. While EMS 8 members have pursued price stability by linking their currencies to a strong D-mark, the United Kingdom and Spain have independently followed a rather similar course. For Spain, the main impetus had been to prepare for its forthcoming full EC membership and subsequent participation in the EMS.

On the part of the United Kingdom, reining in fiscal deficits and inflation has been an essential goal of the Thatcher government. Yet, as it looks now, maintaining economic stability may have become more burdensome under conditions of managed floating. The country is presently more exposed to inflation and rising interest rates than are EMS participants, and it also faces a major current-account deficit.

Current account imbalances and capital flows

The EMS is a system of pegged exchange rates, but does not rule out parity adjustment as a means of correcting external imbalances. In the first years of the EMS, some of its members experienced large current-account deficits, and parity adjustments took place more frequently. With respect to frequency and size of currency realignments, the bulk of parity adjustments took place between October 1981 and March 1983. Since then, realignments have become rarer and the margins of adjustment have narrowed.

Starting in 1983, balances of current account have improved for most EMS countries. This particularly applies to countries such as Belgium, France, Ireland and Italy which had formerly had a deficit and which experienced a downward correction of their currencies in previous EMS realignments. Current-account imbalances have widened in intra-EMS transactions, however, as West Germany's trade surpluses with other EC members have increased during the last four years. Yet, with the exception of a slight depreciation of the lira when it was brought into the inner margin of the EMS exchange rate mechanism in January 1990, the EMS saw its last currency realignment as long ago as January 1987. Since them, EMS members have not considered a new currency realignment to be a suitable means of correcting external imbalances and neither have currency markets expected a realignment to occur.

Regarding the role of the exchange rate in the overall process of bringing about economic adjustment, the EMS now functions in a completely different way than the exchange rate management of the Group of Seven which evolved from the Plaza and Louvre accords. With respect to the latter, the particular emphasis is on bringing exchange rates into line with the requirements of reducing current-account imbalances. The external value of the dollar is a key variable in this process. Accordingly, in view of the persistent US trade deficit, the question of how far the dollar should decline in relation to the currencies of the major surplus countries in order to support the restructuring of the US economy is a major issue in the current domestic discussion in the United States.[7]

On the contrary, EMS members presently tend to consider the exchange rate as a standard to which the domestic economy has to perform rather than as an instrument to bring about easier adjustment of the current account. The overall emphasis now seems to be on restructuring the domestic economy with a view towards dealing with the challenges of 1992. As competition among countries has generally shifted from foreign trade to all kinds of foreign economic activities, where the exchange rate matters less, this applies even more to the internal market. Furthermore, regarding 1992, the attractiveness of a country for European investments depends on the overall performance of the domestic economy, and currency depreciation is considered detrimental in this context. With an eye to 1992, the French emphasis with respect to the EMS, for instance, is now on making the French franc as strong as the D-mark.

Also, as long as currency markets do not expect large realignments in the EMS, capital movement works for exchange-rate stability rather than to destabilize the EMS. While France and Italy have been removing foreign exchange restrictions – a process which started in 1986 – this has not destroyed the system, as some observers feared, but actually bolstered confidence in these respective currencies. As realignments have diminished in frequency and size, private capital flows have functioned as a means for the financing of current-account deficits and for exchange-rate stabilization. The system has become more like a monetary area in which external imbalances between regions are compensated for by financial transfers rather than corrected by exchange-rate adjustments. This can be looked at as an indicator for intensified monetary integration.

Nevertheless, in view of present current-account imbalances (with a German surplus of more than 5 per cent of GNP in 1989), some parities may have to be adjusted. Such a decision is, however, not visible on the political horizon in early 1990. Moreover, within the inner core of the EMS, currencies have become very coherent and their adjustment is not regarded as necessary.

To secure capital imports, countries with weaker currencies have to keep interest rates at higher levels. Compared with West Germany or the Netherlands, domestic nominal interest rates have been very high in some EMS countries, largely reflecting differences in the rate of inflation. Moreover, interest rates have been higher in all EC countries except West Germany and the Netherlands than in the United States. This illustrates the force of capital drains from Western Europe and other parts of the world into the US in the 1980s.

For France, Belgium and Denmark, from 1985 onwards interest rates were on lower levels than in the United Kingdom. Real interest rates were below UK levels in some EMS countries as well. Obviously, exchange markets no longer expected major EMS realignments at that time. As confidence in the system strengthened, it shaped conditions for capital inflows which were more favourable for members belonging to the inner core of the EMS. UK policy was to keep the pound sterling in a sound relationship between the dollar and the D-mark in those years. Yet, as the currency was not anchored, interest rates probably had to be higher to cover the risk of currency fluctuation.[8] This experience may also suggest that managed floating is not a sound option, even for a country the size of the United Kingdom, and that autonomy in monetary policy is, in fact, rather limited.

Solidarity: regional compensations

The fundamentals on which an economic and monetary union could be built up are the Common Market, including capital liberalization, the EC insitutions and the EC Structural Funds. The last of these could be considered as a nucleus for regional financial compensations. Such compensations are indispensable if economic coherence is to be achieved between centres and peripheries as laid down in the Single European Act.

Disparities in regional income and levels of economic development can be a major obstacle to economic and monetary integration. Mutual assistance of central banks in exchange-market interventions and credit mechanisms for the financing of balance-of-payments deficits are common instruments in all systems of pegged exchange rates. They were (for instance) employed in the monetary system of Bretton Woods.

When the EMS was introduced in 1979, special credits for regional compensation were temporarily granted to Italy and Ireland to secure EMS membership for these countries. Leaving these short-term relief measures aside, the EMS does not possess the means to allow for specific regional compensation for countries participating in the pegged exchange rate combine. The European Community, however, is in a position to take such measures.

Compensations are aimed at strengthening the economic and social coherence among regions within the Common Market. In 1975, the European Fund for Regional Cooperation was established as a part of the bargain on the implementation of the second stage of the European currency snake. In 1986, the Integrated Mediterranean Programme was concluded in support of structural adjustment in the Mediterranean regions of France and Italy, as well as in Greece. At that time, emphasis was placed on providing compensation for the detrimental effects of the southern enlargement of the Community. The largest payments at that time went to Italy, followed by the United Kingdom and France.

With the southern enlargement of the EC, regional disparities within the Community have increased. The least developed regions now are on the new periphery, primarily Ireland, Greece, Portugal and Spain. In accordance with the decisions of the European Council in February 1988, the financial assets of the EC Structural Funds will almost double by 1993. Compensation will be provided in particular for the fringe regions. If there is a European identity, it cannot be confined to monetary rules and intensified market transactions. Identity is also associated with solidarity, and the overall framework for achieving solidarity is not the EMS but the EC.

The European space

The global dimension of monetary cooperation

More than international trade, the globalization of capital markets has linked national economies more closely than ever. Financial transactions are now 25 times larger than trade in goods and services, and capital flows know no

Table 4.1 Share of national currencies in total identified official holdings of foreign exchange

	1979	1988
US dollar	73.2	63.3
Yen	3.6	7.2
D-mark	12.0	16.2
Pound sterling	1.8	3.1
French franc	1.3	1.7
Guilder	1.0	1.1
Swiss franc	2.4	1.5

Source: International Monetary Fund, *Annual Report*, 1988 and 1989.

boundaries. Western Europe is closely integrated into this highly inter-dependent international economic system. The United States is still the key currency country in the global system, although it may have ceased to be the super-core. The dollar ranks first in the composition of official reserves and international financial transactions. The D-mark and the yen are the main counterparts to the dollar because these currencies are mostly used as altern-atives for currency diversification (Table 4.1).

The US has accumulated huge current-account deficits and external debts in the course of the 1980s. Japan emerged as the main and most visible individual creditor of the United States in these years. Yet the West European net creditor position with the US amounted to $437 bn at the end of 1988, more than three times what it was for Japan ($128 bn).[9] Moreover, Western Europe has been in a creditor stance towards the United States since at least the early 1970s. Due to its own adjustment problems and its external indebtedness, the US itself now has to rely on international cooperation. The main partners are Japan, Canada and the major European industrial countries – the UK, France, West Germany, Italy – as well as the European Community regarding trade policy.

Starting with the Plaza Accord in September 1985, global monetary coopera-tion has been revitalized. It currently centres on managing the dollar rate within sound margins. Rapid shifts in capital flows from one country to another cause large fluctuations in exchange rates. In order to calm currency fluctuation, central banks work together in the management of floating exchange rates on a global basis. There are inner and outer circles in the pursuit of monetary policy coordination, namely the informal G2 or G3 (the United States and Japan plus West Germany) and regular meetings of the G7 (which is the G3 plus Canada, the United Kingdom, France and Italy). The next circle is the G10, already established in 1962.

The most important currency relationship in the global system at present is the G3. Shifts in the exchange rate of the dollar almost immediately push the D-mark or the yen in the opposite direction. As the D-mark is the key currency in the EMS, it also serves as a link between the dollar and other EMS currencies.

Table 4.2   International claims of banks located in main financial centres ($ bn)

	1984	1987	1988
Britain	489.3	875.6	883.6
Japan	126.9	576.9	733.7
USA	409.6	508.9	555.8
Offshore centres:			
Asia			598.3
Caribbean			421.4
Other EC 12:			
France	141.5	266.4	275.9
Germany	64.2	206.0	206.0
Luxembourg	85.6	182.3	188.6
Belgium	68.3	164.8	142.8
Netherlands	56.5	115.3	122.3
Italy	36.7	63.4	62.8
Spain		25.5	24.3
Denmark		17.1	19.8
Other W. European:			
Switzerland	52.8	130.2	117.0
Austria		54.9	50.3
Sweden		17.1	14.9

Source: Bank for International Settlements, 55th/58th/59th *Annual Reports* (German edition).

The Werner Plan failed when the depreciation of the dollar moved European currencies apart. In the early years of the EMS, large fluctuations of the D-mark with respect to the dollar were most likely to cause strains in EMS exchange rates. Yet, when the dollar was brought down (starting in 1985), EMS currencies had already become more converging.

Moreover, in the case of dollar disturbances, a close coordination of exchange-market interventions and interest rates has been achieved on the part of all West European central banks concerned. Coordination has been particularly strong between the Bundesbank and its counterparts in Switzerland, Austria, the United Kingdom and in the EMS. In comparison with the 1970s, Western Europe has become a more stable and coherent monetary area.

Centres and periphery: the financial network

Financial Europe is not on the fringe of the global system. The Euromarket for money and capital functions as a switchboard for private capital flows all over the world. European financial centres serve as a platform for the global activities of international banks. London is a pre-eminent international banking place. In regard to the dimension of foreign activities of financial institutions

Table 4.3   Composition of international claims by the national origin of banks ($ bn)

	1985	1988
USA	590.2	675.2
Japan	706.2	1756.4
Britain	192.8	238.6
France	244.0	384.1
Germany	191.2	353.8
Others	789.1	1190.1

Source: Bank for International Settlements, 59th *Annual Report* (German edition).

located there, London ranks far above financial centres in the US or continental Europe. Yet, foreign activities of banks located in Japan came very close to those of London banks in 1988 (Table 4.2). Offshore centres in East Asia and the Caribbean have also gained in importance recently.

Moreover, competition between London and the financial centres of the continent increases in view of 1992. The British financial community is now urging the Thatcher government to join the inner circle of the EMS because this would give London a stronger foothold in the internal financial market. Also, when international claims are examined with respect to the national origin of financial institutions, British banks rank below French and German banks (Table 4.3). Regarding the currency composition of international bank positions, the pound sterling is behind the Swiss franc. The D-mark is the most used European currency in this field, comparable with the yen, but far behind the dollar (Table 4.4).

In continental Europe, financial centres are roughly equivalent in size. France holds the first rank, followed by West Germany, Luxembourg, Belgium and the Netherlands. Each of them ranks above or is comparable to Switzerland, which can be viewed as the main European financial centre outside the EC. Total international activities of EC continental financial centres exceed the international activities of banks located in the United States or Japan.

These figures indicate, first of all, that Western Europe and the European Community certainly play more than a peripheral role in the global dimension of financial interactions. Although London is the main banking centre in Europe, the dimension of international activities of banks with origins in other EC Member States or in Switzerland, and the currency composition of financial transactions, suggest that intra-West European financial relations are shaped more by mutual interdependence than by unilateral dependence on one single financial centre.

The financial cores are on a north-south axis, within an area stretching from the United Kingdom over the Benelux countries, France and Germany to Switzerland. Smaller West European banking places, ranking second to the major centres (and whether located within the EC or not), can hardly be considered as belonging to the fringe, however, due to their own involvement in the Euromarket.

Table 4.4 International claims of banks by currency composition ($ bn)[a]

	1988
US dollar	1818.0
Other currencies	1647.5
of which:	
Yen	503.7
D-mark	438.4
Pound sterling	146.1
Ecu	86.0
Swiss franc	168.9

[a] Euromarket positions and external positions in domestic currencies.

Source: Bank for International Settlements, 59th *Annual Report* (German edition).

Europe as a financial space has no clear-cut boundary lines. Capital flows have a global orientation and are rather volatile. Capital flows tend to follow short-term incentives in money and security markets. They can change direction quite rapidly. Germany has recently experienced net capital exports with respect to all Western industrial countries. The destination of German capital outflows may thus be looked on as an indicator of financial interactions. German short-term capital flows went mainly to the financial centres of the Euromarket, where they may have been recycled to other destinations inside and outside the EC or Western Europe, The main destinations were the UK and Luxembourg, and to a lesser extent France, the Netherlands, Switzerland and Austria. In 1987, a large portion of German short-term capital export directly went into the US as well (Table 4.5). Looking at German direct investment abroad, a major part went to the United States and a steady stream to West European countries (Table 4.6). These figures also demonstrate recent capital drain from Europe to the US. Yet financial flows may become more favourable for Europe when the internal market offers more attractive opportunities for investment.

Dynamics of monetary integration

When the Werner Plan failed in the early 1970s, the snake became the framework for a closer monetary cooperation of West European countries within the global system. The snake was a fairly stable monetary system centred on the D-mark. It was, however, not aimed at achieving more ambitious goals of economic and monetary integration among its members.

As the EMS replaced the snake in 1979, the immediate emphasis was not on economic and monetary unification but on re-establishing exchange rate stability in support of domestic price stability. Yet, the smooth functioning of

Table 4.5 German balance of capital account, short-term (bn DM)

	1985	1986	1987	1988
All industrial countries	−37.7	−108.0	−18.0	−25.4
EC-12	−28.2	−100.0	−6.1	−16.4
Britain	−9.8	−44.9	−1.4	−5.0
Bel/Lux	−13.7	−39.5	−3.4	−8.0
France	−4.5	−5.8	−0.6	−2.4
Italy	−1.3	−2.4	−1.5	−0.9
Netherlands	1.7	−6.7	0.3	1.4
Spain	−0.7	0.7	0.3	−1.5
Other W. European				
Switzerland	−4.6	−3.7	1.6	−2.0
Austria	−4.2	−4.2	−1.0	−2.0
Sweden	2.0	−1.0	−1.1	−0.4
Norway	0.4	−0.5	−0.8	0.4
USA	1.6	0.8	−7.6	−0.5
Japan	−2.7	0.7	−2.0	−5.3

Source: Deutsche Bundesbank, *Statistische Beihefte (Beilage)*, Series 3, No. 7, July 1989 (for 1985 EC-10).

the system enlarged prospects for further steps in West European integration. It is hard to imagine that the 1992 initiative would have been feasible at a time when the main EC currencies largely diverged from each other. The perspective of the internal market has now revitalized the objective of Economic and Monetary Union. When the Community achieves a single market, going ahead with Economic and Monetary Union seems to be a logical step within the overall economic and political destination of West European integration. However, when EC members agreed at the summits in Hanover and Madrid to advance economic and monetary integration, this only became feasible by virtue of past EMS success.

So far, monetary integration in Western Europe has centred on the D-mark, which was the leading currency in the snake and has become a key currency in the EMS. Austria and Switzerland did not officially participate in the European currency snake but followed, and still pursue, a stability-oriented monetary course that keeps their currencies close to the D-mark. The D-mark has gained such a pre-eminent role because it offers a strong currency option favoured by other countries in accordance with their own price stability goals. This is particularly so in the case of smaller West European countries. Furthermore, since the introduction of the EMS, the number of countries pursuing a course oriented towards price stability has increased. Thus, when the core of strong EMS currencies strengthens further, relations between members may become more balanced rather than being dominated by one single strong-currency country.

Table 4.6 German balance of capital account, direct investments (bn DM)

	1985	1986	1987	1988
All industrial countries	−11.7	−18.2	−11.0	−16.3
EC-12	−2.4	−5.3	−3.5	−4.2
Other W. European	−0.9	−0.7	−0.0	0.2
USA	−8.5	−11.5	−7.3	−11.5

Source: Deutsche Bundesbank, *Statistische Beihefte (Beilage)*, Series 3, No. 7, July 1989 (for 1985 EC-10).

Moreover, the success of the EMS would not have been possible if the EMS partners had not pledged themselves to a strong currency position.[10] The Bundesbank cannot swim against the stream, but can only achieve price stability in the EMS when other participants are also committed to this goal. With the mandate from the Hanover and Madrid meetings, the issue now is to ensure a common understanding on the principles and goals of a European monetary policy over the long term. As the EMS functions continuously as a zone of monetary stability, it will also provide an anchor for monetary policy of other West European countries following similar goals.

When the EMS replaced the snake, participation in the exchange rate mechanism was not ruled out in principle for third European countries that are closely linked economically and financially with the European Community.[11] The countries most closely connected with the EC are the EFTA states. A large portion of their foreign trade is destined for the EC. It thus goes without saying that the external value of EFTA currencies with respect to EC currencies is most significant. Yet, although some EFTA members (Norway and Sweden) were formal members of the snake, no EFTA member has so far applied for formal participation in the EMS.

Norway and Sweden dissociated from the D-mark when they assumed a more expansionary monetary course in order to counter unemployment in the early 1980s. They now peg their exchange rate to a currency basket representing a composite of the main currencies used in foreign trade. The same holds for Finland. Switzerland has renounced formal links with the EMS for reasons of autonomy. Austria is now considering EMS participation in line with its application for EC membership. As the EFTA states and the EC aim to deepen economic relations in accordance with the elimination of boundaries within the internal market, market integration may also work for an intensifying monetary relationship.

In summary, the evolution of the EMS can be considered as an illustration of the dynamics of West European integration. In 1979, the introduction of the EMS was a response to monetary disturbances in the international system. The emphasis was on creating a European zone of monetary stability and on making European currencies less vulnerable to external shocks. Yet, private capital flows can easily destroy a system of pegged exchange rates if diverging economic policies erode confidence in the system. The most remarkable aspect of the EMS is thus that the common understanding on price stability goals was strong enough to make the system sustainable.

The European business community pushed the 1992 project because a unified market offers gains in economic growth and international competitiveness. It now favours a single European currency because this would further rationalize Common Market transactions. Moreover, as an inner circle of EC countries has moved ahead by reconciling economic policies, prospects for West European economic and monetary unification have improved. There are still considerable obstacles to overcome. Yet, as the core of EMS members now aim at Economic and Monetary Union, the worst policy for other EC countries would probably be to keep apart. Starting from an inner circle, the dynamics of economic and monetary integration thus draw all EC members into the process and may eventually also spread beyond EC boundaries, if the project succeeds.

Notes

1. See also DeAnne Julius, *Global Companies and Public Policy: the Challenge of the New Economic Linkages* (London, RIIA, 1990).
2. The rescue package also included a smaller credit from the German Bundesbank and the Bank of England. See Susan Strange, *International Monetary Relations* (London, Oxford University Press, 1976), p. 133 and Andrew Shonfield, (ed.), *International Economic Relations of the Western World 1959–1971*, Vol. 2 (Oxford: Oxford University Press/RIIA, 1976).
3. See also John B. Goodman, *The Domestic Impact of International Regimes: France, Italy and the European Monetary System*, paper delivered at the Joint Annual Convention of the British International Studies Association and the International Studies Association, London, 28 March–1 April 1989.
4. See also Daniel Gros and Niels Thygesen, *The EMS: Achievements, Current Issues and Directions for the Future* (Brussels: Centre for European Policy Studies, 1988), CEPS-Paper No. 35.
5. Elke Thiel, 'From the Internal Market to an Economic and Monetary Union', *Außenpolitik*, Vol. 40, No. 1 (1989), pp. 66–75.
6. EC Commission, Annual Economic Report 1988–9, Com (88) 591 endg.; vol. 1, p. 15.
7. See e.g. 'All Exports Aren't Created Equal', *The Wall Street Journal*, 3 July 1989, p. 1.
8. See also Andrew Scott, 'Britain and the EMS: an Appraisal of the Report of the Treasury and Civil Service Committee', *Journal of Common Market Studies*, Vol. 24, No. 3 (March 1986), pp. 187–201.
9. *Survey of Current Business*, Vol. 69, No. 6 (June 1989), p. 42.
10. The Delors Report attributes the success of the EMS to the following three achievements: 'the participants' willingness to opt for a strong currency stance'; 'the flexible and pragmatic way in which the system has been managed'; and 'the role played by the D-mark as an anchor for participants' monetary and economic policy': Committee for the Study of Economic and Monetary Union, *Report on Economic and Monetary Union in the European Community*, 12 April 1989, p. 2.
11. Conclusion of the European Council on 5 December 1978 in Brussels on the establishment of the European Monetary System, cipher 5.2.

Part II
Centre and periphery

5 Patterns of production and trade
Per Magnus Wijkman

The aim of this chapter is to draw an economic map of Europe – defining its economic core and its periphery – as a background to the development of economic institutions.

The geographic concentration of economic activity in the countries of Western Europe, and the close network of commodity trade between them, delineate Western Europe as a relatively homogeneous and highly integrated economic region. This economic unity is often obscured by the division of most of Western Europe into two trade groupings, the European Communities (EC) and the European Free Trade Association (EFTA).[1] This division reflects different political preferences and constraints, which prevent the countries in these two groups from participating in one and the same institution. Indeed, the fact that countries working under different political constraints are already closely integrated economically poses a special institutional challenge. How much institutional pluralism is compatible with the application of uniform rules for economic activity – a uniformity that is necessary if integrated markets are to be achieved?

This chapter goes some way towards providing an answer by illustrating how the interaction between changing economic interdependence and political constraints has formed institutions for economic integration in Europe over the past 30 years. This process of institutional evolution has not yet run its course – *vide* recent developments in Eastern Europe – and additional changes can be expected.

An economic mapping

Both the pattern of production and that of trade identify the 18 countries of Western Europe as a distinct economic region. These distinguishing patterns single out the present 18 members of the EC and EFTA as forming a true European Economic Space (EES).

In a global perspective, the economic size of Western Europe is disproportionate to its landmass. In 1985, for example, Western Europe produced more than the USSR and Japan together and about as much as North America, albeit with a somewhat larger population.

The difference between East and West Europe is striking. Each of the six planned economies of Eastern Europe produces about as much as one of the smaller countries of Western Europe, but has about four times as large a population. The EFTA countries with a population of 32 million produce as much as the six Eastern European countries with 110 million. In addition to the sharp difference in per capita income, the planned economies of Eastern Europe have been based on different economic principles from those of the market economies of Western Europe. During the postwar period, this difference in economic systems has drawn a sharp borderline between West and East Europe, in part explaining the variations in productivity.

Within Western Europe, economic activity is concentrated in the central region, forming an economic core. Sixty per cent of the gross domestic product of the EES countries is produced within a triangle formed by the harbours of Bristol, Genoa and Hamburg. Most of the geographic area of the original six EC members lies within this core as do Switzerland and south-east England. Here lie Western Europe's major agglomerations of population and production and its major regions with high per capita incomes.

Outside this triangle lies the periphery: the Fenno-Scandinavian and the Iberian peninsulas, the Celtic fringe, southern Italy, Greece and perhaps Austria. An important distinction between the Community and the Association is apparent here. While the EC is more core than periphery, EFTA is more periphery than core.

Finally, geography, economics and history combine to make Cyprus, Malta, Turkey and Yugoslavia truly the 'orphans of Europe': peripheral, poor and politically complex.

Trade flows between the countries of Western Europe also delineate Western Europe as a distinct economic entity. The share of intra-regional trade is high and has grown during the past three decades, reflecting increased regionalization. An EES country conducts on average close to three-quarters of its trade with the other EES countries. (See Figure 5.1.) This heavy dependency on trade with their neighbours distinguishes EC and EFTA countries from others. Turkey and Yugoslavia have the lowest shares of intra-European trade.

Trade flows are evenly spread among countries within the EES and it is not possible to group them into two separate trading blocs on the basis of the direction of their trade. All EES countries buy more from the EC than from the EFTA, reflecting the larger size of the former. But EFTA countries on average take as large a share of their imports from the Community as do EC countries themselves. Those EC countries with the lowest share of imports coming from the Community (the UK, Germany and Denmark) buy more from EFTA. Likewise, those EFTA countries taking a low share of their imports from EFTA (Austria and Switzerland) tend to buy more from the EC. As a result, the share of imports from the EES is high and relatively even for all West European countries except Turkey and Yugoslavia.

In summary, the European Economic Space is characterized by the relatively free play of market forces, large 'economic mass', high per capita incomes, and large intra-regional trade flows. Nowhere else in the world can one find such

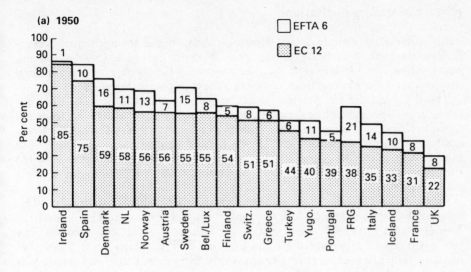

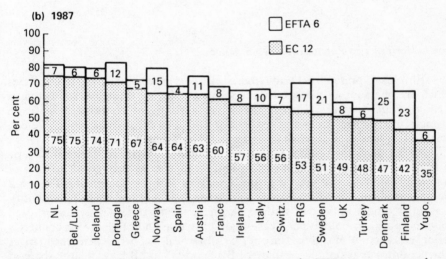

Figure 5.1 Exports from West European countries to the EES (as percentage of total exports)

high economic interdependence between a large number of sovereign states. Except for Greece, it is a contiguous area with a core largely formed by the original six EC members. All EFTA countries except Switzerland lie outside this core, as do the southern EC members. However, the peripheral countries in the north as well as in the south are tied closely to the core through trade. Thus, the 18 countries stand out as an affluent economic unit with strong internal cohesion.

History of trading institutions

Economic variables alone do not determine institutional arrangements. Nevertheless, the pattern of trade flows within Western Europe is a useful starting point when considering economic institutions. The course of institutional design since 1958 has run from competitiveness to complementarity.

The EC and EFTA started as competing organizations with different economic scope and political ambitions but of roughly equal size. In response to the creation by the six core countries of a customs union in 1958, EFTA was created as an organization with more limited objectives to provide those outside the EC with a free trade area for industrial goods until a broad European solution could be achieved. Until 1972, two competitive trade systems existed in Europe.

In 1972 the United Kingdom and Denmark left EFTA for the EC. The enlarged EC entered free trade agreements with each remaining EFTA country. This created a broad European system for industrial goods encompassing the two sub-systems represented by the EC and EFTA, which became complementary rather than competing organizations. However, this broad system was centred on the dominant EC sub-system through bilateral agreements and lacked an institutional identity of its own.

The pattern of symmetric trade dependence

The stimulus to preferential trade liberalization is especially strong in countries which are one another's best customers, since reducing trade barriers between them provides strong reciprocal benefits.[2] Groups of countries which are strongly interdependent in trade, therefore, tend to form trade blocs. We can observe this tendency at work over the years in Western Europe.

Table 5.1 gives the trade matrix for individual countries of Western Europe in 1958.[3] It shows the share of each country's total exports of goods to each of the other countries the year after the Treaty of Rome was signed. (Table 5.2 gives the trade matrix for the same countries in 1987.) In order easily to identify a country's most important trading partners, the three largest shares in each column appear in bold type. These highlights thus indicate a given country's major markets in Western Europe. Symmetrical export dependency arises when country A takes a large share of B's exports, and B takes a large share of A's. Such trading partners are likely to form preferential trading areas, especially if exports account for a large share of GDP.

A clear pattern emerges in Table 5.1 delineating three mutually exclusive groups of countries. The two large boxed-in areas group those countries which tend to depend mainly on each other as markets for exports. A first group ('Northern Periphery') is formed by the British Isles and the Nordic countries. The United Kingdom is the pivot in this group in the sense that it is a major export market for all the other countries in the group. Exports constitute a larger share of GDP for this group of countries than for the other two groups in 1958 (Table 5.3). A second group ('Core Europe') is formed by

Table 5.1 Trade matrix for Western Europe, 1958
Country composition of exports (in per cent of total exports)

From → To ↓	Iceland	Finland	Norway	Sweden	Denmark	UK	Ireland	FRG	Netherlands	Belg-/Lux.	France	Italy	Switzerland	Austria	Portugal	Spain	Greece	Yugoslavia	Turkey
Iceland	—	0.5	0.3	0.1	0.6	0.1	0.0	0.1	0.1	0.0	0.0	0.0	0.1	0.0	0.0	0.3	0.0	0.0	0.0
Finland	3.3	—	1.2	2.8	1.3	1.0	0.0	1.3	0.8	0.7	0.6	0.7	0.8	0.4	0.1	0.6	1.0	0.3	0.7
Norway	1.4	0.7	—	10.5	4.8	2.0	0.2	2.9	2.3	1.3	0.9	1.3	1.1	0.7	0.8	2.3	0.8	0.1	1.2
Sweden	5.2	3.3	9.8	—	7.4	3.2	0.3	6.1	4.5	2.7	1.6	1.5	3.1	1.9	2.3	2.5	0.5	1.7	0.5
Denmark	2.3	2.9	6.2	5.9	—	2.4	0.1	3.0	2.6	1.6	0.7	0.8	1.6	0.8	1.2	1.7	0.3	0.2	1.6
UK	7.6	21.6	19.4	16.3	25.9	—	78.7	3.9	11.9	5.7	4.9	6.8	5.6	2.4	11.3	27.0	7.6	7.8	6.6
Ireland	0.6	0.9	0.1	0.3	0.3	3.5	—	0.3	0.4	0.3	0.2	0.1	0.1	0.0	0.3	0.7	0.1	0.0	0.0
FRG	10.5	10.8	14.1	14.2	20.1	4.2	2.2	—	19.0	11.6	10.5	14.3	16.2	25.1	7.7	23.3	20.5	9.5	18.3
Netherlands	0.1	0.8	2.3	4.5	2.6	11.9	0.5	8.1	—	10.5	2.0	2.5	3.6	2.8	2.5	3.1	2.0	1.9	4.5
Belgium/Lux	0.1	3.6	2.9	4.3	1.2	5.7	0.8	6.6	15.0	—	20.7	2.9	3.9	1.7	3.7	2.8	1.0	1.0	1.7
France	0.9	6.2	4.0	4.4	3.0	4.9	0.8	7.6	4.9	10.6	—	4.2	7.5	3.0	6.6	13.4	6.0	3.7	4.4
Italy	3.2	1.8	2.6	3.2	5.3	2.1	0.4	5.0	2.7	2.3	3.4	—	7.8	17.0	4.2	2.0	12.8	12.2	5.8
Switzerland	0.0	0.7	1.0	3.1	1.5	1.1	0.1	5.6	2.5	2.9	3.8	6.9	—	4.2	1.3	3.1	0.9	4.4	1.6
Austria	0.0	0.2	0.6	0.6	0.5	0.5	0.0	5.0	1.0	0.6	0.7	2.9	3.0	—	0.6	1.1	2.9	4.3	2.2
Portugal	4.1	0.1	0.6	0.6	0.3	0.7	0.1	0.9	0.4	1.1	1.1	1.3	0.6	0.6	—	0.3	0.1	0.0	0.1
Spain	2.1	1.1	1.7	0.5	0.8	0.8	1.0	1.2	0.8	0.7	1.7	2.0	2.8	1.3	0.8	—	0.1	0.3	0.5
Greece	0.0	0.6	0.7	0.8	0.3	0.6	0.2	1.3	0.6	0.8	0.6	2.0	0.5	0.9	0.6	0.1	—	3.1	0.9
Yugoslavia	0.0	0.2	0.2	0.3	0.2	0.3	0.1	0.9	0.3	0.2	0.4	1.6	0.8	2.9	0.0	0.1	4.0	—	0.5
Turkey	0.0	0.2	0.4	0.1	0.1	0.3	0.0	0.7	0.2	0.3	0.3	0.6	0.4	1.1	0.1	0.3	0.3	0.5	—
World	100.0	100.0	100.0	100.0	100.0	100.0	100.0	100.0	100.0	100.0	100.0	100.0	100.0	100.0	100.0	100.0	100.0	100.0	100.0
EC 6	16.5	26.7	27.2	31.0	31.8	13.8	4.7	27.3	41.5	45.1	22.2	23.9	39.2	49.6	24.7	44.7	42.3	28.3	34.7
EC 9	27.0	52.1	52.9	53.6	58.0	19.6	83.5	34.5	56.5	52.8	28.0	31.6	46.5	53.0	37.6	74.2	50.5	36.4	43.2
EC 12	33.2	53.9	55.9	55.5	59.4	21.8	84.8	37.9	58.3	55.4	31.1	34.9	50.9	55.6	38.9	74.7	50.9	39.8	44.4
EFTA 9	24.0	29.9	38.5	38.0	42.2	10.9	79.6	28.9	26.2	16.6	14.0	22.0	16.3	10.9	17.5	39.2	14.1	18.9	14.6
EFTA 6	10.0	5.3	12.8	15.1	16.0	7.9	0.7	21.0	11.2	8.2	7.6	13.7	8.1	7.2	5.0	10.0	6.1	10.7	6.3
N. Periphery	20.4	29.8	37.0	36.0	40.3	12.1	79.4	17.6	22.7	12.3	8.9	11.7	12.4	6.4	16.0	35.3	10.5	10.2	10.9
Core Europe	16.5	27.6	28.8	32.7	33.7	15.4	4.8	37.9	45.0	48.7	26.6	33.7	42.2	53.8	26.5	48.9	46.1	36.9	38.5
S. Periphery	6.3	2.2	3.5	2.4	1.7	2.8	1.4	5.1	2.3	3.1	4.1	7.5	5.6	6.5	1.5	0.9	4.5	3.9	2.1

Source: OECD.

Note: The highlights in the first two groups tend to fall along the main diagonal. This is because neighbouring countries tend to be placed beside each other in the row and column headings. It indicates the importance of being neighbours for the countries in these two groups.

Table 5.2 Trade matrix for Western Europe, 1987
Country composition of exports (in per cent of total exports)

From \ To	Iceland	Finland	Norway	Sweden	Denmark	UK	Ireland	FRG	Netherlands	Belgium/Lux.	France	Italy	Switzerland	Austria	Portugal	Spain	Greece	Yugoslavia	Turkey
Iceland	–	0.2	0.6	0.3	0.7	0.2	0.1	0.1	0.2	0.1	0.1	0.1	0.1	0.1	0.1	0.1	0.1	0.1	0.1
Finland	1.7	–	2.0	6.3	2.3	1.0	0.6	1.2	0.7	0.6	0.5	0.7	0.9	0.9	1.7	0.5	0.7	0.2	0.1
Norway	1.9	4.8	–	11.2	7.6	1.6	1.2	1.1	1.2	0.8	0.7	0.7	0.8	0.9	2.0	0.5	0.4	0.5	0.2
Sweden	2.0	14.9	10.8	–	11.6	3.0	2.0	3.1	2.0	1.5	1.4	1.4	2.0	2.0	4.7	1.2	1.3	1.0	0.7
Denmark	3.9	3.9	5.2	7.5	–	1.6	1.0	2.2	1.6	1.1	1.0	0.9	1.3	1.2	2.5	0.8	1.0	0.4	0.5
UK	19.5	11.3	26.7	10.2	11.3	–	34.2	8.9	10.4	8.4	8.8	7.5	7.5	4.6	14.1	9.5	8.3	2.4	5.4
Ireland	0.2	0.6	0.4	0.6	0.5	4.9	–	0.5	0.6	0.4	0.4	0.3	0.2	0.2	0.5	0.4	0.3	0.1	0.2
FRG	10.0	10.8	15.0	11.8	16.4	11.8	11.3	–	27.5	19.9	16.7	18.6	21.3	34.9	15.4	12.1	24.5	11.7	21.5
Netherlands	1.0	3.6	7.3	5.0	4.2	7.4	7.3	8.8	–	15.1	5.1	8.1	2.8	2.7	6.6	5.4	3.9	1.1	2.8
Belgium/Lux	1.2	1.8	1.4	4.2	2.0	4.9	4.8	7.4	14.5	–	9.3	3.4	2.3	2.4	3.0	3.1	3.1	0.7	3.2
France	5.4	5.3	5.1	5.4	5.4	9.8	9.3	12.1	10.9	20.6	–	16.4	9.2	4.5	15.9	18.8	8.7	3.7	5.0
Italy	3.1	2.6	2.3	3.8	4.7	5.2	3.7	8.8	6.5	6.5	12.2	–	8.3	10.4	4.0	8.9	16.3	13.1	8.4
Switzerland	2.7	1.8	1.0	2.2	2.3	2.3	1.6	6.1	1.8	2.2	4.3	4.7	–	7.5	2.3	1.8	1.4	1.1	3.5
Austria	0.1	1.2	0.7	1.3	0.9	0.6	0.7	5.4	1.1	1.0	0.9	2.6	3.9	–	1.1	0.7	1.2	3.7	1.9
Portugal	9.4	0.4	0.6	0.7	0.6	0.9	0.3	0.8	0.6	0.5	1.1	1.1	0.7	0.5	–	4.6	0.4	0.1	0.1
Spain	3.0	1.3	0.7	1.9	1.5	2.9	1.8	2.9	1.8	2.0	5.4	3.7	1.9	1.9	9.4	–	1.5	0.6	0.7
Greece	1.1	0.6	0.3	0.4	0.8	0.6	0.4	1.0	1.0	0.5	0.8	1.5	0.6	0.6	0.3	0.7	–	1.6	0.7
Yugoslavia	0.1	0.4	0.2	0.5	0.3	0.3	0.2	1.2	0.3	0.2	0.4	1.3	0.7	2.0	0.1	0.2	1.0	–	1.3
Turkey	0.2	0.4	0.3	0.4	0.2	0.7	0.1	1.0	0.5	0.7	0.5	0.9	1.1	0.7	0.2	0.6	1.6	1.3	–
World	100.0	100.0	100.0	100.0	100.0	100.0	100.0	100.0	100.0	100.0	100.0	100.0	100.0	100.0	100.0	100.0	100.0	100.0	100.0
EC 6	20.5	23.8	30.9	30.0	32.4	38.9	36.2	36.9	59.2	61.9	43.1	41.4	43.8	54.7	44.7	48.0	56.0	30.0	40.6
EC 9	44.0	39.4	63.0	48.1	44.1	45.2	71.3	48.3	71.6	71.6	53.2	49.9	52.6	60.6	61.6	58.6	65.5	32.7	46.4
EC 12	57.3	41.6	64.4	51.0	46.8	49.5	73.7	52.8	74.9	74.5	60.4	56.1	55.6	63.4	71.2	63.8	67.3	34.8	47.8
EFTA 9	40.9	38.0	47.5	38.9	36.8	10.8	41.2	28.4	19.1	15.8	18.4	19.2	16.7	17.2	28.1	19.2	14.4	8.9	12.0
EFTA 6	8.2	22.6	15.2	20.7	25.0	8.4	5.8	16.7	6.8	5.9	7.6	9.9	7.4	11.1	11.6	4.5	4.8	6.1	6.2
N. Periphery	28.9	35.4	45.7	35.5	33.7	11.9	38.7	16.7	16.3	12.5	12.6	11.2	12.4	9.6	25.2	12.6	11.8	4.2	6.7
Core Europe	23.3	26.6	32.5	33.3	35.5	41.8	38.4	48.3	62.1	65.0	48.2	48.6	47.6	62.1	48.0	50.5	58.6	34.6	45.9
S. Periphery	13.6	2.8	1.7	3.6	3.1	5.2	2.7	6.5	4.0	3.7	8.1	8.3	4.7	5.4	9.7	5.9	4.3	3.4	1.5

Source: OECD.

Table 5.3   Exports as a share of gross domestic product (percentages)

Country	1958	1987
Iceland	16.10	25.65
Finland	18.90	22.39
Norway	18.17	25.91
Sweden	17.33	27.95
Denmark	24.98	24.40
UK	14.70	19.42
Ireland	22.56	54.34
Northern Periphery	**16.09**	**22.67**
France	8.82	16.26
W. Germany	14.85	26.28
Italy	7.88	15.42
Belgium/Lux	28.79	57.27
Netherlands	33.20	43.57
Switzerland	21.19	26.51
Austria	17.35	23.18
Core Europe	**13.81**	**23.58**
Portugal	13.57	24.89
Spain	3.39	11.79
Greece	7.41	13.75
Yugoslavia	5.90	17.50
Turkey	1.97	14.98
Southern Periphery	**4.26**	**14.09**
Total Western Europe	**13.24**	**22.43**
EC6	13.38	
EC 12		17.00
EFTA 7	16.26	
EFTA 6		25.57

Source: OECD National Accounts. The figure for Yugoslavia in 1987 is an EFTA Secretariat estimate.

the original six EC members plus Switzerland, with Austria as a possible addition. Germany is the pivot in this group. The remaining group – comprising Portugal, Spain, Greece, Yugoslavia and Turkey ('Southern Periphery') – does not evidence a pattern of symmetrical export dependency. These countries are characterized instead by one-sided dependence on trade with Core Europe, in particular with Germany. They are of negligible importance as a market for each other and for other countries in Western Europe. Exports constitute a low share of GDP for all countries in this group except Portugal.

These three groups differ in two important respects: relative size and cohesion. Core Europe is the major economic group. The countries there

Table 5.4 Major country groups' share of GDP (%)

	1958	1973	1988
Northern Periphery	29.0	21.9	23.9
Core Europe	58.1	68.0	66.0
Southern Periphery	12.9	10.1	10.1
Total Western Europe	100.0	100.0	100.0

Source: OECD, National Accounts; EFTA Secretariat estimate for Yugoslavia.

produced twice as much GDP in 1958 as the Northern Periphery, which in turn produced twice as much as the Southern Periphery. The share of Core Europe grew to two-thirds during 30 years of integration.

Core Europe is not only the largest, but also the most cohesive of the three groups. Six of the 21 pairwise trade relations in this group are cases of mutual trade dependence in that each country in the pair is among the other country's three most important export markets in Western Europe.[4] Six are cases of one-way trade dependence,[5] while the remaining nine cases are characterized by non-dependence.

The Northern Periphery was less cohesive than was Core Europe in 1958. Of the 21 pairwise trade relations in this group, only three evidence mutual trade dependence (Sweden/Norway, UK/Sweden, UK/Ireland). Six are cases of one-way trade dependence (of Nordics on the Swedish and UK markets).[6] The remaining 12 country pairs are characterized by lack of dependence. The high frequency of non-dependence reflects the preponderance of relatively small countries in this group.

The pattern of dependency within – but not between – each of these two groups is schematically illustrated in Figure 5.2. The interdependence pattern between four of the Core Europe countries (counting Belgium and Luxembourg as one country) creates a close-knit web of interdependency between France, West Germany and the Benelux countries. These countries constitute the focal point of the European core. Appropriately, at the centre of this web, Brussels stands as a European capital. No similarly dense web of mutual dependency exists in the first group.

The Southern Periphery in 1958 is strikingly different from the first two groups. One-way dependence on Core Europe is the predominant pattern. Trade dependency within the group is low. Trade flows are relatively unimportant even between neighbours, for example Portugal and Spain, Greece and Turkey.

In summary, West Germany is the pivot country for all other countries, with the UK serving as a pivot for the EFTA Nordics. Together with France, Benelux, Italy, England and Switzerland, Germany forms the economic core of Western Europe. The periphery is tied closely to the core through trade.

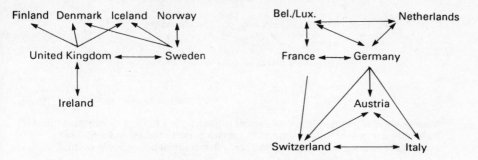

Note: An arrow pointing from, for instance, Switzerland to Austria indicates that Switzerland is one of the three most important export markets in Europe for Austria. A two-headed arrow thus indicates that trade dependency is mutual.

Figure 5.2 Webs of dependency in 1958: the Northern Periphery and Core Europe

Overcoming political constraints

In practice, the formation of trade blocs differed from that delineated in Table 5.1. The strong economic interlinkages between France, West Germany and the Benelux countries were reinforced by the political objective of Franco-German reconciliation, in which the Low Countries and Italy were also involved. This overriding political goal led these six countries to set up a close economic union aiming at greater political cooperation. Other countries chose less far-reaching forms of economic cooperation. For reasons involving neutrality and sovereignty, Switzerland and Austria did not join the EC when it was formed in 1958, although they were more closely integrated with these countries than with the five other countries with which they formed a free trade area for industrial products, EFTA.[7] Portugal, excluded at the time from EC membership by its non-democratic government, joined the looser organization EFTA.

This division of Western Europe into the Inner Six and the Outer Seven was not a natural economic one, and Table 5.1 explains why it proved to be a transitional arrangement. First, the two groups were not symmetrically balanced. EFTA's cohesive power was less than the EC's. Its web of mutual dependence was weak and was created entirely by Scandinavia-UK trade.[8] This web is schematically illustrated in Figure 5.3. Finland became an associate member of EFTA in 1961 and Iceland a full member in 1970.[9] The three medium-sized countries (Switzerland, Austria, Portugal) were at least as dependent on trade with the EC as on trade with other EFTA countries.

Secondly, the importance of the United Kingdom and West Germany as pivots was not confined to each country's respective bloc. West Germany was a major export market for each EFTA country, as well as for each of the six EC members. The United Kingdom was a major market for two of the Inner Six (Italy and the Netherlands). Thus, the pivot country in each bloc was important also for countries in the other bloc. In fact, West Germany served as a pivot for all of Western Europe. Consequently, the smaller countries in each

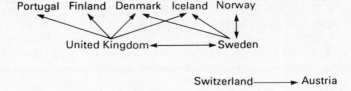

Note: An arrow pointing from, for instance, Switzerland to Austria indicates that Switzerland is one of the three most important export markets in Europe for Austria. A two-headed arrow thus indicates that trade dependency is mutual.

Figure 5.3 Web of dependency in 1958: EFTA countries

bloc were anxious to avoid a situation where they were forced to choose which pivot country to group around. *Both* pivots were important for them.

Thirdly, each of the two pivot countries was itself more dependent on exports to members of the other trade bloc than on exports to its co-members. West Germany was more dependent on the EFTA countries as an export market than on its partners in EC 6, due to the importance of neighbouring Austria, Switzerland and Sweden. Similarly, the EC 6 countries were more important export markets for the United Kingdom than were other EFTA countries.[10] The leading EC member, therefore, had a strong interest in reaching an agreement with EFTA, while the leading EFTA member had an interest in reaching an agreement with the EC.

These economic factors combined to produce an agreement in 1972. The following year the United Kingdom and Denmark left EFTA and, together with Ireland, joined the EC.[11] By itself this step would have required the UK and Denmark to reintroduce tariffs on imports of industrial goods from their former EFTA partners. To avoid this, each remaining EFTA member concluded similar free-trade agreements with the enlarged EC. Thus, accession by Denmark and the UK was not so much a defection from EFTA as an extension of free trade in industrial goods to include all EC countries. This ended the division of Western Europe into two different trade blocs and confirmed institutionally that the area was a single economic space. It was the origin of the EES.

In summary, the EC and EFTA started as competitive institutions. Because of the close economic interdependence between countries in the two groups, they were ultimately linked together through bilateral free trade agreements. Both groups thus became sub-systems of a single trade system, at least for industrial goods. However, these sub-systems lack a formal higher-level system with common institutions for decision making.

Trade policy really matters!

While patterns of trade influence institutions, institutions also influence trade patterns. The institutional changes described above affected intra-European

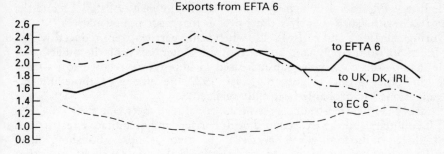

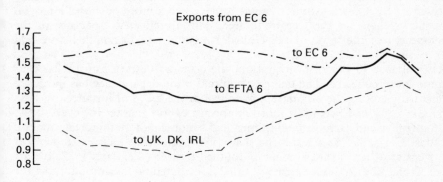

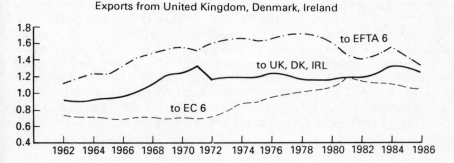

Figure 5.4 Export intensity coefficients for manufactures

Source: EFTA Secretariat. See also Amund Utne, 'Free trade and growth of trade in Western Europe', in *Free Trade in Europe, A commemoration of EFTA's 25th Anniversary*, Geneva 1985.

Note: The coefficients express the share a given country has of a given market relative to its share of the world market. If the first share is larger than the second, the coefficient is greater than 1, expressing a greater than average trade intensity.

trade flows. Figure 5.4, which shows the relative intensity of EFTA's and the EC's trade with each other over time, proves that trade policy matters.[12]

During the 1960s and early 1970s, when trade barriers were reduced within the Inner Six on the one hand and within the Outer Seven on the other hand, trade inside each country group increased in importance relative to its trade with the other group (Figure 5.4). By 1972 the effects of these internal liberalizations had probably been fully realized.

From 1973 the free-trade agreements concluded between the remaining EFTA countries and the EC reduced tariff barriers and quantitative restrictions on trade in industrial goods *between* the two groups, abolishing them completely by 1984. In this period, trade between the original six EC countries and the remaining EFTA countries grew, while internal trade within each grouping became relatively less important. The closer form of integration represented by a customs union seems to have had a more powerful effect on trade flows than did the free trade area. This is reflected especially in the development of the trade of the United Kingdom and Denmark before and after joining the EC 6.[13]

After almost 30 years of integration, the core of Western Europe has thus become more cohesive. The degree of mutual trade dependence has increased dramatically among the original six members of the EC. For instance, by 1987 West Germany had become a more important export market for every other EC 6 member and each of them in turn had become a more important market for West Germany. As a result the share of exports from each EC 6 member that went to other members roughly doubled between 1958 and 1987. It now ranges from 37% in West Germany to 62% in Belgium-Luxembourg. At the same time, the share of exports in GDP has increased, making the EC 6 increasingly interdependent. In addition, the core has become larger. The United Kingdom has reoriented its trade and trebled its share of exports to continental Europe (though its importance for the other EC members has not increased as much, reflecting partly its relatively slow economic growth).

Through trade, this enlarged and more cohesive core exerted a strong gravitational pull on the periphery of the European Economic Space, eventually absorbing the Southern Periphery, whose export dependency had increased dramatically (Table 5.3). Most EFTA countries also became more dependent on the EC 6, especially Austria and Switzerland. As a result, the Nordic and Alpine countries within EFTA remained relatively loosely connected to each other. The cohesion of EFTA weakened and its dependence on the enlarged EC grew.

Institutional geometry in the new Europe

Economic integration is a dynamic process, in which one step invites another. Creation of a trading bloc changes the competitive position of outsiders and sets up pressures for further change. When a country's major competitors and major markets join to form a trade bloc, economic incentives encourage it to join too. The establishment by 13 nations of the EC and EFTA presented the other European countries with a choice either to stay outside or to apply to join one or other organization. Political factors influenced this choice but political constraints change. As they changed, countries moved from outside into one group or from one group to the other. In 1960 there were 11 outsiders in Western Europe (including Cyprus and Malta). To-day only the four orphans remain outside.

However, economic fundamentals change too, striking a new balance of costs and benefits. This can alter the outcome even if political constraints are given. The successive enlargements of the EC dramatically changed the relative economic weights of the EC itself and also of EFTA. At present, the EC produces 85% of the GDP of Western Europe. By virtue of size alone, it exerts a strong economic attraction on all countries in its proximity. In addition, the successive deepening of integration within the EC increases its competitiveness relative to outsiders.

As a result, the EC increasingly dominates the course of European integration, setting its direction and its pace. Where the EC leads – as in completing its internal market – others feel compelled to follow. Enthusiastically or reluctantly, other countries find themselves cooperating with the EC on the EC's own terms. The EC has emerged as the European hegemon. Will it present other European countries with the choice of becoming either full members or satellites? Or will a more general system emerge of which the EC, EFTA and other countries form sub-systems?

Three major questions on the institutional agenda illustrate the need for a variable institutional geometry in Europe. The first concerns the creation of institutions for decision making in the EES. The second question is how the four orphans fit into the European picture. The third concerns the options open to countries in Eastern Europe.

The dilemma of the favourite sons

EC-EFTA relations are a major concern for both sides but with an important difference. The EFTA countries as a group are the EC's largest trading partner, more important than the United States and Japan combined. Nevertheless, relations with EFTA are not high on the Community agenda. The EC is more preoccupied with internal than with external relations; intra-EC trade accounts for 59% of total EC trade.

By contrast, the EFTA countries' primary concern is relations with the EC while intra-EFTA relations are secondary. When the original EFTA members lost their pivot country, the United Kingdom, EFTA's centre was effectively transferred to inside the EC. For each remaining EFTA country, at least two of its three most important export markets in Europe are now located in the EC. The EFTA countries are present in the EC as invisible members. The time has come to design institutional frameworks that give the invisible members form and voice on matters of common concern.

This task is complicated by a fundamental difference between the two organizations. The Association lacks the legal basis and institutional capacity of the EC to act as an entity on behalf of its members in external commercial policy matters. Each EFTA country has traditionally dealt bilaterally with the

Table 5.5   Major country groups' share of GDP (%)

	1958	1973	1988
EC	54.1	78.5	85.3
EFTA	31.7	12.2	12.4
Other Europe	14.2	9.3	2.3
Total Western Europe	100.0	100.0	100.0

Note: The EC consisted of the Six in 1958, plus Denmark, Ireland, UK in 1973, plus Greece, Portugal, Spain in 1988. EFTA consisted of the Seven in 1958, minus Denmark and UK, plus Finland and Iceland in 1973, minus Portugal in 1988. Other Europe consisted of Finland, Iceland, Ireland, Greece, Spain, Portugal, Turkey, Yugoslavia in 1958, minus Finland, Iceland, Ireland in 1973, minus Greece, Spain, Portugal in 1988.

Source: OECD, National Accounts; EFTA Secretariat estimate for Yugoslavia.

EC. Furthermore, EFTA is a typically intergovernmental organization, making decisions by consensus and with limited Secretariat powers. By contrast, EC institutions possess important supranational powers of surveillance, enforcement and decision-making.

Thus, the EFTA countries are bound to the Community by common economic concerns but have a different institutional preference. This institutional difference is more important than the disparate size of the organizations. EC-EFTA relations are characterized by asymmetric institutional powers in what is basically a complementary economic relationship. This poses a dilemma for the EFTA countries. Is institutional 'harmonization' the price for deepened integration with the EC?

In January 1989, President Delors proposed that the EC and EFTA countries investigate a more structured partnership with common decision-making and administrative institutions for the EES. Such common institutions would tie together the existing two subsystems, expanding free movement in the EES to include services, capital and persons in addition to industrial goods.

The EFTA side welcomed this proposal and declared its preparedness to speak with one voice in forthcoming negotiations and to strengthen its internal structure as warranted by the results of the negotiations. However, strengthening EFTA will not go so far as to convert the Association into a mini-EC. This would remove the justification for its continued existence. It will remain as a smaller but also a different organization. What is needed to solve the EFTA dilemma is an institutional framework that can combine the institutional diversity represented by the Community and the Association with the application of uniform rules necessary for integrated markets for goods, services, capital and persons.

Return of the prodigal sons

The collapse of non-democratic regimes in Eastern Europe and the erosion of the Iron Curtain have overnight enabled the East European states to join the group of European outsiders. Several of them have already expressed a desire to 'return to Europe'. A precondition for this return is the introduction of the principles of pluralistic democracy and market economy in former Peoples' Democracies. Thus, they face a major process of systemic change. The democratic market economies of the West can support them in this difficult process.

Like other western countries, members of EFTA and the EC already contribute to the process of systemic change in Eastern Europe through existing organizations. The World Bank, the IMF, the OECD, the Group of 24 assistance and the new European Bank for Reconstruction and Development are central institutions for this task. However, countries in Eastern Europe are likely to expect more of their European neighbours. In particular, they may wish to be part of the existing European trade system.

This trade system provides the East European countries with several options. EFTA provides a free trade area for industrial goods, encompassing, through bilateral agreements, also the EC countries. The EC will in 1993 provide a single market in which the four freedoms are realized in the framework of an economic and monetary union. Finally, the European economic space will provide free movement of industrial goods, services, capital and persons between all EC and EFTA countries in an institutional framework yet to be determined. These options represent differing degrees and scope of integration.

When East European countries consider these options they will want to know the conditions for their possible participation. The best contribution to systemic reform that the EC and EFTA can make is to state clearly in advance the conditions on which they are open to East European countries. Membership is perhaps not for today. The Eastern countries must first accomplish the difficult process of systemic change. The EC must first complete its internal market and conclude an EES treaty with EFTA. Nevertheless, East European countries may desire some form of participation already now as an assurance for the future. EFTA may well have a special attraction for these countries because it represents a looser form of integration limited to industrial goods. Free movement of capital and persons between Eastern and Western Europe has implications for which neither side may be ready at the moment.

Whether ultimately an East European country chooses to return to Europe through the door of EFTA or through the door of the Community, trade diversion in Europe should not be allowed to result. In order to avoid this, the EFTA countries and the EC will have to coordinate their policies towards Eastern Europe. For instance, membership in EFTA could be accompanied by free trade agreements with the EC in industrial goods, just as membership in the EC would give East European countries access to the EFTA countries through the EES.

Owing to the political constraints of the past fifty years, current levels of East-West trade in Europe are low. However, geographic proximity and historical ties suggest that it has great potential. In a couple of decades,

Czechoslovakia, Hungary and Poland may well be as integrated with the EES
countries as the countries of its Northern or Southern Periphery are today. An
'Eastern Periphery' of the European core will emerge. Now is the time to
consider the institutional arrangements necessary to accommodate this likely
prospect.

Adopting the orphans

The absence of symmetric trade dependence for Cyprus, Malta, Turkey and
Yugoslavia makes it difficult for these countries to gain access either to the EC
or to EFTA. In a bargaining situation based on reciprocity, they have little to
offer but much to gain. President Delors's description of them as the orphans
of Europe appears singularly appropriate. They are located on the borderline of
Europe – in some cases there is even doubt as to whether they are indeed
European. They are poor compared with even the poorest EC members. They
are fraught with political problems. Turkey and Yugoslavia are less dependent
on the EES market than other West European countries and are relatively
unimportant for them.

The role of these countries in European integration will be determined by
political and not by economic considerations. Like the other poor in Europe,
they can lay claim to 'cohesion'. Their democratization is as worthy of
protection as that of the southern EC members. Yugoslavia rounds out the EES
as a contiguous area. Yet all this is probably insufficient to convince the
Community or the Association to adopt the orphans. Some looser form of
association is more likely.

Looking to the future

After thirty years of integration in Western Europe, the classical integration
issues are still at the centre of the stage but now on a larger European scene.
Symmetric trade dependency, the driving force behind integration in Western
Europe, will make realization of the EES inevitable in spite of institutional
difficulties. Thereafter, its force may be temporarily exhausted until the
ongoing systemic change in Eastern Europe creates new trade patterns in
Europe. Economic and monetary unification will strengthen Germany's role as
the core country of Europe. It will exert a growing attraction on its neighbours,
both in EFTA and in the East. New patterns of symmetric trade dependency
between Germany and these countries are likely to give renewed momentum to
European integration and change its course, in spite of institutional differences.

As in the past, this course will be both constrained and reinforced by
political factors. Postwar reconciliation, so powerful a factor determining the
scope and the form of integration in Western Europe, may prove to be a
reinforcing factor. Reconciliation – long overdue – may well occur between a
European Germany and its Eastern neighbours with similar economic effects as
previously in the West.

A restraining factor is once again likely to be countries' differing preferences for sharing sovereignty. Institutional diversity will be needed for several decades. To be robust, the institutional framework for economic integration must accommodate some diversity. Achieving uniformity of basic economic rules within such a framework is the same challenge as before, but now facing a broader Europe.

Notes

The author alone is responsible for the views expressed in this chapter. A fuller version can be found in EFTA Occasional Paper 32, Geneva.

1. The original EC 6 were Belgium, France, West Germany, Italy, Luxembourg and the Netherlands. Denmark, Ireland and the UK joined in 1973, Greece in 1981, and Portugal and Spain in 1986. The original seven members of EFTA were Austria, Denmark, Norway, Portugal, Sweden, Switzerland, and the UK. Finland became an associate member in 1961 and a full member in 1986. Iceland became a member in 1970.
2. The same principle of reciprocity lay behind liberalization through GATT negotiations which took place between principal suppliers on a product-by-product basis. However, in GATT negotiations concessions were extended to all GATT members and not just to the reciprocating partners, they usually concerned a limited number of products, and they were seldom reductions to zero rates.
3. Cyprus and Malta have not been included owing to their small size.
4. West Germany/France, West Germany/Netherlands, West Germany/Belgium-Lux., Belgium-Lux./France, Switzerland/Italy, Belgium-Lux./Netherlands.
5. West Germany is important for Italy, Switzerland and Austria; France for Switzerland; Italy for Austria; and Switzerland for Austria.
6. Sweden is important for Iceland and for Denmark; the UK for Denmark, Finland, Iceland and Norway.
7. The Republic of Ireland already had a free trade agreement with the UK, which made EFTA membership superfluous.
8. Of the 21 trade relations in EFTA, two were characterized by mutual dependence, five by single dependence, and the remaining 14 by no dependence.
9. Note, however, that a decision to accord Iceland's main export (fish products) complete free-trade treatment was not reached until 1989.
10. However, the UK's traditional overseas orientation meant that Europe was less important for the UK in this period than for other countries in the table.
11. The importance of agriculture in the Danish economy and of the UK as a market for Danish agricultural exports persuaded Denmark to follow the UK into the EC. The Norwegian government negotiated membership in the EC at the same time. This was rejected in a popular referendum in 1972 and Norway remained a member of EFTA.
12. Anyone doubting this need only consider the development of trade between countries in Eastern and Western Europe. The difference in economic systems now constitutes an institutional discontinuity which inhibits trade between neighbours that once were traditional trading partners.
13. Denmark's and the UK's exports to their former EFTA partners declined strongly in relative terms after 1973, while trade with their new partners in the EC increased. Similarly, current EFTA members lost market shares in the three new EC members, particularly in the UK, while the EC 6 gained.

6 The European Community and its sub-systems
Philippe de Schoutheete

The decision-making process in the European Community is governed by the legal framework of the Treaties and by the institutional framework they have created. This arrangement, which is more complex and more elaborate than that of any other international institution, allocates powers, lays down rules and procedures, sets time-limits and provides for appeals. At first sight it looks as if everything has been foreseen and laid down in written rules which put all Member States on an equal footing even if their votes are weighted. Nevertheless in the Community, as in any political organization, the written law and the institutional mechanisms do not adequately describe everyday reality. In the first place, there are certain sectors of European activity, such as political cooperation, which lie largely outside the legal constraints and function independently of the institutions set up under the European Treaties. But even within the Community's own field of action, conflicting interests, ideological affinities, differences of view, and sometimes even personal relations allow of, or impose, a kaleidoscope of alliances or oppositions which, in the course of time, are made and unmade according to whatever the subject may be. This is the other side of the decision-making process: the political manoeuvering which breathes life into the legal and institutional structures.

So long as such political manoeuvering does not go beyond the forming of temporary alliances in the quest for short-term interests, it is of limited importance. Tactics are a natural and essential element of all multilateral diplomacy. The analyst can neglect them, for they do not alter the system; they are part of its normal functioning. But at times such alliances take on a more durable nature, one that is deeper and more highly organized. Under certain conditions of duration, intensity and formality, an alliance of that nature becomes a strategic option: 'The negotiating process changes if a particular bilateral coalition becomes a durable and predictable feature.'[1] In such a case, and only in such a case, it is worthy of the analyst's attention because it exerts a more or less effective and more or less lasting influence on the functioning of the whole. It becomes a sub-unit, an identifiable sub-system.

This chapter sets out to enquire into the existence of such sub-systems within

106

the Community, to define the criteria by which they may be recognized, and to pinpoint actual cases.

We will not consider as a sub-system those elements of flexibility which have been introduced in the Community framework itself. For example, the management of the European Monetary System has some of the aspects of a sub-system, regrouping those Member States who participate in the exchange rate mechanism. However, great efforts have been made to keep it formally within the Community institutional framework and not to present it as a sub-system. As things now stand it can be accepted as an accidental and flexible solution to a specific problem. Such would also be the case if (as seems to be the Commission's intention) greater use were made of Article 130 L to initiate research policy programmes with a limited number of Member States. The management mechanisms would probably need to have some of the aspects of a sub-system (excluding those Member States who do not wish to pay for the programme) but in fact it would be nothing more than an ad hoc solution to a practical problem.

On the other hand we will take the word 'Community' to cover not only those activities that are conducted in the legal framework of the Paris and Rome Treaties but also activities of the Twelve in political cooperation. This assimilation has a legal basis in the Single European Act and corresponds more and more to the way European affairs are, in fact, conducted. By broadening the classical analysis of the European Community and examining the sub-systems which influence its internal functioning we hope to obtain a fuller and more balanced view of the European System as a whole.

The definition of a sub-system

Before studying practical cases it may be useful to attempt a definition of the criteria by which a sub-system may be identified. To that end we need to consider the motivations of the actors.

Why do certain participants in the multilateral game make the effort to set up a syb-system inside a larger whole? No doubt in order to enable them to play a particular role in it. But the roles envisaged may differ, and at least three spring to mind:

- there are those people who feel that, together with certain others, they are called upon to play a leading role. The sub-system, in this case, is intended to give form to that collective leadership; this is what is, inter alia, covered by the term 'directoire';
- others may wish to preserve certain positions acquired prior to the joint effort. The sub-system then serves to defend and manage these positions; it plays a conservative part. This is one of the aspects of Benelux; and
- lastly, there is the similar yet distinct case of those who wish to press forward in a specific field at a time when not all are ready to follow them. The sub-system serves to manage that part-process; the concepts of a 'two-speed' or 'variable-geometry' Europe give expression to this.

Whether the sub-system enables those who participate to play a leading role, to preserve acquired positions, or to go off in advance of the rest, it must be based on a *special relationship* between the participants which differs from that which they have with the other members of the whole. This presupposes a certain intensity in the relationship, a certain variety in the subjects dealt with, and a certain depth in the way they are approached.

The second characteristic is that of *duration*. By definition we are speaking here of something which goes beyond the purely temporary and tactical in order to seek long-term results. This cannot be done without an enduring effort going beyond the good personal relationship which may at a given moment exist between two leaders or two teams. There cannot, therefore, be any sub-system without lasting relationships between the participants.

As a rule any social relationship which is both privileged and durable is reflected in a written agreement, whether it be between individuals, in the world of business, or in that of international relations. It is, of course, not essential that all the sub-systems which we shall endeavour to identify should have a legal basis (in the form of either a treaty or an agreement), but we shall see that this is often the case, simply because this is the normal way in which to ensure a durable relationship between parties subject to international law. Even where there is no such legal basis we will have to look for a minimum of organization. we must, therefore, take it that a certain *formalization* is a necessary characteristic of a sub-system.

There is also a requirement of *effectiveness*. In order to be able to speak of a sub-system, the relationship must exert a noticeable influence on the whole. where a sub-system exists, it must be possible to identify it by the practical results which it has brought about or to which it has contributed in the course of time.

Finally, there is the requirement of *acceptability* which is a corollary of the above. Collective action by a limited group within a wider whole can be effective only if its existence and, above all, its fruits, are accepted or at least tolerated by the other participants. They do not have to like it (and often they won't) but they must not reject it. If group efforts automatically provoke rejection, they will be counter-productive and will paralyse the system rather than advance it. Helen Wallace explains this with regard to the Franco-German pair: 'Whether such a development is functional or dysfunctional will depend on the extent to which the predominant coalition produces results which give adequate political satisfaction in terms of the other partner's substantive interests.'[2]

The Franco-German relationship

When one turns to sub-systems within the European Community, the first case which springs to mind is, of course, the relationship between Paris and Bonn. This goes back to the pre-history of European institutions: in 1950 it was to occupied Germany that the speech of Schuman and the démarche of Monnet were addressed. Because this relationship has been extensively studied, we need examine only briefly how it fits in with the criteria set out above.

There can be no doubt about the exceptional character of the relationship. An IFRI study of the Franco-German pair concludes: 'Les deux parties sont parvenues, au fil des années, à créer au sein de leurs élites et de leurs opinions publiques la conviction solide que la France et l'Allemagne ont entre elles une relation très spéciale et privilégiée.'[3] Giscard d'Estaing puts it in more lyrical terms: 'L'intimité naturelle et confiante qui a existé entre Helmut Schmidt et moi, est sans doute un cas unique dans les rapports entre les responsables des grands états contemporains.'[4] Lyricism or no lyricism, the privileged nature of the Franco-German relationship is beyond dispute.

And so is its duration. To the initial complicity between Monnet and Hallstein in the 1950s, there succeeded in the 1960s a majestic relationship between de Gaulle and Adenauer, then intimacy between Giscard and Schmidt, followed by the relaxed relations between Mitterrand and Kohl. Throughout these years governments and administrations on either side acquired and maintained the habit of meetings and concertation, whatever political party was in power. 'These habits and attitudes have survived the major changes of government and personalities remarkably well in recent years.'[5]

As to formality, this relationship is unsurpassable. The Elysée Treaty of 1963, concluded with the solemnity that de Gaulle knew how to bestow upon public occasions, constitutes the closest possible of bilateral alliances. It has given rise to a level of consultation, the breadth and rhythm of which are unprecendented and which has lasted for a quarter of a century. The legal commitment even seemed so formal that the Bundestag felt it necessary to introduce a preamble to the Treaty reflecting and confirming Germany's ties with the Atlantic Alliance.

From the point of view of effectiveness, Giscard remarks, writing of his close intimacy with Schmidt: 'Elle a permis de faire avancer l'Union de l'Europe.'[6] He refers no doubt to the European Monetary System and it is true, as Peter Ludlow has ably shown,[7] that the document approved by the European Council of Bremen in July 1978 is largely a Franco-German plan which emerged from lengthy concertation inspired by the two leaders. A further example can be found in the Franco-German proposal of a treaty on political cooperation submitted to the European Council of Milan in 1985 and which to some extent influenced the negotiations concerning that part of the Single Act. The 'Eureka' initiative is yet another case in point, even though its final outcome probably did not fully come up to the initial expectations of Mitterrand and Kohl. Lastly, the activation of the military clauses of the Elysée Treaty, realized by the protocol signed on 22 January 1988 in Paris, is considered by some – even outside France and Germany – as one element of a possible solution to the problem of European defence. We may therefore say that over the years Franco-German initiatives in fields of such fundamental importance as monetary policy, diplomacy, research and defence have been at least partly successful in the European framework.

The question of acceptability is perhaps the most interesting. How is it that such an enduring and close a relationship (sometimes described as the Bonn-Paris Axis) has been reasonably well accepted by most of the other Member States, even though in London, and sometimes elsewhere too, it has from time to time caused nervousness or displeasure? The answer to this question is twofold.

The first element is historical. From the outset, Franco-German relations appeared so fundamental in the negotiations for the first European Treaties that from this fact they derived a kind of original legitimacy. The memoirs of Jean Monnet bear witness to this. Moreover, reconciliation between France and Germany was the first, the most political and the most visible dividend of the European Community project so far as, for instance, the Benelux countries were concerned. 'It is the fate of small and relatively weak countries to be trampled on when their large neighbours make war and to have their interests squeezed when these neighbours make up . . . The beauty of the Schuman and subsequent proposals was that they held out the prospect of guarantees of equality undreamt of in previous attempts at European cooperation.'[8] In addition, it seemed, at least since the Elysée Treaty of 1963, that the Franco-German relationship was the best means of containing within acceptable limits the danger emanating from Gaullist ideas on European affairs and Atlantic solidarity. For all these reasons the original Community of Six met the Paris-Bonn compact with an approval which subsequent enlargements have not completely buried.

The second consideration has more to do with substance: Franco-German proposals, at least those which prospered, were always made in a direction where the support of several partners was virtually assured.

- The case of the EMS is typical and well-documented. The need for a monetary initiative appeared in the Tindemans Report, was taken up again by the Belgian presidency at the beginning of 1977, and also by President Jenkins at the same time. Its technicalities had been carefully examined by J. van Ypersele, then President of the Monetary Committee. At the end of that year, therefore, a Franco-German initiative could count on some support.
- The idea of putting in legally binding terms the rules of political cooperation, which also appears in the Tindemans Report, was supported by several Member States when the Genscher-Colombo proposals were discussed. A watered down echo can be found in para. 4.3 of the Stuttgart Solemn Declaration on June 1983. The Franco-German proposal made at Milan in 1985 could therefore expect to fall upon fertile ground.
- Extension to the EFTA countries of the Community's technological activities had already occurred to a modest degree in Community programmes such as 'Comett'. The need to develop further this aspect of European activity was not disputed by anyone and so, in 1984, the 'Eureka' initiative, jointly launched by Mitterrand and Kohl, was supported in principle by all Community countries.
- As to European defence, the climate in the early 1980s was ripe for new ideas and any reasonable initiative (such as the activation of the military clauses of the Elysée Treaty) was likely to attract support.[9]

These points do not aim to diminish the merits of Franco-German initiatives. On the contrary, the protagonists have had the political will and skill to select their subjects and their timing so as to put forward proposals which met the concerns of several of their partners and which were in tune with a certain logical development in the construction of Europe. That being so, the Commission and several Member States found in these proposals 'adequate political satisfaction in terms of their substantive interests' (to use the words of Helen Wallace).[10] This eased the passage of these proposals, however unorthodox or irritating the procedure might have been. It helped greatly to make acceptable something that, given a less felicitous choice, might not have been so.

It is clear, therefore, that the Franco-German relationship constitutes a subsystem in the European whole.

Other bilateral relations

Franco-German relations have served as an example for other bilateral relations within the European Community. For several years now Heads of Government meetings, involving the participation of a number of ministers, have been organized between the United Kingdom and France and between the United Kingdom and Germany. Similar arrangements exist between France and Italy, France and Spain, Germany and Italy, Germany and Spain, and Italy and Spain. We may say today that the existence of relationships of this type has become a 'status symbol' for the larger countries in the Community and that they attach importance to them. Spain, as a new member, regards these arrangements with particular satisfaction.

Not one of these bilateral relations has a formal juridical underpinning which could be compared with that provided by the Elysée Treaty for the Franco-German pair. As a rule they are based on arrangements agreed at a first meeting, which therefore have the normal weight of a diplomatic undertaking. They are regular, in certain cases they have been going on for some time, and they always take place at a level higher than that which is customary in international relations. We may therefore accept that they meet the criteria of formality and duration as defined earlier on. On the other hand there is no evidence that they reflect any really privileged relations. Certainly, through them is established a type of meeting which does not, in general, exist either with countries of comparable size outside the Community or with smaller countries within it. But even though it may seem that such meetings have an exceptional character, it is not clear that the relationship thus created is indeed exceptional. In no case does it even approach the 'very special and privileged relationship' that exists between France and Germany. Neither the national administrations nor public opinion in the various countries perceive them as such. We must conclude, therefore, that one of the criteria for a sub-system is lacking.

The criterion of effectiveness is also absent. In no case (excepting what will be said later with regard to the Genscher-Colombo initiative) can any significant initiative undertaken over the past years within the community's field of action, or outside it, be attributed to or in any way linked with one of these bilateral relations. This is in significant contrast to the record of Franco-German proposals. Such absence of effectiveness or of genuine weight in the life of the Community probably explains why this network of relations, though apparently disciminatory, has not in general given rise to nervousness or displeasure among those who were excluded. On the whole, the reaction of smaller countries in the Community to the burgeoning of such meetings is one of more or less well-disposed indifference.

This leads to the conclusion that, other than the Franco-German axis, no bilateral relationship can qualify as a sub-system in the European whole; a conclusion which is both surprising and thought-provoking. The case of Spain is rather special: a new arrival on the European multilateral scene, after many years of isolation. We should not yet expect to find Spain at the hub of the power game' but the same does not apply either to Italy or to the United Kingdom.

In the Europe of the Six Italy might, at the beginning, have seemed the weak link: characterized by a less diversified economy, regional under-development, political instability, and a strong communist party. But these weaknesses have been gradually overcome over the years. Diplomatically, the Franco-German bond and Benelux solidarity left Italy somewhat isolated. Such a position is not necessarily disadvantageous because it opens the option of bringing one's weight to bear on one side or the other according to circumstances and timing. This no doubt explains why, while continuing its active commitment to the construction of Europe, Italy has never forged a privileged link with any of its partners. Italy's views are often close to those of the Benelux countries who broadly share Italian thinking on the future of Europe; sometimes Italy tends towards France or Germany on a particular issue, and it often finds itself in agreement with the new southern members of the Community. But though frequent coalitions of Mediterranean interests can be observed in Community business, there is no attempt at systematic consultation, no organization, no trace of a Mediteranean sub-system. It must also in fact be said that frequent changes of Prime Ministers and Foreign Ministers (even though the same names turn up again at intervals) do not help to establish those lasting personal relations which play such a role in the Franco-German context.

At one specific moment, however, Italy did take an active part in a bilateral initiative which became a significant event in the construction of Europe: the *Genscher-Colombo* proposals. These emerged from two speeches, one delivered by Genscher in Stuttgart on 6 January 1981 and the other by Colombo in Florence at the end of that month. Both recommended a strengthening of political cooperation and an endeavour to elaborate a common defence policy. They also spoke of providing a cultural dimension for Europe. Based on the similarity of views, contacts took place over several months and led to a common document submitted to their partners at the end of 1981. The solemn Declaration of Stuttgart (June 1983) which was the achievement of discussion between the Ten shows no more than a faint link with the original German-Italian proposals; the security dimension in particular had been much watered down. But this Solemn Declaraction does for the first time define the functions of the European Council and endeavours to bring political cooperation closer to the community structures. In retrospect one may say that it looks like a first sketch of what later became the Single Act. However, from the angle which concerns us here, it appears as an isolated event. Nothing of its kind went before or came after it; it rested upon the coincidence of two ministers holding identical views rather than on any systematic and enduring will of two countries to cooperate. The fact that in France a government of the Left was at that moment pursuing policies which did not please Bonn, with, as a consequence, a temporary weakening of Franco-German cooperation, may have been relevant.

In many ways the case of the United Kingdom is more extraordinary. Everything suggested that this country, once in the Community, would endeavour to play a guiding role in it. Its political weight, its economic strength, its historic links, the excellence of its diplomacy, enable it to aspire quite naturally to become a force at least equal to France or Germany. And indeed the United Kingdom does evidently play an important role in the Europe of today. But it has never sought to establish the kind of privileged relations which have frequently enabled France and Germany to initiate joint proposals.

On the one hand such a relationship presupposes a common view of the long-term future, and the United Kingdom has remained hesitant on that point. 'There has been considerable ambiguity in British thinking about the future of the EC. Part of the difficulty has been the absence of an overall philosophy for European integration against which to judge these strategies.'[11] There is indeed no strategic option. 'A l'élaboration d'une politique à long terme est préférée un recherche d'avantages à court terme, le tout dans un contexte dominé par l'obsession de la souveraineté nationale.'[12] We have seen, however, at the outset that a sub-system can only be sustained as a long-term option.

But it is also a matter of tactical choice. Any lasting alliance does in some way tie the hands of those committed to it. British diplomacy has preferred to keep its hands free, to examine each case on its merits and only then to look here or there for the support needed to succeed. The European Council of Milan in June 1985 illustrates this point well. There were two draft agreements before it for the codification of political cooperation: one had been presented by Germany and France, the other by the United Kingdom. The agreements had the same purpose, which was to occupy the ground and to direct the discussion about to begin on the follow-up to the Dooge Report.[13] The fact that Germany and France opted to submit their draft together, while the United Kingdom did so alone, reflects a different tactical choice.

From the point of view of the theory of the European institutions, the British approach is perhaps the more orthodox. Moreover, on several occasions the United Kingdom has been concerned to limit the disadvantages which might result from the Franco-German axis functioning too effectively. But in practice, the fundamental point to bear in mind is that neither from the point of view of a long-term strategic option nor from that of routine diplomatic tactics has Britain been willing to accept the constraints inherent in a sub-system.

The 'directoire'

Our analysis shows that apart from the Franco-German pair there does not exist any lasting operational alliance between any two Member States within the European decision-making process. The same analysis seems also to demonstrate the non-existence of any 'directoire', that is to say an operational alliance regularly composed of the *large* Member States. No important decision taken over recent years, and major draft put up for discussion, bears the stamp of an initiative undertaken by the three or four or five largest Member States. On the contrary, in many of the most important instances one of these states found itself in isolation. This was true of the United Kingdom in the European Councils of Milan in 1985, Brussels in 1987 and Madrid in 1989.

Of course, this does not mean that the weight of all Member States is equal in decision-making. 'There are observable hierarchies of political influence and economic weight.'[14] Quite apart from the weighting of votes, it is clear that the political and economic clout of Member States plays a part when it comes to the making of Community decisions. It is easier to set aside the opposition of a small country than that of a large one. This is self-evident and a matter of Realpolitik; it applies to any multilateral organization and perhaps even to human society as a whole. One cannot deduce from it the existence of a privileged decision-making mechanism.

It is often said, especially in the United Kingdom, that the future of Europe depends mainly on the relationship between Bonn, Paris and London. Even if one accepts this, however, it is not quite clear what conclusion one is to draw from it. In essence the statement reflects the idea that nothing very substantial can be done in the Community or in European affairs in general against the will of one of the large partners. That is a reasonable working hypothesis, even though it is essentially negative. The positive counterpart to it would be that the large countries, aware of the responsibility placed upon them, should organize their relationships accordingly – which they have never done.

It is surprising that this should be so. The decisive role played by the Franco-German relationship in the early stages of European construction might have developed further into a triumvirate. This did not happen. The famous overture in that direction made by de Gaulle to Soames in 1969, whether it was sincere or not, foundered in an atmosphere of recrimination and distrust. At one stage in 1978 the preparations for the European Monetary System seemed to bear the mark of what Ludlow calls 'The Gang of Three', but the underlying reality was Franco-German and so was the outcome. 'The document that was distributed to the Heads of Government on 6 July was to all intents and purposes a Franco-German plan.'[15] In 1981 the directors of four prestigious research institutes proposed the establishment of a kind of directoire for certain sectors of political cooperation.[16] This idea of 'principal nations' met with no more success than its predecessors and there is no trace of it either in the documents or in the present practice of political cooperation.

Of course, the level of consultation, especially in the political field, is higher between the large countries than it is between them and the smaller ones. The reason for that lies in the greater sophistication of their diplomatic apparatus, in the bilateral consultation process discussed earlier, and in reciprocal interests. It is more interesting to consult with those who have more to contribute in terms of knowledge and political weight. In times of tension such consultations may multiply to a point where some may see in them the beginning of a directoire. 'Under the pressures of the successive international crises of 1980/1981 the three Foreign Ministries worked together extremely closely on a trilateral basis, operating as an informal European directoire in responding to American concerns and demands.'[17] It is possible that something like that did happen, but in that case the arrangement was so discreet that it is impossible to attribute to it any visible initiative or any precise result which could compare with those attributable in the European field to Franco-German cooperation. The personal commitment of Lord Carrington and the shared concern of influencing a new American administration created for a few months a special atmosphere in the relations between Bonn, London and Paris. At any rate, the change of government in France in 1981 and the hateful climate created by the British budgetary row from 1981 to 1984 meant that this privileged cooperation was of short duration.

Thus we may conclude that although several proposals for a directoire were put forward, no such attempt has been seriously undertaken, and there is no question of success. This may be because it is felt that any arrangement of that type would have a very negative effect on the construction of Europe in view of the reactions it would provoke in the other Member States. That is what William Wallace seems to suggest in the case referred to above. Many of those who have a practical experience of Community life doubt the basic assumption underlying the idea of a directoire, which is that in a way it might be easier for the big countries to agree by discussing matters among themselves only. Experience would seem to show, rather, that efforts at compromise undertaken by the small countries are often necessary either to bring about a decision or form the adoption of common positions, in political cooperation just as much as in Community affairs. It also shows that when the large countries manage to agree among themselves, the solution adopted is sufficiently close to the general interest for it to be acceptable to the small countries too. Why, therefore, run an institutional risk by excluding them from the discussions? For all these reasons one may doubt whether a directoire will ever be an operational reality in European affairs except for a few special instances which sometimes arise in political cooperation (on the issue of Berlin, for example or, more discreetly, on Cyprus).

Before going further into specific cases, it may be useful to note that transnational political parties have not, as a rule, proved to be an effective factor in shaping European policies. One might have expected that socialist parties or christian democrat parties, present in all or most of the Community countries, would organize themselves to wield power within the Community. This is what parties usually do at the national level. And it is true that the transnational groupings of these parties exert influence, but not great influence, on European affairs. But there is nothing that even resembles a sub-system. This may be due to the fact that the same parties are not in power at the same time in different countries. It may be due to internal differences of opinion (between the British Labour Party and continental socialists or between French and Italian communists, for example). It may be due to the relative lack of power of the European Parliament which would be one of the natural means of exerting power on a party basis. But the fact remains that there is no ideological sub-system working in European affairs.

Benelux

The association between the three Benelux countries is one of the oldest and best-documented European sub-systems. The initial agreements were concluded in London between the governments in exile before the continent was liberated. The first monetary agreement goes back to 1943, while the agreement on the establishment of a customs union is dated 5 September 1944. From 1948 onwards specific agreements set up a common commercial policy (1950), the liberalization of capital movements (1954) and the free movement of workers (1956). These measures were based upon the monetary and customs arrangements through which Belgium and Luxembourg had been associated ever since 1921. Nevertheless, in the difficult years immediately after the war they constituted a pioneering effort on the road to the economic integration of sovereign states. The effort bore fruit: between 1948 and 1958 trade between the three countries increased by an average of 13% annually. To safeguard this achievement, despite the broader prospect of the Common Market of the Six, the Benelux countries concluded in February 1958 (i.e. after the Treaty of Rome) a Treaty of Economic Union which codifies and extends the commitments entered into over the preceding decade. In parallel to this they had inserted into the Treaty of Rome Article 233, which specifies that 'The provision of this Treaty shall not preclude the existence or completion of regional unions between Belgium and Luxembourg, or between Belgium, Luxembourg and the Netherlands.' The main purpose of this provision was to safeguard the arrangements agreed between these three countries before the Treaty of Rome (though they were of necessity discriminatory against the other Member States) in the fields of the free movement of goods, persons and services. It is, therefore, a protective provision. Its other purpose was to enable this collaboration to be carried on at a pace different from that of the European Community. And indeed, although the activities of Benelux were largely eclipsed by the very much more spectacular activities of the community and were intentionally kept from the limelight, they went on over the years. Even today the level of integration between these three countries is higher than that attained in the Community as a whole.

The practice by which a single document records goods crossing a frontier, which has been in force among the Twelve since January 1988 and is one of the first practical results of the Commission's 1992 Programme, has been operated in the Benelux countries since 1984. The opening up of the road haulage market, which has been justly praised as one of the great successes of the German Presidency in 1988, has existed between Belgium, Luxembourg and the Netherlands since 1960. The abolition of frontier controls within the Community, which is one of the European objectives for 1992, has existed between the Benelux countries since 1960 for persons and since 1971 for goods.

Cooperation between the Benelux countries serves the further objective of maximizing their influence within the European institutions. To this end, administrative contacts between them are numerous and regular. Their Heads of Government engage in formal consultation before each European Council. Frequently there is ministerial contact before an important Council meeting. As far as closeness and regularity are concerned, these contacts are equal, if not superior, to those in the Franco-German relationship. This practice of informal consultation between those responsible at various levels, which generally occurs outside the Benelux Secretariat General and its institutional structures (Committee of Ministers, Union Council etc.) ensures at least a good knowledge of the respective points of view and, as a rule, an adequate degree of coordination and common action. The habit goes back to the beginnings of the Community. With reference to the negotiations for the Treaty of Rome, Spaak notes: 'L'accord des trois ministres bénéluxiens allait se révéler efficace. Il est permis d'affirmer que le succès de la conférence de Messine est dû en grande partie à leurs initiatives et à leurs actions communes.'[18] At the milestones in the life of the Community (the empty chair in 1965, the crises of British membership, the budgetary quarrel, the enlargements, the negotiations for the Single Act, or the Delors package) we very regularly find the Benelux countries acting together to defend common positions.

This summary clearly shows that Benelux meets the requirements of a sub-system within the Community:

- the relationship is obviously privileged and is perceived as such: the first international activity of every newly constituted government of a Benelux country is to pay a visit to its two partners (just as French and German governments do with each other);
- it has been in existence since 1943;
- it has been formalized by treaty;
- it has proved effective both as a vanguard and as a partner in collective negotiations; and
- it enjoys full acceptance, since it is the object of a special Article in the Treaty of Rome.

It is the sub-system par excellence!

The Schengen agreement

On 14 June 1985 Germany, France and the Benelux countries signed at Schengen in Luxembourg an agreement for the gradual abolition of frontier controls between them. This agreement is in line with what was laid down a year earlier by the European Council at Fontainebleau; it pulls together the efforts to simplify frontier controls undertaken bilaterally between France and Germany and, for many years, between the Benelux countries. It lists short-term measures, to be adopted before 1 January 1986 (for instance, for the passage of tourist cars) and other longer-term measures, to be adopted if possible before 1 January 1990 (such as the harmonization of legislation on drugs, arms and explosives). The objectives which the partners have set themselves can, for the most part, be found in the Commission's White Book on the Internal Market which was also published in 1985. The preamble to the Schengen agreement, moreover, expressly refers to the necessity of ensuring that in the long run all frontiers within the Community shall be wholly opened 'in order to ensure an ever closer union between the peoples of the Member

States'. In the sensitive area of the 'Europe of the citizens' progress, at first
limited to five Member States, was to be ensured.

The implementation of the Schengen agreement was entrusted to a Committee
of Undersecretaries of State (Secrétaires d'Etat) meeting twice annually. These
meetings are prepared by a central negotiating group which in turn supervises
four special working parties: security and police, movement of persons,
transport, and movement of goods. The Member States take the chair in turn.
The European Commission attends as an observer the Undersecretaries'
meetings and those of the central negotiating group. Italy has let it be known
officially that it is interested in joining the agreement (which would mean that
in one particular field the original Community of Six would be restored).

The Schengen agreement led fairly quickly to the adoption of a number of
measures which, while not insignificant, are largely symbolic: the green disc to
ease the passage of tourists' cars, joint checkpoints, facilities for the control of
rail traffic and of inland waterways. These provisions have not made any
fundamental change. The more ambitious measures set out in Part II of the
Agreement presuppose the harmonization of existing regulations on visas, the
right of asylum, immigration, drugs, arms and frontier-crossing traffic. They
also assume agreement between the Member States on the controls to be
implemented at the Community's external frontiers, so that there may be
free movement within the participating countries while respecting the non-
discrimination clauses of the Treaty of Rome. The work is going on. The
ministerial meeting, which in June 1988 celebrated the third anniversary of the
agreement at Schengen, declared itself satisfied with the progress made. It is not
yet known whether the participants will succeed in anticipating or even going
beyond the measure which the Twelve must in any case adopt if the internal
market is to become a reality.

The Schengen agreement displays several of the characteristics of a sub-
system. It certainly does establish a *privileged* relationship in a particular field,
it was concluded with a view to *durability* and is in the *legal form* of an
international agreement. The other Member States have never questioned
its *legitimacy*, and the presence of the Commission as an observer would
presumably suffice to reassure those who might have doubts. On the other
hand one may still entertain some doubt with regard to the *effectiveness* of the
agreement. A tourist crossing an internal Community frontier will be very well
aware of the existence of Benelux because there is no frontier control at all. The
effect of the Schengen agreement is less evident. Therefore this agreement can
be described as a sub-system *in statu nascendi* which will not attain its full value
until it produces the results which its creators expect from it.

Western European Union

Western European Union (WEU) has always been committed in principle to
the ideal of European unification. Article VIII of the Brussels Treaty as
amended lists among the aims of the organization 'd'encourager l'intégration
progressive de l'Europe'. Taken literally, WEU texts could always be interpreted
as establishing an institution which was at the same time the European pillar of

the Atlantic Alliance and the 'security' branch of the European integration process. But historically and in fact WEU has been of little significance and of no great weight in the Atlantic framework and, apart from a brief period of activity during the difficult years of the British negotiations, it was also insignificant in European affairs. As a result of the failure of the European Defence Community initiative, the Community became an exclusively civil enterprise and WEU was left to eke out an obscure existence in the shadow of NATO. 'Clearly WEU is historically, legally and politically embedded in and subordinate to the Atlantic Alliance.'[19] In 1980 any mention of WEU as a sub-system in the construction of Europe would certainly have caused a smile.

That is no longer the case. The efforts at reactivation undertaken over the past years have succeeded in turning an institution subordinate to NATO into one which is in a way complementary to the Community. This evolution is due in the first place to a need which arose at the beginning of the 1980s for a European forum to discuss matters of defence.[20] Secondly, it was an answer to the repeated failures of attempts to introduce the security dimension into political cooperation, especially the relative failure of the Genscher-Colombo initiative. The former Secretary General of WEU writes: 'Il me parait que c'est l'accumulation des échecs et des semi-échecs enregistrés à chaque effort fait pour assurer aux Dix des possibilités réelles de travailler de concert dans le domaine de la sécurité qui est pour l'essentiel à l'origine des tentatives tendant à la relance de l'Union.'[21]

From 1983 onwards the idea that WEU could and should become part and parcel of the effort towards European integration attracted support and credibility. An important report published collectively by several research institutes recommended that course.[22] Leo Tindemans wrote: 'Une évolution de ce genre introduirait au moins provisoirement dans le domaine de la sécurité une notion d'Europe "différenciée" analogue à celle que le système monétaire européen établit dans le domaine monétaire.'[23] This idea was very successful in France and even penetrated into the Gaullist milieu. Jacques Chirac has said: 'L'UEO, et c'est à mes yeux sa raison d'être essentielle, à vocation à devenir tôt ou tard l'une des pièces maitresses de la construction européenne.'[24]

This gradual integration of WEU, an organization previously held to be moribund and outdated, into an accepted intellectual framework for the future of the European Community is an interesting phenomenon; its evolution can be traced step by step in a number of texts. The Rome Declaration of October 1984, which is the first attempt at reactivation, does not mention the other European institutions. In April 1985 in Bonn the WEU ministers announced their resolve to reinforce Europe's technological capacity. This was the first contact with Community activities. Meanwhile, the members of the Community had received the Dooge Report which (with some reservations on the part of the Danes, the Greeks and the Irish) spoke of the WEU as a framework for security discussions, acknowledged that this framework was being strengthened and considered that this strengthening should enable WEU to enrich its contribution to the debate on security. The Single Act (February 1986) declared formally that it saw no obstacle to closer cooperation in the field of security between certain contracting parties within WEU. This testimonial of respectability enabled the WEU ministers meeting in Venice in April of that year to recall 'the importance of WEU in the construction of Europe'. Finally, at The Hague in October 1987 the 'platform' adopted by WEU ministers declared that the integration of Europe would not be complete if it did not extend to security and defence, and that the amended Treaty of Brussels was 'a major instrument towards the attainment of that goal'.

The reactivation of WEU is interesting in itself: its gradual conversion from a dormant institution into a 'major instrument' and a 'corner-stone' confers upon diplomacy the fascination of a fairy tale! But from the angle which concerns us the main point is the absorption of WEU into the European concept. Since the 'platform' adopted by the WEU ministers at The Hague in October 1987, this absorption seems to have become an established fact and we may speak of WEU as being a European sub-system.

The criteria which we set for the definition of a sub-system apply quite easily:

• the relationship established is without doubt a privileged one: the commitment to mutual assistance is stronger under the Treaty of Brussels than under the Atlantic Alliance;
• it has been in existence since 1954;
• it has been formalized by a Treaty (and more recently by The Hague platform); and
• it has been accepted by the other partners under Article 30, Section 6, of the Single Act.

Opinons may differ concerning the criterion of effectiveness, but it is a fact that since 1984 the WEU countries have set up a system which comprises:

• joint meetings of the Ministers of Foreign Affairs and Defence;
• regular contacts between political directors;
• working parties on politico-military questions; and
• a direct communications network (WEUCOM) similar to COREU (the confidential communications network which links foreign ministries for the purposes of European Political Cooperation).

The structure has evidently been modelled on that of political cooperation. It makes it possible for the Seven (now Nine) to do what the Twelve cannot – to hold regular consultations on security matters. This they have done on issues such as the US Strategic Defence Initiative, the various possibilities of the zero option on missiles, and the means of ensuring the safety of shipping in the Gulf. Thus WEU can be considered part of the European whole, on a par with political cooperation, of which it is a 'differentiated' form. It is undoubtedly a sub-system.

Conclusions

The first conclusion is self-evident: sub-systems do exist. Some (such as Benelux and the Franco-German pair) date back to the beginnings of the

Community. Others were set up to meet special needs (WEU for defence and Schengen for the movement of persons in the countries bordering on the Rhine and the Meuse). But there are fewer sub-systems than one might have assumed. This is largely because the criteria to which they have to respond in order to be effective are very demanding. Sub-systems imply a common commitment to a long-term goal, which is something that certain countries, such as the United Kingdom, hesitate to undertake. They offer obvious advantages in the multilateral power game, in terms of greater influence and increased chances of furthering agreed views, but there is also a price to be paid: options are more limited and prior compromises have to be made with the privileged partner. For this reason, perhaps, sub-systems are rare.

The fact that they exist adds precision and nuance to the objective image one may have of the decision-making process in the Community, but it does not basically change that process. In particular the idea, seeminly cherished by some, that Community decisions are to a large extent pre-determined by bi- or trilateral arrangements is unsupported by any evidence. Obviously, the juridical structure of the Community, like any other political structure, covers a gamut of concurrent political and economic influences and interests. In this interplay some like to join in a sub-system and feel happy in it; they believe that by so doing they can maximize their influence and stand up better for their interests. Others remain aloof and are also quite happy; they believe that in this way they will be better able to defend their freedom of action and independence. Moreover both sides occasionally depart from their general line of conduct in specific circumstances. It is true that at least one sub-system, the Franco-German pair, has exerted a significant influence on the development of European affairs. But the constant refusal of the United Kingdom, in the 1950s as well as later on, to seek privileged partners with whom to engage resolutely in ambitious long-term action in European policy fields has without doubt brought an even more significant influence to bear. The negative decision was at least as important as the positive. The Franco-German sub-system has been important to the extent that, and in the instances where, it has given expression to a joint fundamental option. The sub-system is at first an effective way of maximizing the chances of success of that option. But later the mere existence of an accepted and well-known sub-system increases the pressure and therefore the chances of arriving at common points of view. Like the system itself, the sub-system is not static.

We must also rid ourselves of the idea that the existence of these sub-systems is in any way contrary to the Community spirit. 'To the Community purist the notion that bilateral, let alone trilateral, relationships are an intrinsic feature of the system smacks of heresy.'[25] It is possible that there are purists who set their sights so high; every political idea engenders its orthodoxy. But the founders of the community, as well as being men of vision, were experienced practitioners in the field of international affairs. In April 1951, on the eve of the signing of the Paris Treaty, Jean Monnet felt uneasy about the child of his imagination that was on the point of being born, and in his memoirs he notes: 'Je me rendis à Bonn pour m'assurer que les positions de la France et de l'Allemagne seraient pour l'essentiel identiques et résisteraient à l'offensive prévisible des pays du Benelux.'[26] We identify there, in the pre-history of the construction of Europe, two of the sub-systems which exist to this day. Far from being offended by them, Monnet always knew how to use them.

We note, moreover, that those who take part in these sub-systems consider themselves not less, but *more* 'European' than the others. Franco-German cooperation was designed as an axis for the construction of Europe. The Benelux countries like to look upon themselves as the guardians of the Community spirit. Those involved in the reactivation of WEU and in the Schengen agreement believe they are acting as an enlightened vanguard. To a certain extent it is attachment to the central aims of the construction of Europe which seems to have motivated the special arrangements described above.

We must certainly bear in mind that the European structure which has been evolving over the past 30 years is considerably more flexible than the rigour of the texts and the ambition of the purist make it appear at first sight. Within the Community, that flexibility shows itself in the practice of differentiation, or two-speed Europe (an example being the EMS). It is also shown in the existence of sub-systems. The decision-making apparatus set up by the Treaties remains the fundamental feature without which it is clear that nothing would be possible. But from the very beginning that apparatus has adapted itself to a powerful Franco-German complicity and to the solidarity of Benelux. It has not been weakened – quite the contrary – by the gradual and pragmatic emergence of a parallel apparatus, that of political cooperation in the field of foreign relations. After several setbacks, security matters have found at least a provisional forum for discussion in WEU, which seems to satisfy not only those who take part in it but also those who do not wish to do so. Each one of these sub-systems (and others which never saw the light of day, such as the directoire) has provoked disquiet and sometimes even alarm. Yet not one of them has seriously weakened the Community's institutions. Some of them strengthen gradual movement towards the integration of Europe. Such flexibility, of course, leads to complexity. 'La communauté des années 1980 est un ensemble complexe imbriquant des réseaux plus ou moins étroits d'intégration et de concertation.'[27] Without flexibility and complexity the countries of Western Europe would not have been able, over the years, to tackle together an ever-growing number of problems.

The most important (though not unexpected) conclusion to be drawn from an analysis of the sub-systems in the construction of Europe is the central nature of the Community and its institutions. At no time has any sub-system sought to replace the Community. On the contrary, they all take the Community as their point of reference. It is possible that in General de Gaulle's mind it was the purpose of the Elysée Treaty to replace by an exclusive alliance the 'international aeropagi' whose influence he deplored. He certainly felt no sympathy with the 'soi-disant exécutifs, installés à la tête des organismes communs en vertu des illusions d'intégration qui sévissaient avant mon retour.'[28] But the preamble voted by the Bundestag at the time of ratification in 1963 set the record straight. At no time has there been a bilateral Franco-German agreement the content of which could have endangered the existence of the Community. And the same goes for the other cases in point. The Benelux countries intentionally put a damper on their own efforts at integration. WEU and the Schengen agreement were firmly placed into a long-term

Community perspective, and even the directoire which never saw the light of day was intended not to destroy the Community (which indeed might have been its effect) but to manage it better. Everybody has gradually come round to the implicit agreement that 'la légitimité européenne est détenue par la Communauté, dont les institutions constituent le noyau dur, l'"axe de l'unification".'[29]

At the end of the day, it seems that in the construction of Europe sub-systems are rejected if they represent a serious threat to the cohesion of the whole (like the directoire or certain Gaullist views of the Franco-German axis) but are tolerated where they serve temporarily to overcome an obstacle, to preserve acquired positions, to open up new ways, or simply to maximize the normal interplay of interests – always on the condition, which is accepted also by political cooperation, that the central role and higher legitimacy of the community is recognized. One is reminded of the image that Fernand Braudel employed to throw light upon the history of capitalism: 'Les diverses zones d'une économie-monde regardent vers un même point, le centre: polarisées, elles formant déjà un ensemble aux multiples cohérences.'[30]

Notes

1. Helen Wallace, in Roger Morgan and Caroline Bray, (eds), *Partners and Rivals in Western Europe: Britain, France and Germany* (London, Tower, 1986), p. 156.
2. Ibid.
3. Karl Kaiser and Pierre Lellouche, *Le Couple franco-allemand et la défense de l'Europe* (Paris, Travaux et Recherches de l'IFRI, 1986), p. 317.
4. Valery Giscard d'Estaing, *Le Pouvoir et la vie* (Paris, Compagnie 12, 1988), p. 124.
5. Helen Wallace, art. cit. (above, n. 1), p. 145.
6. Giscard d'Estaing, op. cit. (above, n. 4), p. 124.
7. Peter Ludlow, *The Making of the EMS* (London, Butterworth, 1982).
8. Christopher Tugendhat, *Making Sense of Europe* (London, Viking Penguin, 1986), p. 36.
9. On the proliferation of ideas on the subject of European defence at the beginning of the 1980s, see Ph. de Schoutheete, 'Neue Ansätze für eine Europäische Aussen-politik', *Integration*, April 1981.
10. See above, n. 5.
11. Helen Wallace, *Europe: The Challenge of Diversity* (London, Chatham House Papers No. 29, 1985), p. 5.
12. Françoise de la Serre, *La Grande Bretagne et la Communauté européenne* (Paris, Presses Universitaires de France, 1987), p. 104.
13. J. De Ruyt, *L'Acte unique européen* (Brussels, Editions de l'Université libre de Bruxelles, 1987), pp. 57–60.
14. Helen Wallace, op. cit. (Above, n. 11), p. 27.
15. Ludlow, op. cit. (above, n. 7), p. 105. We know from Roy Jenkins that, at the time, the British Prime Minister felt 'miffed' because he had not been more closely consulted by the French and German governments. Roy Jenkins, *European Diary 1977–81* (London, Collins, 1989), p. 283.
16. Karl Kaiser et al., *La Securité de l'Occident. Bilan et orientations* (Paris, Travaux de l'IFRI, 1981), paras 5.12–5.20.
17. William Wallace, in Morgan and Gray, op. cit. (above, n. 1), p. 221.

18. P.H. Spaak, *Combats inachevés* (Paris, Fayard, 1969), Vol. II, p. 65.
19. A. Pijpers, in Panos Tsakaloyanis, (ed.), *La Relance de l'UEO, implications pour la CE et ses institutions* (Maastricht, Institut européen d'administration publique, Documents et travaux), 1985–4, p. 82.
20. See above, n. 9.
21. A. Cahen, in Tsakaloyanis (ed.), art. cit. (above, n. 19), p. 7.
22. Karl Kaiser et al., *La Communauté européenne: déclin ou renouveau* (Paris, Travaux et Recherches de l'IFRI, 1983), para. 4.62.
23. In *Le Monde*, 23 December 1983.
24. Speech to WEU assembly, 2 December 1986.
25. Helen Wallace, art. cit. (above n. 1).
26. Jean Monnet, *Mémoires* (Paris, Fayard, 1976), p. 414.
27. Ph. Moreau-Desfarges in Tsakaloyanis, (ed.), art. cit. (above, n. 19), p. 49.
28. Ch. de Gaulle, *Mémoires d'espoir* Vol. I, p. 192.
29. Ph. Moreau-Desfarges, art. cit. (above, n. 19), p. 50.
30. F. Braudel, *Civilisation matérielle, economie et capitalisme* (Paris, Armand Colin, 1979), Vol. III, p. 25.

7 Nordic cooperation
Carl-Einar Stålvant

There are grounds for regarding the northwestern corner as a stable subsidiary area of Europe. The five small Nordic countries display a combination of domestic stability with dense, amicable and predictable interregional relations. Indeed, this comforting image is often projected onto the region's links with external powers as well. A theory of Nordic stability in the midst of superpower rivalries and high politics has been expounded. It serves both as a rationalized description of the combined effect of five national decisions concerning viable security strategies, and as a source of normative considerations in new circumstances. Hence the same attribute is claimed to pervade all three layers of politics, underscoring a certain uniqueness in the Nordic pattern of parallel national developments, neighbourhood cooperation and defusion of bloc antagonism.

As with other shorthand and sweeping judgements, the reality is much more complex and conditional. What may appear as an outstanding feature in a crude international comparison, may be broken down into an array of distinct and separate conditions. But let us assume that, by and large, developments in the Nordic countries are less sporadic, extreme and, for that matter, imaginative than they may be in other parts of the world.

An examination of the Nordic pattern benefits from a comprehensive multi-layered view: its peculiarities are not only manifest on the level of regional formation but also embedded in national conditions and decisions. Earlier chapters in this volume have suggested some tools and vantage points. One is that of geographical location, a perspective that is useful both for understanding the Nordic legacy and for appreciating the countries' role in power politics. A second departure is provided by Philippe de Schoutheete's list of criteria for delineating sub-systems within Europe (Chapter 6). A third derives from the answer to a question: When established political, economic and social alliances in postwar Europe are under strain, how do the Nordic countries, individually and collectively, adapt themselves to altered and less predictable environments? Both disintegration and integration are strong secular trends. Ethnic national reawakening in the East entails prospects of new divisions and alliances. The building of market-regions in West Europe poses challenging questions about

the long-term viability of the Nordic pattern and its relationship to the
European centres.

The background

A conventional image of the Nordic region depicts the five members as small,
homogeneous, affluent, secularized, industrially advanced and (with the
exception of Denmark) sparsely populated states. The five countries have
similar political and economic institutions, as a result of mutual influences and
diffusion, and also of simultaneous exposures to leading international ideas and
models. Party systems overlap considerably. And, of course, there are common
roots in language (with the exception of Finnish and Inuit), culture and history.

Each Nordic country remains distinct, however, and it is important not to
overstress the homogeneity. Indeed, a trans-Nordic community was not
achieved until the postwar era, when the five members had firmly established
their independence. In considering the Nordic future, it is useful also to look at
the past and to trace the evolution of the Nordic configuration within a wider
European context.

The Norwegian sociologist Stein Rokkan explained the variegated nature of
European politics by a conceptual map, a 'typological topology' of variations in
territorial systems.[1] Basically, he distinguished between a North-South and an
East-West axis. The first concerns itself with relations between states and
culture, indicated by degrees of independence from Roman Law and the
Catholic Church. The second axis has two features, characterizing state-
economy relationships: first, the strength and nature of city networks; and
secondly, the degree of centralization brought about by the incorporation of
primary-producing peripheries.

The five Nordic countries occupy the upper tier of the North axis. As a unit,
they broke with the Catholic Church after 1517. The framework of the
Hanseatic League, which had been dominated by German cities, was quickly
absorbed by the emerging territorial systems of Denmark and Sweden. These
dual cores subjected other parts of the north to long spells of dependence. The
rivalry for regional hegemony was in part a competition for control of Russian
trading routes. Shifts of alliances, conquering and reconquering of provinces,
and dynastic intrigues were part of a Baltic pattern, in turn reinforced by a
diversity of religions, cultural and linguistic affiliations on the eastern borders
of the region. Traces of these remain: the name of the Estonian capital, Tallinn,
is derived from the Finnish words *Tanskan Linna* and literally means the
Danish village; and St Petersburg was constructed on the ruins of a Swedish
fortress. In due time, the two kingdoms contracted territorially. Sweden lost its
colonial possessions in Germany in 1803. The Danish king held a seat in the
inner circle of the German Conforederation until 1864. Since then, much of the
Baltic-Nordic politics has been governed by the changing nature of German-
Russian relations and links to the global balance of power.

The five countries can be ranged along the East-West axis roughly as follows:

Table 7.1 Origins of the Nordic countries

Seaward Periphery		Successful empire-nations Seaward Landward		Landward periphery
Weaker cities, once independent, later a subject territory:	Stronger cities, medieval empire, later reduced to dependence:	Stronger cities, continuous independence:	Weaker cities, continuous independence:	Weaker cities subject territory:
Iceland	*Norway*	*Denmark*	*Sweden*	*Finland*

Source: Stein Rokkan (see note 1).

The legacies of these origins are still valid. It is no coincidence that the influence of the EC diminishes on the Atlantic side of the region.[2] The secession of Greenland in 1985 and the unwillingness of the Faroe Islands to accept the Treaty of Rome (in connection with Denmark's entry) bear witness to this. In the same context, the Stockholm Convention may symbolically be seen as a counterbalance to the Treaty of Rome in the struggle over integration strategies.

The 'Europeanization' of the 1980s went beyond political and economic questions, such as the EC-EFTA dialogue and negotiations on the European Economic Space, to influence cultural and even spiritual matters.[3] The Nordic countries have re-established diplomatic relations with the Holy See, and the Pope made his first-ever visit (which caused some controversy) to this part of Europe in 1989. Shortly before, the Finnish government played host to the Patriarch of Constantinople.

Links with the East

It is estimated that the Orthodox Church has about 60,000 followers, most of them of Karelian origin. Language also connects Finland eastwards with Karelia and across the Bay of Finland. Both Ingrian – the vernacular of the region southwest of Leningrad – and Estonian are allied to the Finnish-Ugrian language family. Consequently, a long experience of common cultural and economic links with Russia and the Soviet Union has resulted from Finland's geographical proximity: with a shared border of 196 kilometres along the Pasvik River. Likewise, despite strains in Swedish-Soviet relations since 1981, a solution was found in 1988 to a long-standing disagreement concerning economic and fisheries zones in the Baltic. A compromise giving 75% to Sweden and 25% to the Soviets is an accord as yet unmatched in other disputed areas along the Soviet coastline.

In a polar projection, 'Scandinavia is the Western part of Siberia',[4] and this naturally has implications for defence. The straight missile trajectory from Sverdlovsk to Washington crosses the peninsula. More important still, the technological and marine conditions for the superpowers' deterrence strategies extend considerably the potential theatre of conflict.

A special pattern?

Students of Nordic regionalism are struck by the formal limits that divergent foreign policy solutions and traditional ideas of state sovereignty impose on the form and content of Nordic integration. Yet most observers have found such impediments elastic and possible to circumvent. A common outlook on international developments outside core commitments balances centrifugal pressures. The unanimity rule does not always imply that the will of the least eager member prevails – it may, conversely, bolster natural political cohesion if the alternative formula is thought to create resentment. Although Sweden's central location and economic strength gives the country a pivotal position in most pan-Nordic projects, there is no clear pattern of regional leadership. Social and cultural conditions are particularly conducive to the building of a transnational community.[5] Economic modernization and industrial restructuring have led progressively to a regional division of labour and increased interdependencies between the economies.

If anything, the 'Nordic route' exemplifies how incremental achievements add up to an accumulated structure of links on all levels of society. According to Nils Andrén, the resulting network exerts a significant influence on joint policy outputs and the formulation of broadly similar national policies.[6]

The Nordic experience contradicts a few assumptions in integration theorizing. There is little support for the assertions that economic integration and common institution-building lead gradually to coordinated foreign policies and eventually to common security; and little for the collateral idea that coordination should be accompanied by a decrease in formal dependency on extra-regional powers. Rather, respect for divergence boosts internal interdependence of policies.[7] Formal affiliation with outsiders enhances the need for coordination in order to preserve a state of affairs that is deemed to bring more collective advantages than a situation where major commitments to outside powers threaten to divide the region. In this sense, Nordic cooperation offers a defensive adjustment mechanism to offset challenges that may undermine national and regional autonomy. A certain ambiguity is built into the system of checks and balances, since the Nordic area does not completely fit into any regional bloc pattern. It is militarily fragmented across the East-West divide. It falls within the wider Western Europe area, with specific conditions attached to Finland's Eastern trade. But nevertheless it is split between EC and EFTA.

It thus seems useful to examine the Nordic pattern as an outcome of political dynamics at different levels, with a clear division between high and low politics.

Security and mutual considerations

Since the formation of blocs in Europe in the late 1940s the configuration of the Nordic countries has displayed the same fundamental features. Denmark, Iceland and Norway are members of NATO. Neither Denmark nor Norway has nuclear weapons or allied troops on their territories in peacetime. The Swedish policy of non-alignment in peace aims at neutrality in case of war, while the neutral foreign policy of Finland is conducted with due regard to the framework provided by the Treaty of Friendship, Cooperation and Mutual Assistance (FCMA) with the Soviet Union.

The result is said to form a pattern of alignments and constraint that for a long time kept Northern Europe as a low-tension area. The military build-up in the high north and the growing strength of the Soviet northern fleet retroacted only slowly on the national positions. The pattern was interpreted as a political rather than a military arrangement, the best-known exposition of the internal dynamics being Arne Olav Bruntland's analysis of the 'Nordic balance'.[8] He demonstrated how existing premises for each country were conditioned by unchanged policies on the part of its Nordic neighbours. The supposed linkages were most convincingly shown to work in the Finnish-Norwegian relationship as a result of, or in anticipation of, an activation of the military consultation article in the Finnish FCMA treaty with the Soviet Union.

The regional balance-of-power reasoning that sustains the dissuasion mechanism is most evident in Swedish thinking: 'Although the situation as regards security in the North European area is not insusceptible to change, it may be assumed that both sides realize that attempts to alter the fundamental security pattern in the Nordic area in their favour are likely to meet with countermeasures from the other side.'[9] The limitations in Finland's obligations and conditional nature of Norway's and Denmark's unilateral limitations are claimed to be facilitated by Sweden's relatively strong defence and non-alignment. Furthermore, the view that the Nordic pattern somehow was in the hands of smaller powers gained ground. Changes in the strategic environment and in domestic politics have nevertheless undermined the conviction that the Northern flank stays aloof from the central balance. Rather, three levels of relationships operate in the area: a superpower 'overlay', linkages to the central balance and the CSCE process, and a Nordic level.

Cold water politics

During the Reagan administration the combination of the new American marine strategy and the presence of strong Soviet navies west of the Scandinavian peninsula changed threat perceptions in the North. Russian 'defensive expansionism' and the proclamation of 'horizontal escalation' seemed to signify precisely the opposite to Nordic thinking: rather than promoting barriers to increased presence, the situation in the North could be used as a springboard for introducing tensions in the area. The strategic competition resulted both from technological factors and from the particular role that the Kola peninsula plays in nuclear deterrence. Increased Soviet marine activities, including two cases of intrusions into Swedish territorial waters that have led to formal protests, could accordingly be viewed as a Baltic reflection of the 'strategic' North.[10] Confidence-building measures and naval disarmament in the Nordic area have been more tricky to discuss than arms control measures on the continent. Soviet diplomacy has offered fewer surprises than in Central Europe. The Nordic region's importance for Soviet strategic interests was further underlined by Gorbachev's Murmansk speech of October 1987, when he claimed that the militarization of this part of the world was assuming 'threatening dimensions'.

So, maritime complexities are very much an American-Soviet preoccupation. From a US perspective the Norwegian Sea might even be the central front. Asymmetrical force reductions, changes in military doctrine and a contraction of obligations in relation to continental allies are all conceivable steps in the reconstruction of the European post-Cold War order. Such measures, however, are likely to retroact only slowly on the situation in the North as long as so much of the two powers' bilateral security is invested there.

Europeanization and defence

Europeanization expresses an awareness that Nordic security is embedded in larger frameworks. Norway is attracted by the EPC process, for political reasons, by the revitalized WEU, which offers a counterweight to the pre-dominance of US interests in the North. The CSCE process offers possibilities for Norway (not a member of these organizations) to link its views with mainstream views held in Europe. The CSCE talks are equally important for the neutrals, and some concern has been expressed at the exclusion of these neutrals from the CFE forum where the important military matters for the future are settled.

In a period of unilateral moves and reduction of standing forces, a few local factors in the North at are play as well, although military glasnost is less evident here. Promises of force reductions in the Leningrad district have acted as incentives for the Norwegians to launch a 'Nordpolitik'. A series of embarrassing accidents at sea made Soviet authorities give assurances of early notification to Norway. The Defence Committee of the Norwegian Storting was invited in 1989 to visit the Murmansk base complex. Despite such overtures, the general cautiousness that characterizes asymmetrical relationships between small states and big powers is likely to prevail. Norwegian authorities outline the balance of deterrence and reassurance versus the Russians by maintaining the right to draw on the broader patterns of Western security.

Sweden and Finland stand out as being very cautious in the restructuring process. The catchword for their policies is stability, and for two reasons they avoid overtures that could be interpreted as changes in established positions. First, they argue that their roles are an integral part of the European pattern, and secondly they see few signs of changed military positions on the part of the predominant power in the immediate vicinity. Defence and non-provocative defence postures may be less reassuring than offensive doctrines for small countries inside the strategic perimeters of big power defence. Continuing 'brown water activities' and violations of Swedish territorial waters add ambiguity to local imbalances.[11]

Interpreting the pattern

Two notions of theoretical significance express the link between the otherwise divergent views on security of the Nordic countries. They are an example of

Karl Deutsch's *security communities*.[12] War between them is unthinkable. Conflicts of interests have been solved by arbitration or negotiations, such as the dissolution of the Swedish-Norwegian union in 1905, the settlement of the status of Aaland Islands in 1921, and the peaceful solution of the disputed territories in East Greenland in 1933. Extension of economic and territorial waters has also led to bilateral disagreements, but all cases of overlapping claims have eventually been solved. More important still, the people identify with each other to the extent that their confident expectations of each others' orderly behaviour are self-fulfilling.[13] The Nordic group is a pluralistic, non-amalgamated security community, blending national independence with a system of conditional and restrained links with the main adversaries and the broader pattern of security arrangements.

Barry Buzan has suggested the term 'security complexes' for 'a group of states whose primary security concerns link together sufficiently closely that their national securities cannot realistically be considered apart from each other'.[14] A regional system approach acknowledges the interaction between two sets of mechanisms. One describes the macro overlay, the second proximate relations. Within the broader category, security communities constitute successful 'mature anarchies' – that is, groups of states which succeed in combining political fragmentation with satisfactory management of collective goods. The Nordic experience relies on the conjunction of interest between East and West and the Nordic states. The prospect of rapid shifts in great power relations has revealed vulnerabilities that are beyond the influence of small actors. Europeanization could be one strategy to restore and maintain the status quo.

The Nordic sub-system

Although Nordic community-building differs in many ways from the EC system, there are some structural similarities. The division between high and low politics coincides with the distinction between intergovernmental process and the work carried out within the common Nordic institutions, centred on the Nordic Council. Outside the agreed set-up, recurrent meetings between Prime, Foreign and Defence Ministers confirm that treaty-bound cooperation lacks the more topical and emotive appeal of foreign policy issues. Nordic affairs have been domesticized by the habit of appointing functional ministers as coordinating members of the Nordic Council of Ministers.

A feature that deviates from EC design is the weak legal foundation that exists for joint collective behaviour in foreign policy or international issues. The codifying Helsinki Treaty treats the subject by omission rather than by inclusion, though it does acknowledge the close interrelation between domestic Nordic concerns and *external cooperation* (arts. 22, 33, 34, 35, 36, 40). In the absence of a firm legal doctrine, Nordic cooperation is built on norms of good faith and converging interests. As an example, cooperation in the foreign economic field is formulated in terms closer to the rather vague diplomatic language of EPC regulations than on those articles in the Treaty of Rome which deal with common commercial policy. Article 22 reads: 'In issues of international commercial policy the Contracting Parties shall, both separately and jointly, endeavour to promote the interests of the Nordic countries and shall consult together with this purpose in view.' A second formal source that bears witness to Nordic collective action is actually not Nordic at all. In a footnote to the Single Act, the Danish government declares that section 3 does not affect 'Denmark's participation in Nordic foreign policy cooperation'.

In many ways the Nordic countries can be regarded as a sub-unit, possessing contours clear enough to separate them from the rest of the world. Following Philippe de Schoutheete's criteria for delineating sub-systems, the Nordic record could look like this:[15]

Special relationship

Few traces of Nordic nationalism are left since the heyday of romantic Scandinavianism more than a century ago. What remains is the collective small-state pride in postwar achievements, resulting in rather egalitarian welfare states with comparatively good records for solving socio-economic issues. Sweden, in particular, poses as *the* model of the social-democratic conception of society.

Within the Nordic area, the attitude to group cooperation is favourable. Public opinion surveys reveal a generally positive and tolerant attitude towards Nordic neighbour states, which facilitates policy diffusion and broadly identical outlooks.[16]

Duration

The comprehensive social and organizational links that sustain the Nordic community are enduring. Of 436 non-governmental organizations which had at least three members in 1972, 40% could trace their origins to prewar times. In many respects Nordic cooperation is a forerunner of regional integration on the continent. For almost any type of transaction except trade, the intra-Nordic flows were already intensive in 1952, some significantly more intensive then than external exchanges.[17] The institutional structures for public cooperation were set up at about that time. Three major cooperation ventures – the passport union, national treatment of Nordic citizens in the social security field and the common labour market – were in existence before the Treaty of Rome was signed.

Formalization

The Nordic preference is for informal contact and communication – reflected even in a regional inclination to use the telephone rather than the postal system. The formalization and inevitable bureaucratization of the many joint ventures set up during the past 20 years cannot primarily be explained as an institutional adjustment to a change in scale. Both the general tendency towards 'organizing in' new public tasks and a political motive to maintain what had been achieved against external pressures contributed to the birth of a Nordic Council of Ministers in 1972. The accompanying build-up of secretariats and high-level working groups in all policy areas symbolized the continuing importance of Nordic cooperation after Denmark's EC entry. A side-effect was increased governmental control of the process. A Fund for Industrial Development and a joint Nordic investment bank were also created. Other small, permanent bodies have been added to the Council network. In 1975 the Nordic budget enumerated 85 institutions; ten years later the number was 112. A similar formalization has occurred in grouping allied parties and polarizing the various groupings in the Nordic Council. The entire network is run by approximately 450 'Nordocrats'.

Effectiveness

Identifying practical results in a political field means that one should be able to evaluate achievements in relation to the actors' own aspirations. One should also be able to see evidence of regional influence on a larger whole.

As constitutional unity is not an overriding aim of Nordic cooperation, other more mundane and pragmatic motives are salient. Many institutions represent a cost-reducing pooling of resources. Others are coordinating mechanisms that enhance the prospects for reaching goals that one country cannot achieve on its own. The most politically important motive, however, the quintessence of the achievements and conditions described earlier, is the use of Nordic instruments to sustain the ideals of these small democratic states.

The second criterion is less tangible. Owing to the countries' differing priorities, there is no easily defined target for assessing influence. The cohesiveness of the bloc can be judged both in UN voting behaviour and in the different informal or formal agreements that guide the countries in multilateral diplomacy. Table 7.2 summarizes the main categories of behaviour. In traditional diplomacy, the countries have been less successful in representing each other.

Table 7.2 Examples of Nordic foreign policy cooperation in international organizations

Joint representation	Rotation of posts	division of tasks	Joint resolutions/statements	Informal coordination
IMF ad hoc meetings	World Bank	UNESCO	UNDP	UNGA†
UN Commissions	ECOSOC	GATT*	UNEP	UNCTAD
Conventions	Subsidiary		ILO	WHO
Consortia in	ECOSOC			
scientific	bodies			
organizations				

* despite Denmark's participation in the EC.
† A series of studies confirms high voting cohesion for Nordic states: at the 38th session of UNGA, 78% of the votes of the group of Nordic states were unanimous, compared with 30.1% for EC member states; at the 40th session the figures were, respectively, 70.8% and 41.5%.

Suggestions regarding joint embassies or common Nordic representation have been made in the Nordic Council but have never been realized (apart from the utilization of common facilities).

Coordination of views and exchanges of information are standard procedures between field offices abroad as well as among domestically based staffs. Nordic interests are then furthered in different ways. The execution of joint policy comes close to the EC prescription for concerted action. What is lacking are the centralized instruments of EC foreign relations: there is no Commission, no Nordic presidency and, for that matter, no delegated treaty-making power. Absence of such structures has not impeded a high degree of policy integration, however.

Acceptability

Nordic cooperation seems widely accepted. Only the Soviet Union has at times expressed misgivings in accordance with its policy of discouraging regional cooperation in which it takes no part. Strong Soviet signals have been sent to indicate limits of acceptability to Finnish participation and to the use of Nordic countries as a bridge to the EC. Otherwise only the Scottish National Party and members of the Peoples' Fronts in the Baltic states have displayed active interest in developing relations with the Nordic Council. However, the 'new political thinking' under Gorbachev led to a reassessment of the value of Nordic cooperation. Gorbachev's Finlandia speech of 26 October 1989 suggested direct contacts between the Supreme Soviet and the Council, and proposed cooperation between republics in the western part of the Soviet Union, including the Baltic republics, and the Nordic Council.

Russett ranks Nordic regionalism on a par with Benelux, the EC sub-system par excellence.[18] Historically, the two groupings of small states have been exposed to the benevolence or active protection of neighbouring major powers. Their fortunes have depended on their ability to work together to increase freedom of manoeuvre and to safeguard autonomy despite changes in external constraints. Postwar developments transformed the situation fundamentally for the Benelux countries. Their initial conception of community-building as a *strategy* has tended to be displaced by one of organization and rules, following the growth of the EC. Yet one can observe a threshold condition – of foreign and security policy commitment – which resists adding a neutral country to the EC formula of rights and obligation. It is easier for EC members to accommodate new members operating like themselves within the broader patterns of West European cooperation and alliance understandings.

Membership overtures from the neutrals (like Sweden in 1970–2 and Austria in 1989) tend to raise opposition. Clear exceptions to the system of commitments are likely to decrease their ability to mitigate pressures from stronger neighbours through strong institutions: a means to avoid coming empty-handed, to phrase Paul Henri Spaak. Nordic regionalism, as noted, has not been framed within one overriding foreign context. The Nordic countries' course is much marked by an effort to preserve stability in the North while adapting to prevailing conditions and the challenges from new departures in

European integration. In this game, the role of the Nordic countries becomes much more ambiguous. Packages tend to be formulated and implemented over cycles of 10–15 years. On each previous occasion, changed relations between the UK and France have mattered most.

Social and economic interaction

The Swedish geopolitician Rudolf Kjellén was one of the first to ponder the dialectics of high and low politics. Writing about changes in the pre-world War I pattern, he tried to relate changes in big power relations to the foreign policies pursued by each of the Nordic countries. He observed the strength of attracting and repelling forces: each of Sweden's three small neighbours occupied locations of strategic interests to their proximate big power.[19] Influences were felt even more strongly by a small country if trade relations, cultural affiliations and strategic dependence ran in the same direction. As the other Nordic countries had easily identified core areas in the east, south and west, the net result was that the centrally placed country, Sweden, although the region's largest, had to accept that it was neither a superpower nor a small, weak country. Today, it is still asked how factors internal to the region are offset by extra-regional dependence. We have already discussed this in relation to security and will now look at the patterns of social communication and economic interests.

Social communication

Inter-Nordic travel and transport are intense. The impression is that inward-looking orientations predominate. A few qualifications need to be made. Denmark's role in travel and tourism is oriented more towards the continent and towards Germany in particular. It is more a receiver of flows from the North than a sender. The bilateral relationships between Sweden and Finland

Table 7.3 Ratio of domestic and Nordic scheduled flights to total number of passengers

Company	Domestic routes			Inter-Nordic routes			Total
	1967	1977	1987	1967	1977	1987	
SAS	40			20			60
		40			26		66
			45			25	70
Finnair	57			20			77
		59			19		78
			55			18	73

Source: Nordic Statistical Yearbook, 1968, 1978 and 1988.

and between Sweden and Norway, respectively, are dense. Iceland appears to be much oriented to the US, and Sweden seems to be something of a node. Air transport figures show that European and international journeys have declined in proportion to domestic and intra-Nordic ones.

Migration flows are also largely confined to intra-Nordic movements, although substantial numbers of immigrants have arrived from other areas as well, mostly to Sweden and Denmark.[20] It is estimated that labour mobility across the borders amounted to about 1.4m persons for the period 1954–86. Within the common labour market about two-thirds of the movement is between Sweden and Finland. Originally the high level of migration was explained by the pull effects that an expanding Swedish industry exerted on the Finnish labour force. As modernization of agriculture came rather late to Finland, migration offered the easiest solution to the surplus of workers. In times of recession, large numbers have moved back again or have resorted to long-distance commuting. Despite a growth of available jobs in Swedish industry in the late 1980s, the overall trend is levelling off.

Economic orientation

The trading and production system of the Nordic countries is examined by Per Wijkman.[21] Sweden has an important role in some areas. For instance the Volvo sub-supplier network links distant parts of the Scandinavian countries. Strategic alliances are created between big multinationals from Scandinavia and companies on the continent. The ABB merger, the Volvo-Renault connection, takeovers by Electrolux of Italian household equipment companies and the purchase of a majority position by Europe GM in the SAAB personal cars division reveal diversities of approach.

Table 7.4 Nordic and European home markets: Export intensity for manufactures

Country	Nordic share of total exports	Surrounding Nordic market/ habitants	Export- intensity
	A	B	A/B
	%		
Denmark	28.7	17.6	1.63
Finland	24.1	17.9	1.35
Iceland*	10.7	22.5	0.47
Norway	32.8	18.6	1.76
Sweden	25.1	14.4	1.74
——	EC share	EC market	
EC-Denmark average est.	50.0	317.3	0.158

* Total exports.

Source: Nordic Statistical Yearbook and Carl Fredriksson, *Ekonomisk Integration i Norden.*

Table 7.5 Swedish investments abroad (A) and foreign investments in Sweden (B), 1986–8 (kronor, m)

| | (A) three main target countries (Europe) | | | | (B) three main investor countries (Europe) | | |
| | A | | | | B | | |
To	1986	1987	1988		1986	1987	1988
Total	25,380	24,508	44,471		6,746	4,322	7,902
EC	7,597	12,458	25,261		1,620	1,424	1,847
EFTA	3,888	5,489	10,803		3,693	1,754	4,833
Rank of	UK	Nor	NL	Investors	Nor	Nor	Fin
receivers	Fin	UK	Swi		Fin	Fin	Swi
	Nor	FRG	UK		Fra	NL	NL

Source: Sweden-EFTA-EC 1988, (Stockholm: Foreign Ministry, Department of Trade, 1989).

Wijkman's figures indicate a slow but discernable growth for the Nordic area as a home market for the five countries. Not surprisingly, this very notion has been adopted as a policy guide for developing Nordic economic cooperation parallel to the internal market programme and its EC/EFTA derivative, the 'Economic Space'.

The EC area takes between 57% (Norway) and 45% (Finland) of the countries' exports. EC countries supply more than 50% of Nordic imports. But the market picture is *concentric*. Commercial relations are perhaps governed more by what could be gained than what could be preserved. In this respect the Internal Market programme has had an impact on investment figures. Denmark's role is as a bridgehead to the continent: the northern neighbours' interest is not reciprocated. It is also obvious that great structural changes are taking place within and between the countries. Finnish and Norwegian investments are geared towards Sweden, while Swedish capital – although it dominates foreign ownership in both Finland and Norway – is to a large extent invested in the EC area. The 1988 figures for Europe, or for EFTA Europe, are exceptional owing to the ASEA/Brown Boveri merger. Swedish direct investments in the EC are several times the amount of EC countries' investment into Sweden (Table 7.5).

Nordic countries seem to diversify into their neighbours' markets not so much to acquire new market shares and areas of operation as to strengthen an overall Nordic home-market resource as a strategic asset in Euro-wide operations.

In areas such as trade in services and finance, the Nordic area is almost negligible – the EC members are main suppliers. The overall impression is nevertheless that the EC-EFTA regime is neutralizing one-sided economic pressures. West Germany is centrally placed as a supplier, but its dominant position is not overwhelming. The Nordic countries will be affected by financial and monetary change in the enlarged D-mark zone, but they are not alone in that.

Nordic cooperation has registered setbacks with schemes of comprehensive economic agreements.[22] Exclusive Nordic measures carry less weight than the European framework and forces of autonomous restructuring. Nevertheless, the EC-EFTA agreements and continuous dialogue have created beneficial side-effects for the region. The absence of one simple long-term solution or formula for the five countries does not mean that regional solidarity fights an uphill battle with forces of fragmentation.

As a result, all governments and the Nordic Council have monitored the content of Nordic cooperation and assessed its relations to the items in the European Community's Internal Market Programme. While it is undeniable that the EFTA framework is the main instrument for furthering non-members' interests in shaping the European Economic Space, the Nordic framework offers a back-up position. On some issues, such as personal mobility, it is an *acquis* that the governments would like to preserve within a wider Western Europe.

The future

The events of 1989–90 in Eastern Europe have had important implications for the Nordic countries, especially as the Baltic republics begin to establish closer links with their nearest Western neighbours. Latvia and Estonia, in particular, are beginning to reorient much of their external interests to their Nordic neighbours. Twin-town relationships were conspicuously absent some years ago (with the exception of Finnish-Soviet Friendship Associations) but have been established in great numbers since 1988. Transport links, by air and sea, have been re-established. All major political parties in Sweden have developed contacts at party level with newly formed groups in the Baltic states.

The two Nordic neutrals consider that it is their stabilizing influence that has opened up opportunities and enabled these republics to pursue their courses towards self-determination and monetary reforms. The planned convertible

Table 7.6   East-West trade in northern Europe: Shares of export to other economic systems as a percentage of total exports to Baltic riparian states

Country	1965	1975	1985
Denmark	8	6	4
Finland	45	40	42
West Germany*	17	29	25
Poland	17	22	29
Sweden	7	12	5
USSR	18	30	34
East Germany*	15	24	—

* Intra-German trade not included due to 'low transparency'

Source: Unto Vesa, calculations in Pertti Joenniemi and Unto Vesa (eds), *Säkerhetsutveckling i Östersjöområdet* (Tampere, Tampere Peace Research Institute, 1988).

Estonian currency is to be called the krona. However, the Baltic republics are not alone in turning towards the West. Soviet reformists plan to re-establish Leningrad as 'an international city' and to exploit its potential for research and development according to the 'technological village' concept. Likewise, the first-ever Russian free economic zone has been constructed in the vicinity of the Finnish border at Svetogorsk.

In a long-term perspective one can discern four historical regions re-emerging along the East-West divide that artificially kept Europe's halves apart for a long time: the Balkans, *Mitteleuropa*, the German nation and the Nordic-Baltic region. To a certain extent the contours of such a formation are visible in trade flows. Riparian countries in the East Baltic Sea area tend to trade primarily with other riparians in the region. The same holds for company joint ventures and for investment in Eastern Europe.

In general, the Nordic countries as a unit are likely to cooperate increasingly in different ways with the various other groupings of European countries, East and West. Potential problems are most evident in the pay-offs that must be worked out in relation to the demands of security and the interests of civilian society in dealings with the East.

Notes

1. Stein Rokkan, 'The Growth and Structuring of Mass Politics' in Erik Allardt et al., eds, *Nordic Democracy* (Copenhagen: Det Danske Selskab, 1981).
2. A separate body for furthering cooperation between the Nordic islands in the Atlantic has been established in the Nordic cooperation network.
3. See Toivo Miljan, *The Reluctant Europeans* (London and Montreal: C. Hurst & Co., 1977).
4. Bernt Hagtvet and Erik Rudeng, 'Scandinavia: Achievements, Dilemmas, Challenges', in *Daedalus*, vol. 113, no. 2, Spring 1984.
5. Bengt Sundelius, *Managing Transnationalism in Northern Europe* (Boulder: Westview Press, 1978).
6. Nils Andrén, 'Nordic Integration: Aspects and Problems', in *Cooperation and Conflict*, vol. 2, no. 1, 1967.
7. Håkan Wiberg, 'The Nordic Countries: A Special Kind of System?', in *Current Research of Peace and Violence*, no. 1–2, 1986.
8. Arne Olav Bruntland, 'Nordisk Balanse för og nå', *Internasjonal Politikk*, no. 5, 1966.
9. *Sweden's Security Policy Entering the 1990s*. Report by the 1984 Defence Committee, SOU 1984:23 (Stockholm: Ministry of Defence, 1984).
10. *Countering the Submarine Threat*, SOU 1983:13, enumerates a number of conceivable motives and relationships (Stockholm: Ministry of Defence, 1983).
11. This category of operations in coastal and archipelago areas, estuaries, harbours, etc., was introduced in the UNGA *Study on the Naval Arms Race*, doc.A/40/535.
12. Karl Deutsch et al., *Political Community and the North Atlantic area* (Princeton, NJ.: Princeton University Press, 1957).
13. Johan Jörgen Holst, 'The Pattern of Nordic Security', in *Daedalus*, loc. cit.
14. Barry Buzan, *People, States and Fear* (Brighton: Wheatsheaf, 1983), p. 106.
15. See above, Chapter 6.
16. Lauri Karvonen, *Med Vårt Västra Grannland som Förebild* (Åbo: Stiftelsens Åbo Akademi Forskningsinstitut, 1984).

17. Bengt Sundelius, op. cit., Chapter 2.
18. Bruce Russett, *International Regions and the International System* (Chicago: Rand McNally, 1967).
19. Rudolf Kjellén, *Politiska Essäer*, Tredje Samlingen (Stockholm: Gebers, 1915).
20. Carl Fredriksson, *Ekonomisk Integration i Norden* (Copenhagen: Nordisk Ministerråd, Nord 1988:111, 1988). See also below, Chapter 10.
21. See above, Chapter 5.
22. Carl-Einar Stålvant, 'Nordic Political Cooperation', in *Nordic Journal of International Law*, no. 4, 1988.

8 The Central European dimension
Richard Davy

From the late 1940s to the end of the 1980s the sharpest and most important boundary in Europe – in terms of social and economic exchanges as much as of political and security alignments – was that between the countries of OECD Europe and those of the Warsaw Pact. This was not a natural division; it did not emerge from any traditional differences of culture, religion or politics. Nor did it make any sense in terms of geography or economics. It merely marked the demarcation line which the victorious armies of the superpowers had agreed to establish as they rolled across Germany in 1945.

As this chapter will show, the evidence of interactions across this East-West divide in the 1980s strongly suggests that the distortions imposed by political controls and increasing economic divergence were beginning to give way even before the collapse of communism. The underlying identity of Central Europe was beginning to re-emerge. To an increasing extent, Europe's customary traffic was penned behind political barriers and waiting to be released.

The division had nevertheless gone very deep, largely because of the thoroughness with which the Soviet Union imposed its political control over Eastern Europe. Traditional patterns of trade, travel and culture were sharply interrupted. Wartime and postwar deportations had already reduced the overlap of languages and cultures. The East European economies were now reoriented to the East, personal contact with the West broken, personal travel largely stopped. New political elites were imposed, new institutions created, and cultural links severely reduced. The result was a sharper interruption of contacts than had been imposed on Europe by most of the imperial and religious divisions from which the continent has suffered over the centuries. In spite of the modest relaxations of the 1980s, only a mere trickle of the potential traffic of interchange was passing across this artificial boundary before the end of 1989 – though some aspects of interchange, particularly immigration, had been increased by the division.

Any mental map of greater Europe (East, West and neutrals) is therefore bound to be confused. On one level it consisted of two clearly defined blocs that have taken very different paths over the last 40 years, with a few Western-oriented neutrals floating between. At another level it was still an untidy assembly of contrasting nations with very different histories, cultures and levels of political and economic development, some of which are emerging again as confrontation diminishes. For instance, the line between the empires of Rome and Byzantium is still visible, as are old lines between Catholic and Protestant traditions. Russia and Turkey do not know whether they belong to Europe, and the rest of Europe shares their uncertainty. Also revived is the debate on central Europe, the heart of the Habsburg empire, which for many of its inhabitants defines the essence of old Europe. Some people would exclude Germany from full membership, most would exclude Russia, and some would now include the Baltic nations. Today's central Europe is in part an artificial result of common resistance to Soviet domination and might not survive its removal. Finally, there are the divisions between the developed and the underdeveloped, the powerful engine of the West German economy next to the relatively backward East German, the crumbling, antiquated ruin of Czechoslovakia next to advanced Austria, the failed modernization of Romania beside the relative rural success of Bulgaria and the reforms of Hungary, and, looming over all, the huge, sprawling, backward muddle of the Soviet Union.

All this suggests a long period of difficult adjustment even if reforms continue to move forward throughout Eastern Europe. Meanwhile, over the past decade, some of the blocked arteries of greater Europe were gradually being freed, particularly to the movement of people and ideas, and very slowly in economic relations too. The figures show various forms of East-West contact rising fairly sharply in recent years, though some countries, notably Romania, chose to exclude themselves.

Economic relations

Probably the slowest change has been in economic relations. While the intensity of trade within each area has risen, the intensity of East-West trade has been much less than would have been the case without political constraints. Europe's 'natural' trading patterns suffered two sharp knocks in this century. The first was in the 1920s, when trade between Europe and the Soviet Union dropped by half and national barriers were raised within Europe.[1] The second came when the Soviet Union captured the economies of Eastern Europe and switched them eastward. In 1937, Eastern Europe accounted for 8.2% of West Europe's trade. By 1953 its share had sunk to 1.8%, rising to a peak of about 4% in 1967[2]. Then it entered a long-term decline, interrupted only by a temporary rise in Eastern Europe's share of Western Europe's exports between 1966 and 1975.

Overall, in the 1980s, Eastern Europe accounted for only 2% of total OECD exports and about 4% of world trade if inner German trade is excluded. Its trade with Western Europe remained well below the average level of each area's trade with the rest of the world. By 1984, excluding inner German trade, Eastern Europe accounted for some 2–3% of the EC's exports and 3–4% of EFTA's. In 1988 only 2.9% of West Europe's exports went to Comecon Europe (including the Soviet Union and East Germany) and only 3.2% of its imports came from the area.

Table 8.1   East-West trade

	1960	1972	1984	1988
West European exports to Comecon Europe as % of total exports				
Western Europe	4.2	4.3	3.6	2.9
EC 12	3.7	4.0	3.2	2.6
EFTA 6	7.3	6.3	6.2	5.0
West European imports from Comecon Europe as % of total imports				
Western Europe	4.1	4.0	5.4	3.2
EC 12	3.7	3.7	4.9	3.0
EFTA 6	6.4	5.5	8.3	4.5
Comecon exports to Western Europe as % of total exports				
Comecon 7	18.4	19.2	25.3	20.7
Bulgaria	12.5	12.2	7.7	6.2
Czechoslovakia	15.6	17.7	14.7	14.4
East Germany	20.0	20.5	28.7	26.0
Hungary	21.6	23.4	30.5	31.8
Poland	26.8	26.2	28.0	28.7
Romania	20.7	31.7	32.4	23.2
Soviet Union	16.4	15.1	26.5	18.2
Comecon imports from Western Europe as % of total imports				
Comecon 7	19.1	22.2	20.3	20.9
Bulgaria	13.2	14.0	12.5	13.8
Czechoslovakia	18.0	21.4	14.0	16.4
East Germany	21.8	29.0	25.5	26.4
Hungary	24.0	26.4	32.5	38.8
Poland	19.1	28.5	24.2	25.5
Romania	23.4	35.2	14.9	10.1
Soviet Union	17.7	16.2	18.8	17.0

Source: European Affairs 2/89, p. 14.

Eastern Europe was much more dependent than Western Europe on East-West trade. (See Table 8.1.) In 1988, 20.7% of Comecon's exports went to Western Europe and 20.9% of its imports came from Western Europe. Hungary was the most dependent on this trade, with 31% of its exports and 38% of its imports accounted for by Western Europe. East Germany and Poland also ranked high. These figures are, however, based on East European statistics which are not reliable. In general, Western Europe's dependence on trade with Eastern Europe has been declining while Eastern Europe's dependence on trade with Western Europe has risen very slightly since 1960. (See Table 8.2.) In 1987, Eastern Europe took about 2% of Western Europe's (EC and EFTA) exports to all Europe and accounted for about 2.3% of total imports from all Europe.

Table 8.2 West-East trade

	1962	1972	1984	1987

West European* exports to Eastern Europe as % of exports to all Europe (excluding inner German trade)

	1962	1972	1984	1987
Albania	0.02	0.02	0.03	0.01
Bulgaria	0.20	0.26	0.29	0.27
Czechoslovakia	0.78	0.76	0.46	0.43
East Germany	0.48	0.46	0.34	0.31
Hungary	0.49	0.61	0.52	0.47
Poland	0.94	1.10	0.56	0.46
Romania	0.58	0.66	0.22	0.12
Total	3.49	3.87	2.41	2.06
Plus Soviet Union	2.24	2.03	3.31	2.11
Total	5.73	5.90	5.72	4.17

West European* imports from Eastern Europe as % of imports from all Europe (excluding inner German trade)

	1962	1972	1984	1987
Albania	0.01	0.01	0.03	0.01
Bulgaria	0.24	0.22	0.15	0.10
Czechoslovakia	0.78	0.75	0.61	0.45
East Germany	0.46	0.42	0.48	0.33
Hungary	0.44	0.61	0.49	0.42
Poland	1.17	1.01	0.75	0.58
Romania	0.47	0.59	0.54	0.40
Total	3.56	3.61	3.06	2.28
Plus Soviet Union	2.69	2.01	5.07	2.61
Total	6.25	5.62	8.13	4.89

Source: Compiled by J. Lisiecki, St Antony's College, Oxford, using COMTRADE data from UN, Geneva.

* EC 12 plus EFTA 6 plus Yugoslavia, Turkey, Malta and Cyprus.

West Germany stands out among OECD countries as having had the greatest stake in East-West trade, with 3.4% of its exports going to Comecon, excluding East Germany. If inner German trade is included, West German exports to Comecon were probably well over $10 billion, or about half the EC's total exports to Comecon. A significant indicator is that West Germany's machinery exports to the Soviet Union are higher than would be indicated by West Germany's competitive position in world markets, which suggests that political preference was a factor.[3]

In the 1980s East-West trade tended to decrease. Between 1980 and 1987 Western exports to Comecon dropped by about 12% in nominal terms and by

40% in real terms. This is explained partly by the sharp fall in raw material prices and partly by Eastern Europe's attempts to reduce its debt burden. In addition, growth rates in Eastern Europe were tending to fall. The cutback in imports did, however, enable Eastern Europe to achieve a trade surplus of $13 billion by 1984 and thereby to reduce its debt burden a little. Nevertheless, Eastern Europe's share of the Western market in nominal terms continued to slide, partly because of lower fuel prices but also because of stronger competition from Asia. By the end of 1988 there was a small improvement in Eastern Europe's trade surplus with the West. The upturn reflected strengthened growth in most countries, led by Poland and Hungary, and growing Western import demand.

Tourism was also becoming a more important source of hard currency earnings for some countries. Czechoslovakia's gross income from tourism rose from $172m in 1980 to $302m in 1987. Hungary's gross receipts rose from $364m in 1986 to $553m in 1987, though net receipts declined because of the steep increase in Hungarians spending money abroad.[4]

The intensity of East European trade with EFTA was stronger than with the EC. This was partly because some EFTA members, such as Austria and Sweden, border East European countries, partly because trade barriers with the EC were higher, and partly because EFTA countries tended to have more stable political relations with Eastern Europe.

The most intense trade has been between East and West Germany. It accounted in 1988 for 30% of West Germany's trade with the Comecon area, but the trend was generally down because of the steep rise in West German trade with other Comecon countries. Between 1968 and 1985 trade between East and West Germany increased from DM 2.9b to DM 15.5b, averaging 11% growth a year. In 1986, however, this trade dropped by 8%, in 1987 by 1.7% and in 1988 by 2%. The main reason was that East Germany was gradually becoming less competitive, particularly in capital goods, in relation not only to West Germany but more especially to Asian exporters. Its earnings per unit of mechanical engineering delivered were only one-sixth of that of West Germany in 1987. Its share of the market for machine exports to OECD countries dropped from 3.9% in 1973 to 0.9% in 1986. Taiwan's share, for instance, was 20 times higher[5].

Nevertheless, although total trade between East and West Germany declined, East Germany achieved a surplus in direct trade with West Germany in 1988. Its imports from West Germany fell 7% to DM 6.8b while its exports to West Germany rose 3% to DM 7.3b. But these figures include goods and services. In goods alone West Germany remains in surplus of DM 446m, though East German deliveries rose by 2%. The decline in West German exports to East Germany was in the investments good sector, which dropped by 20% to DM 1.7b.[6]

East Germany was in effect subsidized by West Germany. Official estimates put the net transfer at about DM 2.5b a year. Unofficial estimates put it at more than double that figure.[7] The biggest lump sum was the payment of transit fees for Germans travelling to Berlin. This rose from an average of DM 188m in the early 1970s to DM 860m in 1989. In the 1988 agreement the government committed itself to paying DM 860m a year for the next decade. On top of this there were road fees (in effect a toll) for the use of East German motorways, and West Germany also had to pay for road repairs. Visa and entry fees accounted for DM 30m.

Payments to buy out political prisoners and other East German citizens were mostly put under the heading 'furthering special supportive measures for Germany as a whole'. Expenditure under that heading was DM 290m in 1987 and 320m in 1988. The Berlin Senate paid for waste and sewage disposal, but the federal government also invested directly in sewage plants in East Berlin. East Germany clearly received more favourable treatment in this respect than Czechoslovakia. In addition West Germany contributed to railway building and was investing more and more in pollution control.

East Germany was the only East European country that had no formal provision for joint ventures with capital participation, but various forms of industrial cooperation were increasing. For instance, East Germany made shoes for the West German Salamander company and engines for Volkswagen. In both cases part of the product went to West Germany and part to East Germany.

There were some other oddities in East-West German traffic. Scarcely any East German scholars, students, scientists or managers came to West Germany for further training or education. In this area, the other East European countries were far ahead. However, West Germany bought a surprising number of patents from East Germany – considerably more than went in the other direction, though the trend was generally down. The reason for this imbalance was not that East Germany was unusually inventive but that it could not afford to buy more patents from the West. Far more important in the trade balance was the rise in West German payments for the disposal of waste in East Germany.

East-West trade was closely related to Western lending to Eastern Europe, which borrowed heavily in the 1970s and then cut back after 1981, when net debt began to fall, largely as a result of cutting imports. Deteriorating terms of trade in 1986–7 caused the debt to rise again, partly because the devaluation of the US dollar increased its nominal value. According to the Bank for International Settlements, 60% of the increase in bank claims on Comecon between 1985 and 1987 was due to the devaluation of the dollar. There was a slight upturn in 1988.

Eastern Europe's trade surplus in convertible currencies grew to about $4b, but the widening deficit in invisibles, due to rising interest rates and higher average debt, resulted in a marginal contraction of Eastern Europe's current account surplus to about $1b in 1988.[8] Net indebtedness declined from nearly $76b in 1987 to $73b at the end of 1988, largely because of the appreciation of the dollar.

In economic relations, therefore, the basic picture is of two adjacent areas doing much less trade with each other than would be considered 'normal' by world standards. Western Europe could do without Eastern Europe altogether except, perhaps, for energy imports. Eastern Europe was relatively more dependent on East-West trade, and particularly dependent on credits from the West, but in manufacturing it was losing out to Asian competition.

Population movements

Human contacts between the two parts of Europe were reduced to negligible levels by the cold war. They did not start to increase significantly until the 1960s. Between 1970 and 1973 the number of Western visitors to Eastern Europe doubled from 7m to 14m, while tourism also intensified within Eastern Europe. In the second half of the 1970s the growth curve flattened, partly because of limited capacity in Eastern Europe but also because of cooler relations between East and West. There is a clear correlation between improvement in political relations and the growth of tourism.[9] From 1980 there was a period of stagnation. Worsening political relations reduced organized exchanges, while the Polish crisis discouraged individual travellers not only to Poland but also to neighbouring countries. Later Chernobyl also cut visits. However, by the middle of the 1980s the number of visitors exceeded that in the late 1970s.

Asymmetry has been a constant feature. It is partly the result of vastly different population sizes – there are 395m West Europeans to 135 million East Europeans; the latter figure including Albania and Yugoslavia and excluding the Soviet Union – but it also reflects political factors. In the 1970s there was three times as much traffic from West to East as in the other direction. By the 1980s there was roughly four times as much. In 1988–9 there was a sharp change because of freer travel from Poland, Hungary and East Germany. It is possible that by the end of 1989 the total flow had been reversed if brief shopping trips by Hungarians and Poles are included. There has also been a qualitative difference. West Europeans visit Eastern Europe largely for recreation, though family connections and political interest also play a role. When political factors do not intervene, the market largely determines the traffic, which responds to prices, availability of accommodation and rates of growth in the West.

Flows in the other direction until the end of 1989 were determined largely by the level of political restraint and the availability of hard currency. East Europeans came proportionately less for recreation and more for shopping or in search of temporary work to earn hard currency, though some were on the way to permanent emigration and some were visiting relatives.

Eastern and Western Europe still had in 1989 far more intense traffic movements within their own areas than across the East-West border. Only around 20% of the people who entered East European countries did so from the West. In 1981 a total of 40.8 million people entered East European countries (excluding the Soviet Union, East Germany and Romania), and of them 7.4m (18%) were from the West. In 1986 there were 47m travellers, of whom 10.1m (21%) were from the West. The traffic in the other direction was generally much lower in the past. In 1981 2.4m East Europeans (excluding East Germans) went to the West, in 1982 1.5m, and in 1986 2.6m.[10] Visitors from Eastern Europe made up only 0.5% of West European hotel visitors in 1987. This under-represents actual numbers of travellers because many stay in private accommodation, but the proportion is still very small.

The most intense traffic was between the two parts of the Germany. In 1987 there were 5.5m crossings from West Germany and West Berlin to East

Germany and East Berlin, of which about half were day trips. This is nearly double the number of 2.9m in 1967.[11] There was also a huge increase in telephone traffic. The number of calls from West Germany and West Berlin to East Germany rose from 700,000 in 1970 to 35.5m in 1987. (Calls from East to West were estimated at about 25% of those from West to East.)[12] In the other direction traffic rose considerably. The East Germans allowed pensioners to travel, the number rising from 1.1m in 1967 to 2.2m in 1987.[13] In the late 1980s the authorities became more liberal towards people of non-pensionable age, though whole families were seldom permitted to travel together. The total number of East Germans allowed to travel for 'urgent family reasons' rose from 11,000 in 1972 to 573,000 in 1986 and then made a sudden jump to 1.2m in 1987.[14]

Permanent departures from East Germany varied according to the state of political relations. In 1977 the figure was 12,078; in 1987 17,711, of whom 11,459 were legal.[15] The West German government expected a record number of about 90,000 to leave East Germany legally in 1989. By the middle of June, according to the Ministry for Inner German Relations, the figure had already reached 30,000, compared with 143,917 in 1959 just before the wall was built. In addition about 10,000 came out illegally through third countries. However, there was still enormous pent-up demand. According to Church authorities, the number of applications for departure was 250,000 in the autumn of 1988, compared with about 50,000 at the beginning of 1987. Most were from whole families, so the number of individuals would be 3–4 times higher.

There was naturally very intense traffic between West Germany and West Berlin by Germans and foreigners. The total number of journeys (by road, rail or air) rose from 13.9m in 1971 to 31.3m in 1987. (In 1987 total food traffic amounted to 16.1m tonnes.)[16] Journeys made by Germans and foreigners from West Germany into East Germany and through to third countries rose from 3.6m in 1979 to 4.1m in 1987. There was also intense traffic in local border regions, though this fell from 415,941 West German crossings into East Germany in 1979 to 336,700 in 1987. West Germans also formed the majority of travellers to other countries. In 1987, 961,000 went to Hungary, 551,000 to Czechoslovakia, 132,000 to Poland, 268,000 to Bulgaria and 132,000 to Romania. The total number of travellers from Britain, France and Italy to Eastern Europe was on average about one-third the number of West Germans, though national statistics often give conflicting pictures.[17]

The Austro-Hungarian border was also much crossed. In 1987, according to Austrian statistics, a total of 3.3m foreigners arrived in Hungary from Austria, of whom 823,000 were tourists. In the other direction, 448,000 Hungarians travelled to Austria.[18] Hungarians statistics differ, however. The intensity of traffic across the Hungarian border with Czechoslovakia was much greater, with 4.9m foreigners coming into Hungary and 2.6m Hungarians going out.[19]

Unquantifiable numbers of East Europeans had begun to shop across borders when permitted, in spite of currency restrictions. In the first week of April 1989, 200,000 Hungarians tourists spent $143m shopping in Austria.

Asylum-seekers

Another growing category of travellers from East to West was that of asylum-seekers. The flood of applications for asylum hit West Germany particularly hard because of its very liberal asylum laws. West German border authorities cannot refuse entry to an applicant for asylum unless he or she has already been granted asylum in another country. The procedure for granting asylum is long and thorough, often taking about two years. By that time it has become extremely difficult to expel even those whose applications are refused. Most other West European countries have greater powers to refuse entry at the border. As a result West Germany has had a steady increase in asylum-seekers in recent years, except for a brief drop in 1987 when East Germany agreed not to allow foreigners unrestricted transit to West Berlin. Thereafter, instead of coming in through Berlin, most arrived at Frankfurt airport. In 1988 there were 103,076 applications for asylum in West Germany, compared with 57,379 in 1987, a rise of 80%. Of these, 35,718 came from Eastern Europe, compared with 20,483 in 1987, but the proportion from Eastern Europe remained about the same at 35%. Of the total, 29,023 came from Poland, 20,812 from Yugoslavia, 14,873 from Turkey, 7,867 from Iran, 4,233 from the Lebanon, and 3,383 from Sri Lanka.[20] The number of applicants accepted fell from 9.4% in 1987 to 8.6% in 1988. In other words, more than 90% were judged to have come for economic reasons and not to be genuine victims of political persecution. Of the Yugoslav applicants only 0.3% were granted asylum. The numbers from Turkey were limited by visas which were introduced in 1980. Controls were also under discussion for Yugoslav travellers in 1989, whose numbers had increased dramatically and overtaken those from Poland.

Austria has been the second major destination for asylum-seekers. It has taken a steady stream since the end of the war, with surges after the Hungarian uprising in 1956, the supression of the Prague Spring in 1968 and the imposition of martial law in Poland in 1981. Between 1945 and 1983 nearly 2m people sought refuge in Austria, of whom about 590,000 stayed in the country, equivalent to about 8.8% of the Austrian population. Between 1956 and 1986 the total number of applicants was 368,000. The flow has been very uneven. The number in 1977 was 2,566, rising to 8,639 in 1986, with a surge to 34,557 in 1981. In 1987, 1,460 applicants came from Romania, 2,705 from Czechoslovakia, 667 from Poland, 402 from Yugoslavia, 4,689 from Hungary and 93 from Bulgaria. Of the total of 11,406, about 10% were from outside Europe.[21] Large numbers of emigrants and refugees have also passed through Austria to other destinations, many of them Soviet Jews. Numbers have fluctuated enormously even over the past ten years, rising from 14,061 in 1976 to 50,202 in 1979 and dropping to 901 in 1986.

There is now growing pressure in the EC to harmonize asylum laws and regulations before 1992, which really means that West Germany will have to come into line with the others.

German resettlers

West Germany has also had to cope with a growing influx of ethnic German groups from Eastern Europe and the Soviet Union. This problem had its origins in the nineteenth century when German settlers spread out through most of Eastern Europe and into Russia. The rise of nationalism drove many of them back, but by 1939 there were still 8.6m Germans outside the borders of the Reich. Some returned under the Nazis but the biggest movement was after the war, when millions of Germans were expelled from Poland's new eastern territories, the Sudetenland and other areas, many dying on the way. The result was to reduce the number of Germans in Eastern Europe to about 4m by 1960. Nevertheless, the exodus has continued, helped on by various agreements with the governments concerned, some of which have involved substantial payments of hard currency.

The number of ethnic Germans arriving in West Germany has fluctuated according to the political climate, rising to a peak of 132,233 in 1958 as a result of agreements with the Soviet Union and falling to 18,949 in 1970. The figure was 58,130 in 1978, of whom 36,102 came from the Polish areas, rising to 200,000 in 1988, mainly from Poland and the Soviet Union. Some 343,000 arrived in 1989.[22] Official sources say that about 60% of the resettlers are regarded as having German citizenship while the rest, mainly those from the Soviet Union, belong culturally to the German nation and therefore have the right of abode in West Germany. Of the total in 1988, 43% were under 25 years old, and 4% over 65.

According to the Red Cross there are still about 3 million potential emigrants among ethnic Germans in the Soviet Union and Eastern Europe, of whom 1.9m are in the Soviet Union, 750,000 in Poland, and 200,000 each in Romania and Hungary. This pent-up demand could create enormous political, social and economic problems. Already the political backlash has found expression in votes for the right-wing Republican Party.

In theory all these immigrants would have the right of abode throughout the European Community but it seems unlikely that more than a very small minority of ethnic Germans would wish to move on from West Germany to other European countries. If they went anywhere else it would be to the United States, Canada or Australia.

Broadcasting

The most dramatically intensive traffic across the East-West frontier is in the form of radio and television broadcasts. According to Radio Free Europe, the Munich-based American station, a total of 95.5m people in Eastern Europe (excluding both the Soviet Union and East Germany) listen to at least one of the five main Western radio stations transmitting to Eastern Europe – Radio Free Europe, Voice of America, the BBC and Deutschlandfunk/Deutsche Welle. (See Table 8.3.) In addition, about 15m East Germans regularly watch West German domestic television, while Austrian television has substantial audiences in Hungary and Czechoslovakia. Jamming of Western radio stations declined in recent years and ceased entirely in March 1989.

Table 8.3   Listeners to Western radio stations, 1989 (millions)

Country	RFE	VOA	BBC	DLF/DW
Czechoslovakia	3.9	5.7	2.8	1.1
Hungary	4.6	2.1	1.6	0.5
Poland	15.0	14.2	10.8	1.6
Romania	9.9	4.9	3.9	2.5
Bulgaria	2.5	1.6	2.0	1.3
Total	35.9	28.5	21.1	7.0

RFE: Radio Free Europe
VOA: Voice of America
BBC: British Broadcasting Corporation
DLF/DW: Deutschlandfunk/Deutsche Welle

Source: East European Area Audience and Opinion Research, Radio Free Europe, Munich, July 1989.

This is one area where the West Germans do not dominate, except in broadcasting to East Germany. The airwaves are dominated by the American stations, with the BBC in a very strong second position (though RFE is admittedly difficult to categorize as it is an American station on German soil which most East Europeans regard as a domestic station in exile). This huge and largely one-way traffic is probably far more intense than listening or viewing across borders within Western Europe. It has clearly played a major role in maintaining the fabric of pan-European consciousness, in spite of the dominance of the American stations.

In the other direction, Western audiences for East European broadcasts have been negligible, though some films and other programmes have been exchanged through official channels. There has also been intense cultural interchange, partly through an official market in books, films, and cultural visits in both directions, and partly through large unofficial networks which smuggled unapproved writings across borders in large but unquantifiable numbers.

The environment

Environmental pollution does not respect frontiers. It is carried in both directions across the East-West frontier by wind and water and forms a burgeoning area of East-West cooperation. West Germany, East Germany, Czechoslovakia and Poland are responsible for about 70% of Europe's sulphur dioxide emissions, 40% of nitrogen dioxide, and much of the pollution of the North Sea, the Baltic, the Danube and the Black Sea. The situation in Eastern Europe has deteriorated rapidly over the past 15 years. Poland's gaseous emissions have doubled, East Germany's sulphur dioxide emissions more than doubled. East Germany is a very heavy polluter of rivers, particularly the Elbe, which also carries industrial waste from Czechoslovakia. However, nitrous oxide emissions in Eastern Europe are generally lower than those of Western Europe because there are fewer cars. West Germany produces 2.9m tonnes of nitrous oxide compared with East Germany's 800,000 tonnes, but West Germany produces 2.5m tonnes of sulphur dioxide compared with East Germany's 5.5m tonnes. Since the prevailing wind blows from west to east, the main tendency is for West Germany's pollution to be carried into Eastern Europe, but because Eastern Europe's pollution is so much heavier the balance is more than rectified during the periods when the wind blows from east to west.

A network of agreements on pollution crosses the East-West frontier. West Germany is the most involved. It has agreements with every East European country except Albania and Yugoslavia. Lower Saxony and Bavaria also have local agreements with East Germany. Many agreements involve West Germany paying for anti-pollution measures or contributing technology. For instance, West Germany has spent DM 86m on water purification in East Berlin and Thuringia, and it signed an agreement with Czechoslovakia in October 1987 which set up working groups to study pollution and instigated West German cooperation in new cleaning plants. The UK has environmental agreements only with Poland and the Soviet Union but is selling anti-pollution equipment in Eastern Europe and building a cleansing plant in East Germany. France has agreements only with Albania, Hungary, Romania and the Soviet Union.

Conclusion

In spite of the modest growth of East-West traffic, Europe was still deeply divided at the end of the 1980s. Trade and travel were far more intense within each half of Europe than across the divide. But the enormous surges of travel across the East-West boundaries when political restrictions were lifted in the winter of 1989–90 demonstrated the potential for far more intensive contact.

Writing in the early months of 1990, it is impossible to discover how much of the old Central Europe has survived 40 years of division. But it seems likely that the process of reintegration will go far beyond restoring the old patterns and historical identity of prewar Europe. The integration of Western Europe has been a response not only to shared history but also to the requirements of modern economic development and to the opportunities provided by efficient means of transport and communications. The same pressures of economic development and technical change will pull Eastern and Western Europe together.

There are, however, countervailing pressures which will delay integration. Eastern Europe between the wars suffered the disintegrating pressures of competing nationalisms, suppressed rather than resolved since then. Admittedly the pressures were somewhat reduced by the massacres and expulsions of the war and postwar years. For tragic reasons, there are now fewer disputed frontiers and aggrieved minorities in Europe than before the war; political and ethnic frontiers more nearly coincide. But there are still enough problems to cause trouble and to retard interchange. Eastern Europe has not been permitted the political and economic evolution that might have enabled its societies to grow naturally together beyond these rivalries.

In addition, the relatively long period of enforced separation has created differences of economic structure, working habits and levels of development that will take many years to overcome. As ideological differences dissolve, authorities on both sides may feel the need to retain some barriers in the interest of transitional stability. East European economies could not survive an abrupt confrontation with the rigours of the world market. The dependence of all East European economies on the European Community and its Western partners is already evident. The terms of reintegration, and the conditions attached to closer economic interchange, will therefore be set largely by those on the Western side of the previous divide, where there may be some pressure for protection against cheap goods from Eastern Europe.

Both sides will also have problems in coping with the movement of people. In the longer run reform in Eastern Europe should reduce pressures for emigration. But in the short term it will increase them by releasing pent-up demand. Even if change remains peaceful, many people in Eastern Europe are too sceptical of the prospects and too impatient for a better life to resist an opportunity to emigrate if it is offered. If the first effects of economic reform are – as so often – to depress living standards, larger numbers will look to find permanent or temporary work abroad. And if change proves not to be peaceful, the flood of refugees could create a major crisis.

The relationship between West and East Germany in the winter of 1989–90 provided what may prove to be a model for West European support for East European economic reform. Faced with the prospect of large-scale emigration, with the consequent threat of strain on local services, housing and employment, the West German government had little choice but to pay its Eastern neighbours generously enough to persuade them to stay at home. The pressure for emigration from other East European countries will be much less because of linguistic and cultural differences, but it could still be sufficient to demand a costly response from Western Europe.

Notes

1. A. Maizels, *Industrial Growth and World Trade* (Cambridge: Cambridge University Press, 1965).
2. *Economic Bulletin for Europe*, vol. 37 no. 4 (Pergamon Press, 1986), pp. 371–406.
3. Information from Michael Kaser, St Antony's College, Oxford.
4. *Economic Bulletin for Europe*, vol. 40 no. 3 (1988), p. 398.
5. Harry Maier, *European Affairs*, 2/89, p. 13.
6. *Frankfurter Rundschau*, 2 March, 1989.
7. Information from Jurek Lisiecki, St Antony's College, Oxford.
8. *Economic Survey of Europe in 1988–1989* (Geneva, Economic Commission for Europe), p. 187.
9. Norbert Ropers, *Der Tourismus zwischen West und Ost und seine politischen Implikationen*, (Gustav Stresemann Institut e.V., Bonn), p. 8.
10. Ibid.
11. Joachim Nawrocki, *Die Beziehungen zwischen den beiden Staaten in Deutschland* (Holzapfel: Verlag Gerb., 1988).
12. Ibid.

13. Ibid.
14. Ibid.
15. Ibid.
16. Ibid.
17. Ropers, op. cit., above n. 9.
18. *Statistisches Handbuch für die Republik Österreich, 1988.*
19. *Statistical Pocket Book of Hungary, 1987.*
20. Information from Federal Ministry of the Interior.
21. Austrian official statistics.
22. Information from Federal Ministry of the Interior.

9 The Mediterranean dimension
Roberto Aliboni

Momentous changes are taking place in East-West relations, harbingers to no less momentous changes in inter-European relations. This chapter asks how the Mediterranean Space will enter the coming equation; where the Mediterranean frontier will be drawn; and how Mediterranean identities and solidarities may affect changes that are under way in Europe.

In addressing this question, the first step will be to define Mediterranean patterns of solidarity. Then we will ask how effective they are. Finally, we will discuss the relationship between patterns of Mediterranean solidarity and the changing European Space.

Patterns of Mediterranean solidarity

Regional Mediterranean solidarity

Let us first refer to what one could define as the 'regional' pattern of Mediterranean solidarity, that is one including South European, North African and Near Eastern countries. This notion has its roots in a shared cultural and historical heritage that gives Mediterranean peoples a sense of community and 'spécificité'. This heritage, however, is not reflected in their present political, economic and military arrangements.

The 'regional' Mediterranean solidarity is directed at regaining political autonomy. Marginal actors seek to unite against those new political and ideological forces that have defeated the old Mediterranean centrality and reduced ancient and sophisticated cultures to sub-cultures. This applies to nations such as the Catalans, the Sicilians or the Sardinians which have been absorbed by the modern, centrally organized Mediterranean nation-states. The same is true of the Arab and Islamic nations in relation to the powerful, technologically advanced Western countries. Finally, it covers the situation of the less developed Mediterranean regions, both in South European and Arab countries, in relation to the sudden change in values and social order imposed by Western modernization.

155

When looked at from such an angle, 'regional' Mediterranean solidarity is nothing other than one form of non-alignment or a sort of North-South tension that cuts across Arab as well as European solidarities at both national and international levels.

Inter-regional Mediterranean solidarity

A second kind of Mediterranean solidarity is concerned with the different sets of 'Mediterranean association agreements' and the Euro-Arab Dialogue (EAD). This time Mediterranean solidarity goes beyond the Mediterranean basin, reaching the Northern EC countries on the one hand, and the Gulf countries on the other. One can talk about an 'inter-regional' Mediterranean solidarity.

Whereas the 'regional' pattern of solidarity identifies a South-South region, more or less in conflict with the North and cutting across European solidarity, the 'inter-regional' pattern is a regular North-South frame whose aims are explained by definition in terms of cooperation for attaining development. However, differing perceptions about the rationale of this 'inter-regional' solidarity may affect the ordinary cooperative character of the pattern and give way to conflictual 'inter-regional' patterns of solidarity.

At the end of 1973, when a team of Arab ministers went to propose the EAD to the European ministers gathering in Copenhagen, what they had in mind was a Euro-Arab trade-off: Arab oil in exchange for European support of the Arabs in disputes with Israel and the USA. As in the case of the 'regional' pattern of solidarity, we again discover a form of North-South tension under a Mediterranean cover. However, this conflictual pattern – cutting across both Atlantic and European solidarities – has failed to materialize. The EAD has never really taken off.

Still, many Mediterranean Arab countries remain firm in their belief that the European countries, and specifically the EC, are sensitive to their aims and grievances and that this could help put pressure on the USA. This belief is supported by the existing network of commercial and economic agreements; by the 1980 Venice resolution whereby the EC governments recognized the Palestine Liberation Organization as the representative of the Palestinians; by the tendency of the EC countries to emphasize political and local factors in managing Mediterranean crises (as opposed to the US tendency to emphasize global and military factors). This perceived pattern of solidarity, based as it is on the assumption of an Arab-European 'spécificité' with respect to the USA, is close to that related to the EAD. However, on political grounds, it is very different, because here the Euro-Arab combination is expected to help persuade the USA not to attack it or separate the EC from it.

In conclusion, while the early Arab motivations for the EAD put forward a conflictual pattern of solidarity that cuts across Atlantic and European alliances, Euro-Arab relations as a whole – always characterized by the second Arab goal of enjoying the Europeans' good offices with the Americans – constitute a case of a cooperative pattern of 'inter-regional' solidarity.

South European patterns of solidarity

We come now to South European solidarity, that is the specific identity that would link the Southern members of the EC: France, Greece, Italy, Portugal and Spain.

The first point to consider is whether this group of countries perceives itself as having a separate identity with respect to other internal EC groupings. The second point is that some South Europeans feel they have a special role to play within the 'inter-regional' patterns of Mediterranean solidarity, that is between EC Northern countries and non-EC Mediterranean countries. As a consequence, South European solidarity can be both a 'domestic' cross-cutting pattern – when it works as an EC grouping inside the EC – and a factor in the 'inter-regional' patterns of Mediterranean solidarity. It can also act on both grounds.

The rationale for Southern 'domestic' solidarity often claimed by the South European leaders is the advantages which would accrue to the South European EC countries if they united to balance the influence of the Northern members inside the EC. During the process of the enlargement of the EC to Greece, Portugal and Spain, the shift in the balance of power inside the EC which would result from their entry was one of the standard arguments of the debate in the South European countries.

This position, firmly held by the socialist parties – which for a short period happened to head all the South European governments – is not shared by all political forces. Whenever effective, this 'domestic' cross-cutting pattern of solidarity would be a conflictual one.

As for the role the South European countries are expected to play within the extra-EC patterns of Mediterranean solidarity, the argument is that their natural sensitivity to the problems and claims of the South Mediterranean countries would push them to represent and to support the latter inside the EC.

As a matter of fact, because of their agricultural interests the South European countries compete fiercely with the South Mediterranean countries to preserve their preference in the EC market. However, the 'regional' sense of community existing among the countries concerned and the definite importance on bilateral grounds of their multiple economic and political ties make this solidarity credible. Recently, the role of the South European countries was defined as that of 'mentors' of the Maghreb countries with respect to the EC.[1]

This means that within the 'inter-regional' pattern of Mediterranean solidarity EC Southern solidarity plays a positive role, and that it contributes to reinforcing the cooperative brand of the 'inter-regional' pattern. However, the corollary is that the Southern members of the EC may look on the 'mandate' entrusted to them by the Mediterranean countries as a factor reinforcing their bargaining position within the EC policy framework. This would bring us back to the conflictual pattern already noted in the discussion about 'domestic' South European solidarity.

We will now consider fully both the cooperative and the conflictual cross-cutting patterns of South European solidarity and will discuss in less detail the cooperative 'inter-regional' pattern of Mediterranean solidarity. Because they are highly improbable, we will not consider the conflictual types of 'inter-regional' solidarity or the pattern of 'regional' solidarity.

Table 9.1   Shares of selected areas in Southern EC countries' total imports and exports, 1980 and 1986

	Northern EC countries	Southern EC countries	non-EC Mediterranean countries
Imports			
1980	28.5	14.6	6.2
1986	38.9	18.4	5.8
Exports			
1980	30.4	18.9	9.3
1986	47.3	26.1	8.4

Source: Courtesy of Dr Mauro Scarfone, Ente Nazionale Idrocarburi.

How effective are Mediterranean solidarities?

Trade

Trade is an important item for Mediterranean relations, both inside the EC – as part of the enlargement negotiations that brought the new South European members into the EC – and as a component of the preferential 'association agreements' between the EC and the South Mediterranean countries.

Table 9.1 shows the shares of Northern EC countries, Southern EC countries, and the non-EC Mediterranean countries in the total imports and exports of the Southern EC countries. Figures are provided for two years, 1980 and 1986, to demonstrate the impact of the enlargement of the EC to Greece, Portugal and Spain.

The first conclusion suggested by Table 9.1 is that the Southern EC countries are being integrated into the EC to a very remarkable extent. If the figures for Northern and Southern EC countries are combined, it emerges that the Southern EC countries increased their import share from the EC as a whole by 14.2 points and their export share to the EC by 26.1. If one distinguishes the two areas, it is evident that the Southern EC countries' trade with their Northern partners is increasing more than their mutual trade inside the Southern EC region. This may suggest that the 'pull' comes from the Northern EC countries and that the perceived solidarity of Southern EC countries is not supported by a special importance of their commercial relations.

The second conclusion is that trade relations of Southern EC countries with the non-EC Mediterranean countries are stagnating, in startling contrast with their relations inside the EC. This stagnation is confirmed by data related to the EC as a whole (not included in Table 9.1): the shares of the non-EC Mediterranean countries in the total import and export of the EC diminished from 4 to 3.7 and from 5.4 to 4.4 respectively.

For our purposes it would be helpful to ascribe this adverse tendency affecting the non-EC Mediterranean countries to the fall in oil prices or to the displacement effect caused by the entry of Greece, Portugal and Spain into the

EC. George N. Yannopoulos is explicit about the adverse consequences affecting the Southern Mediterranean countries, especially the Maghreb countries:

> It may be argued that entry has undermined the EC's system of preferences for associated non-EC Mediterranean countries . . . Although agreement has been reached that their exports will be maintained at 1986 levels . . . the expanding EC market has been denied to the Maghreb states . . . In response to this situation a number of countries (Cyprus, Malta, Morocco and Turkey) have applied for EC membership or requested closer links.[2]

Table 9.1 shows, finally, that the enforcement of the EC preference is redirecting considerable amounts of the new South European members' trade towards the EC. As part of their integration into the EC, these countries are increasing their trade within the South European region itself. This 'sub-regional' trend, however, is less – and not more – important than the general trend towards an increased integration into the whole of the EC.

The accession of the new South European members, coupled with the decrease in the price of oil, is diminishing the already modest importance of the South Mediterranean countries to the EC trade, whereas the importance of trade in the reverse direction is not diminishing – and it may even be growing.

In other words, Southern EC countries seem to form less of a unit than do EC countries as a whole. Furthermore, the EC-South Mediterranean solidarity is weakening and its future appears linked less to an inherent economic logic than to political options. This is the meaning of the applications made by Cyprus, Malta and Morocco and of the insistence of Turkey on speeding up its accession to the EC.

Table 9.2 gives a more detailed insight into Mediterranean trade relations. It shows the shares of the five Southern EC countries, West Germany and the USA in the total 1987 import of the Mediterranean countries, both EC and non-EC.

The importing EC and non-EC Mediterranean countries are divided into four groups, according to the dominance of four exporting countries: West Germany, Italy, the USA and France. France is the most important partner of the three Maghreb countries. Italy is an important partner for Libya, and for a heterogeneous group including Cyprus, the Lebanon and Malta. The USA has a special relationship with Egypt, Israel and Jordan, clearly brought about by the regular aid programmes to these countries. West Germany is the first partner of all the Southern EC countries and of Turkey and Yugoslavia. Moreover, in every group it is second to the dominant partner and, normally, extremely close to it – as in the case of Italy.

What is remarkable is that the central role in Mediterranean trade relations is played by two non-Mediterranean countries, West Germany and the USA. Another notable feature is the parallel between trade relations and traditional political links, with the UK's role being substantially taken over by the USA. Fifteen years ago Marcello De Cecco[3] came to the same conclusion. Following his analysis, one can still note that West Germany shows a surplus in its trade balance in relation to all the EC and non-EC importing countries listed in table 9.2, except for Algeria and Tunisia. The Southern EC countries show surpluses

Table 9.2 EC and non-EC Mediterranean countries: Imports from selected EC countries and the USA as share of their total imports, 1987

To/From	France	Greece	Italy	Portugal	Spain	FRG	USA
France	–	0.4	11.7	1.0	4.3	19.6	7.1
Greece	8.0	–	13.1	0.2	1.7	22.1	2.8
Italy	14.6	1.0	–	0.3	2.2	21.1	5.3
Portugal	11.1	0.03	8.7	–	11.8	14.7	4.9
Spain	12.8	0.3	8.8	1.7	–	16.1	8.3
Turkey	4.9	0.7	8.4	0.1	1.5	19.1	11.7
Yugoslavia	4.2	0.4	10.6	0.04	0.4	22.4	2.9
Cyprus	4.6	7.6	11.5	0.5	2.4	9.2	4.5
Lebanon	15.0	3.3	19.8	0.2	4.8	10.9	10.2
Libya	5.3	0.8	24.7	0.04	2.8	11.3	. . .
Malta	3.4	1.5	18.9	0.3	1.8	17.4	10.7
Syria	10.3	1.7	10.7	0.06	3.4	9.9	5.8
Egypt	8.0	1.1	6.7	0.07	1.5	9.5	19.6
Israel	3.8	0.2	5.2	0.2	0.9	10.7	13.4
Jordan	3.3	0.4	4.9	0.03	0.9	6.7	8.8
Algeria	29.8	0.5	11.8	0.3	5.2	10.3	6.5
Morocco	22.8	0.1	5.6	0.6	9.1	6.0	9.2
Tunisia	27.3	2.4	11.3	0.2	4.5	12.6	5.9

Source: IMF, *Direction of Trade*.

only in relation to other Mediterranean countries (though less regularly than West Germany does). The way deficits are paid gives a very clear picture of the Mediterranean economy and its international integration. In fact, they are offset by tourism and labour. While tourism is exported by all the countries concerned, labour is now emigrating from the less developed non-EC Mediterranean countries more than from the Southern EC countries – showing a recent reversal of the position.

These observations seem to suggest that the Southern EC countries' role in representing non-EC Mediterranean countries in the EC is highly debateable. The non-EC Mediterranean countries are highly integrated with the EC as a whole, especially with West Germany, though in a frame of generally dwindling relations. The notable exception seems to be France's solidarity with the Maghreb. Its current attempt to associate the Southern EC partners in institutionalizing a specific West Mediterranean solidarity[4] may be aimed at opposing this strong German teleology in the Mediterranean. If France were to succeed in its endeavour, it would give substance to a South European solidarity that would cut across the EC.

Immigration

From what we have just said about the structure of the Mediterranean economy, it can be argued that migration is an outstanding issue in the 'inter-regional' Mediterranean frame. Moreover, migration is going to increase sharply because of growing demographic differentials between the EC countries and the non-EC Mediterranean countries.

According to several studies and especially the UNEP's *Blue Plan*,[5] the demographic structure of the Mediterranean is undergoing a sweeping change. In 1980, the northern shore held 56% of the total Mediterranean population. In 2020 it will account for no more than one-third of it.

This trend is coupled with an increase in the proportion of youngsters in the non-EC Mediterranean countries. The slow economic growth foreseen for these countries will not allow younger generations to be fully employed and so will induce a large number of people to migrate to the EC. As a result the migration pattern already inherent in the Mediterranean economy will be markedly emphasized. According to Massimo Livi Bacci,[6] the non-native workforce will amount to an average of 10% of the total West European workforce, i.e. about 250,000 immigrants per year.

Until now, only the Northern EC states, especially West Germany and France, have acted as receiving countries for migrants. Today, the Southern EC countries, especially Italy and Spain – historically countries of emigration – are becoming the destination of migrants. Source countries are changing too. To Turkey and the Maghreb countries must be added other non-EC Mediterranean countries like Egypt and the Lebanon. Furthermore, there are new and considerable extra-Mediterranean flows of migrants now competing with old and new Mediterranean flows. They come from Africa south of the Sahara, south-western Asia and Eastern Europe. Developments in Poland and the growing EC commitment to support East European economies may bring about a large immigration of educated and skilled Poles. For these reasons, not all the 250,000 jobs estimated by Livi Bacci will be available to people coming from the non-EC Mediterranean countries.

Will the 'inter-regional' EC-Mediterranean solidarity work by giving preference to Mediterranean migrant workers? West Germany and, to some extent, Italy will definitely prove sensitive to East European migration. France will try to preserve a preference for immigrants from the Maghreb countries. Different solidarities will cut across the EC.

Will the Southern EC countries unite on the immigration issue? Attitudes and perceptions seem very different, though all of them are interested in maintaining a high degree of openness because of tourism. Italy recognizes that foreign manpower is needed for the working of its economy. Moreover, the government and the political forces have been reluctant to regulate immigration, seeing such regulation as ungenerous discrimination that could lead to racism. The Italian government has declared its willingness to sign the Schengen agreement; but its ambiguous attitude to stricter immigration controls has made the five negotiating governments unwilling to accept it. Portugal and Spain regard immigration as a threat to both domestic manpower and security. In France a strong racist movement has emerged, and the wave of Lebanese-

French terrorism since 1985 has caused fears that immigrants may become involved in terrorist activities.[7] There may be a split on security and immigration between Northern and Southern EC countries, and in any negotiations Southern EC countries will not necessarily act as a group.

Security

In contrast with the issues previously examined, security against the new threats coming from the southern approaches to Western Europe[8] is the field in which a specific South European solidarity may emerge. Differences in South European perceptions of East-West security and of the new threats from the south have been illustrated in detail by a recent set of analyses.[9] Points of agreement may be less clear.

There are two dimensions to West European countries' ever more frequent interventions in the extra-NATO area: first, the geopolitical dimension justifying intervention on the basis of threats to national security interests, and secondly, a dimension which might be called 'transatlantic' that makes Western European countries intervene in situations which they do not necessarily consider threatening, but which the United States does. Clearly, as was seen in the 1980s, very serious inter-Atlantic conflicts can arise in this dimension.

Another, no less important, aspect of out-of-area intervention concerns the specific organization of West European allies. The West European countries' recognition of their common economic interests and the resulting institutionalization in the framework of the EC has made it possible to define common objectives in this area and to organize communitarian policies, agreements and institutions, which have certainly had considerable impact south of Western Europe. The absence of a common security concept and common defence institutions, along with the institutional weakness of European Political Cooperation (EPC), has meant that an analogous politico-military EC presence in the out-of-area sphere has never been developed.

Another important consequence of the lack of European political integration is the West European countries' weakness in negotiating American requests and motivations in the 'transatlantic' dimension of extra-NATO intervention. Within this context, what may unite South European countries is the fact that they are particularly exposed to the conflict implicit in the 'transatlantic' dimension and to the weakness of the EC's political-military institutions.

Where the institutional framework of the Alliance is lacking, as in out-of-area operations, bilateral relations between the United States and its European allies result, and it is no coincidence that these are more important between the US and South European countries than they are in the north of the continent.

In this situation, the South European countries may develop two kinds of policies. They may recognize a common interest in fostering a stronger EC presence in the Mediterranean and, more generally, in the south of the NATO area, on economic as well as on political and military grounds. In this case they will evolve a South European solidarity to try to direct EC and other European policies towards a renewed and stronger alliance with the South Mediterranean countries. On the other hand, they may reinforce their bilateral relations, as they are doing at present – though this development is currently limited to the south west European countries, especially France, Italy and Spain, because of the conflict prevailing between Greece and Turkey in the Eastern Mediterranean.

The difference between the two courses of action – which, obviously, are not mutually exclusive – is that, as regards EC solidarity, the multilateral course shows concerted action by the South European countries, whereas the bilateral course may emerge as a conflictual pattern, to the extent that European multilateralism may include Greece, whereas bilateral relations have a tendency to leave that country in dangerous isolation.

An enlarged Mediterranean EC?

Economic relations

With respect to the present evolution of the EC, the Mediterranean dimension, with its various alliances, is competing with two other dimensions, that of EFTA and that of Eastern Europe.

The completion of the Single European Market planned for 1992 is prompting a number of EFTA members to consider full EC membership,[10] and so a stronger EC-EFTA alliance may emerge at the expense of the non-EC Mediterranean countries. So far the proximity of the large industrialized area of the EC, giving free and/or preferential access to the manufactured products of less developed countries, has proved beneficial to those non-EC Mediterranean countries (like Turkey) which are embarking on industrialization programmes and pursuing export-led growth policies. By contrast, the Maghreb countries have proved unable to take advantage of EC markets because of their accentuated agricultural specialization (Morocco and Tunisia) or inward-looking and ambitious industrialization policies (Algeria), and also because of the existence of strategic limitation on export to the EC of textile and petroleum products. As a result, if the EC were to admit further industrialized countries, while maintaining its present 'protectionist' policies, new difficulties would be created for the Maghreb countries, with a corresponding increase in the advantages currently enjoyed by other non-EC Mediterranean countries. In particular, the admittance of some EFTA countries would provide new markets for Spain's agriculture, but it would deny further markets to the Maghreb countries and to other non-EC Mediterranean countries specializing in agricultural products.

The evolution of the EC and the whole of Western Europe with respect to East (and especially Central) European countries is a more competitive process than that discussed above. Besides commerce, it competes with the Mediterranean dimension on migration, investment – both private and public – and even food aid. The tendency to divert developmental and economic resources towards the Eastern countries is reinforced by strong political and emotional factors.

Developments both in EFTA and in Eastern Europe will worsen the position of the non-EC Mediterranean countries in relation to the EC unless the 'inter-regional' EC-Mediterranean alliance and/or the help of the Southern EC countries works in some way in their favour. Too strong a diversion of resources away from the non-EC Mediterranean countries, despite the EC unanimity on the need to facilitate change in East European countries, may bring about some splits among EC members. Some of the Southern EC countries, especially France, may feel that their interests are at risk and, most of all, fears may arise as to the overall imbalance between Northern, Central and Southern approaches brought about by a concentration of resources in Eastern and Northern Europe. This reaction might result in a concerted effort by the Southern EC states to give special advantages to the Maghreb countries with the creation of a 'Western Mediterranean Community'. This would be a divisive decision with respect to the EC, but the Community might then assume an enlarged form, as a new type of 'overall Mediterranean policy'. One should not overlook the fact, in the end, that West Germany has more economic interests in the wider Mediterranean area than has France, Italy or Spain. Such a decision on enlargement would be a political one, with no truly economic motives.

Where to draw the line

One important aspect of this probable development in the Mediterranean is the question raised by the recent multiplication of membership applications. Turkey and now Morocco wish to become members of the EC as a means of asserting their secular and democratic identity, though this motive is definitely more powerful in Turkey than in Morocco. Malta, with the change in its leadership, wants to join in order to rebuff the neutralist policies adopted by the previous government and thereby to assert its Western and European identity. Cyprus is looking for an EC guarantee in the dispute between Greece and Turkey. If a policy of renovation and reinforcement of the Mediterranean grouping of countries were decided upon, where would the EC draw the line?

Moroccan membership seems out of the question. The application is most of all a rather ironical way of complaining about the consequences of EC enlargement. Furthermore, after having applied to the EC, Morocco has signed the treaty setting up the Union of the Arab Maghreb (UMA), an important attempt at Arab unification.

As for Malta, its membership of the EC would entail a decision about its neutrality, a status that is unilaterally guaranteed by Italy. By contrast with Austria's application, which seems to be conditional on maintaining its neutral status, Malta's present leadership appears open to change or prepared to qualify the island's status. However, neutrality is not a specific Mediterranean problem, nor is it new to the EC. The compatibility of neutral status with membership of the EC must be clarified on general grounds. The outcome will also affect applications of countries other than Malta.

The most complicated question concerns extension of the EC in the Eastern Mediterranean. A success in the CFE (Conventional Forces in Europe) talks would probably weaken Western motives for reinforcing Turkey's alliance by integrating it into the EC and the wider circle of Western institutions. The weakening of such motives would combine with existing strong opposition to

Turkey's entry into the EC. On the other hand, the application of Cyprus is fully linked to the dispute between Greece and Turkey and to Turkey's possible membership of the EC. If Cypriot membership becomes a factor in the rapprochement between Greece and Turkey, no one will oppose it. The same would be true if Turkey were to become a full member of the EC – possibly having settled its dispute with Greece.

In conclusion, we can foresee two possible developments. The first would enlarge the EC by admitting Turkey, Cyprus and, possibly, Malta. The second would leave these countries outside the EC. In any case, it remains to be seen what the status of the non-EC Mediterranean countries will be in relation to the EC: whether it will involve a new attempt at setting up a single 'overall Mediterranean policy'; differentiated individual statuses; or a special status for the Maghreb/UMA countries under cover of the EC or that of a 'Western Mediterranean Community'.

Security relations

Like economic relations, security relations are tied to developments in Central Europe. Though it may be very difficult to foresee the East-West evolution in Eastern Europe, what is apparently happening in the region is a form of reverse 'finlandization'. Whereas Finland is a 'Western' country that maintains a special political and security relationship with the USSR, East European countries – and especially Poland and Hungary – are maintaining their security and political relationships with the USSR but are 'westernizing' their political and economic systems. If carried out fairly, this process may warrant detente and disarmament without implying destabilization of the wider East-West framework.

This perspective will understandably attract the best of the West European political forces and consequently distract them from the Mediterranean. This is not to say that it will obscure the necessity for the EC to rearrange its Mediterranean policies. However, it will make more difficult and laborious a process that, as indicated above, is already difficult in its own right.

Disarmament measures expected from the CFE talks, besides nuclear measures which have already been agreed and which may multiply in the future, are going to have special consequences for the Mediterranean situation. If we look on the Mediterranean basin as the southern flank of NATO, two scenarios may be envisaged: first, an increase of tension on the northern and southern wings of the central European front, unless arms control, political understandings and confidence-building measures are expanded (for example, to naval arms); second, the propagation of the central front's detente as the consequence of a wider East-West understanding (such as an understanding expanded to regional crises).

The second scenario would contribute to an attitude of neglect with respect to the Mediterranean. The first would expose initially the Southern EC countries and Turkey, while pushing the Northern EC countries to the back of the stage. This differentiation would not be without consequences for the EC alliance. The alliance would be tested further because the special Mediterranean exposure of the Southern EC countries would create a closer association between them and the USA, the dominant power in the area. This association would bring about cooperation and conflict, as in the past, and would not, on the whole, facilitate any 'inter-regional' EC-Mediterranean relationship.

Exposure of Southern EC countries to Mediterranean tension and to American 'bilateralism' might also emerge in a situation of decreasing East-West tension in the Mediterranean basin. If the out-of-area threat were to continue or increase, and if the Southern EC countries were left alone to tackle it in a framework in which NATO's perception of the East-West threat was diminishing, this would again be a factor in dividing Southern and Northern EC members.

In conclusion, the most evident Mediterranean question that may arise from the new detente in Central and Eastern Europe is the isolation of the South European countries in dealing with threats south of NATO, both in the East-West and in the out-of-area frameworks. As indicated above, this predicament may be combined with a difficult bilateral relationship with the USA. If an alliance of the Southern EC countries must be established in order to tackle Mediterranean problems, it must be done with the aim of strengthening EC political and military union and enforcing EC rather than South European policies.

Notes

1. In the final resolution approved by the second Forum of the Western Mediterranean countries on 25–28 May 1989 in Tangiers.
2. *Southern Europe in Transition: Roles in Nato and Integration into the European Community*, Wilton Park Papers, 6, 1988, pp. 5–7.
3. 'Sulla vocazione mediterranea dell'economia italiana: una nota', *Prospettive Settana*, I, 1, 1975, pp. 5–9.
4. This proposal is being put forward by France at diplomatic level and through the forum mentioned above, n. 1.
5. PNUE, *Le Plan bleu. Avenirs du bassin méditerranéen. Résumé et orientations pour l'action* (Centre d'Activités Régionales du Plan Bleu pour la Méditerranée, Sophia Antipolis, 1988).
6. *Demographic Trends: Consequences for the Labour Market*, paper presented at the Third Conference on the Mediterranean, World's Crossroads: The Approach to Mediterranean Development, Aspen Institute Italia, Barcelona, June 1987.
7. See the special issue of the *Revue française de science politique*, 37, 6, December 1987 on 'Les Musulmans dans la société française'.
8. Gianni Bonvicini, 'Out-of-Area Issues: A New Challenge in the Atlantic Alliance' and Reinhardt Rummel, 'Political Perceptions and Military Responses to Out-of-Area Challenges, in Joseph I. Coffey and Gianni Bonvicini, (eds), *The Atlantic Alliance and the Middle East* (London: Macmillan, 1989), pp. 1–16 and 193–226.
9. See John Chipman, (ed), *Nato's Southern Allies: Internal and External Challenges*, The Atlantic Institute for International Affairs (London and New York, Routledge, 1988), and Douglas T. Stuart, *Politics and Security in the Southern Region of the Atlantic Alliance* (London, Macmillan, 1988).
10. See Kari Möttöla and Heikki Patomäki, (eds), *Facing the Change in Europe. EFTA*

Countries' Integration Strategies (Finnish Institute of International Affairs, Helsinki, 1989); Helen Wallace and Wolfgang Wessels, *Towards a New Partnership: The EC and EFTA in the Wider Western Europe* (Geneva, EFTA, Occasional Papers, 28, March 1989).

Part III
Social dynamics

10 Cross-border population movements
Federico Romero

Movements of people across European borders have mushroomed over the past three decades. The scale of the phenomenon is readily observable, but it is less easy to measure, or to chart its growth, features and directions. Movements are constantly changing over time. They are of a different nature but tend more and more to intertwine, particularly inside the European Community. They also flow around with little respect for formal borders – at least inside Western Europe. If a core can be detected in West Germany, it is not so much for a neat converging of directions and numbers, but rather for the cumulative overlapping of multiple trends. France and Britain, the smaller nations, and the South European countries all play decisive, albeit different, roles in an extremely complex picture. Besides, statistical data generally lack precision, consistency and comparability. Thus, most of the figures have to be considered as useful approximations and trend indicators, rather than as precise accounts of that intricate network of population movements across Europe whose complex details still largely elude our understanding.

Tourism

The vast majority of the people moving across West European borders each year are tourists: they are estimated to account for 75% of all travellers.[1] Even though in most countries most holiday-makers are domestic tourists – 92% in West Germany, 83% in Italy, but only 36% in Spain[2] – foreign visitors are everywhere in staggering numbers. In Western Europe, more than in any other area of the world, their massive migrations dwarf any other kind of population movements. Worldwide, international tourist movements have grown from 25 million in 1950 to 285 million in 1980 and 333 million in 1985: slightly more than half of them were in Western Europe. The astonishing rate of growth of the early postwar period has obviously decreased in the last two decades (see Table 10.1), but Western Europe was less affected by the slowdown than was the Eastern part of the continent. With 157.9 million international tourists in 1981 and 185.8 million in 1985, Western Europe has increased its share of the

Table 10.1 Tourists from abroad in Europe (millions)

1950	1960	1970	1980	1985
16.8	50.4	113	196	224.5

Source: World Tourism Organization, *Yearbook of Tourism Statistics 1986* (Madrid, WTO, 1986).

world total from 54.7% to 55.8%. Most significantly, about 80% of all Western Europe's international tourists are estimated to be 'intra-regional': that is to say, coming from another West European country. This means that cross-border tourist movements in Western Europe amounted in 1985 to 148.6 million, or 45% of world tourism! (A disproportionately large share: 'intra-regional' movements in a geographically and economically comparable area, the US, are obviously accounted for as domestic tourism).

Even though incomplete and not always directly comparable, the best available data (see Table 10.2) emphasize a few major trends. International tourism continues to grow, although at a slower pace, and is especially important in Mediterranean countries. The traditionally big host countries – France, Italy and Spain – hold their positions or grow at a steady pace, while the new, secondary resorts in countries such as Turkey, Portugal, Greece and Yugoslavia are receiving booming numbers of North European tourists. The rate of growth is rather fast also in the UK but it has substantially diminished in other traditional host countries: Austria and Switzerland. Yet in absolute terms these are still major receivers, together (surprisingly) with Germany, after the big three and the UK. According to OECD, the only losers are the Nordic countries where – even if the data cannot show it – international tourism is stagnating or declining. Three main trends can thus be summed up: (1) a booming flow towards the new South European destinations; (2) a steady growth of the huge flows towards the nations of art and history and the established Mediterranean resorts (with the exception of Italy, whose tourist intake is no longer growing); (3) a significant but stabilized flow to the Alpine nations.

In absolute terms, the only figures with an acceptable degree of reliability are those from category (a) 'registered arrivals at all types of accommodation', while the category (b) 'bednights' figure does not allow for any comparison and can only be used in determining a single country's trend. Category (c) 'arrivals at frontiers' is probably reliable for the UK and the other island nations, but can only be a very vague indicator for the other countries: even with these precautions, however, it conveys the sheer magnitude of the movements (not only of tourists but also of short-stay visitors from neighbouring nations) on the borders of Italy and Spain.

These statistical problems become more complex when examining the origins of the tourist flow. Data on arrivals at frontiers inevitably inflate the proportion of visitors from bordering nations; when they are the only available data (as for Spain), figures about visitors from neighbouring nations have to be deflated in order to have an arbitrary but not completely unrealistic estimate of the

Table 10.2 International tourists in West European countries

		Absolute figures (millions)				Percentage growth		
		1960	1970	1980	1987	1960–70	1970–80	1980–87
Austria	(a)	4.59	8.86	13.88	15.45	93	57	11.3
Belgium	(b)	–	6.89	7.17	10.06	–	4	40.3
Denmark	(b)	–	6.20	8.23	8.20	–	32.7	−0.1
Finland	(b)	–	–	2.05	2.21	–	–	7.8
France	(a)	5.61	13.70	30.10	36.82	144	120	22.3
FRG	(a)	5.48	7.71	11.29	12.78	41	46	13.2
Greece	(a)	0.34	1.41	4.80	7.56	315	240	57.5
Iceland	(c)	–	0.05	0.07	0.13	–	24.5	85.7
Ireland	(c)	2.04	1.82	2.26	2.04	−11	24.2	−9.8
Italy	(a)	9.10	12.72	22.19	21.32	40	74	−3.8
Italy	(c)	–	–	47.80	52.72	–	–	10.3
Netherlands	(b)	–	6.10	6.14	6.59	–	0.6	7.3
Norway	(b)	–	–	–	1.78	–	–	–
Portugal	(c)	–	1.58	2.71	6.08	–	71.5	124.3
Spain	(c)	6.11	22.66	39.65	50.54	271	75	27.5
Sweden	(b)	–	–	–	7.08	–	–	–
Switzerland	(a)	4.95	6.84	8.87	9.32	38	29.7	5.1
Turkey	(c)	–	0.45	1.29	2.86	–	186.6	121.7
UK	(c)	1.67	6.73	12.42	15.44	303	84	24.3
Yugoslavia	(b)	–	22.56	36.98	52.30	–	63.9	41.4

(a): registered arrivals at all types of accommodation
(b): nights spent in all types of accommodation
(c): arrivals at frontiers

Sources: Brian W. Ilbery, *Western Europe: a systematic human geography* (Oxford, Oxford University Press, 1981); OECD, *Tourism Policy and International Tourism* (Paris, OECD, 1988).

number of actual tourists (see Table 10.3). Figures for non-bordering countries remain certainly overestimated in relation to movements into other nations which register tourists at accommodation, but at least they have a useful internal consistency. As may be expected, Germany is by far the main generating country, followed by the UK and a more distant France, but its contribution to international tourism has remained rather stable in recent years. Between 1982 and 1987 the fastest growing source has been the UK, whose tourism in the OECD increased from 100 to 163; French travellers went up to 116, while Germans achieved a modest growth to 108. Tourists from these countries are dispersed all over Europe. In this respect, however, the position of the Germans is unmatched. In all the neighbouring countries, but also in Yugoslavia, Turkey and especially Italy they account for the largest share, often overwhelmingly so; in every destination they are among the three largest groups (see Table 10.4). The French are more thinly distributed and show a proportionally stronger liking for Mediterranean resorts (but also for the UK). British travellers form the largest share in Greece and are numerous in

Table 10.3 International tourism. Major flows to main West European destinations in 1987 ('000s)

		Aus	Bel	Fra	FRG	Ita	NL	Swi	UK	US	E.Eur (d)	Scan (e)
Austria	(a)	–	350	694	8,589	708	1,300	578	765	671	419	649
France	(a)	312	3,091	–	8,809	3,157	3,923	3,358	6,368	1,802	180	745
FRG	(a)	488	437	688	–	636	1,857	606	1,175	2,072	547	1,841
Greece	(c)	305	140	510	1,205	465	345	172	1,980	260	670	784
Italy	(a)	1,334	461	2,145	7,096	–	580	1,232	1,376	1,961	515	799
Italy	(c)	5,543	990	9,042	9,618	–	1,839	10,452	1,999	1,482	–	1,884
Netherlands	(f)	–	274	331	1,688	157	–	89	682	430	–	318
Portugal	(a)	41	88	421	568	144	218	110	725	238	12	222
Spain	(c)	282	1,266	11,671	6,596	1,193	1,685	1,030	7,550	866	292	2,202
Spain			(est. tourists:	(2,766)								
Switzerland	(a)	189	326	725	3,020	595	511	–	668	1,117	130	277
Turkey	(a)	106	35	492	833	172	65	49	152	95	96	72
UK	(c)	127	463	2,008	1,644	683	855	403	–	2,800	247	1,072
Yugoslavia	(a)	799	138	407	2,786	1,185	444	135	700	232	1,122	365
Total	(g)	3,983	7,069	11,187 (20,092)	42,834	9,095	11,783	7,762	22,141	12,544	4,230	9,346
USA	(c)	85	99	544	952	319	202	239	1,362	–	116	420

(a) registered arrivals at all types of accommodation; (c) arrivals at frontiers; (d) Bulgaria, Czechoslovakia, Hungary, Poland, Romania, USSR, Yugoslavia; (e) Denmark, Finland, Norway, Sweden; (f) registered arrivals at all types of accommodation, 1985; (g) based on arrivals at accommodation for Italy, while the number of French tourists in Spain has been estimated on the assumption of a similar ratio between arrivals at frontiers and at accommodation as in Italy.

Source: OECD, *Tourism Policy and International Tourism* (Paris, OECD, 1987); author's own calculation.

Table 10.4   International tourists: shares by nationality (%), 1987

| | | | | | Tourists' nationality | | | | | | | |
	Aus	Bel	Fra	FRG	Ita	NL	Swi	UK	Scan	W.Eur	E.Eur	US
Austria	–	2.3	4.5	55.6	4.6	8.4	3.7	5.0	4.2	89.8	2.7	4.3
France	0.8	8.4	–	23.9	8.6	10.7	9.1	17.3	2.1	85.3	0.5	4.9
FRG	3.8	3.4	5.4	–	5.0	14.5	4.7	9.2	14.4	64.8	4.2	16.2
Greece	4.1	1.9	6.7	15.9	6.1	4.6	2.3	26.2	10.9	80.1	7.9	3.4
Italy	6.3	2.2	10.1	33.3	–	2.7	5.8	6.5	3.7	76.0	2.4	9.2
Netherlands												
(1986)	–	5.7	6.9	35.0	3.3	–	1.8	14.1	6.6	79.1	–	8.9
Portugal	1.1	2.3	11.0	14.8	3.8	5.7	2.9	18.9	5.8	84.8	0.4	6.2
Spain	0.6	2.5	23.1	13.1	2.4	3.3	2.0	14.9	3.3	89.9	0.6	1.7
Switzerland	2.0	3.5	7.8	32.4	6.4	5.5	–	7.2	3.1	72.0	1.4	12.0
Turkey	4.0	1.4	18.5	31.3	6.5	2.4	1.8	5.7	2.7	78.2	3.5	3.6
UK	0.8	3.0	13.0	10.6	4.4	5.5	2.6	–	7.0	58.6	1.6	18.1
Yugoslavia	9.0	1.5	4.6	31.3	13.3	5.0	1.5	7.9	4.3	81.8	11.1	2.6
US	0.3	0.3	1.8	3.2	1.1	0.7	0.8	4.6	1.4	15.4	0.4	–

Source: OECD, *Tourism Policy and International Tourism* (Paris, OECD, 1988); author's own calculation.

Germany and the Netherlands. Their largest and densest flow, however, is in the Western end of the continent: through France and then into Spain and Portugal, a massive flow of Britons outnumbers the Germans in the Iberian market. Another striking feature is the density – in relation to total population – of tourists from the small, high-income countries of central Europe and Scandinavia. Swiss, Danes, Swedes, Dutch, Belgians and, to a minor extent, Austrians, travel throughout Western Europe in exceptionally high numbers. With the exception of the Dutch, whose presence is significant in France and Germany but also evenly spread throughout the continent, geographical proximity seems in this case to be the main determinant. Austrians are particularly prevalent in Italy and in the Balkans; the Swiss in France, Italy and Germany; the Belgians in France and the Netherlands. This factor reflects also a statistical distortion: presence in bordering countries is overemphasized by registration in various types of accommodation while on the way to a more distant destination in another country. This probably explains the high rate of Scandinavians in Germany, their favourite foreign country after Spain and before the UK, in a range of rather evenly visited countries. It is worth noting the small but significant presence of East Europeans not only in Yugoslavia but also in Austria, Italy and especially Germany. The border-density effect has to be taken into consideration, but their shares probably depend more on a one-country short-trip pattern of holiday, since they drop very sharply in distant countries. Quick visits from Eastern to Western Europe are rapidly increasing, with a particular concentration in Austria and Western Germany: it is estimated that in 1988 East Germans made five million trips to Western Germany and Hungarians about 4 million to Western Europe, mainly to Austria.[3] Finally, the large presence of US tourists has to be emphasized: they make up the third largest national group; their total is higher than the (presumed) figure of French tourists. The Americans are widely spread, are the largest national presence in the UK and Germany, the second in Switzerland and the third in Italy, and are poorly represented only in Spain and Yugoslavia. The existence of a privileged UK-US relationship operates both ways: Britons go to the US in almost the same numbers as to Italy and nearby Germany, and no other European country comes close to their share of the American market, even though Scandinavians, Dutch and Swiss have a disproportionately dense presence.

On the receiving end, the visible feature is the general, all-round attraction of France to tourists from every corner of Western Europe. Italy and Switzerland show a similarly comprehensive inflow, but with a greater density of Germans and extra-European travellers. Germany and the UK share rather low rates of West European tourists, above-the-average shares of Americans, and a particularly dense presence of North Europeans. Compared with the rest of Europe, these two countries are evidently more accessible to East Europeans and extra-Europeans respectively. Spain and, at a much lower level, the new Mediterranean destinations stand out for a high density of holiday-makers from the three big sending countries and a rather strong appeal to Scandinavians, Dutch, Swiss and Belgians. Italy is still a major receiver but its tourist inflow is stagnating and has altogether missed the cycle of growth enjoyed by all the other destinations; on the other hand, Italians are taking holidays abroad in fast-growing numbers.

Student exchange

Data collected by UNESCO on enrolment in universities provide us with a broad picture of foreign students' distribution patterns over the last decade. Moreover, the new ERASMUS programme for exchanges among EC universities offers very interesting indications about new flows activated by integrative policies. The growth of foreign student population over the last decade – even though it is a global trend in industrialized countries – has been quite uneven (see Table 10.5). The number of foreign students stagnated in Italy and Denmark and diminished quite rapidly in Greece, Ireland and, until 1983–4, in the UK. On the other hand, Belgium, Austria, Germany and France (as well as the US) markedly increased their role as educational hosts. Inside such a trend – and taking into account the expansion of the EC from 9 to 12 – the presence of EC nationals increased very rapidly both in America and in several European countries. Besides, this latest trend has been further accelerating in the most recent years, indicating a growing exchange across the Atlantic and, more conspicuously, inside the EC. Between 1983 and 1986 West Germany has overtaken the US as the major recipient of European foreign students; and even the UK – where the foreign student population is growing again after collapsing in the early 1980s – attracts increasing numbers of EC students. In spite of these recent trends, the latest data (see Table 10.6) show that student exchanges inside the EC are still relatively limited. Austria and Switzerland have the highest ratios of EC citizens among their foreign student populations. The US hosts more EC nationals than any Community country.

Table 10.5 Foreign students in main host countries: rate of growth

		Foreign students		
		Total growth	% of Europeans	% of EC nationals
Belgium	1975–6	100	–	29.9
	1984–6	206	48.6	46.6
USA	1975–6	100	8.1	–
	1984–6	172	9.1	7.1
Austria	1975–6	100	68.0	–
	1984–6	154	64.8	55.7
FRG	1975–6	100	39.3	13.8
	1984–6	147	40.7	24.8
France	1975–6	100	17.7	7.8
	1984–6	132	16.9	14.3
Switzerland	1975–6	100	68.8	–
	1984–6	111	71.9	60.3
Italy	1976	100	67.2	4.0
	1983	99	57.3	52.5
UK	1975–6	100	12.3	4.2
	1984–6	87	17.6	14.0

Source: UNESCO, *Statistical Yearbook* (Paris, UNESCO) various years.

In analysing the determinants of the distribution of foreign students (see Table 10.7), patterns immediately appear to be shaped by three relevant factors: geographical contiguity, cultural and linguistic similarity, and the existence of an established community of immigrants. While the former two elements are visible in any movement, the importance of flows based on traditional migratory links can be clearly detected in the distribution of Mediterranean students (the heavy presence of Italians in Belgium; of Turks and Yugoslavs in Germany and Austria; of Spaniards and Portuguese in France). Among these, the case of Greece is unique for the exceptionally high rate of student emigration and for the concentration of these students in Italy, but subsequent options (West Germany and the US) stress once more the relevance of migratory patterns. In general, South European countries host small numbers of students and very few Europeans, but often play a major role as senders of their own students abroad. As an opposite case, Austria, Switzerland and the Benelux nations host conspicuous groups of foreign students and record-high shares of EC nationals, mainly from neighbouring nations of common linguistic and cultural heritage or from Southern countries of emigration. Other sub-areas of dense interaction are represented by the UK and Ireland (in a triangular relation with the US), and by the Scandinavians, whose mutual exchanges are very substantial but not at all exclusive of other relations, particularly with the English-speaking nations.

Table 10.6 Foreign student population (most recent of the years 1983–86)

	Total	EC nationals	%	Europeans	%	US nationals	%	First 3 nationalities (Eur. or US)					
EEC	334,627	74,551	22.3	96,893	28.9	13,750	4.1	Gre	24,881	USA	13,750	Tur	12,263
USA	349,610	24,805	7.1	31,804	9.1	–	–	UK	5,507	FRG	4,490	Gre	3,742
FRG	79,354	19,702	24.8	32,303	40.7	4,042	5.1	Tur	10,060	Gre	6,693	USA	4,042
France	126,782	18,090	14.3	21,427	16.9	3,398	2.7	FRG	3,705	USA	3,398	Gre	2,905
Italy	28,068	14,752	52.5	16,090	57.3	976	3.5	Gre	12,222	FRG	1,740	USA	976
Belgium	20,095	9,359	46.6	9,760	48.6	262	1.3	Ita	2,435	NL	1,738	Fra	1,366
Austria	15,740	8,775	55.7	10,196	64.8	391	2.5	FRG	4,468	Ita	2,994	Tur	816
Switzerland	13,576	8,190	60.3	9,756	71.9	516	3.8	FRG	3,066	Ita	1,744	Fra	1,441
UK	48,686	6,800	14.0	8,560	17.6	3,386	6.9	USA	3,386	Gre	2,141	FRG	1,527
Netherlands	5,704	2,803	49.1	3,387	59.4	306	5.4	FRG	1,271	Bel	444	Tur	374
Sweden	10,401	1,843	17.7	7,216	69.4	304	2.9	Nor	839	Gre	440	FRG	359
Ireland	2,684	1,105	41.2	1,283	47.8	287	10.1	UK	982	USA	287	Fra	51
Spain	10,997	978	8.9	1,220	11.1	614	5.6	USA	614	FRG	208	Fra	195
Denmark	3,167	716	22.6	2,483	78.4	187	5.9	Nor	663	FRG	320	Swe	269
Greece	6,683	139	2.1	267	4.0	252	3.8	Tur	427	USA	252	UK	58
Portugal	2,407	107	4.4	113	4.7	40	1.7	Spa	46	USA	40	FRG	23

Source: UNESCO, *Statistical Yearbook* (Paris, UNESCO, 1988).

Table 10.7 Geographical distribution of students abroad (1983–86)

Country of origin	Total in EC	Major destinations								
Greece	24,881	Ita	12,222	FRG	6,693	USA	3,742	Fra	2,905	UK	2,141
USA	13,750	FRG	4,042	Fra	3,398	UK	3,386	Ita	976	Spa	614
Turkey	12,263	FRG	10,060	USA	2,200	Aus	816	Fra	753	Gre	427
FRG	9,433	USA	4,490	Aus	4,468	Fra	3,705	Swi	3,066	Ita	1,740
Italy	6,979	Aus	2,994	Bel	2,435	FRG	2,266	USA	1,765	Swi	1,744
UK	6,067	USA	5,507	Fra	2,009	FRG	1,960	Irl	982	NL	362
Spain	5,941	Fra	2,793	USA	1,807	FRG	1,659	Bel	930	Swi	502
France	5,727	USA	3,454	FRG	2,654	Swi	1,441	Bel	1,366	UK	908
Netherlands	4,771	FRG	1,985	Bel	1,738	USA	1,313	Fra	531	UK	357
Austria	4,417	FRG	3,960	Swi	436	USA	372	Fra	195	NL	90
Portugal	3,651	Fra	2,538	USA	553	FRG	501	Bel	228	Spa	171
Luxembourg	3,069	Bel	1,042	Fra	974	FRG	958	Aus	340	Swi	150
Yugoslavia	2,864	FRG	2,068	USA	539	Aus	409	Fra	375	Swe	256
Switzerland	2,808	FRG	1,302	USA	896	Ita	520	Fra	460	Aus	228
Norway	2,792	USA	1,691	UK	889	Swe	839	FRG	808	Den	663
Belgium	2,325	Fra	823	USA	683	FRG	586	NL	444	UK	293
Sweden	1,301	USA	1,335	FRG	493	Fra	284	Den	269	Swi	140
Ireland	1,044	USA	942	UK	609	Fra	200	FRG	171	NL	22
Denmark	663	USA	525	Swe	349	FRG	269	Fra	192	UK	105

Source: UNESCO, *Statistical Yearbook* (Paris, UNESCO, 1988).

The main patterns of student exchange, however, gravitate around the world-leading host countries: the US, Germany and France. Their foreign student population is vast, increasing and of global origins: among large groups of Asians and Africans, European students are a relatively small but growing minority. More importantly, these nations are the core of an expanding mutual exchange among the most advanced industrial states. (Japan attracts very few foreign students.) The US and Germany, in particular, stand out as key actors of unmatched prominence: they are always among the first choices for students from every European country; their own students abroad are spread over all destinations; their mutual exchange is the densest one. France has a similar role as host country, but the presence of its own students abroad is rather thinner. The UK is perhaps on the way to join this leading group, if it continues to recover a major role as educational host after the drastic reduction of the early 1980s: and particularly so since its share of European students – traditionally very low – is expanding fast and is already equal to that of France. We can thus visualize an inner circle of four most advanced large nations, increasingly at the core of international student exchanges. Their mutual interaction is particularly dense: the ratio of concentration in the three other leading countries, among all those studying abroad in Europe and America, is 78.7% for the Americans, 69.8% for the Germans, 76.4% for the French and 81.8% for the British! The core function of these countries is further evinced by their growing appeal to students from the most diverse European nations. The numbers of their

Table 10.8   ERASMUS: student mobility by destination (%) 1988–9

Home country	Bel	FRG	Den	Spa	Fra	Gre	Ita	Irl	Lux	NL	Por	UK
Belgium	–	12.2	2.6	10.5	20.8	1.7	8.4	3.5	0.0	25.3	1.1	13.8
FRG	1.8	–	0.2	9.1	32.1	1.1	5.0	3.3	0.0	5.4	1.5	40.5
Denmark	3.9	9.4	–	8.2	6.9	0.7	4.8	13.5	0.0	11.2	1.1	40.2
Spain	3.7	14.1	0.9	–	38.4	0.1	8.8	2.0	0.0	3.9	1.3	26.7
France	2.5	23.9	0.3	14.0	–	0.9	4.7	3.0	0.0	1.9	1.3	47.4
Greece	3.8	30.3	2.2	0.4	27.9	–	4.3	0.8	0.0	4.4	0.0	25.9
Italy	6.2	17.5	0.9	13.1	23.6	1.6	–	2.1	0.0	7.8	2.3	24.9
Ireland	4.5	26.0	8.1	6.2	32.1	0.7	5.4	–	0.0	4.1	0.9	12.2
Lux.	0.0	100.0	0.0	0.0	0.0	0.0	0.0	0.0	–	0.0	0.0	0.0
Neth.	14.0	23.6	3.4	8.6	11.4	0.9	10.2	2.4	0.0	–	2.3	23.2
Portugal	5.2	18.7	1.1	9.5	29.8	0.0	12.7	5.4	0.0	5.1	–	12.5
UK	1.6	27.1	1.6	9.9	44.8	1.0	6.7	1.3	0.0	5.3	0.7	–
Total	3.3	17.9	1.1	9.6	25.3	0.9	5.9	2.5	0.0	4.9	1.3	27.3

Source: Internal estimates of Erasmus Bureau, Brussels.

Spanish, Irish, Belgian, Italian, Dutch, Austrian, and Portuguese guest students are steadily increasing (while such a long-standing major host as Switzerland has recently been losing its attraction). Around these expanding flows towards the leading countries (and among themselves) the most interesting trend is the relatively faster growth of the host role played by the EC. Between the two latest sets of data (1982–4 and 1984–6) the global foreign student population grew by 3.5% in the EC and by 2.1% in the US, and American students in the EC went up 45.7%, against a more modest 11.4% increase of EC nationals in America.

Thus, if the perimeter of international higher education is primarily defined by the Atlantic area, inside its boundaries a gradual shift is taking place towards the EC, particularly its German core. Such a trend can be strengthened by specific programmes aimed at enhanced levels of formal integration. This, in fact, seems to be the early effect of the new Erasmus programme for short-term exchanges among EC universities. Growing very rapidly, from 3,260 students involved in 1987–8 to 12,800 in 1988–9 and an anticipated 25,000 in 1989–90, Erasmus exchanges point to patterns (see Table 10.8) which confirm the larger trend – concentration on the three leading nations – but also introduce a few novelties: the lesser role of Germany by comparison with Britain and France; the relatively high attraction of Spain and the Netherlands; the disproportion-ately minor role of Italy. The primary host function played by the UK and France is certainly due also to the international status of their languages (especially given their own high mutual exchange). But the rapid success of the scheme reveals a potential demand for intra-EC exchanges which might very well steer the overall flows to the leading nations away from the US and more heavily into the EC. It is certainly not by chance that the students attracted in

Table 10.9   Foreign residents in European countries

	1950 '000s	%	1970 '000s	%	1982 '000s	%	1986 '000s	%	
Austria	323	4.7	212	2.8	291	4.1	283	3.9	(1987)
Belgium	368	4.3	696	7.2	896	9.0	898	9.0	
Denmark	–		38	0.8	102	2.0	136	2.6	(1987)
Finland	11	0.3	6	0.1	12	0.3	–		
France	1,765	4.1	2,621	5.3	3,680	6.8	–		
FRG	568	1.1	2,977	4.9	4,667	7.6	4,513	7.5	
Greece	(31	0.4)	(93	1.1)	(260	2.7)	98	1.1	(1985)
Ireland	–		-		69	2.0	88	2.5	(1984)
Italy	(47	0.1)	–		211	0.4	–		est. 1,300 2.3
Liechtenstein	3	19.6	7	36.0	9	36.1	–		
Luxembourg	29	9.9	63	18.4	96	26.3	97	26.3	(1985)
Netherlands	104	1.1	255	2.0	538	3.8	568	3.9	
Norway	16	0.5	–		86	2.1	109	2.6	(1987)
Portugal	21	0.3	–		64	0.6	86	0.8	est. 100 0.9
Spain	(93	0.3)	(291	0.9)	(418	1.1)	293	0.8	est. 650 1.7
Sweden	124	1.8	411	5.0	406	4.9	391	4.6	
Switzerland	285	6.1	1,080	17.2	926	14.2	956	14.7	
UK	–		–		1,638	2.9	1,736	3.1	
Europe (est. in millions)	5.1		10.2		14.4		14.2	or	15.4

Sources: Denis Maillat, 'Long-term Aspects of International Migration Flows. The Experience of European Receiving Countries', in OECD, *The Future of Migration* (Paris, OECD, 1987), pp. 38–63; Eurostat, *Demographic Statistics* (Brussels, EC, 1988); SOPEMI, *Continuous Reporting System on Migration* (Paris, OECD, 1987); various national statistics; Rinus Penninx, 'International Migration in Western Europe since 1973: Developments, Mechanisms and Controls', *International Migration Review*, XX, 4 (Winter 1986), pp. 951–72.

the highest numbers to France and the UK are the French and the British themselves, together with Germans, Spaniards and Danes: the same groups that, on the larger UNESCO data (see Table 10.7), usually give priority to studying in the US! Moreover, the high proportion of business and foreign language studies (51.2% of the total student-months) among the disciplines covered by the scheme points towards the possible emergence of European alternatives for the internationalization of education traditionally searched for in the US. ERASMUS is at too early a stage to indicate definite trends, but its features already anticipate a major advance of transnational education in the EC.

Immigration and foreign residents

A threefold increase in foreign residents has been the most relevant population change in postwar Europe (see Table 10.9). Immigration has evolved through

Table 10.10   Stocks of immigrant population in selected countries (Most recent year '000s)

	in Bel 1984	in Fra 1982	in FRG 1986	in NL 1986	in Swe 1986	in Swi 1986
Nationals of:						
Austria	–	2.7	174.2	3.0	2.8	28.8
Finland	–	1.0	10.1	0.6	134.2	1.4
Greece	20.7	7.9	278.5	3.8	8.0	8.5
Italy	269.3	333.7	535.5	17.0	3.9	388.4
Portugal	10.4	764.9	77.0	7.5	1.5	39.2
Spain	55.1	321.4	151.0	18.2	2.8	110.4
Turkey	72.5	123.5	1,425.7	160.6	21.9	52.8
Yugoslavia	5.3	64.4	591.1	11.6	38.4	77.8
Algeria	10.8	795.9	5.4	0.6	0.5	1.9
Morocco	123.2	431.1	51.0	122.7	1.0	1.6
Tunisia	6.8	189.4	23.6	2.6	0.7	2.2
Other countries	323.5	644.2	1,158.8	219.8	175.1	243.4
Total	897.6	3,680.1	4,482.6	568.0	390.8	956.0

Source: SOPEMI, *Continuous Reporting System on Migration* (Paris, OECD, 1987).

three different stages, marked by distinct patterns of flow. Up to 1973, the growing flow of 'guest-workers' from the south brought into the northern economies of Western Europe a large number of foreigners. When the consequent social costs and political tensions interacted with the oil recession and the new trends towards the dispersal of industrial production, restrictive measures were enacted in order to arrest the inflow. But a complex chain had by then been set in motion: migration did not stop, it just changed nature and scope. Inflows of 'guest-workers' gave way to new movements: first of family reunification, and then of refugees.[4] Transfers from southern to northern Europe turned into more temporary, fluctuating and complex movements between various labour markets. Stocks in the receiving countries expanded due to the low death- and high birth-rate of immigrants, while clandestine migration spread throughout Europe's unofficial labour markets.[5] Through its various stages, the long migratory chain established multiple interactions of the receiving countries not only with southern Europe but with the whole Mediterranean basin. After the 1973 restrictions, migration from southern Europe decreased unevenly. From Greece and Spain outflows were rapidly reduced to a trickle, and vastly outnumbered by returns, as in Yugoslavia. Migrations from Portugal and Turkey increased at first, but lately migrations from Portugal have decreased sharply and from Turkey they have almost ceased. (Turkish workers have been emigrating instead to the Middle East.) Italian migration slowed down and became more cyclical, but has not ceased completely: thanks to free circulation in the EC, flows have assumed a rotating nature (especially with West Germany), with about 60,000 movements a year

Table 10.11 Inflow of foreign labour to selected countries, 1977–86 ('000s)

	1977	1978	1979	1980	1981	1982	1983	1984	1985	1986
Belgium	4.7	3.9	3.4	3.8	3.5	2.3	1.8	1.7	1.9	2.2
France	22.8	18.4	17.4	17.3	33.5	97.0	18.5	11.8	11.0	11.2
Germany	29.7	19.5	37.9	82.6	43.9	25.9	24.4	27.5	33.4	37.2
Switzerland	19.7	21.9	25.5	32.3	35.3	33.0	24.0	24.9	25.5	29.4

Source: SOPEMI, *Continuous Reporting System on Migration* (Paris, OECD, 1987).

but no net loss of manpower; migrants are now mostly young workers moving between various temporary jobs in different EC labour markets.[6] Even though returns outnumber departures, the large communities established abroad (see Table 10.10) ensure a continuous two-way flow of considerable proportions between southern and northern Europe: in the 1980s there have been around 200,000 departures a year from the six Mediterranean members of OECD.[7]

Although the phase of family reunification with the 'guest-workers' of the 1960s and 1970s has ended, the demographic potential for emigration from Mediterranean countries remains rather high. Movements are small because of legal restrictions and saturated labour markets. But West European economies still have a limited, diversified and shifting (yet deeply ingrained) need for new migrants to fill low-level jobs, particularly in years of rapid expansion. In conjunction with the large potential supply – and through the chains of communication and movement offered by the established migrant communities – this structural demand generates recurrent peaks of new arrivals, which can be significant at any surge of the European economy and are expected to remain as a permanent feature in the future.[8]

Table 10.11 makes this evident and signals a new wave of arrivals, in West Germany and Switzerland, and possibly in Belgium, beginning in 1984–5. What this data cannot visualize, however, is the large and rapidly expanding phenomenon of illegal immigration not only in the traditional receiving countries but, above all, in southern Europe. The demographic pressure originating from the south Mediterranean coast and from Africa and Asia is pushing a new inflow of unregistered migrants into illegal employment in Spain, Portugal, Greece and, above all, Italy. The latest estimate (1985), certainly already outdated, put their number at about 2 million, half of them in Italy, which seems to serve also as a staging post for further movements beyond the Alps; in 1988, foreigners in Italy were already estimated at 1.3 million, 5% of the labour force.[9] The surge of illegal immigration has to be seen in connection with the other major migratory phenomenon of the 1980s: the increasing number of Third World refugees (and lately East Europeans) asking for asylum, and seeking employment and residence, in the richest economies, particularly West Germany, Sweden and Austria.[10]

Ever since 1969, the EC-12 area has had an overall positive migratory balance – largely due to the inflow of foreigners – with significant peaks in the early 1970s, in 1978–81 and, probably (though statistics are not yet available), from 1985 to the present. In the 1980s every country except Belgium, Ireland and the UK reported a positive balance; and the UK's negative balance has been reversed since 1984.[11] Calculations are uncertain but it is fairly clear that foreign residents are almost everywhere on the increase again, especially since 1984. By and large, this applies also to the non-EC states, with the single exception of Sweden where new inflows of East Europeans and non-Europeans are more than offset by the return home of Finnish migrants. Flows from the customary recruitment areas of the 1960s – Finland for Sweden, the Commonwealth for the UK, and southern Europe for all the other economies – are now low or have a negative value, and this often entails an overall decrease of foreign labour. On the other hand, arrivals are increasing from more distant areas.

The new inflows can be broken down in the following way: (1) arrivals from the southern coast of the Mediterranean and from Africa are the most widespread, with significant concentrations in Italy, France, Belgium, the Netherlands and West Germany; (2) numbers of Asians are increasing in West Germany, Belgium, the Netherlands and all the Scandinavian countries; (3) East Europeans are moving into West Germany, Austria and Sweden. In most cases, these migrants arrive as refugees, as family dependants, or with a semi-clandestine status. This not only implies new political and administrative problems, but also explains the apparent paradox in the statistics of many receiving countries, where foreign population is on the increase but foreign employees are diminishing (as in West Germany, Austria and the Netherlands). New migrants face competitive or closed labour markets and are increasingly pushed into unregistered jobs, thus further aggravating the dichotomy between official unemployment and illegal work. The noticeable exceptions are Switzerland and Britain. In the former, recruitment has simply shifted to new areas of the south European belt (away from Italy and into Portugal and Yugoslavia). In the UK, where the overall balance has become positive since 1983, after almost 20 negative years, settlement from former colonies has been reduced and Commonwealth immigration overtaken by arrivals from highly industrialized areas: the US, Japan and the EC.[12] Finally, the Swiss and Austrian tourist sectors still attract seasonal labour from neighbouring countries, and so does French agriculture (from Spain and Portugal).

The inflow of non-European refugees and clandestine migrants has major economic and demographic implications, and it has a special urgency in southern Europe, in West Germany and, probably, in France.[13] But the most interesting trends are taking place inside Europe. The first concerns East-West relations, and is focused mainly on West Germany. After the restrictions of 1974, overall net migration of foreigners into West Germany followed a fluctuating pattern (see Table 10.12). Between the two peaks of 1980 and 1986, however, the composition of the inflow changed drastically: the Turks seem to have completed their cycle of family reunification, and Asians have become by far the largest portion of the inflow, while Poles and East Europeans are taking an increasing share (see Table 10.13). Migrations from Poland had a net positive balance in 1980–86 of 273,640. Migrations from Eastern Europe also include the 'ethnic Germans' who are not enumerated in these tables. From East Germany alone, their net total inflow, already high at 150,700 in 1980–86, has

Table 10.12 Net migration of foreigners to West Germany ('000s)

1975 − 234.0	1978 + 50.4	1981 + 85.6	1984 − 213.9
1976 − 128.1	1979 + 179.2	1982 − 111.6	1985 + 31.5
1977 − 29.2	1980 + 245.6	1983 − 151.7	1986 + 130.6

Source: Statistisches Bundesamt, *Gebiet und Bevölkerung* (Wiesbaden, SB, various years).

boomed in 1988 and especially in 1989. Immigrants from the East also go to Sweden (a constant flow of Poles with a peak of 4,000 in 1981 and a recent increase in the number of Romanians) and Austria. Here, where refugees account for the total growth in foreign population since 1985, 89,975 asylum-seekers entered the country in 1980–87: 39,328 of these were Poles, with a peak in 1981, later substituted by Hungarians and Romanians.[14]

The other new trends concern flows within Western Europe. Here we tread on much thinner ground, because many movements, particularly inside the EC, do not appear in any statistics. (Work permits are no longer required and residence permits not always so.) With the exception of southern immigrants, foreign residents in Europe, in any case, form rather small communities (see Table 10.14). Only in Belgium, Ireland, Luxembourg, Switzerland and Spain do EC nationals reach 50% of the foreign population. As far as trends are concerned, EC foreigners are generally declining, due to the return of ex-migrants to the south. Still, if we focus our attention on the north European citizens (and keep in mind the structural underestimation of these statistics), a few interesting trends begin to appear. First, there is an increase of exchanges between France, the UK, West Germany, Denmark and the Benelux countries. In various proportions, immigrants from these countries are growing in numbers in the Netherlands (French, Belgians and British up to 1984); in France (more British and Dutch); in Luxembourg (French and Belgians); in Denmark (British and Dutch). An increased exchange with Britain and among themselves seems also to be taking place in the other Scandinavian countries. European population in Belgium is relatively stable but Belgians are moving out, particularly to the Netherlands and Germany. Numbers of West Germans are increasing slightly in France and, up to 1985, also in the Netherlands. But it is in West Germany and Britain that these new trends, however small, become clearly visible and comprehensible. With the exclusion of the southern migration countries, the net inflow of EC citizens into West Germany has increased

Table 10.13 Inflow of foreigners to West Germany, main shares (%)

	Turkey	Asia	Africa	EC	Poland	Rest of Europe
1980	55.4	15.6	4.5	5.2	5.8	8.3
1986	7.8	49.6	7.0	6.1	17.2	10.2

Source: Statistisches Bundesamt, *Gebiet und Bevölkerung* (Wiesbaden, SB, 1987).

Table 10.14 Foreign residents in selected European countries ('000s, most recent year)

Origin	Bel 1985	Den 1986	Irl[a] 1981	Fra 1982	FRG 1986	Gre 1985	Ita 1981	Lux 1981	NL 1986	Por 1986	Spa 1987	UK[b] 1984-6	Nor 1987	Swi 1986
							Country of residence							
Belgium		0.3	0.5	50.2	19.2	0.8	7.0	7.9	22.8	0.8	8.6	–	–	–
Denmark	1.9		0.4	2.4	13.6	0.6	13.0	0.8	1.2	0.3	4.7	–	16.8	–
Ireland	1.3	0.9		1.9	7.0	0.3	0.6	0.2	2.6	0.2	1.3	542.0	–	–
France	103.2	1.7	2.0		76.7	4.2	23.0	11.9	7.0	2.6	21.2	25.0	–	47.2
FRG	27.6	8.3	3.5	43.8		7.1	14.8	8.9	41.0	3.6	34.1	37.0	3.7	80.3
Greece	20.1	0.4	–	7.9	278.5		6.1	0.2	3.8	–	0.5	11.0	–	–
Italy	269.0	2.0	1.3	333.7	537.1	4.9		22.3	17.8	1.0	12.2	77.0	–	338.4
Luxembourg	5.7	–	–	3.5	5.0	–	0.4		0.3	–	–	–	–	–
Netherlands	66.3	1.7	1.7	14.0	109.0	1.6	3.1	2.9		1.3	12.1	21.0	2.4	–
Portugal	10.4	0.3	–	764.9	78.2	0.2	–	29.3	7.5		28.7	–	–	39.2
Spain	55.1	0.9	–	321.4	150.5	0.6	–	2.1	19.0	7.0		29.0	–	110.4
UK	22.3	10.0	187.0	34.2	90.0	10.5	11.2	2.0	38.5	3.1	46.9		12.6	–
Total EEC	583.9	26.6	–	1,577.9	1,364.7	30.9	79.2	88.6	161.6	22.5	170.3	754.0	35.5	–
Yugoslavia	5.3	8.3	–	64.4	591.2	0.8	5.0	1.5	11.7	–	0.2	–	–	77.4
Turkey	72.5	22.3	–	123.6	1,434.3	–	–	0.1	156.4	–	–	12.0	3.7	52.8
Rest of Europe	17.0	28.9	–	110.8	434.1	11.9	39.7	2.2	12.3	1.5	18.1	109.0	27.7	–
Total foreigners	897.6	128.2	232.4	3,680.1	4,512.7	295.8	211.0	95.8	552.6	87.0	293.2	1,736.0	109.3	956.0

[a] Persons born abroad. [b] Average for the years 1984–6, data unavailable for groups below 10,000.

Sources: EUROSTAT, *Demographic Statistics* (Brussels, EC, 1988); various national statistics.

rapidly from 2,288 in 1984 to 4,609 in 1985 and 8,306 in 1986. Of this latest figure, 33% were French, 30% British, 16% Dutch and 7.8% Belgians.[15]

In the UK (while the balance with the rest of Europe is stable at around zero) exchange of residents with the EC, traditionally negative and with small flows, has risen sharply since 1982 when it increased by 16,600; then 1,500 in 1983; 10,800 in 1984 and 23,500 in 1985 (40% of whom are British citizens). The most remarkable feature, however, is that most of these people are classified as managerial or professional (67% of the inflow and 59% of the outflow in 1985). And this is the only category, apart from housewives and children, with a positive balance of migration, not only from the EC but from the US and Japan as well.[16] It seems very likely that a good part of the movement into West Germany and between the Benelux countries and France also concerns professional and highly qualified workers. Overall data on sectors of employment for foreigners indicate a global shift away from manufacturing and construction and increases in financing, insurance and other services (particularly in France, the UK, Benelux and, since 1985, also in West Germany). The structural shift probably accounts for this initial, small but significant influx of foreign managers and professionals.[17] Specific studies on the transfer of managerial and professional workers also indicate a steady intra-European movement, a strong inflow to West Germany and a concentration in finance, trade and leisure services. As a determinant of these movements, there is particular emphasis on the growing role of intra-company transfers connected with careers inside business organizations with an international structure. If data are disaggregated, the ratio of foreign workers coming from non-Mediterranean EC countries is very high in Luxembourg and Belgium (46% and 25% respectively), and quite significant in the Netherlands, Sweden and Switzerland (between 19% and 17%).[18]

The second noticeable intra-European trend is the growth in numbers of foreign residents on the EC Mediterranean coast. In Greece, between 1981 and 1985, numbers of German, French, British, Dutch, Danish and Belgian residents have grown, on average, by 36%. Poor statistics do not provide as clear a picture for Italy, but new applications for residency by German, Swiss, French and British citizens increased in the early 1980s especially in Tuscany and Sicily. In Portugal, after sharp ups and downs in the 1970s, figures for Dutch, Austrian and, above all, British and German residents have all gone up since 1981.[19] But it is especially in Spain that a new flow of north Europeans is so large and so rapid as to appear more than a byproduct of the intensification of trade across Europe (see Table 10.15). The close connection with the pattern of tourism growth, and its wide geographic origins across all of Western Europe (inside and outside the EC) suggest that we are witnessing the emergence of a European version of the Sunbelt phenomenon. Part of the flow is undoubtedly accounted for by the spouses of returned migrants. In general, however, the low rate of economic activity among foreign residents, and their concentration in tourist areas, seem to point towards a growing propensity by north Europeans to move and retire to the Mediterranean coast. Mutual exchanges among citizens of Mediterranean countries are growing as well, but at a rather slower pace and with no such clear direction: one noticeable phenomenon is the large presence of Portuguese in Spain, presumably new migrants attracted by sustained growth.

Table 10.15 Foreign residents in Spain, by nationality (and percentage growth, 1980–86)

	1980	1982	1984	1986	% growth
Austria	1,279	1,530	1,670	1,925	50.5
Belgium	4,625	6,127	7,110	8,553	84.9
Denmark	2,583	3,491	3,913	4,718	82.7
France	16,262	15,349	16,925	21,162	30.1
FRG	20,878	23,609	27,052	34,065	63.2
Ireland	528	650	843	1,329	134.7
Norway	899	1,020	1,238	1,625	80.8
Netherlands	6,342	8,350	9,740	12,139	91.4
Sweden	3,427	3,844	4,490	5,449	9.0
Switzerland	4,367	4,619	5,141	6,264	43.4
UK	22,678	28,537	35,263	46,914	106.9
Europe	119,169	133,338	149,028	188,528	58.25

Source: INE, *Anuario Estadistico de España* (Madrid, INE, 1987).

Conclusion

Western Europe is open to dense interaction in every direction. The trans-Atlantic tourist and business flow is the most prominent, but also the least problematic. Population movements which affect the Continent increasingly converge on it from three main geographical areas. First, there is a growing flow of Asian refugees into West Germany, Scandinavia and the Benelux countries. Secondly, Eastern Europe is sending increasing numbers of refugees, migrants and even tourists into Austria, Sweden and, again, West Germany. Third and most important, the Mediterranean basin and Africa have become the major frontier for Western Europe. On the basis of huge economic and demographic differentials, their long-established migrations into France and Belgium, and the more recent ones to West Germany, Switzerland, the Netherlands and Scandinavia, have now spilled over into large unregulated flows to southern Europe and the whole Continent.

Inside Western Europe, population flows are large, diverse and often intertwined. The most conspicuous ones take place on the north-south axis. A massive movement of tourists towards the Mediterranean coast is accompanied by a dense two-way flow between south European countries and their migrant communities beyond the Alps and the Pyrenees. The countries around the North Sea and France form a second area of intense interaction: tourist, student and professional exchanges are large, growing and multi-directional. A similar, horizontal dimension of interaction, though much less intense, is beginning to emerge among the Mediterranean nations. Finally, there are several regional sub-areas of specific exchange: the Alps, Benelux, Iberia, Scandinavia, and the British Isles.

At the centre of this network of multiple flows is West Germany, which takes part in *all* types of movement, often with a prominent role. It is the junction with Eastern Europe; the largest receiver of refugees; the main actor in exchanges with the Mediterranean basin; the largest all-round exporter of tourists; and even its interaction with the US equals that of Britain. In every category examined West Germany shows the densest interaction with the surrounding smaller states, with France, Italy and most southern countries, with Scandinavia and, on most indicators, with Britain as well. In close relation with this German core, France and the Benelux countries share a variety of intense flows. Belgium and the Netherlands export an astounding number of tourists to all destinations – and are cross-roads of European migration, together with Switzerland. France is the second most active country in tourist, student and migrant movements, as well as the second most important destination, but its spread is more circumscribed: while it is the main partner in exchanges with Africa and Iberia, it has a less active role than West Germany in other directions.

Italy and Spain relate very intensely, in every movement, with all the continental countries and also with Britain and Scandinavia in the sphere of tourism. Italy, in particular, has the densest interaction with all the core countries and is emerging as the central focus and funnel for North African migrations into the whole of Western Europe.[20] Britain is the only major country which does not have a large migration exchange with the Mediterranean. However, the UK is a major partner in the new flows of professionals and students between the northern economies and is becoming a superpower as far as tourism is concerned. Besides, exchanges with North America and Asia remain a prominent feature of Britain's population movements. Finally, it has to be stressed how deeply integrated in almost every flow are the non-EC countries: in varying proportions, Switzerland, Austria and Scandinavia are closely interlinked with the core countries, with the Mediterranean, the UK and also Eastern Europe.

The image of Western Europe projected by these population movements is that of a large unified area whose external openness appears increasingly problematic, and whose internal integration is primarily determined by informal developments rather than by political regulations. Tourist, student and resident exchanges are not driven or limited by EC rules, just as past migrations from the south were not shaped by the existence of the Community: its Mediterranean extension actually sanctioned an already established common space. Substantial discriminations begin to apply at the frontiers of Western Europe rather than inside it. In the West European area, however, the EC forms a privileged inner space whose lack of restrictions affects not freedom of movement as such but, rather, the possibility of combining various types of movement. In a common space of intense, revolving and multifarious flows of people, the abolition of work and residence permits allows for greater elasticity and an increasing overlap among the diverse determinants of flows. Harmonization of legal, commercial and financial procedures will obviously further enhance this process. When foreign students can pick up jobs, tourists buy real estate and go into business, migrants move between various labour markets, managers pursue an international career and so forth, we are already in a new dimension of diversified, interlinked and largely unmeasurable patterns of exchange. They feed each other, blending and probably growing much faster beyond some invisible threshold: cross-national social contacts are then multiplied and can activate entirely new types of flow, in a sort of chain reaction process. The pace and direction of this process are hardly predictable but its first signs have emerged, particularly in the tourist regions, around the most flexible occupations and in the big cities, where the features of a multinational European society in the making are already perceptible.

This, however, does not point towards the emergence of homogeneous spaces of supranational societal integration bound to supersede national differences. It looks much more likely – and is perhaps already apparent – that a few urban and tourist regions will diversify into areas where the cumulative juxtaposition of multinational elements is going to coexist, and occasionally to clash, with the persistence of national and provincial features. Particularly so since the open character of the common EC space can – at least potentially – affect the middle and working classes even more directly than the already less differentiated elites. Whether by wealth or education (and usually both) social elites have always enjoyed higher levels of internationalization, especially in Europe; while labour migrations, even though very extensive, have rarely been able to transcend the geographical patterns defined not only by market demand but by political and administrative restrictions as well. The freedom not only to circulate but to work, reside and transfer social benefits, has opened up the EC as a large space where young workers can move among various local and national markets in a growing range of temporary, precarious jobs. And this can be variously combined with tourism, study or other activities without the difficulties incurred by non-EC citizens. This phenomenon of multiple mobility, though hardly detectable in the statistics, is clearly visible in areas of increasing multinationalization, and it prefigures the emergence of new social groups which might progressively recognize concrete meanings in the formerly abstract concept of 'European citizenship'.

However, it remains evident that these new flows are still limited and that most population movements are determined by economic and social factors largely independent of EC laws. External migrations, tourism, student exchanges and professional mobility depend on structural processes of economic transnationalization and can take place in a framework of political cooperation, not necessarily of direct integration. Integration in Western Europe is extended primarily by informal factors. The formal level of integration – although not a prerequisite for most of these phenomena – can, however, activate a more complex interplay among various flows, which will ultimately alter their nature and extend their range. Moreover, formal integrative policies, like ERASMUS, are already proving effective in redirecting and enlarging transnational flows with long-established informal origins and motives.

Notes

1. Douglas G. Pearce, *Tourism Today. A Geographical Analysis* (London, Longman, 1987).
2. Allan M. Williams, *The Western European Economy. A Geography of Postwar Development* (London, Hutchinson, 1987), pp. 226–39.

3. *The Guardian*, 28 November 1988; *The Economist*, 28 January 1989.
4. See Stephen Castles, 'The Guest-Worker in Western Europe – An Obituary', *International Migration Review*, XX, 6 (Winter 1986), pp. 761–78; Dave Edye, *Immigrant Labour and Government Policy: The Cases of the FRG and France* (Aldershot, Gower, 1987); SOPEMI, *Continuous Reporting System on Migration* (Paris, OECD, 1987).
5. See OECD, *The Future of Migration* (Paris, OECD, 1987).
6. See M.L. Gentileschi, 'Comment se modifie l'Emigration italienne en Allemagne Occidentale', *Hommes et terres du nord*, special number, 1981, pp. 723–42.
7. OECD, *The Future of Migration*, above, n. 5.
8. Denis Maillat, 'Long-Term Aspects of International Migration Flows. The Experience of European Receiving Countries', in OECD, *The Future of Migration* (Paris, OECD, 1987); Rinus Penninx, 'International Migration in Western Europe since 1973: Developments, Mechanisms and Controls', *International Migration Review*, XX, 4 (Winter 1986), pp. 951–72.
9. *La Stampa*, 29 November 1988.
10. OECD, *The Future of Migration*, above, n. 5; SOPEMI, *Continuous Reporting System*, above, n. 4.
11. EUROSTAT, *Demographic Statistics* (Brussels, EC, 1988).
12. Office of Population Censuses and Surveys, *International Migration 1985* (London, HMSO, 1987).
13. AA.VV., *Abitare il pianeta*, vol. I (Turin, Ed. Fondazione G. Agnelli, 1989).
14. SCB, *Befolkningsförändringar 1986*, part 3 (Stockholm, SCB, 1987); OSZ, *Statistische Nachrichten*, XLIII/8 (Vienna, OSZ, 1988).
15. Statistisches Bundesamt, *Gebiet und Bevölkerung 1987* (Wiesbaden, SB, 1989).
16. See OPCS, *International Migration 1985*, above, n. 12.
17. See EUROSTAT, *Employment and Unemployment* (Brussels, EC, 1988).
18. John Salt, 'High-Level Manpower Movements in Northwest Europe and the Role of Careers: An Explanatory Framework', *International Migration Review*, XVII, 4 (Winter 1986), pp. 951–72; SOPEMI, *Continuous Reporting System*, above, n. 3.
19. EUROSTAT, *Demographic Statistics* (Brussels, EC, 1988); ISTAT, *Statistiche Demografiche* (Rome, ISTAT, 1988); INE, *Anuário Estatistico 1983* (Lisbon, INE, 1983).
20. See *Studi Emigrazione*, special issue on migration of foreigners in Italy, XXV, nos. 91–2 (1988).

11 Cultural linkages
Bruno de Witte

Integration can, generally speaking, be measured in three different ways: in terms of social interaction, in terms of political decision-making and in terms of common identity or consciousness.[1] Accordingly, West European integration in the field of culture may also be assessed along those three dimensions. I propose to examine briefly the first dimension, and then, somewhat more extensively, the second. The discussion on European identity will not directly be addressed, but will be present in the analysis both of 'informal' and of 'formal' interaction.

Informal interaction

Mapping the observable patterns of interaction within Western Europe, and with the outside world, is not an easy task. Before trying to analyse informal 'culture flows', we must first ask some perplexing preliminary questions: what sector of human activity do we define by the word *culture*; how can we define *flows* of culture; how can we *measure* those flows and how, finally, can we assess their *effects*?

'Culture'

Cultural interaction is one form of human interaction, which may be 'economic' or 'social', but also has some less obvious special features of its own. 'Cultural activities' (and 'cultural policy') are continental European concepts that are hardly used in countries like the United States or Britain where one prefers to use terms like 'the arts' or 'the media'. Yet, there are some justifications for attempting to analyse education, the media, and the arts under the common heading 'culture'.

With this broad meaning, the term is used extensively in international law and international relations, at the various geographical levels. In Unesco's official designation, culture is one of the catchwords alongside education and science but it has become common to use the term 'culture' for defining Unesco's scope of activity as a whole (that is, including education and science). The same has happened at the bilateral level. Agreements have been signed on quite a number of different topics in the cultural field. Yet, a practice has developed among states to conclude, alongside any specific agreements, also a treaty which covers the exchange of culture as a whole and which is simply called 'cultural agreement' or 'cultural cooperation agreement'[2] and includes schemes in the fields of education, the arts, and science. At the regional European level, finally, 'culture' has emerged as a similarly global denominator for a whole sector of activity.

The concept of culture adopted here is not founded merely on the pragmatic consideration that a number of fields happen to be considered together in relevant fora of international cooperation. It is also based on the assumption that the objects and processes brought under the heading 'culture' have some unifying characteristics. In much of sociological theory, culture is perceived as a societal (sub-)system whose specific function is the symbolic (as opposed to the material) reproduction of society, the creation of meaning in human society. All human activity, of course, shapes the pattern of life and therefore belongs, in the wide definition used by anthropologists, to culture. But one may also single out a number of specialized agencies (schools, the media, art institutions) that have been created for this specific purpose and therefore constitute the cultural system in a more narrow sense.

There is a paradox in this functionalist approach to culture: the specific function of the cultural sub-system is, to a large extent, to counterbalance excessive social differentiation by producing a collective *identity* overarching the functional roles in society and guaranteeing the cohesion of the nation or country as a whole. But in modern society, cultural institutions appear to be much less preoccupied with (collective) identity building and to act more often towards increasing mobility and individual differentiation.[3] Hence the tendency in recent years for governments once again to develop policies for fostering the national identity and for limiting the differentiating impact of transnational culture flows.

Culture 'flows'

The domain of culture, as defined above, is relevant to the study of international relations, because many cultural expressions can move across state borders. The term 'culture flows' is perhaps too expressive for these interactions, as it conveys the impression that one can observe a number of material events happening at the state border which, put together, constitute the flow of culture between any two countries. This may be true for *cultural goods* such as works of art, records and audio-tapes, films and videotapes, books and periodicals; and for *persons engaged in cultural activities* like art performers, students and teachers. There are also a large number of what could be called invisible operations: *capital flows* (like the remuneration of copyright holders)[4], trade in *services* (like broadcasting)[5] which are still to a certain extent encapsulated within international trade statistics. But a number of activities and practices have no transfrontier element but nevertheless involve a process of transnational diffusion, like the teaching of foreign languages, or the diffusion of books or films on foreign cultures.

Measuring culture flows

Transnational flows have definitely increased in recent years, although the degree of internationalization varies considerably. Among the various means of cultural expression, music and visual art travel more easily across cultural (and therefore also national) borders than does language. It is not surprising, therefore, to find a largely international market for records, for films and especially for modern art, while the market in the publishing sector is much more compartmentalized along national or linguistic lines. A second noticeable element is that the balance of culture flows very often does not correspond to the general balance of trade. France and Britain are major exporters of cultural goods, while West Germany and Japan are not; the United States has an immense trade surplus in this area, which contrasts with its overall trade situation.[6]

It is difficult to move beyond those general remarks and provide, even approximately, a quantitative view of culture flows. We have already seen that cultural trade statistics sometimes give an inaccurate view. They may also be unreliable, for a number of reasons. A first difficulty is that, in establishing international trade statistics, one needs rules of origin for deciding on the 'nationality' of the goods involved. The result very often does not reflect the cultural content of the product,[7] but rather business strategies of production and distribution.[8] Secondly, there are many *artificial* flows which do not supply a genuine demand for cultural products from the exporting state but are generated in order to circumvent regulations of the importing state. There are, probably, even more *illegal* flows that occur in breach of the law of either the importing or the exporting state and are, of course, unreported: the musical sector and the trade in antiquities[9] are prominent examples of this.

Despite all those problems, interesting statistics exist for selected sectors, such as student flows and broadcasting.[10]

Effects of culture flows

If the contours of the notion of culture and of culture flows, and the quantitative dimension of transnational cultural interaction, are so controversial, then it would seem extremely hazardous to venture into an analysis of the effects of this interaction. Yet many interpretations have been offered on this subject, and the formal regulation of culture, which will be examined in the rest of this paper, is indeed largely based on such interpretations.

There is the classic view of liberal internationalism that 'the exchange of ideas, and possibly also of artistic and literary productions, is one of the most promising methods of fostering the development of world understanding and a sense of moral and cultural community among the peoples of the world.'[11]

Another and opposed view, which has gained some prominence more recently, particularly in Unesco thinking, is that unchecked flows of culture turn the world into a 'global market' for cultural goods which jeopardizes the autonomous development of national cultures.[12]

Both these views may be said to focus excessively on the production-diffusion side of culture flows and on the strategies of the 'emitters', and to consider the final 'receivers' as more or less passive objects. Others emphasize the fact that the message may be reinterpreted or rejected by its receivers.[13] According to this view, the impact of many forms of cultural interaction is limited because they are caused not so much by the cultural preferences of the receivers as by financial convenience or economic market domination.

Formal regulation

The map of *formal interaction* in the field of culture does not correspond at all to the map of informal interaction. Formal cooperation is neither a natural outgrowth nor the direct source of informal interaction. There is a striking contrast, for instance, between the importance of informal flows across the Atlantic and the almost total absence of formal links, in this field, between the United States and European countries. Another major cultural link, that between the European core and its southern periphery which was caused by mass migration, is hardly institutionalized either. On the other hand, relations *between* Western European countries appear, generally speaking, less intense at the informal level than the pattern of institutionalized cooperation would lead one to think.[14]

This is not to deny that there is a link between formal and informal interaction. In fact, formal regulation is often intended precisely to redirect observable patterns of informal interaction. But the relation frequently works the other way: formal regulation comes about on the initiative of influential private actors in order to facilitate their transnational activities. In other words, some of those formal rules are *restrictive*, that is, they purport to limit culture flows that are considered undesirable; others are *permissive*, that is, designed to facilitate certain flows by removing existing obstacles. *International* rules are more often of the latter sort; they tend to expand cultural movement by removing national restrictions and to create a framework allowing for unhindered informal interaction between private actors. Typical sets of permissive rules are those of the GATT and, as will be shown below, of the EEC Treaty and many Conventions adopted within the Council of Europe. But in recent years 'European' regulation is also increasingly directed at limiting the interaction with non-European countries, either directly (for instance, the proposed quota of European programmes as a condition for allowing transfrontier television) or indirectly, by trying to redirect existing flows. Thus, common educational initiatives like the 'Erasmus' programme or the European University Institute in Florence may, in part, be considered as offering plausible alternatives for student flows that used to be directed towards the United States.

The Council of Europe

At the regional West European level, the Council of Europe is the main forum for day-to-day cultural cooperation. Culture is expressly included in the Council's field of activity, according to article 1(b) of its statute.[15] It is not valid to conclude from this, however, that the West European states wanted to locate their cultural cooperation within the framework of the Council of Europe, to the exclusion of any other (existing or future) multilateral institution such as the European Community. It is, rather, for the Member States of the Council to decide whether *specific* problems in the field of culture can more adequately be dealt with at the level of the Europe of the 23 or the Europe of the 12 or any other configuration.

The historical importance of the Council has, first of all, been to provide an institutional framework within which are elaborated and adopted international treaties whose purpose is to facilitate the free flow of culture.[16] Those, of course, are 'classical' instruments of international law, binding only those states which choose to sign and, subsequently, to ratify them; they are not comparable to EC regulations or directives that are binding for, and enforceable against, all the members of that organization.

Alongside those conventions, there is one which organizes future cultural relations between its signatories. This is the European Cultural Convention of 1954 which was also signed by a few non-members of the Council. Its article 3 provides that 'the Contracting Parties shall consult with one another within the framework of the Council of Europe with a view to concerted action in promoting cultural activities of European interest.' A number of intergovernmental bodies have been set up to undertake this 'concerted action': the Council for Cultural Co-operation,[17] the Standing Conference of European Ministers of Education, and a bewildering array of other, more specialized bodies[18] of which the most important, in recent times, has been the Steering Committee on the Mass Media.

This cumbersome institutional set-up provides a forum for the exchange of views and sharing of experiences in the field of cultural policy. The output consists mainly of studies, conferences, exhibitions and publicity, and sometimes also of formal but non-binding rules like resolutions and declarations (what is sometimes described as 'soft law'). The Council of Europe may optimistically be considered as a laboratory of ideas with some indirect influence on subsequent national policy-making. But it can hardly claim to have a cultural policy of its own; it remains very much a tool in the hands of the member governments who may choose to keep it dormant for some time and resurrect it for some new purpose, such as, recently, the regulation of transfrontier television, and cultural relations with Central and Eastern Europe.

The European Community

The general aim of the European Community is to facilitate *economic flows* between its member countries by the creation of a common market for goods, persons, services and capital. It was not obvious, at first, that this could have any consequences for cultural policies. Indeed, the EEC Treaty makes no mention of the words 'culture', 'education' or 'broadcasting' – not even after the recent amendment by the Single European Act.

Yet, it has now clearly been established, mainly through a number of judgments of the European Court of Justice, that there is no clear separation between economy and culture, and that the economic-sounding concepts used in the EEC Treaty may affect cultural goods and activities in so far as these have an economic dimension (which most of them have). Therefore, the EEC Treaty has had a 'cultural programme' from the very beginning (although this was only recently acknowledged): the *elimination of national obstacles against the free flow* of cultural goods and activities within the territory of the Community.

Thus, the *free movement of goods* (articles 30 to 36, EEC Treaty) applies, in principle, to cultural goods as to other goods. Article 36 allows, it is true, for an exception to free movement for reasons of 'protection of national treasures possessing artistic, historic or archaeological value', but there would have been no need for a provision excepting a limited category of cultural goods if the basic principle of free movement did not apply to all cultural goods in the first place. Indeed, the European Court of Justice confirmed early on that all products forming the object of a commercial transaction come under the rules on free movement of goods, whatever their other qualities.[19]

The same subordination of culture to general economic concepts occurs with the *freedom to provide services*, which, again according to the European Court of Justice, includes among other things the cross-border transmission of broadcasts.[20] This judicial move enabled the Commission to launch an ambitious project to (de)regulate transfrontier broadcasting which was first outlined in the Green Book *Television without Frontiers*, and then given concrete form in a Directive on transfrontier broadcasting which was adopted recently after several years of negotiation.[21]

The same happens with the free movement of persons. *Freedom of establishment* in other Community countries is, in principle, guaranteed to professionals and to self-employed operators or firms in the cultural and educational sector, as in any other sector of economic life. To facilitate this, the EEC Treaty expressly empowers the Council to adopt directives on the mutual recognition of diplomas and study certificates. The specific directives already enacted, and even more the recent directive on general recognition of diplomas in higher education,[22] will probably have a major influence on national educational policies.[23] The *free movement of workers* confers the right to take up employment in the cultural or educational sectors. Community nationals, for instance, cannot be excluded from employment as teachers in the national educational system of any Community member.[24]

All these rights are part of so-called 'negative integration', which is the process of abolition of existing national barriers to the mobility of goods and persons. Beyond that, the Community institutions have also developed 'positive integration' by adopting legislative acts which harmonize national rules and sometimes create autonomous Community rules. The two elements are often linked, both legally and politically, as can be illustrated by the example of the directive on transfrontier television. Its primary purpose is to eliminate existing

national rules impeding the free provision of broadcasting services from other
Community countries ('negative integration'); but the Commission thought at
the same time that this deregulation would only be acceptable if accompanied
by some measure of European 're-regulation' consisting of limited harmonization of broadcasting standards on such issues as advertising, the protection of
youth, and 'European' content ('positive integration').[25]

The growing involvement of the European Community in culture and
education would seem to provide an excellent illustration, and partial vindica-
tion, of functionalist theories of integration. 'Spillover' into the cultural sphere
takes place, roughly speaking, as follows.[26] Market integration for economic
activities implicitly but directly affects culture in its material form, but thereby
also indirectly in its symbolic significance. National cultural policies are limited
by those rules on market integration much more effectively than by any other
explicit form of cultural cooperation. This limitation of national powers may,
in turn, lead to the perception that some forms of regulation, to be effective,
must be transferred to the European level, in order to counterbalance the
undesirable effects of market integration. All this constitutes a dynamic process
which does not, at any given time, present a perfect equilibrium between the
'negative' and 'positive' dimensions of integration, but instead is marked by
major integration deficits which keep the process in motion.

Bilateral relations and sub-systems

There is a vast network of bilateral agreements on cultural matters between
almost all countries of the world, and across economic and ideological barriers.
While those agreements constituted only a marginal feature of international
relations until about 30 years ago, they are now one of the most frequent and
typical forms of intergovernmental cooperation.

Cultural relations between Western and socialist or Third World countries
tend to be based prevalently and almost exclusively on bilateral instruments
which allow for close control and easy withdrawal by the contracting parties.
They are sometimes 'the only device available to make large-scale cultural
exchange at all possible'.[27] This is not the case in the relations *between* Western
European countries. The free flow of culture is largely guaranteed both by the
ideological compatibility of their political systems and by the existence of
regional 'free-flow' arrangements like those examined in the preceding sections.

Still, even the multilateral European system is not an atomic structure. Each
of its member countries is also part of smaller networks that limit its freedom of
action and steer its activity within the multilateral system. Cultural relations are
marked, even within Western Europe, by the existence of special relationships
between two or more countries in which cultural exchange and cooperation is
more intense, to the extent of constituting in some cases a small *sub-system*.[28]
The striking thing about most of those special links is that they link EC
Member States with non-members. Cultural links therefore tend to cut across
political and economic links and this fact may go a long way in explaining some
of the difficulties facing the European Community in this area.

The social and historical reality underlying a first group of those special relationships is the existence of a *linguistic or cultural community* across state borders.

The *Dutch* language area is the only one of those situated entirely within the European Community. It is slowly emerging due to the disintegration of the Belgian nation-state which has provided the Flemish community with a large amount of autonomy in cultural matters, including their 'external' aspects. However, despite the creation of a veritable (bilateral) international organization, the *Nederlandse Taalunie*,[29] the Dutch language area has so far not become a sub-system with clear political contours. Linguistic unity masks profound cultural differences between the two partners.[30]

The *German* language area and the *Nordic* cultural community, on the other hand, consist of countries situated both inside and outside the Community. At the informal level, there are strong links between West Germany, Austria and Switzerland,[31] but formal ties are few and mainly recent.[32] Cooperation between West and East Germany is, of course, an entirely different matter. The free flow of culture has, for a long time, been severely restricted from the Eastern side, with the major exception of broadcasting.[33] Formal exchange of cultural activities between the two countries has increased since the signing of the cultural agreement of 1986, and the most recent events may give a fresh boost to both formal and informal cooperation, and lead to the emergence of a genuine cultural sub-system within Europe.

Within the *Nordic Council* (discussed in more detail in Chapter 7), the fully fledged multi-purpose organization of the five Nordic countries, culture plays a relatively much more important role than in the Council of Europe or the European Community. There is a special Secretariat for Nordic Cultural Co-operation, alongside the general Secretariat, and the cultural budget is only slightly lower than the general budget supporting all other forms of cooperation. The Council has dismantled some barriers to cultural mobility (for instance, in the area of recognition of diplomas), and has financially supported the exchange of culture and sponsored cooperation in (satellite) broadcasting.

Special relationships are also based on the existence of a *colonial legacy*. At least three countries of the European Community are linked to a multitude of non-European countries over which they have exercised colonial power and to which they brought their language and other forms of cultural expression.

The *Commonwealth* links Britain to many of its former colonies in the form of a general-purpose international organization which promotes educational exchange but is very timid in other cultural sectors.[34] The *informal* cultural influence of Britain in the world is, in any case, vastly superior to anything done through the formal channels provided by the Commonwealth.

The *Hispanidad* is not a formal international organization,[35] but only a political reality which starts to emerge from the network of bilateral cooperation agreements linking Spain to its former American colonies, which are being reactivated in recent years.

Unlike those two clusters, the *Francophonie* both specializes in cultural relations and is strongly institutionalized, around the *Agence de Coopération Culturelle et Technique*.[36] Politically, it is somewhat more ambiguous: it perpetuates the colonial legacy by promoting the cultural links between France and its former, mainly African, colonies; but it is also to a large extent a language-based movement including some very active industrialized states other than France.[37] It is sometimes considered an impediment to Europe-wide cooperation because of its perceived French nationalism, but is probably less centrifugal than the Commonwealth. Much of the thinking about American cultural imperialism and the need for multilateral cooperation in order to protect national identities was initiated within the Francophone world and was later transferred, and almost officially accepted, at the European level.

There is one bilateral cultural sub-system situated within the European Community which does not belong to any of the preceding categories but can be considered as the mere reflection and instrument of an underlying *political* sub-system: the *Franco-German relationship*. This began with a cultural agreement in 1954, but did not depart from the usual model of bilateral cultural cooperation until the Elysée Treaty of 1963. This treaty not only established a formal international organization between the two countries, the *Office franco-allemand pour la jeunesse*,[38] but also made cultural cooperation into a major instrument for reinforcing the political entente and the economic solidarity between the two countries.[39] Franco-German relations have been at their best where culture merges into technology (the media) or into 'personal relations' generally (youth exchange schemes, town twinnings), but much less effective in the core areas of cultural policy like educational cooperation or language learning.[40]

Interactions within Western Europe

Cultural policy shows very clearly that there is what William Wallace calls a 'discontinuity among the network of regimes'. The pattern of formal cultural cooperation, unlike cooperation in the economic field, is not strongly centred on the European Community. But things are rapidly changing in this area. I will end this contribution by making two rather contradictory statements about the recent evolution. On the one hand, there is a growing overlap between the various networks and a bewildering resort to the so-called 'variable geometry'. On the other hand, the European Community, which had been entirely absent from this area, is now gradually assuming a role which is more adjusted to its general political predominance within the network of West European regimes. The contradiction between those two trends is perhaps apparent rather than real: the trend may be towards a non-homogeneous system of cultural cooperation, in which the European Community is an initiator, leading actor and point of reference, but does not always provide the institutional framework of action.

The prevalence of 'variable geometry'

To start with, it may be useful to illustrate the bewildering accumulation of levels of cooperation by examining recent efforts in one particular and now fashionable area, that of *media regulation* in its various aspects.[41]

The regulation of transfrontier *broadcasting* of television has been the object of a race between the Council of Europe and the European Community. A proposal for regulating it had been under consideration by the Commission since 1984. Only much later, at the Vienna Conference of Ministers in 1986, was it decided that the Council of Europe should work out a convention on the same theme. Political agreement was first reached within the Council of Europe framework, and the Commission's 'defeat' was made official when the European Council of Rhodes in December 1988 considered it 'important that the Community's effort should be deployed in a manner consistent with the Council of Europe Convention' and noted that 'the Commission will adapt the proposal in the light of the Council of Europe Convention'.[42] While the Council of Europe Convention was adopted and opened for signature in the spring of 1989, the EC Directive met with some additional opposition and was finally adopted, in a considerably watered down version, in October 1989.[43]

The saga of the creation of a *common European television channel* also features several actors. The European Parliament has repeatedly expressed the wish that such a channel should be set up,[44] but without as yet convincing either Commission or Council to take strong action. Within the European Broadcasting Union,[45] the satellite programme 'Europa TV' was produced for some years by five members but was broadcast rarely and was discontinued when its initiators lost (financial) interest. The French- and German-language public broadcast services each transmits a common programme on satellite, TV-5 and 3-Sat. The latest initiative was taken within the framework of the Franco-German alliance; in a common declaration of 4 November 1988 on the occasion of a Franco-German summit, the French government and the German *Länder* agreed to create a common cultural channel to be broadcast by one of the satellites which the French and Germans have been launching together for some years now.[46]

There is a strong motive for European countries to cooperate in the area of *audiovisual coproduction*, to pool resources for large production budgets comparable to those of the United States, and to ensure at the same time a wide distribution of the product. There has been, for many years now, a very dense network of *bilateral* agreements on film production, based usually on formal treaties between the countries concerned; even now, bilateral cooperation both for cinema and for television production is much more common than multi-lateral European ventures.

Still, the latter have multiplied recently, and it is useful to list some of them. In 1985, the Commission proposed a European Community aid scheme for non-documentary cinema and television coproductions.[47] The proposal was not adopted by the Council of Ministers because several countries, among them Denmark and the UK, had misgivings about the substance or about the Community's competence to act in this field.[48] Subsequently, the Commission proposed a more modest 'action programme' which later developed into the 'Media' project: a rather small fund aiding what are defined as 'European' low-budget films in the production and distribution phase, and which is now (1989) gaining momentum.[49]

The more glamorous part of the Commission proposal was taken up again by the French government in the Council of Europe orbit and became the 'Eurimage' project. This is a more classical form of international cooperation grouping most of the EC Member States and a few non-EC countries like

Switzerland and Sweden; however, its budget is very modest and consists of separate national contributions.[50] At the same time, the European Community and the Council of Europe jointly organized in 1988 the European Cinema and Television Year which featured a number of disparate and mainly symbolic activities. Still in 1988, a European Fund for Multilingual Production was set up jointly by the 'Media' programme, the European Broadcasting Union and the 'European Alliance for Television and Culture'.[51]

Fearing that all those global European programmes might pay insufficient attention to their needs, 12 small and medium-sized public-service broadcasting organizations established, also in 1988, a 'Group for the Development of an AudioVisual Identity for Europe' ('David') to improve the exchange and production of television programmes.[52] Finally, the so-called 'Audiovisual Eureka', launched by the President of France, and endorsed by the European Councils of Hanover and Rhodes in 1988, was to be prepared by a large 'Audiovisual conference' in the autumn of 1989 and to come into operation in 1990. It is the most ambitious of all the projects[53] and seems intended to incorporate 'Media', 'Eurimage' and any other scheme to be proposed by an undefined number of states from the whole of Europe[54] under very loose institutional arrangements inspired on the existing 'technological' 'Eureka' programme.[55] While the political initiative clearly lies with the countries of the European Community, the intention is to keep the operation of the programme outside the ordinary Community decision-making process.

The audiovisual scene offers an extreme example of 'variability' in which 'geometry' seems entirely lost. Yet, the tendency is present in other fields of cultural cooperation as well. The French government chose it as its general approach when it presented, in 1986, its *Livre bleu* on cooperation in the field of education and culture. It proposed to concentrate on a number of substantive policy goals and to allow the maximum possible flexibility both in the choice of the appropriate forum (European Community, Council of Europe, or any other possible organization) and the participating states.[56] This idea was, to a certain extent, officially endorsed by France's Community partners at the June 1988 meeting of the Ministers of Culture of the EC where it was decided that cultural cooperation could henceforth take place in three alternative settings: including all Member States, as cooperation 'à la carte' with less than 12 participants, or as cooperation with non-EC states.

How is this tendency to be explained? The realist school of international relations may emphasize the political will of governments not to be constrained by over-rigid institutional mechanisms and their wish to lead parliamentary and other control organs astray in the intergovernmental thicket. Organizational sociologists may want to point to the tendency of every international organization and its members (whether they are international officials or representatives of the national governments) to expand its own reach without considering the need for overall harmony.[57]

But why does this happen above all in the cultural sector? Could it be because this is a sector of symbolic politics in which it matters more for governments to be seen taking numerous initiatives in various settings rather than developing effective and coherent forms of regulation? However this may be, the multiplication of new shapes of cooperation, although it may be convenient for politicians, and perhaps for some industrialists as well, has its own costs. The democratic deficit, which is generally the weak side of the European integration process, is particularly gaping here.

The EC's expanding role

Relations between the European Community and the Council of Europe in the cultural sector[58] have evolved from mutual ignorance and duplication of efforts to a situation of diffuse rivalry. Lip-service is repeatedly paid to the need for a division of labour and for respect for the identity and comparative advantages of each institution, but reality shows, instead, a constant tendency for the stronger organization – the European Community – to invade the territory of the weaker. The Council does not possess the organizational resources of its rival and depends entirely on the decision of the national governments to prefer, in a particular instance, the broader forum of the Europe of the 23.[59]

The Council's role in education has already been marginalized. The results achieved in a few years within the European Community, on matters like the recognition of diplomas, the equal treatment of foreign nationals, the mobility of students and teachers, and international exchange programmes, are more impressive than anything that has happened in 30 years of the Council of Europe.[60]

Nevertheless, the Council of Europe is still sometimes regarded favourably by national governments: its encompassing geographical scope is better suited to problems which cannot be confined to the territory of the 12; its open-ended field of activity is undisturbed by qualms about competence; its primarily non-economic nature allows cultural policy arguments to be duly considered; it permits a variety of regulatory constructions; and its rules are comparatively less incisive and 'threatening'. All those factors may have contributed to its resounding but as yet precarious[61] 'victory' over the European Community on the regulation of transfrontier television. The same factors may also give the Council a new lease of life as the forum for the construction of a 'common European house'. Culture is an appropriate area to start this intensified cooperation between Western and Central-Eastern Europe.

The increasing cultural role of the European Community is also revealed by the attitude of its members. Culture and education have recently developed into particularly sensitive areas in which the Member States resent Community involvement and stress the need for 'subsidiarity'. There is a diffuse unrest in many Member States, but three in particular have expressed considerable reluctance to move forward in this area: Denmark, West Germany and the United Kingdom.[62]

The motives for this uneasiness vary. There is the general opposition to the extension of Community powers and the corresponding loss of 'national sovereignty' which becomes particularly vivid for policy areas that are not even explicitly mentioned in the founding treaties. There is the fear, which is more specific to the field of culture, that market integration in this area may erode national identities (the smaller countries) or existing privileged links with non-member countries (Denmark and West Germany). There is also the concern of

regional institutions that growing involvement of the Community may affect
their autonomy in one of the few areas which they were hitherto able to shield
against central interference. Whether or not all those misgivings are well-
founded, they certainly affect the possibility of further developments at the
Community level. The recent struggles around, for instance, the 'Erasmus' and
'Lingua' programmes[63] illustrate those difficulties.

Not only does the Community affect the capacity of its Member States (and
sub-state actors) to conduct autonomous cultural policies, but it also displaces
existing *bilateral* programmes between them. This was shown explicitly by the
European Court of Justice in the *Matteucci* case of 1988. Candidates for
scholarships awarded in the framework of the German-Belgian cultural agreement had to be, as in almost all agreements of this type, citizens of one of the
two partner states. Such a provision, the Court ruled, is contrary to European
Community law in so far as it excludes Community workers, or members of
their families, living in another Member State. Miss Matteucci, who was the
daughter of Italian migrants living in Belgium, and was herself employed in
Belgium, could therefore not be denied the right to apply for the scholarship.
The European Court also firmly rejected the view, defended (among others) by
the French government, that cultural relations between states were a 'domaine
réservé' in which the Community should not interfere.

Not only do Community rules directly affect the operation of bilateral
cooperation agreements, but the EC has also set up its own educational
exchange programmes, namely 'Erasmus', 'Comett' and now 'Lingua', which
tend to displace similar bilateral programmes.[64] The development of European
audiovisual cooperation programmes (inside or outside the formal Community
framework) may in future have the same effect on bilateral coproduction
arrangements.

European integration, culture and identity

The process of economic unification in Europe has certainly affected the
informal patterns of cultural interaction, even if it has not redirected them in a
fundamental way. On the other hand, a decision was made in the 1950s to
separate the economic and cultural spheres on the formal level, and to launch
a process of economic integration which would leave unaffected national
competences in culture and education. Intergovernmental cooperation would
be possible in this area (mainly within the framework of the Council of
Europe) but no transfer of competences would take place to the supranational
level. This initial choice was never formally revoked, not even at the time when
the EEC Treaty was globally amended through the Single European Act.[65]
Nevertheless, as we have seen, the European Community has recently been
making considerable inroads in the cultural field.

One possible reaction is to welcome those developments as a happy
consequence of the classic European spillover mechanism. According to this
view, the decision to omit culture from the European Community treaties was
a strategic but not a substantive choice. Cultural initiatives could gradually
grow from economic interdependence. Indeed, cultural initiatives may even be

instrumental in fostering a feeling of loyalty, a sense of 'European identity', which in turn may bring forward the process of economic and political unification. This strategy, which was attempted rather clumsily in the late 1970s and early 1980s,[66] is strongly present in a number of recent initiatives of the Commission that are grouped under the heading 'a People's Europe'.

On the other hand, there are those who think that the separation between economy and culture was a substantive policy choice which is still valid and should be respected. They reject the idea of creating a 'European identity', and stress that European integration is original precisely because it attempts to provide peaceful coexistence, economic unification and (possibly) political cooperation without affecting the cultural identity of the Member States, that is, without creating a nation-state on the nineteenth-century model.

Even if one accepts the latter view, one must recognize that a separation of the economic and cultural spheres is becoming increasingly artificial, and that one should therefore attempt not merely to *prevent* the Community from entering the field, but also to *steer* its policy into the appropriate direction. Both national and regional identities may sometimes better be protected by closer formal interaction at the European level than by the separate policies of each Member State.

Notes

1. For this tripartite distinction, see Daniel Frei, 'Integrationsprozesse. Theoretische Erkenntnisse und praktische Folgerungen', in Werner Weidenfeld, (ed), *Die Identität Europas* (Bonn, Bundeszentrale für politische Bildung, 1985), pp. 115–31.
2. See the many hundreds of bilateral treaties going under those names in the *World Treaty Index*, 2nd edn, vol. 5, keyword index.
3. See Alain Touraine, 'Les deux faces de l'identité', *Quaderni di sociologia*, 1979, no. 2, pp. 407–19.
4. Capital flows constitute, of course, a negative indicator of culture flows: the money goes to the country exporting its cultural product.
5. In the framework at least of European Community law, transfrontier commercial broadcasts are considered as 'services'. See further below.
6. It has been suggested that there may be a causal connection between the specific pattern of cultural trade and the overall trade pattern. Culture importers obtain a detailed knowledge of the exporting country's culture; they can adapt their market strategies accordingly and start a successful economic counter-penetration (see René Jean Ravault, 'Défense de l'identité culturelle par les réseaux traditionnels de coerséduction', *International Political Science Review*, vol. 7, 1986, pp. 251–80, at p. 264 ff).
7. A few random examples: records exported from the UK need not feature British artists; books published in Germany may be written by Swiss authors; a Belgian ballet company may have few Belgian dancers. Films have, for most legal and statistical purposes, the nationality of their producer, but their director, main actors and technicians may well be citizens of other countries.
8. Some cultural sectors, like film and television production, are dominated by multinational enterprises which can organize production and distribution according to their economic or fiscal convenience, rather than according to the cultural

characteristics of the products concerned. See, for instance, Holde Lhoest, *Les Multinationales de l'audiovisuel en Europe* (Paris, Presses Universitaires de France, 1986).

9. Switzerland, for instance, appears as a major exporter of antiques; yet, many of these objects originate in Italy, or similar countries with severe export restrictions, from which they have previously been illegally exported. In this case, the 'real' culture flow (from Italy) goes unreported while the reported flow (from Switzerland) is 'artificial'.

10. Figures on student flows in Europe appear above, Chapter 10. Broadcasting is discussed briefly above, Chapter 8. More generally, research has been done on two types of television flows. The first type is the trade in programmes between broadcasting corporations and/or independent producers of different countries; see e.g. the six-country study (UK, Ireland, Italy, Norway, Sweden, Finland) by G.P. Chapman, J.H. Johnson & P.R. Gould, *International Television Flows in Western Europe*, 5 vols (Cambridge, Development Policy, 1986). The other type of data refer to actual transfrontier broadcasting by airwaves, cable or satellite and to the viewing habits of its receivers; see Olle Findhal, 'Language in the Age of Satellite Television', *European Journal of Communication*, 1989, pp. 133–59; Els De Bens, 'Cable Penetration and Competition among Belgian and Foreign Stations', *European Journal of Communication*, 1986, pp. 477–92 (and the later article by the same author in *Publizistik*, 1988, pp. 352–65).

11. K.D. Mc Carthy, 'From Cold War to Cultural Development: the International Cultural Activities of the Ford Foundation', *Daedalus*, Winter 1987, pp. 92–117, at p. 97.

12. This question is often addressed in the context of American cultural dominance or 'imperialism'. Several well-known studies of international media flows reflect this view: the 'Mc Bride Report', *Many Voices, One World* (Paris, Unesco, 1980); Cees J. Hamelink, *Cultural Autonomy in Global Communications* (New York, Longman, 1983); Armand Mattelart, et al., *International Image Markets. In Search of an Alternative Perspective* (London, Comedia Publishing Group, 1984).

13. 'Ce n'est pas parce qu'il y a, effectivement, intention de persuasion et existence d'un imposant appareil d'exportation culturelle qu'il y a pout autant et nécessairement "Conquête des Esprits"' (Ravault, op. cit., above, n. 6, p. 255). The same sceptical view is expressed, within the specific context of television flows, by Michael Tracey, 'The Poisoned Chalice? International Television and the Idea of Dominance', *Daedalus*, Fall 1985, pp. 17–56.

14. Writing about cinema and television Jack Lang found that it was 'as if the countries of Europe, encumbered as they are with all sorts of historic, linguistic and sociological barriers, were more or less impervious to each other, while the European market – unified – existed only for the Americans' (Jack Lang, 'The Future of European Television and Cinema', *European Affairs*, 1988/2, pp. 12–20, at p. 18).

15. Article 1(b) proclaims that the Council's aim of achieving greater European unity 'shall be pursued through the organs of the Council by discussion of questions of common concern and by agreements and common action in economic, social, cultural, scientific, legal and administrative matters and in the maintenance and further realization of human rights and fundamental freedoms'.

16. Those Conventions are: the European Convention on the Equivalence of Diplomas leading to Admission to Universities (1953); the European Convention on the Equivalence of Periods of University Studies (1956); the European Agreement concerning Programme Exchanges by means of Television Films (1958); the European Convention on the Academic Recognition of University Qualifications (1959); the European Agreement on the Protection of Television Broadcasts (1960);

the European Agreement for the Prevention of Broadcasts Transmitted from Stations outside National Territories (1965); the European Convention on the Protection of the Archaeological Heritage (1969); the European Agreement on Continued Payment of Scholarships to Students Studying Abroad (1969); the European Convention on Offences Relating to Cultural Property (1985); the Convention for the Protection of the Architectural Heritage (1985); and the European Convention on Transfrontier Television (1989). Some of those treaties have had some impact on cultural and educational exchange; some others not at all. The most recently adopted convention may well prove to be the most important of them all.

17. A survey of the activities of this body can now be found in its annual report, the first of which was published in 1988: *Annual Report 1987 of the Council for Cultural Co-operation* (Strasbourg, 1988).

18. A survey of those bodies, with some useful tables, can be found in the appendix to the *Report on European Cultural Cooperation* presented by Mr Müller, *Parliamentary Assembly of the Council of Europe*, Doc. 5871, 19 April 1988.

19. *Commission* v *Italy*, case 7/68, [1968] European Court Reports 423.

20. *Sacchi*, case 155/73, [1973] European Court Reports 1974, 409, at 427. It is not yet clear from the case law of the Court whether only *commercial* broadcasts are to be considered as 'services' or whether *public service* broadcasts are also to be included.

21. Directive 89/552 of 3 October 1989, in *Official Journal* 1989, L 298/23. The first Commission Proposal for a Directive had been made on 19 March 1986: see *Supplement 5/86 to the Bulletin of the European Communities*.

22. Directive 89/48 of 21 December 1988, *Official Journal* 1989, L 19/16.

23. See Chiara Zilioli, 'The Recognition of Diplomas and its Impact on Educational Policies', in Bruno De Witte, (ed), *European Community Law of Education* (Baden-Baden, Nomos, 1989), pp. 51–70.

24. This point was decided by the European Court of Justice in a recent judgment; case 33/88, *P. Allue & C.M. Coonan* v *University of Venice*, judgment of 30 May 1989 (not yet reported).

25. On the link between negative and positive integration in the field of culture, see more generally, Bruno De Witte, 'Cultural Policy: The Complementarity of Negative and Positive Integration', in J. Schwarze & H.G. Schermers, (eds), *Structure and Dimensions of European Community Policy* (Baden-Baden, Nomos, 1988), pp. 195–204.

26. For general considerations on spillover theory and its relevance to the recent evolution of the European Community, see below, Chapter 16.

27. Thomas Oppermann, 'Cultural Agreements', in *Encyclopedia of Public International Law*, vol. 9, 1986, pp. 56–8, at p. 57.

28. For the notion of 'sub-system', see above, Chapter 6.

29. The *Taalunie* was created by a treaty on 9 September 1980. It is a traditional international organization with its panoply of institutions: a Committee of Ministers, an Interparliamentary Commission, a Council for the Dutch Language and Literature, and a General Secretariat. Its main tasks are common 'corpus' planning of the Dutch language and its promotion abroad. See Rita Hamerlynck, 'De Nederlandse Taalunie', *Revue belge de droit international*, 1986, pp. 80–101.

30. The Dutch language area, of course, does not correspond to the *political* sub-system Benelux, and may indeed be weakened by the existence of the latter. On the other hand, the difficulties of Benelux may be due, in part, to the fear among the French-speaking Belgians that the organization will become dominated by Dutch speakers and their interests.

31. Luxembourg, although linguistically a Germanic country, is part of the formal network of Francophone countries, and keeps its formal links with Germany rather

loose. This little country prefers, above all, informal links 'tous azimuts' through its dynamic broadcasting company CLT.

32. An example of formal cooperation is the Drei-Sat satellite television channel set up by the public service broadcasting organizations of the three countries.

33. In a first phase, from 1952 to 1971, East Germany attempted, by a variety of means, to restrict the reception of West German television. Since 1971, those restrictions have gradually been lifted. It is estimated that almost 90% of East German viewers receive West German programmes, and that the viewing rates for these programmes equal or, sometimes, exceed those for domestic programmes. See Norbert Linke, 'Die Rezeption der Programme von ARD und ZDF in der DDR als Gegenstand der SED-Kommunikationspolitik', *Publizistik*, 1987, pp. 45–68.

34. Among the specialized satellite institutions within the Commonwealth are the Conference of Commonwealth Education Ministers, the Association of Commonwealth Universities and the Commonwealth Foundation. On the latter, see J. Chadwick, *The unofficial Commonwealth: the story of the Commonwealth Foundation, 1965–1980* (London, Allen & Unwin, 1982).

35. But there are a number of non-governmental organizations operating in the field of Hispanic cultural relations; see the list in M. Couderc, 'L'Espagne et l'Amérique latine', in *Problèmes politiques et sociaux*, no. 595, November 1988, pp. 47–8.

36. On the organizational set-up of the Francophonie, see the brief account by Xavier Deniau, *La Francophonie* (Paris, Presses Universitaires de France, 1983). The interesting official report *Etat de la francophonie dans le monde* (Paris, Documentation Française, 1986) provides a detailed account of both formal and informal links between French-speaking countries.

37. Belgium, Luxembourg and Canada are 'Etats membres' of the *Agence*, while Quebec and New Brunswick are 'gouvernements associés' with full rights of participation. Switzerland is a reluctant member. It participates only in the work of non-governmental organizations operating in the shadow of the *Agence*, like the 'Association internationale des professeurs de français' or the 'Association des universités partiellement ou entièrement de langue française'.

38. See Henri Ménudier, *L'Office franco-allemand pour la jeunesse* (Paris, A, Colin, 1988).

39. A comparative analysis of the three bilateral relationships established between Britain, France and Germany clearly shows that the *formal* links between France and Germany are qualitatively superior to those established by either of those two with Britain; for *informal* links, however, the picture is exactly the opposite (Caroline Bray, 'Cultural and Information Policy in Bilateral Relations' in Roger Morgan and Caroline Bray, (eds), *Partners and Rivals in Europe: Britain, France and Germany* (Aldershot, Gower, 1986), pp. 78–101).

40. See the global evaluation by Robert Picht, 'Die Fremdheit des Partners: genügen die kulturellen Beziehungen?', in Picht (ed), *Das Bündnis im Bündnis. Deutsch-französische Beziehungen im internationalen Spannungsfeld* (Berlin, Severin und Siedler, 1982), pp. 193–219.

41. I will deal here only with *formal* cooperation. The situation becomes even more complex when one takes account of the immense network of informal business agreements in this area as well as the internal cross-border arrangements of multinational enterprises. Of course, the preferences and strategies of the private media conglomerates often influence the choice of a specific forum for *formal* cooperation, but we cannot examine those connections in detail here. A useful study of all actors in this industry is that by A. Lange & J.L. Renaud, *L'Avenir de l'industrie audiovisuelle européenne* (Manchester, European Institute for the Media, 1988).

42. European Council of Rhodes, Conclusions by the Presidency, in *Agence Europe*,

special edn, 4 December 1988, p. 4.
43. Directive 89/552 of 3 October 1989, *Official Journal* 1989, L 298/23.
44. See its Resolutions of 12 March 1982 and of 30 March 1984.
45. The EBU is a semi-governmental organization, grouping all West European public broadcasting corporations. In one of its activities, the well-known 'Eurovision' programme exchange scheme, it also includes countries like Yugoslavia, Tunisia and Israel, whereby 'Europe' assumes a very peculiar shape.
46. See 'Gemeinsame Erklärung zum deutsch-französischen Fernsehkulturkanal', in *Media Perspektiven* 1988, pp. 795. On the satellite programme generally, as an example of bilateral technological cooperation, see Simone Courteix, 'Les satellites de télévision directe: un programme commun franco-allemand', *Annuaire française de droit international*, 1981, pp. 648–60.
47. COM(85) 174 final of 29 April 1985, published in *Official Journal* 1985, C 125/85; and the Amended Proposal COM(85) 800 final of 19 December 1985.
48. See *European Report*, 20 December 1985.
49. 'Media' stands for 'Mesures d'encouragement pour le développement de l'industrie audiovisuelle'.
50. The project was set up by Resolution (88) 15 of the Committee of Ministers of the Council of Europe.
51. The latter is a private association whose objective is to raise private funding for the production of scripts (see R. Schenker 'European television. A problem of choice, of intent?', *EBU Review. Programmes, Administration, Law*, September 1988, pp. 36–8).
52. See *EBU Review, Programmes, Administration, Law*, September 1988, p. 46. The members are from Austria, Belgium, Denmark, Finland, Greece, Ireland, the Netherlands, Norway, Portugal, Sweden and Switzerland.
53. The political ideas behind the project are investigated by Jack Lang, 'The Future of European Television and Cinema', *European Affairs*, 2/88, pp. 12–20.
54. East European countries are expressly invited to participate; see European Council of Rhodes, Conclusions by the Presidency, Annex II, in *Agence Europe*, special edn, 4 December 1988, p. 6.
55. Those arrangements have been summarized thus: 'Eureka adopte les règles simples d'une conférence diplomatique permanente, l'organisation légère est extra-communautaire, la souplesse en est la règle fondamentale' (Claude André Colliard, 'Eureka ou une coopération technologique européenne', *Revue trimestrielle de droit européen*, 1988, pp. 6–22, at p. 22).
56. See Jean Vergès, 'La voie intergouvernementale: le "Livre Bleu" français', in Bruno De Witte, (ed), *European Community Law of Education* (above, n. 23).
57. Organizational sociologists have seldom made *international* organizations the object of their concern; but see Gayl D. Ness & Steven R. Brechin, 'Bridging the Gap: International Organizations as Organizations', *International Organization*, 1988, pp. 245–73. They consider (international) organizations as 'live collectivities interacting with their environments' and containing 'members who seek to use the organization for their own ends, often struggling with others over the content and allocation of the product' (p. 247).
58. Michael Palmer's unpublished paper for the Brussels conference of this project explored this relationship in detail.
59. See, for instance, the severe assessment by Müller in his *Report on European Cultural Co-operation* for the Parliamentary Assembly of the Council of Europe (above, n. 18), at p. 6:
'The Council of Europe is in a difficult position in competing with increasing Community activity in the cultural area; the Council of Europe lacks the resources to keep up the pace in activities and representations; it lacks the funds to compete

with grants and publicity; it is gradually losing its separate identity (shared parliamentary seat; flag and anthem; narrowing geographical gap); its initiatives are being regularly taken up in the Community context and its methods (such as intergovernmental co-operation) adopted by the Community. It has begun seriously to lose its interest for governments (civil servants), for young people (youth organizations), for the media and for politicians.'

The obsession with the Community is also borne out by the number of pages devoted, in Müller's report', to the section dealing with the 'Growth of European Community involvement'.

60. For a (legal) analysis of those developments in the EC, see Bruno De Witte, (ed), *European Community Law of Education* (above, n. 23). For a short survey of the Commission's policy, see Sarah Evans, 'Education and Training in the European Community', in J. Jamar and H. Wallace, (eds), *EEC-EFTA. More than just Good Friends?*, (Bruges: College of Europe, 1988), pp. 189–210.

61. The Convention on Transfrontier Television was adopted in May 1989, but will enter into force only after it has been signed by seven states; even then, any state will be bound by this treaty only if it decides to ratify it. Conversely, the EC Directive adopted in October 1989 forces all Member States to bring their legislation into conformity with its rules within a given period of time.

62. But practically all other countries have their own particular reasons to be concerned as well. There was a sudden uproar in France when the 'European quota' provisions in the draft directive on transfrontier television were watered down; the Italians grumble at the Commission's intention to liberalize intra-Community trade in works of art; the Dutch government is preoccupied with the consequences of the internal market for its policy of cultural subsidies; the Irish policy of protecting its national language is currently being examined by the European Court of Justice for its possible incompatibility with Community rules on free movement of workers (in the *Groener* case).

63. The Commission and the Council of Ministers (i.e. the Member States) have fought out their debate about the appropriate legal basis of the 'Erasmus' programme before the European Court of Justice: case 242/87, *Commission* v *Council*, judgment of 30 May 1989 (not yet reported). As for 'Lingua', the part of this Commission proposal which dealt with school exchanges was deleted at Council level on the insistence of the British and German governments that it constituted undue interference with matters of general educational policy (see *Agence Europe*, 24 May 1989).

64. West Germany was reluctant to adopt the 'Erasmus' programme because it felt that its own well-developed student scholarship programmes covered its present needs, and would suffer from the operation of 'Erasmus'.

65. Proposals to include provisions on education and culture in the Single European Act could not find the unanimous agreement of all Member States; see J.W. de Zwaan, 'The Single European Act: Conclusion of a Unique Document', *Common Market Law Review*, 1986, pp. 747–65, at p. 759.

66. At that time, one found a number of proposals in the cultural field which were inspired by the need to reinforce the feeling of loyalty to the Community at a time when economic integration no longer seemed to provide tangible benefits; see Bruno De Witte, 'Building Europe's Image and Identity', in A. Rijksbaron, W.H. Roobol, & M. Weisglas, (eds), *Europe from a Cultural Perspective* (Amsterdam, Nijgh en Van Ditmar, 1987), pp. 132–39.

Part IV
Legal and institutional patterns

12 Making multilateral negotiations work
Helen Wallace

In the European Community (EC) ambitious goals are now matched by substantive progress. The objective of unifying the European market by 1992 made events in Brussels hot news.[1] Other long-term aims, long consigned to the pending tray, have been brought forward for action, notably economic and monetary union and European political union.[2] West European governments have become engaged in serious discussions about collective defence on a more European basis, at the levels of both broad policy and practical cooperation.[3] Other European organizations are producing some solid evidence of joint endeavour – the refurbished European Space Agency (ESA), the Eureka framework and the long dormant Western European Union (WEU) are just three examples.[4] Impatiently sitting on the sidelines, the other European neighbours and associates of the EC are pressing for a share of the action through either accession or redefined association.[5] Since the dramatic events of 1989 in Eastern Europe the EC has emerged even more explicitly as a model of transnational collaboration.

But as a model of what kind? At least part of that model is the apparent ability of the EC to resolve conflicts of interests through collective negotiation and to turn the agreements that ensue into solid common rules and policies, which in turn create shared interests that can be sustained.[6] This chapter argues that by dint of persistent effort and identifiable procedures and habits the EC has acquired a robust and innovative mode of negotiating that goes a long way to explaining both its achievements and its magnetic attraction for other European countries. One could indeed go further and argue not only that this mode of multilateral negotiation is firmly embedded in the EC, but that it has also had an impact on the way business is transacted in many other West European organizations.

Towards an explanation

Where should we search for explanations that pass the test of conceptual coherence and empirical plausibility? Part of the answer lies in a better understanding of the empirical evidence on how bargains are struck in Brussels, and part in an assessment of the accumulated patterns of behaviour of the main protagonists in the process. This chapter summarizes the empirical evidence, recounts the key features of the bargain that became the Single European Act (SEA) and ventures some observations on the patterns of behaviour. The thrust of the analysis is that the robust Community of the late-1980s was no sudden or fragile achievement, but rather, to a significant degree, a return on investments made over many years in establishing a particular style of multilateral negotiation.

The European negotiating process has intensity in the sheer volume and frequency of interactions, and range in the variety of issue areas touched. There are systematic decision rules and emergent codes of conduct and behavioural norms.[7] Moreover, the rules are backed by a legal framework that has proved to be amenable to upgrading, as the adoption of the SEA demonstrated.[8] Negotiators deal simultaneously in several 'currencies', and link accumulated 'credits' and 'debits' across issue areas. They have understandings about reciprocity and these are spread over time, indeed often over quite long time-scales. The shadow of the future impinges markedly on negotiators and seems to push them towards the identification of collective interests, both substantive and systemic.[9]

New members of the negotiating club have been absorbed and socialized more readily than could easily have been anticipated. Outputs are demonstrable, relatively effectively enforced and increasing in number. The results are sufficiently tangible to exert a magnetic attraction for other European countries not as yet part of the club.[10] Perhaps most importantly, mechanisms and devices have been established which permit multilateral negotiations to be conducted recurrently on a fairly stable basis. In particular, coalition behaviour is built into the process, mediating agencies operate and complementary special relationships among the players act as catalysts of movement, as Philippe de Schoutheete argues elsewhere in this volume.[11]

Negotiations among Europeans are not easy, but the empirical evidence and the observable patterns of bargaining suggest that EC negotiations are sufficiently productive for the participants to invest and reinvest in improving their performance. The accepted disciplines about both bargaining and compliance have established commitments to the EC process which reach deeply into the political, economic and judicial systems of the member states. It might in theory be possible for a member state to defect and it is certainly in practice frequently the case that member states jib at the consequences of being locked into a continuous and constraining negotiating process with their European partners. But the inducements to cooperate are much more powerful than the seductive appeal of opting out, except at the margins. The resilience of the negotiating process is manifest from its survival, and even its reinforcement, during the discouraging policy environment of the 1970s. The increased pace of output in the mid-1980s reflected a return on investments made over many previous years and not simply a quick response to a specific and more propitious policy context.

Some underlying trends

To assert that the commitment to cooperate is high and durable, or that the participants have developed sophisticated and relatively effective strategies for pursuing their interests, suggests that the negotiating process is deeply rooted. The games played in Brussels are linked to the outcomes of games played in national capitals and in turn influence the games played in national capitals. But it would be a mistake to see each member state as simply a vertical segment of a multilateral system. Evidence abounds of transnational networks of politicians, officials, political activists, entrepreneurs, even trade unionists and other policy-influential groups. The networks are densest among the member states of the EC, but extend in varying degrees to other West European countries.

The internationalization of the economy has steadily induced changing patterns of behaviour and expectation among entrepreneurs. A critical factor in the emergence of the commitment to the 1992 goal was the momentum generated by European industrialists. From the late 1970s their efforts had concentrated on the need to ensure that the policy framework set by European governments and the EC institutions matched their own European frame of reference.[12] The fact that several of the protagonists in the key groupings of European industrialists were not parochially European, but were focusing on wider international markets as well, helped to guard against narrowly defensive lobbying. The industrial map of Europe has changed dramatically over the last ten years. While there remain entrepreneurs locked into the economy of a single state, more and more are caught up in a mixture of export and import dependence and transnational production or collaboration. This has led to a fundamental reorientation of attitudes on the relevance of European rules, who should set them and how.

Negotiations within the EC are nourished by, but also promote, negotiations in other European fora. This is evident in two ways. The sense of European identity is reinforced by the sheer number and range of European discussions in which political and economic actors participate. Habits of discourse and mutual familiarity facilitate productive discussion. There is a 'can-do' atmosphere, much prompted by the EC experience of turning discussion into substance.

EC bargaining now also explicitly assumes that negotiations inevitably have distributional consequences and that these have to be managed. The politics of regulation are never neutral in their distributional impact, and this was recognized, and indeed feared, by some participants in the European process from the outset. But the language of distribution and redistribution now permeates debate not just in the EC, but in other European fora.[13] The agreement in February 1988 on the Delors package of budgetary measures marked a critical turning-point. Inevitably this development has been accompanied by controversies, as governments and groups compete to secure their interests and to minimize their burdens. But mechanisms are in place to provide a framework of 'equity', principles of burden-sharing and instruments of compensation. The participants in European negotiations are able to make quite specific calculations of the pay-offs to themselves and to their partners.[14] The calculations serve as a means of defining precisely and tangibly the options for settlement.

The institutional context

The highly institutionalized structure of negotiations in the EC has always been one of its distinctive features. Although some other multilateral frameworks share this characteristic in form, the EC case is particularly striking. Three key attributes serve to demonstrate this point. The first is the advanced system of binding Community law which combines tight enforcement mechanisms with expanding reach. Secondly, the budgetary arrangements for direct revenue and supranational expenditure are unparalleled. Thirdly, the institutions have a constitutional character. Indeed much of the debate about EC institutions has been cast in terms familiar from domestic rather than international politics. The constitutional bias has, however, set such high thresholds for the institutions to reach that the underlying dynamics and impact of the negotiating process have often been obfuscated.

The Council of Ministers is, and is likely to remain, the key negotiating forum in the EC. It is here that decisions are endorsed or rejected, and it is within the Council that power is exercised and contested. However, the multifaceted composition of the Council (by nationality and function) gives it an appearance of fragmented incoherence, which is as perplexing to the outside observer as the political process in Washington. The jostling for position and interests is of an intensity that makes it tempting to conclude that stalemate is endemic and the status quo more appealing than radical departures. Moreover, the quasi-federal division of powers between the Council of Ministers and the member states (analogous to the US system, though more like the West German brand of federalism) invites inaction if the participating states fear that their policy competence or their policy advantage may be eroded. The German (or Bavarian) attitude to CAP reform, and the concern of the Danish to protect their high environmental standards, are cases in point. Other such examples abound.

However, the Council has acquired some elements of collective identity. It is obliged to behave as an entity in relation to other EC institutions and vis-à-vis the rest of the world when operating within the sphere of the EC treaties. It has interests of its own as an institution to defend in relation to both policy substance and decision-making powers. Thus ministers from one member state will often defend Council positions which do not follow their own substantive preferences. For example, British ministers, in spite of their distaste for much of the common agricultural policy (CAP), are obliged to defend it in international trade negotiations.

This collective identity in the EC Council is built on the immense substructure below the level of ministerial sessions, through which are conducted both pre-negotiations and many complete negotiations. Committees and working groups, some 200 in number, jostle for space in the Charlemagne building, imposing on the Council Secretariat a logistics exercise of testing complexity. The senior committees – the Committee of Permanent Representatives (COREPER), the Special Committee on Agriculture (SCA) and the Article 113 Committee – each with weekly meetings and long agendas, are locked into virtually permanent session and act as the final negotiators on some 70% of Council business. Alongside them sit other high-level groups, each with its own sectoral or subject remit. While their negotiating output is less impressive in volume, they too act as a countervailing influence to the necessary loyalty of their members to their own governments. Three threads of continuity run through the Council's work: first, the rotating Presidency as manager;[15] second, the Council's own Secretariat as facilitator; and, third, the Commission as goad and mediator.

Thus the division of labour between ministers and officials in the Council is not a simple division between the political and the technical. Every dossier is both political and technical. Each proposal has its own technical complexity and also requires some political choices. Both levels form part of a routinized and serial process of negotiation. The technical character of the texts has the advantage that the Council is not given much opportunity to discuss points of underlying political principle, which removes, or at least defers, a potential obstacle to agreement. Some analogies can be drawn with the use of negotiating texts in fora such as UNCLOS, but the direct legislative impact of EC texts gives them a more robust quality.

The Commission was always intended to play a role which went far beyond the scope of secretariats in other multilateral settings. Power-plays in the EC over the years have not facilitated dramatic extensions of the Commission's constitutional authority. But the Commission has always been a full partner in the negotiating process. The Council really does consist of 13 members (12 governments and the Commission). Any practitioner of negotiation well recognizes the crucial power of the drafter of texts, which remains the Commission's prerogative. The Commission can also bring the Council to a halt by providing no text at all. The Commission is no neutral arbiter, but a player with vested interests of its own to promote and the record of Community legislation to defend. Yet its very partisanship means that the Commission is an activist in the search for solutions and often a mediator, in that one of its key interests is in finding the common ground.

But in all negotiations skill is as important as formal position. The Commission has often been its own worst enemy and dissipated its inbuilt negotiating assets. However, over the last few years the Commission's all-round performance and impact have improved visibly. The correspondence between Commission proposal and Council decision has been close in several areas of high salience, quite apart from the day-to-day matters in which the Commission's impact has been considerable. Two recent cases demonstrate this. First, the final outcome on the 'agro-budgetary' dossier negotiated at the Brussels session of the European Council in February 1988 bore a remarkable similarity to the Delors package.[16] The Commission defined the area and parameters of settlement, and all the member states in the end recognized that they were unlikely to find a more 'yes-able' set of propositions. Secondly, the whole 1992 programme on the internal market became credible and feasible as a result of sustained and focused propositions from the Commission.[17]

The vital role of Community law has already been mentioned. Negotiated decisions in the EC are immediately turned into enforceable legislation, dependent not just on good behaviour by member governments, but on an independent judicial process. Negotiators know from the outset the necessary seriousness of their obligations. This produces pluses and minuses.[18] On the negative side, negotiators often hesitate to agree precisely because they do not want to contemplate the rigours of an agreement, though even this can be a strength in that it provides some brake on the hastily agreed exhortation which is sometimes to be found in other multilateral meetings. It is only at the level of the European Council, which does not as yet directly negotiate the details of legislation, that rhetoric substitutes for action.[19]

The positive side of enforceability is clear, namely that negotiators are able to predict the legal consequences of agreement as regards the substance and as regards other member states' behaviour as well as their own. None of this would have been possible without a strong and independent European Court of Justice (ECJ). Nor can the Council 'fix' the judgments of the ECJ, any more than an American President can determine the behaviour of the Supreme Court. But the fact that the ECJ will sometimes find for the Council against the Commission or Parliament, or for one member state against another, facilitates the confidence of national negotiators in the judicial process.[20]

The European Parliament (EP) used to sit on the sidelines of the European negotiating process, except in the budgetary arena. As one of the two arms of the budgetary authority the EP had (since the mid-1970s) a direct impact on Council negotiations in the annual budgetary cycle. Under the SEA the EP has acquired a role in the legislative process, in so far as the second reading of legislation requires majorities in both Council and Parliament. Only if the Council is unanimous can it escape the impact of the EP. These powers, in force only since July 1987, are new, but parliamentary positions have now begun to bite into the internal debates of the Council and of the Commission.

All of these factors have thus created an unusual form of integrative bargaining at the transnational level. Its emergence is the product of an accumulation of habits, procedures, constitutional rules and constellations of interests developed over three decades. Although the quantity and quality of outputs have been uneven, the substantive rewards, in terms of the interests of the participants, have been sufficient for them to be willing periodically to reinforce the process. Although the other transnational European organizations lack the intensity, range and disciplines of the EC to make for valid comparison, nonetheless the EC bargaining process has become the model against which the others are judged.

However, it is generally agreed that the improvement, both quantitative and qualitative, in the EC negotiating process has come about only since the signing of the SEA. The section which follows seeks to show that the SEA could not have been signed had it not been for a combination of confidence in the basic Community method of bargaining and frustration at its limitations – limitations that were bound to become more pronounced in the context of an enlarged Community and an expanded policy agenda. The SEA was thus about both substance and methods, about both policy interests and political behaviour.

Constitutions and contracts: towards a new deal

What then was the real significance of the SEA? And what were the key features of the process whereby it was agreed? First of all, let us sketch the bones of its history, in order then to draw out the salient points that it illustrates about the negotiating process. Policy and institutional issues have always been interwoven in the development of the EC. For many years institutional reform appeared to be stalled, in spite of periodic attempts to reopen the dossier, such as the Tindemans Report on European Union of 1975 or the Report of the Three Wise Men in 1979. The powers of the European Parliament were extended in the budgetary field in 1975 and the EP did gain an elected base in 1977, but the central power structures of the EC were not fundamentally altered, nor was the division of policy competences between Community and national authorities.

By the early 1980s there was increasing dissatisfaction with the frozen institutional framework. The traditional supporters of strengthened EC institutions were beginning to organize themselves more effectively, mobilized by the 'crocodile' initiative of Altiero Spinelli. In parallel the succession of applications for accession from Mediterranean countries induced a widespread concern that the institutional framework would not stand the strain of enlargement. Moreover, there was a clutch of important policy propositions on the table, both those calling for reform of existing policies (notably agriculture and the budget) and those advocating policy expansion (perhaps most importantly measures to improve industrial competitiveness and the emerging environmental agenda). Initially these three strands, though obviously contiguous, were not viewed generally as part and parcel of a single whole: the first was a somewhat theological debate; the second rested on practical concerns about efficiency; while the third was the normal, albeit testing, business of day-to-day negotiation.

In February 1984 the European Parliament adopted the Draft Treaty on European Union, the fruit of the Spinelli Initiative, a document which called for a substantial shift towards a more federal constitution. The traditional maximalists were delighted and the Benelux and Italian governments voiced their support, but there were few who expected that this would cut the Gordian knot of hard core resistance from the obvious institutional minimalists, notably the British, Danish and Greek governments, or even that the pivotal French and German governments would do more than mouth a few words of polite encouragement. Yet much to everyone's surprise, even that of many of his own colleagues, President Mitterrand in May 1984 made a rousing speech in Strasbourg announcing to the EP that the Draft Treaty should be looked at seriously. Shortly thereafter the European Council met in Fontainebleau, charged with the daunting task of examining the agricultural and budgetary reform dossiers and of resolving the outstanding issues of Iberian enlargement. The heads of state and government made remarkable progress with both: they also set up the Ad Hoc Committee on Institutional Reform, subsequently known by the name Dooge after its Irish chairman.[21] It was at the same meeting that Mrs Thatcher, the British Prime Minister, tabled her own statement about the development of the EC, advocating among other things a real effort to complete the common market.

With hindsight it is evident that from this point onwards the three strands had been woven together, namely constitutionalism, efficiency and the substantive policy issues. It is important, however, to note that this was not to become obvious to all of the participants for another twelve months. Events and proposals then moved pell-mell. They are listed here in no particular order of importance. The Dooge Committee met, and an apparently stark division emerged between those members willing to advocate rather extensive reforms and the British, Danish and Greek members, who entered so many reservations that their countries were labelled 'footnote' countries. The outlook for a new constitutional settlement looked bleak; indeed there was much talk of 'variable geometry' and a two-speed Community. The arrangements for enlargement were completed, but amid mounting concern that the policy consequences would be untenable, as existing member states rushed to protect those of their interests which they feared would be eroded and the acceding countries, notably Spain, firmly signalled that they would bargain hard to insert their own interests into the fabric of the EC.

Meanwhile on the policy front developments moved apace. Fontainebleau had put on ice, but not solved, the agricultural reform conundrum. Everyone knew that a long-term and structural solution had thus far eluded them. An interim arrangement had been adopted on the budget, in the form of a British abatement, a modest revenue increase and a cosmetic restraint on agricultural expenditure, but the arrangement would have to be recast. Rather more positively, the technology programmes of the EC began to take shape and to find surprisingly strong commitment from many of the companies involved. Interestingly, in the autumn of 1984, a 'new approach' to the setting of common European standards emerged. The new Commission, in the early months of 1985, laboured both diligently and imaginatively, the key result being the White Paper on the Completion of the Common Market. In European Political Cooperation (EPC) there was an emerging consensus that the prevailing informal rules to govern foreign policy consultations had reached their limits and that, therefore, the moment might have come to codify the rules. The British formalized this in the Stresa proposal of early June 1985, suggesting a basic text.

The signals emanating from Brussels and national capitals were ambiguous and contradictory. The European Council in Milan at the end of June led to the surprising spectacle of, first, angry exchanges and then an unprecedented vote by majority to establish an Intergovernmental Conference, Community code for a real constitutional conclave. Six months later, when they met in Luxembourg, the same heads of state and government solemnly, and in the end calmly, agreed to the text of the SEA, a document which strengthened the powers and sphere of the EC institutions, incorporated a commitment to meet the needs of the Mediterranean members, firmly endorsed the internal market objective, extended policy competence to the monetary, technological and environmental arenas and codified EPC.

As regards the negotiating process itself, the critical change was the combination of reaffirmed and new policy goals with revised procedural rules. The extension of voting in the Council by qualified majority implied an acceptance that member states' interests could on occasion be sacrificed for the sake of maintaining momentum and provided those who could rally a majority with the means to override the reluctance of those who had isolated idiosyncratic reasons for their dissent. The Commission's scope for influencing the outcomes and for being adventurous was increased by the knowledge that it no longer had to carry all member states along with its proposals. Yet it could ride on the fact that *all* 12 member states had given their assent, followed by their parliaments, to the new deal.

Negotiating practice

The accumulated practice of EC negotiations has thus primarily emerged from the Council/Commission tandem, but conditioned by the ECJ and Community law. Practice is changing as the amendments of the SEA come into effect, and the full implications cannot yet be identified. It is generally accepted that negotiations have subsequently become more productive, but the analysis that follows suggests that this has been a linear progression, not a step-change.

The intensity of EC negotiations is beyond question. The Council meets at ministerial level over 60 times a year, not because ministers like visiting Brussels and Luxembourg, but because they have business to transact. Between 1975 and 1986 the number of proposals put during the year to the Council by the Commission had risen from 339 to 608. The Cockfield White Paper on the internal market of June 1985 set a legislative agenda of some 300 items (reduced by rationalization to around 280). By spring 1990 well over half had been agreed and a rhythm of work established for progressing through the list. On the external affairs side, over the past few years the Council and the Commission have had to agree positions for negotiations with the Maghreb, in the Uruguay Round, with the countries of the European Free Trade Association (EFTA), with the CMEA, the USSR and several East European countries (both before and after the dramas of 1989) and with the US and Japan, as well as the renewal of the Lomé Convention.

The volume of work is large and the frequency of meetings evident. But the negotiations also produce results and much more quickly than is often supposed.[22] In 1975 the average length of time from proposal to decision was 5.3 months; by 1986 it was down to 3.6 months, after Iberian enlargement and before the SEA came into force. Of course the aggregate figures of output conceal a mix of straightforward or routine dossiers and macro-issues which are controversial and time-consuming, but the figures are nonetheless striking.

Turning output into delivered policy on the ground is another matter. Here the evidence is ambiguous. The judicial system serves to facilitate implement-ation, but depends on individual cases being brought forward. Implementation is taken seriously, though practice is imperfect and uneven. One point worth noting is that EC negotiators differ in their attitudes to the implementation stage. Some prefer to be certain of their ability to implement before concluding a negotiation, while others are willing to assent first and think about imple-mentation afterwards. By and large the implementation record of the former is the more successful.

The range of EC negotiation continues to expand both formally and informally. The SEA specifically extended EC competence to cover the environment, technology, cohesion (redistribution issues) and monetary cooperation, though all of these subjects had already been the object of EC legislation or decisions. The internal market programme lies within the area of well-established EC competence, but it is generally agreed that the corollary areas likely to be touched will involve an increasingly wide range of subjects. Already the 1992 objective has provoked a more thorough coverage of the freedom of movement of all four factors of production and the reactivation of a previously stalled debate on a common transport policy. It could even be argued that the neo-functionalists' concept of 'spill-over' is now being vindicated.

The decision-making rules of the EC have been clearly strengthened under the SEA, with the agreement to use qualified majority rules far more extensively. This applies both to the revision of Article 100 for the harmonization of legislation and to the activation of existing Treaty of Rome provisions for qualified majority voting. Thus negotiations over the CAP and the external trade policy of the EC now regularly rely on the possibility and practice of voting. This change of practice was already evident before the ratification of the SEA. Under the Dutch Presidency in the first semester of 1986, over forty decisions were reached by voting, and over fifty during the subsequent British presidency.

Two key points are relevant. First, the relative ease with which the SEA provisions were in the end adopted is in itself an indication of collective frustration in the Council at the consequences of the old consensus-based system, not least in the wake of Greek and Iberian enlargement. This new mood of 'efficiency' spreads further, in that informal evidence suggests that the conduct of meetings has become more business-like. Council sessions have apparently become brisker, papers shorter and discussion more sharply focused. The through-put of work is thus enhanced, making it more feasible for the long 1992 agenda to be technically processed by the Council. Indeed the Council is now admonishing the Commission for not submitting new proposals more quickly.

Secondly, the language of the negotiations is now the language of voting. Officials and even occasionally ministers are prepared to use the vocabulary of majorities and minorities. Thus, for example, in the debate about how open or closed the external trade stance of the EC is likely to be, there are 'blocking minorities' of both protectionists and liberals, with outcomes thus depending on the attitudes of the median group, individual issue by individual issue. This reflects partly the fact that the threshold of 54 votes out of 76 for a qualified majority is high. With the change of language come changes in behaviour and negotiating tactics. The knowledge that the veto is a tactic to be used only *in extremis* means that negotiators have to assess their options in quite a different way from before and thus to evaluate the positions of their partners more subtly. As these changes have taken root, it has become clear that what matters is not whether a vote is actually taken on a particular issue (the figures are unfortunately not readily available), but the knowledge that a vote could be taken.

Negotiating behaviour

Overall, therefore, there is an accumulation of evidence about the working of the decision-rules to indicate that results matter and coalitions are necessary, and that for both these ends the rules have to be made to work effectively. To have reached this stage suggests a degree of confidence in the rules and in the readiness of partners to play the game according to the rules. But this was not the result of a dramatic conversion overnight, as the figures on majority voting prior to ratification of the SEA demonstrate. Codes of conduct have become established over the three decades of the EC's existence. Participants have become willingly socialized into accepting these codes and the behavioural norms which accompany them. Spain and Portugal became almost instantly fully mature members of the negotiating club, as Ireland had earlier. Denmark, Greece and the UK have each in its own way taken rather longer to accept the codes of conduct, but the shift is palpable in all three cases. Their reservations during the Dooge Committee exercise, evident in the footnotes they appended to the report, already marked movement towards acceptance of a more tightly-knit negotiating process than any had previously accepted. Their willingness to exploit the subsequent provisions of the SEA took each a few steps further towards the other member states.

The evidence for this is most visible in the eventual achievement of a global compromise on agriculture and the budget at the session of the European Council in February 1988. The Delors package in the end brought together all member states in support of a wide-ranging and long-term package of reforms, in turn linked to the pressing case for more rapid progress towards the 1992 objective. But the 'success' of the negotiating process has to be seen in perspective. One explanation lies in the accumulation of sophisticated mechanisms for dealing with the diversity of interests among the 12 member states and particular groups within them.[23] Various labels have been coined to identify the flexibility now built in: 'differentiation' permits variegated and phased application of EC legislation; and 'variable geometry' provides scope for some agreements to go ahead (as under the European Monetary System) without all member states being fully on board or with some moving ahead of the pack. These arrangements have been legitimized in the provisions of the SEA and to a certain extent endorsed by the ECJ.[24]

Yet many would argue that this whole process, in relation to both policies and institutions, has demonstrated the momentum generated by the EC's 'core' members pulling along in their slipstream the more cautious or more peripheral. At several stages members of the latter group have been faced with a challenge to cooperate or to defect. It should also be noted that signs, albeit embryonic, of a similar process are in evidence in other European fora. The ESA Council has both consensus rules (for mandatory programmes) and majority rules (for optional programmes). An interesting debate is currently under way among the EFTA countries about, first, whether the decision-rules of EFTA need to be altered, and, second, whether they could contemplate accepting some or all of the EC's decision-rules.

The currencies of negotiation used in the EC have changed in character and their convertibility has improved. Neo-functionalists, in defining a 'Community method' of bargaining, had always looked to the role of package-deals based on positive-sum games as the means of upgrading common interests. As neo-functionalism lost its persuasive power as a tool of analysis, so much of the commentary on the EC discarded this element. Practitioners would repeatedly assert that global package-deals were rare and that the trade-offs which did take place were limited within specific issue-areas, except for the occasional and chance cross-sectoral deals done, when more than one critical dossier surfaced at one time. Meanwhile outside observers recognized that deals were struck, but regarded them as either zero-sum games in which one or more participant lost out or as cynical and short-term manipulations of the negotiating forum to serve parochial interests.

The harsh economic environment of the 1970s reinforced such interpretations. Yet analyses of this kind have proved a poor guide to the outcomes of EC negotiations in recent years, both those over policy and those that deal with the institutional setting. On the contrary, the combination of market liberalization, investment in Community R&D, an active social dimension, resource transfers, CAP reform and budgetary expansion has found EC negotiators willing to handle the linkages among dossiers and to accept the relevance of the political rules to the prospects of particular economic out-turns. So linkages abound within and across sectors: within sectors, facilitated by the vertically organized work of the Council and Commission; across sectors, helped by the European Council at head-of-government level, by the coordinating role of the General Affairs Council (composed of foreign ministers) and by the Commission in its struggles to retain a collegiate identity.

Expectations of reciprocity have thus become embedded in the negotiating process. Since only the most enthusiastic integrationist could argue that all EC games rest on positive sums, notions of reciprocity apply to the distribution of burdens as well as the allocation of benefits. Cross-sectoral linkages permit discussions to be conducted in several currencies simultaneously. Other member states have not welcomed the adjustments to the EC budgetary system to take account of British arguments about net financial contributions. But they have recognized the right of the British to reciprocal treatment. All parties have had to accept that the argument could be resolved only by the simultaneous use of different negotiating currencies. But this has been achieved only because enough negotiators were willing in the end to be satisficers rather than optimizers. Thus a degree of shared realism about what is feasible has been a catalyst of working arrangements for reciprocity. The system of Community law strengthens confidence that understandings about reciprocity will be observed most of the time.

One element of EC bargaining which so far remains beyond the reach of the analysts is the way in which power is exercised. In the halcyon period of Gaullism, power-based assessments of what happened in Brussels were frequent. Hardly anyone would proffer the same kind of analysis nowadays. The Federal Republic of Germany undoubtedly possesses the greatest economic power, but wields it cautiously and resists concomitant political responsibility.[25] No single government plays a hegemonic role in the EC, nor do the prospects of such a development look plausible. Franco-German bilateralism is the only proxy for hegemony, but in practice falls well short of this, since differences of interest between the two are as evident as the complementarities. Instead the power structure is diffuse and every participant can realistically claim a share of the assets to be distributed.

The structure of pay-offs suggests rather that the smaller (i.e. less overtly powerful) players extract disproportionately high pay-offs. These are identifiable in both systemic and substantive terms. In the budgetary arena, where the pay-offs are the most transparent, the net payers are Britain, France and Germany, while all the rest of the member states are net recipients. At the systemic level smaller, ostensibly weaker, member states exercise more power by vigorous participation in an EC negotiating process with guaranteed rights than they could expect to enjoy in detached isolation. This is not to say that the pay-offs are not there for the other players, but that they are expressed in different ways: market access, a larger share of R&D contracts, guarantees of more or less good behaviour between countries where a degree of endemic rivalry persists and some ability to influence and benefit from the support of their smaller partners in other arenas, such as European collective defence or the European space programme.

The time-scale over which negotiations are played out has a considerable bearing on the process. All the literature on negotiations, and not only at the international level, stresses the relevance of serial exchanges to the stability and predictability of the process. Over a period cooperative modes can be established and habits of transacting business entrenched. Pay-offs and reciprocal understandings are spread over a long period and apparently credibly so. As a working goal, 1992 rests on precisely this assumption – as regards both the pain of adjustment and the promise of growth. The agreements of February 1988 on agriculture and the budget envisage long-term phasing of benefits and burdens. Mrs Thatcher accepted the Delors package not because she was enamoured of its immediate returns, but because over the long haul she believed that the overall outcome lay well within her settlement area. For politicians to commit themselves not just to rhetorical goals but to programmed decisions beyond the life of the electoral cycle suggests that an important pattern of expectations can be identified. Nor incidentally are such expectations confined to the overt output from Brussels. Part of the explanation for French enthusiasm about 1992 lies in the belief of many French industrialists and financiers that EC obligations will provide a thread of continuity, strong enough to withstand the vicissitudes of the electoral cycle and their impact on national economic policy.

Functioning coalition patterns are observable within the system, based on a mix of complementary (rarely identical) interests and tactical alignments. Recurrent groupings include the Benelux group (the confidence-builders of the Schengen agreement and border dismantling in general), the Franco-German sporadic duo, and the Mediterraneans (often joined by Ireland and sometimes France). On some issues a north/south division is apparent, on others a liberal/ protectionist split and, more rarely, a right/left cleavage, as in the current debate about the social dimension. There are blocking minorities on many issues, but no recurrent veto group.

These coalitions are a necessary part of a negotiating process with so many players with such wide-ranging and often contrary interests. The coalition system is not, however, rigidly defined, as the examples above show. The key players are frequently the intermediate balancers, of which the Commission is generally a leading representative. Unilateralism is a diminishingly attractive negotiating strategy, except of course in those areas where unanimity rules persist under the treaties, or where to plead the Luxembourg agreement is a credible weapon; but these last cases are extremely rare.

The Community is thus in an up-beat mood about the shadow of the future. Views about what that future should be like differ, with a persistent dichtomy between those who believe that it should contain a large dose of political integration and those who believe that the economic gains on offer are the real prize. But either way a future consolidated by substantive EC decisions looks like a better position than that of today. There was a period when some participants in EC debates seemed more concerned to re-examine the shadows of the past. For the moment, at least, the past casts a long enough shadow to guarantee the roots of the system, while the shadow of the future is believed to be the blossom on the branches.

Conclusions

The European negotiating process has acquired an in-built dynamic observable in the EC and some other fora. It does not follow that there is an irreversible accumulation of agreements in prospect, but it does appear that West Europeans have acquired the negotiating capabilities to pursue, if they so choose, an incremental path. New members have been willing to accept the momentum. The system has a high tolerance for making side-payments to carry along the doubters, though if Europe plunged back into severe recession that tolerance would almost certainly diminish.

Collective interests are perceptibly pursued. This should not be taken to imply that a starry-eyed supranationalism inhabits the portals of state power in Western Europe. However, both governments and the economic groups affected by the current policy repertoire make the careful calculation that a negotiating process that delivers results is more valuable than the frustration of stalled debate. Some member states have a freer ride than others, but at present none wants to walk. Overall therefore, the process has sharpened in its effectiveness, becoming more productive, more stable and more flexible.

Limitations nonetheless persist. Any decision-making process is capable of being highly geared, but misdirected. The EC is capable of taking silly decisions. European negotiators can outstretch themselves, and serious conflicts of goal, ideology and interest will remain testing. The policy delivery system, though impressive in comparison with most other cases of transnational collaboration, is still immature. Underlying differences in economic assets, geography and political orientation remain as impediments to full economic integration and extended political integration. Nor can the negotiating process be judged in isolation. Negotiations take place largely behind closed doors, though the new procedure for cooperation with the European Parliament has brought some of the issues into a more public arena.

Multilateralism can, however, be made to work, to deliver policy regimes, to develop collective policies and to promote shared interests. Political integration is another question, though the issue of 'deepening' the EC or moving towards 'political union' would not be on the table were it not for the bargaining infrastructure that is already in place.

Notes

1. J. Pelkmans and L. Alan Winters with Helen Wallace, *Europe's Domestic Market*, Chatham House Paper No. 43, Routledge for RIIA, 1988.
2. Communiqué of Hanover European Council, June 1988, and Dublin, April 1989.
3. T. Taylor, *European Defence Collaboration*, Chatham House Paper No. 24, Routledge for RIIA, 1984. See also the chapter in this volume by Reinhardt Rummel and Peter Schmidt.
4. See, *inter alia*, M. Sharp and C. Shearman, *European Technological Collaboration*, Chatham House Paper No. 36, Routledge for RIIA, 1987; and *Europe's Future in Space*, a Five-Institute Report, English edition as Chatham House Special, Routledge for RIIA, 1988.
5. See T. Pedersen, *The Wider Western Europe: EC Policy towards the EFTA Countries*, RIIA Discussion Paper No. 10, RIIA, 1988; and J. Jamar and H. Wallace, eds., *EC/EFTA: More than just good friends?*, College of Europe, De Tempel, Tempelhof, Bruges, 1988.
6. See, for example, G. Ciavarini-Azzi, *L'Application du Droit Communautaire par les Etats membres*, EIPA, Maastricht, 1985; C. O'Nuallain (ed.), *The Presidency of the European Council of Ministers*, Croom Helm for EIPA, 1985; H. Siedentopf and J. Ziller (eds), *Making European Policies Work: Implementation of Community Legislation in the Member States*, Sage, 1988; and H. Wallace et al. (eds), *Policy-Making in the European Community*, Wiley, 2nd edn, 1983.
7. One Herculean contribution has come from the European University Institute's series, Cappelletti, Seccombe, Weiler (eds), *Integration through Law: Europe and the American Federal Experience*, De Gruyter, 1986 onwards.
8. The SEA was agreed in December 1985 and operative from 1 July 1987, published in *Bulletin of the European Communities*, supplement 2/86.
9. There is some literature which sketches out parts of the EC negotiating process: this includes F. Scharpf, 'The Joint-Decision Trap: Lessons from German Federalism and European Integration', International Institute of Management, Discussion Paper, Berlin, 1985; H. von Witzke and C. Ford Pinge, 'Agricultural Integration: Problems and Perspectives'; and H. Wallace, 'The best is the enemy of the 'could': bargaining in the European Community', in S. Tarditi et al., *Agricultural Trade Liberalization and Economic Policy Perspectives in the European Community*, Oxford University Press, 1989.
10. Turkey and Austria have already applied for membership; Cyprus and Malta have announced their intentions of following suit. The other EFTA countries and EFTA collectively are actively seeking an upgrading of their relationship with the EC. Central and East European governments are beginning to talk of possible applications.
11. On the Franco-German relationship, see Haig Simonian, *The Privileged Partnership: Franco-German Relations in the European Community 1969–84*, Clarendon Press, 1985, and the series of studies from the Deutsche-Französisches Institut in Ludwigsburg. For both this and the link with the UK, see R. Morgan and C. Bray (eds.), *Partners and Rivals in Western Europe: Britain, France and Germany*, Gower, 1986.

12. Networks include the group of IT companies constituted by Etienne Davignon, the European Round Table of Industrialists, the ecological and nuclear disarmament groups and, increasingly, trade unionists.

13. In the EC case this is reflected in the lengthy negotiations about net contributions from member states and in the debates about 'economic and social cohesion', included in the SEA and developed by the agreement on doubling the 'structural' funds at the European Council in February 1988. See Michael Shackleton, *Financing the European Community*, Chatham House Paper, Pinter, London, 1990. In the ESA case, interestingly, the language and practice was different and rooted in the explicit concept of 'juste retour'.

14. Helen Wallace, 'Negotiating in the European Community: Can Everyone Win?', mimeo, Political Studies Association, 1987.

15. See C. O'Nuallain, op. cit.

16. The Delors package consisted of a series of communications, produced during 1987, on agriculture, EC financing and agriculture. The final package is reported in *Bulletin of the European Communities*, Supplement 2/88.

17. *Completing the Internal Market*, Commission of the EC, Brussels, 1985.

18. See Siedentopf and Ziller, op. cit.; and Alan Butt Philip, *Implementing the Internal Market: Problems and Prospects*, RIIA Discussion Paper No. 5, 1988.

19. S. Bulmer and W. Wessels, *The European Council*, Macmillan, London, 1986.

20. Helen Wallace, 'A European Budget made in Strasbourg and unmade in Luxembourg', in F. Jacobs (ed.), *Yearbook of European Law*, 6, 1986, Clarendon Press, 1987, pp. 263–82.

21. Known as Dooge Committee, but officially Ad Hoc Committee for Institutional Affairs, *Report to the European Council (Brussels, 29–30 March 1985)*, Brussels, 1985.

22. The information which follows on Council output is derived from research by Thomas Sloot, part of which is to be published in a paper co-authored with Piet Verschuren in the *Journal of Common Market Studies*. Thomas Sloot's premature death leaves incomplete a valuable analysis of EC negotiations.

23. See H. Wallace, *The Challenge of Diversity*, Routledge for RIIA, 1985.

24. See the Single European Act, *Bulletin of the European Communities*, Supplement 2/86, Article 8c, and C-D Ehlerman, 'How flexible is community law? An unusual approach to the problem of "two speeds" ', *Michigan Law Review*, 1984, pp. 1274–93.

25. W. Wessels and E. Regelsberger (eds), *The Federal Republic of Germany and the European Community: The Presidency and Beyond*, Europa Union Verlag, 1987.

13 Administrative interaction
Wolfgang Wessels

Basic assumptions and theses

A look at the literature

There is broad consensus that public administrations are as much a 'product' as a 'characteristic feature' of what we call the 'state'.[1] In all phases of the state's formation[2] the changes in its characteristics are closely linked with respective developments of public administrations.[3] Given this salience, the research on the role of public administration was and is of considerable extent and density: several works in the 1980s[4] have dismantled the Weberian model of bureaucracy,[5] stressing more 'cooperative' relations between politicians, interest groups and civil servants.[6] This line of research has included studies comparing several national states but has left out of their research focus all cross-border administrative relations. There was still the hidden assumption that administrations remained fixed on national decision-making and implementation – a focus no longer adequate for states, at least not for those in Western Europe.

Works studying administrative relations within international or European organizations[7] describe and categorize the role and functions of international and national bureaucrats in the policy cycle (preparation, formula and implementation of decisions) of these organizations. Some look at the impact of national civil servants via permanent representations[8] or via the specific functional roles such as presidencies.[9] They also include the role of bureaucrats in decision implementation.[10] The major focus is oriented to the 'autonomy',[11] the 'decision-making modalities'[12] or the capacity to 'integrate' national civil servants[13] into a new system 'superceding' the pre-existing one.[14] A fairly common view is that national bureaucrats are not developing into 'Trojan horses'[15] – destroying the walls of national sovereignity from within.[16] These findings stress that national administrations as such are not really affected by the trans-border activities of some civil servants.

My own view

This chapter takes a view which is contrary both to the 'benign neglect' of the
experts on national administrations and to the 'no-impact' conclusion by the
works on international and European organizations. It contends that we may
be witnessing in the administrative reality of, at least, the European Community
a significant trend towards a mutual 'engrenage', 'interlocking', 'Verflechtung'.
The 'multi-level game'[17] does not add up to zero, but between national and
Community levels there is, at least to a certain degree, a positive sum game.

By participating in Community decision-making the national civil servants
gain 'access' to and 'influence'[18] on EC decision-making and implementation,
thus also increasing their weight inside their respective national systems. The
same general cost-benefit calculation applies to Community officials who gain
access and influence on 'national' domains by opening their policy cycles to the
national colleagues – although traditional federalists and supranationalists
would argue that this is an unacceptable loss in autonomy and independence of
the EC bureaucracy.[19] This cost-benefit analysis by civil servants (*mutatis
mutandis* by heads of state, ministers and interest groups, but not by national
parliamentarians) creates a major dynamic for European integration leading not
to a transfer of loyalty by national officials to a new centre but to a cooperation
of officials into a new system of shared government. This stage of state
evolution is characterized by an increasing degree of cooperation, in vertical
terms between different governmental levels, and in horizontal terms, among
several groups of actors. The 'multi-level' interactions of civil servants of
several national and international administrations thus reinforce trends towards
specific forms of the 'sharing' or 'fusion' of powers between 'bureaucrats and
politicians' which non-EC-related studies have identified.[20]

The inbuilt dynamics of increasing participation are closely linked with
evolutions in the role and functions of states in Western Europe. At least since
the end of World War II the West European states have significantly increased
the trend towards 'welfare and service states'[21] in constellations of increasing
interdependencies[22] and decreasing stability of global hegemonic regimes.[23]
These factors – exogenous to dynamics of administrative interactions – are a
major factor for the overall evolution of the West European integration
process. They will not be dealt with extensively in this chapter, as I have
presented the major thrust of these arguments elsewhere.[24]

Trends in administrative interaction

Methodology

As indicators for administrative interaction we mainly use statistics about the
number of administrative and (to a lesser degree) political bodies such as
councils, committees, expert and working groups, etc., and the frequency of
their meetings. Concerning the validity of these indicators, the basic assumption
is near to some of the starting points used by Deutsch[25]: as attention and time
are 'scarce resources'[26] (for officials also), the priorities of their activities (and

with this the pattern of interactions) are reflected by the intensity of their relative involvement which can be measured by their participation in formal groups. When compared with interview data, these statistics also enable us to identify ex-post-facto historical trends.

The reliability and availability of the relevant data are, however, limited: the 'map' of the administrative network in Western Europe is incomplete, but the bits and pieces are surprisingly consistent and offer some stimulating insights.

By taking statistics on groups and their meetings there is a bias towards formal organization from which at least some data could be collected; informal cooperation patterns are difficult to grasp by this (or any other) method.

Statistics

Table 13.1 presents statistics for several organizations: two of them (NATO and OECD) are Western, and four are in varying formula European. The EC is presented in more detail. Right across the table – except for the half-day sessions within OECD – we observe a significant growth both in number of committees and working groups composed of national civil servants and in the frequency of meetings. These growth trends are even more significant if we include statistics for the preceding period from 1960, though these are not always available. The statistics show no significant ups and downs in these trends of administrative interactions; the growth rate slowed down, however, over at least the first half of the 1980s.

If one adds the horizontal differentiation along issue areas and agenda items, administrative bodies have enlarged the scope of activities of all organizations. More items of 'national' attention and political sensitivity are drawn into international organization.[27] Problems debated in the national frameworks can be forced almost immediately onto the agenda of Western and West European organizations, often appearing in several organizations at the same time. Issue cycles (such as energy issues in the second half of the 1970s and 'environmental' ones in the 1980s) are spreading across the set of these international organizations which quite often compete with each other for political attention and scarce resources.

The involvement of national civil servants is spread over an increasing scope of issue areas and also over all phases of the policy cycle. The 'autonomy' of international civil servants who, in some organizations such as NATO or the EPC secretariat, are 'national bureaucrats on loan' is minimal. This applies especially in 'internal' budgetary and staff decisions. Through specific functions like presidencies, the national bureaucrats further reduce the autonomy of international secretariats. These trends have even increased over the years: the functions of the newly created EPC secretariat (1987) are strictly limited to serve the Presidency and the Political Committee.[28] In most organizations, the number of international civil servants has not grown in the same proportion as committees and their sessions.

The patterns of involvement of national bureaucrats are characterized by another, surprisingly consistent feature: The average rates for the intensity of interactions (frequency of meetings per group) are (a) surprisingly identical

Table 13.1 Evolution of bodies and meetings in selected Western and West European organizations

		1975	1985	growth (%)
A.	**Non-EC**			
1.	*NATO*			
(a)	number of committees and working groups	308	385	25
(b)	half-day sessions	3,800	5,176	36.2
(c)	average intensity of inter-actions (days per year)	6	7	16.6
(d)	number of ministerial meetings (excluding irregular summits)	4	4	
(e)	international civil servants (higher professional level)	252	303	20.2
2.	*OECD*			
(a)	number of committees and working groups	120	200	66.6
(b)	half-day sessions	4,142	3,871	−6.5
(c)	average intensity of meetings (days per year)	17	9.5	−44.1
(d)	number of ministerial meetings (excluding some meetings of technical ministers)	1	1	
(e)	civil servants (higher professional level)	491	488	−0.6
3.	*Council of Europe*			
(a)	number of committees and working groups	122	152 (1987)	24.8
(b)	half-day sessions	1,356	1,672 (1987)	23.3
(c)	average intensity of inter-actions (meeting days per year)	5.5	5.5	
(d)	number of ministerial meetings (at a junior ministerial level)	2	2	
(e)	international civil servants (all ranks)	712	878	23.3
4.	*EPC*			
(a)	political committees plus working groups	5	18	260
(b)	meetings	no data	89	

Table 13.1   continued

		1975	1985	growth (%)
(c)	average intensity of inter-actions (meeting days per year)		5	
(d)	number of ministerial meetings (plus some extra-meetings)	6	6	
(e)	(international) civil servants	–	6 (1987)	
5.	*EFTA*			
(a)	committees and working groups	5	30	500
(b)	sessions	98	205	109.2
(c)	average intensity of inter-actions (meetings per year)	17.6	6.5	−63
(d)	number of meetings on ministerial level	2	2	
(e)	international civil servants (professional staff)	28	31.5	12.5
B.	**EC**			
1.	*General number of translated sessions*	7,245	7,747	6.9
2.	*Expert groups at the Commission*			
(a)	number of governmental experts	10,381	15,652	50.7
(b)	number of groups	no data	537	
(c)	number of session days	no data	3,364 (1984)	
(d)	average intensity of inter-actions (working days per year)		6	
3.	*COREPER* number of sessions	118	117	−0.8
4.	*Other committees and working groups at the Council*			
(a)	numbers	108 (1974)	180	66.6
(b)	sessions	2,078	1,892	−9
(c)	average intensity of inter-actions (meeting days per year)	19	10	−47.4

Table 13.1 continued

		1975	1985	growth (%)
5.	*Council*			
(a)	number of 'Councils'	13	16	23.1
(b)	number of sessions	57	70	22.8
(c)	average intensity of inter-actions (meeting days per year)	4.3	4.3	
6.	*European Council*	3	3	
7.	*Implementation Committees*			
(a)	numbers	91	218	139
(b)	number of 'comités de gestion' for agricultural products	23	26	13
(c)	session days (agricultural 'comités de gestion')	446	388	−13
(d)	average intensity of inter-actions (meeting days per year)	19	15	−21
8.	*Number of civil servants (higher professional level without language sector)*	2,018	2,521	24.9
9.	*Number of civil servants of West German Ministries (higher professional level)*	4,198	4,292	2.2

Sources: Budgets and lists of secretariats of the organizations concerned. Problems with reliability of the data are discussed in the text.

and, (b) stagnating, if not decreasing. Apparently 'Parkinson's Law' of the bureaucratic (over-)expansion is not valid in these organizations; there are limits to the inbuilt dynamics.[29] These admittedly rough figures could be interpreted in the sense that national officials continued to fulfil their national responsibilities to operate effectively on both levels. Therefore they cannot be away from their offices too often; this is a self-limiting factor. The European and Atlantic level is an 'add-on' responsibility, not a replacement.

The increase in the number of committees, taken with a lower growth in the overall numbers of national bureaucrats (see, for instance, B9, Table 1) indicates that more national bureaucrats (in absolute figures), and a higher proportion of them, are involved in common policy cycles, though only to a limited intensity: the frequency of the sessions of each committee reaches a certain 'plateau' after an initial growth phase.

A second feature is relevant for our argument: while the national structures preparing and implementing decisions of international or European bodies vary[30] according to the 'architecture of the state', the involvement of national bureaucrats in all West European countries becomes increasingly differentiated in horizontal (sectoral) as well as in vertical (hierarchical) terms. Among roughly 1,200 'Referate' (basic administrative units) in the ministries of West Germany, about half are also involved (part-time) in international and EC-affairs; around a quarter deal in one way or another with EC subjects. Forty specialize (full-time) in EC matters. These units are well distributed across all ministries; 'technical' and 'internal' affairs ministries are considerably involved.[31] Interaction with colleagues from other states or international organizations thus becomes a regular pattern: it is a normal, although not dominant, part of the day-to-day activities of national civil servants.

A major difference between those organizations is the involvement of political actors. One notes the marked contrast between the 70 sessions of the EC Council (1985) and the one single session of the OECD Council. Heads of government also become involved within the EC and EPC (via the European Council) and in a less regular pattern within NATO. Adding up the 'multiple bilateralism' of heads of government and ministries, as well as other fora like the Western Summit,[32] we can observe that not only national officials but also all politicians with governmental responsibilities have extended their field of activities into the 'international' arena to a quite considerable extent. This feature is not compatible with a model of 'meta-bureaucracy',[33] a byzantine network of national and international 'bureaucrats' excluding (at least de facto) all other actors from the political cycle. Officials in these networks are also closely 'monitored' and influenced by a parallel, quite competitive structure of interest groups, showing organizational and behavioural patterns quite similar to those of bureaucrats: lobbies have reacted smoothly to decision making outside the national system. The 'losers' are the parliamentarians and parties, their patterns of cross-border interactions have not developed resources and forms comparable with those of national officials and (governmental) politicians. Moreover, forms of transnational parliamentary assemblies have not reached a comparable intensity of meetings; the European Parliament, on the other hand, can rival the intensity of meetings of national officials and ministers, but its members lack an adequate involvement in the national political fora.

The administrative style is characterized by an ambiguous double role played by civil servants: on the one hand to push towards positions in conformity with interests known as 'national' and on the other to achieve results in a policy network where consensus is normally seen as a major value in itself, which is supported by doctrines of 'national sovereignty' and 'vital interests'. National and international officials quite often fulfil troublesome and time-consuming roles as active 'brokers'[34] linking the national and international arenas of conflict settlement. Their linking role is crucial, although they are no 'monopolists': members of governments and lobbies also play the multi-level game. Lobbies are particularly important for decision making limited to narrower sectors, with heads of government and ministers coming into the bargaining game when issues of national political consequence are at stake, particularly when cross-sectoral 'package deals' are being concluded.[35]

A closer look at the trends

As an initial survey of part B of Table 1 would indicate, the EC can be characterized as a most complex and differentiated system of interlocking national and international administrative units and procedures. Overall, there are around 8,000 meetings ('reunions') of Commission and Council bodies with simultaneous translation per year (1985) with a slow rate of increase. (Sessions of the European Parliament, the Court of Justice and the Economic and Social Council are not included.) Interaction patterns extend to at least five phases of the policy cycle.

The intensity of meetings varies: COREPER (the Committee of the Permanent Representatives) on both levels meets at least two days per week, some working groups get together weekly, others only twice per year. Besides COREPER, there are other committees preparing the work of sectoral councils, particularly the Special Committee for Agriculture and – in a different way – the Monetary Committee.

For all its drafting work the Commission has installed around 550 groups of 'independent' experts (1987); at least 70% of participants are civil servants from member governments participating in a 'non-official' capacity. The expert groups are spread all over sectors of EC policies. The intensity of meetings depends on the Commission's preference.

The Commission uses this form of 'engrenage' (not meant in a pejorative sense) to collect the necessary information and to prepare the ground for a viable policy. National civil servants try to direct the Commission towards their own positions. This phase is of crucial importance as the issues for the next steps in the decision-making are set down and first areas of consensus and dissent are identified.

In the second phase, national civil servants are the major actors in an intensive bargaining process: under the guidance of the two levels of COREPER, around 180–200 working groups 'digest' the Commission's proposals to prepare the ground for decisions by the Council. Quite a considerable proportion of these (the so-called 'A-points') are adopted by the Council without further deliberations by the politicians themselves; several of these points are even adopted by COREPER without further debate. Thus a major proportion and large details of the EC legislative acts are, de facto, decided on a low bureaucratic level. These working groups of the Council are also extended to all sectors of EC policies.

In the third phase, the Council – national ministers assisted by the permanent representative and in the presence of up to six more national civil servants per delegation – takes the binding decisions.

The Council meets for about 120 days per year in around 21 (1988) sectoral compositions, examples being the environment, transport, research, women's issues, internal market, development, social affairs, education, fishery, health, steel, cultural affairs, telecommunication, energy, budget, Euratom, industry.

The Foreign Ministers (in the 'General' Council) and the Ministers for Agriculture meet at least once a month; if one adds informal sessions, the frequency of their meetings is even higher. This intensity leads participants to the often-quoted remark that these ministers get to see their EC homologues as often as they meet their national cabinet colleagues.

Most other Councils officially meet at least once per half-year presidency and often once per presidency in an informal weekend meeting – normally in a large country house – within the electoral district of the minister holding the presidency. Feeling under indirect pressure by too many civil servants – at normal Council sessions up to 120 persons may be present – ministers also retreat more and more often to informal luncheon meetings with some civil servants of the presidency and the secretariat of Council present. This form of more confidential negotiations creates major problems for the excluded civil servants.

Of a specific importance for the national procedures are the sessions of the European Council in which the French Commission president and the heads of government of the other countries meet at least twice per year. The functions of this body which is formally outside the Rome Treaties (even after the Single European Act) are to set major points for the Community's agenda, to pass general declarations and – an unpopular function which has nevertheless become the major part of the work of the political leaders – to conclude cross-sectoral package-deals which are the major instruments of achieving progress within the EC. These de facto decisions for the EC (which are put into legal form by the 'normal' EC machinery) are generally quite concrete, that is, heads of government bargain over technically worded details from several sectors of EC policies at the same time.[36] Thus the political heads not only pursue some kind of declaratory policy but also negotiate over sums for the regional funds, over formulae for 'own resources' of the EC, over budgetary rebates for the United Kingdom, and over 'set-aside' quotas for the Common Agricultural Policy – all in one package. At sessions of the European Council around 900 civil servants of all kinds may be present.[37]

After a decision has been taken by the Council, national civil servants are also involved in the implementation process. The complexity of those procedures is considerable. There are 14 applied types which the Council wants to reduce to 7 procedures (Council decision of 13 July 87/373). In 'consultative', 'management' and 'regulation' committees, national bureaucrats can – to different extents – influence and control the Commission's discretionary powers in administering the policies decided upon by the Council. The frequency of the meetings of these 250 or so committees varies: managing committees for certain agricultural products – like wheat and milk – come together weekly, others twice per year.

The application of the EC legislatives act is within the responsibility of member countries, which again implies an involvement of several public administrations and agencies. The Commission and Courts have supervisory and adjudicatory roles.

A search for theories and paradigms

The data we have just examined indicate several forms and degrees of intensity of the involvement of national bureaucrats in Western and West European organizations. Within this picture the EC shows the most developed form of cooperation among national and international (i.e. EC) officials.

The policy cycle of the EC is characterized by a high and widely spread degree of 'fusion', of 'interlocking' of national and EC civil servants (as well as of politicians and lobbies). This EC pattern of administrative and political interactions reflects a trend by which Member States 'pool' their sovereignties and mix them with competences of the EC into a system to which the notion of 'cooperative federalism' can be applied.[38] Competences are not shifted from the national to the EC level without any compensation (a federal solution corresponding to the traditional notion), but a different pattern can be observed. The more intensive are the forms and the stronger are the impacts of the common policy making, the more extensive and intensive are the organizational devices for access and the influence which national officials and politicians preserve for themselves.

The term 'cooperative' thus signals two closely linked patterns of administrative interaction: the way state administrations develop their national policy-making style in a 'horizontal view',[39] and the way several national and international administrations shape common policies in a 'vertical view'. These trends are mutually reinforcing.

Such an analysis evokes a major desideratum for further work: it concerns the yardstick by which to evaluate these administrative trends. The process identified in the evolution of West European states might be seen as a 'modern' way to tackle problems in an interdependent society and world. The administrative interactions increase the mutual calculability and the confidence in the actions of partners or other actors such as the Commission. Civil servants develop norms and rules of working together, reducing the fear of being exploited by co-players.[40] The stability of interaction systems and the overall productivity of decisions are enhanced. All actors concerned are participating in a pluralistic and 'consociative' way.[41]

From an alternative perspective this process of administrative fusion creates considerable problems. The administrative and political 'labyrinth' changes the established and accepted ways and capacities to tackle political problems in democracies. By its complex procedures it reduces efficiency when measured by the time taken to reach a decision and by the quality of the output: national governments and administrations are moving into 'joint decision traps' achieving only sub-optimal outputs;[42] by shifting the major parts of the de facto decision making to anonymous bodies, it diffuses responsibilities and reduces transparency; traditional democratic and parliamentary norms are eroded. Governments become less responsible for the decisions affecting the citizens by whom they are elected. For the normal citizens the 'state' becomes less and less a clear object of 'identification'.[43] National politicians still offer a certain degree of legitimacy, but the mechanism (or assumption) behind this notion is no longer valid: in such an interlocked system politicians cannot be responsive to nor responsible for their electorate. 'Fusion' means 'diffusion' of responsibilities, and undermines the very basis of Western democracies without replacing it with a real EC democracy. This perspective warns against a 'legitimacy gap' which gets wider and wider within the process of interlocking. The European Parliament is not (yet) an equivalent replacement for this growing deficit.[44]

The preliminary results and the debate on its evaluations indicate the need both to develop more comprehensive theory (or theories) on the dynamics of European integration and to discuss the 'paradigms' from which to evaluate those developments.

Notes

1. See, for example, Gabriel A. Almond and G. Binding Powell, *Comparative Politics: A Developmental Approach* (Boston, 1966), p. 35; Ernst Forsthoff, *Der Staat der Industriegesellschaft, dargestellt am Beispiel der Bundesrepublik Deutschland* (Munich, 1971), pp. 11 et seq.; Charles Tilly, 'Reflections on the History of European State-Making', in Charles Tilly, ed., *Formation of National States in Western Europe* (Princeton, 1975), pp. 31 et seq.; Renate Mayntz, *Soziologie der öffentlichen Verwaltung* (Heidelberg and Karlsruhe, 1985), pp. 12 et seq.; Gérard Timsit, 'L'Administration', in *Traité de science politique*, Madeleine Grawitz and Jean Leca, vol. 2 (Paris, 1985), p. 446.
2. See especially Stein Rokkan, 'Dimensions of State Formation and Nation-Building', in Charles Tilly, ed., op. cit., p. 571 et seq.
3. Jost Delbrück, 'Internationale und nationale Verwaltung, inhaltliche und institutionelle Aspekte', in Kurt G.A. Jeserich et al., eds., *Deutsche Verwaltungsgeschichte, Vol. V, Die Bundesrepublik Deutschland* (Stuttgart 1987), p. 398; Thomas Ellwein, 'Geschichte der öffentlichen Verwaltung', in König et al., eds., *Öffentliche Verwaltung in der Bundesrepublik Deutschland* (Baden-Baden, 1981), p. 49.
4. See especially Joel D. Aberbach et al., *Bureaucrats and Politicians in Western Democracies* (Cambridge, MA. and London 1981); Renate Mayntz, 'German Federal Bureaucrats: Functional Elite between Politics and Administration', in Ezra N. Suleiman, ed., *Bureaucrats and Policy Making, A comparative Overview* (New York and London, 1984), pp. 174–206; Gérard Timsit, op. cit., pp. 446–51.
5. Max Weber, *Wirtschaft und Gesellschaft, Grundriß der verstehenden Soziologie* (Cologne and Berlin, 1956).
6. See especially Joachim Jens Hesse, 'Aufgaben einer Staatslehre heute', in Thomas Ellwein et al., eds., *Jahrbuch zur Staats-und Verwaltungswissenschaft*, Vol. 1, (Baden-Baden, 1987), p. 77 et seq.
7. See especially Robert W. Cox et al., *The Anatomy of Influence: Decision-Making in International Organizations* (New Haven, 1973); Reinhard Lohrmann, 'Multinationale Entscheidungsprozesse in der Verwaltung der Europäischen Behörden', in *Regionale Verflechtung in der Bundesrepublik Deutschland, empirische Analyse und theoretische Probleme*, Schriftenreihe des Forschungsinstitut der deutschen Gesellschaft für auswärtige Politik (Munich and Vienna, 1973), p. 193 et seq. and p. 213 et seq.; Helmut Schmitt von Sydow, 'Die Zusammenarbeit nationaler und europäische Beamter in den Ausschüssen der Kommission', in *Europarecht*, Vol. 9 (1974), pp. 62–3; Harold K. Jacobson, *Networks of Interdependence, International Organizations and the Global Political System* (New York, 1984); Giuseppe Ciavarini Azzi, 'Les Experts nationaux, Chevaux de Troie ou partenaires indispensables?, in Joseph Jamar and Wolfgang Wessels, eds., *The Community Bureaucracies at the Crossroads* (Bruges, 1985), p. 59 et seq.; Sabino Cassesse, Theoretical Sketch of the Cooperative and Multidimensional Nature of the Community Bureaucracy', in idem. p. 39 et seq.; Wolfgang Wessels, 'Community Bureaucracy in a Changing Environment: Criticisms, Trends, Questions', in idem, p. 9 et seq.

8. See especially Gerda Zellentin, *Les Missions permanentes auprès des organisations internationales: conclusions théoriques* (Brussels, 1976).
9. See especially, Geofrey Edwards, Helen Wallace, *Die Präsidentschaft im Ministerrat* (Bonn, 1978); Colm Ó Nualláin, ed., *The Presidency of the European Council of Ministers, Impacts and Implications for National Governments* (Beckenham, 1985); Axel Vornbäumen, *Die Präsidentschaft im Ministerrat der Europäischen Gemeinschaft als Führungsinstrument* (Bonn, 1985).
10. Heinrich Siedentopf and Jacques Ziller, eds., *Making European Policies Work, The Implementation of Community Legislation in the Member States* (London, 1988).
11. Zellentin, op. cit, p. 125 et seq.
12. Jacobson, op. cit.
13. See, for example, Theodor Holtz, 'Die Europäischen Behörden und die nationale Bürokratien – Probleme der Zusammenarbeit und der Personalstruktur', in: *Regionale Verflechtung in der Bundesrepublik Deutschland, op cit.* p. 214; Wessels, 'Community Bureaucracy in a changing Environment: Criticism, Trends, Questions', in: Jamar, Wessels eds., *op. cit.*
14. See Ernst B. Haas, *The Uniting of Europe* (Stanford, 1968), p. 5.
15. See, for this term, Guiseppe Ciavarini Azzi, op. cit. pp. 99–105.
16. See especially, Zellentin, op. cit.
17. See, for this term, Robert D. Putnam and Nicholas Bayne, *Western Summits* (Bonn, 1985).
18. See, for these terms, Glenn H. Snyder and Paul Diesing, *Conflict among Nations, Bargaining, Decision-Making and System Structure in International Crises* (Princeton, 1977).
19. See, for example, the lively debate on the so-called 'comitology'.
20. Aberbach et al., op. cit.; Mayntz, *Soziologie der öffentlichen Verwaltung*, third edn. (Heidelberg and Karlsruhe, 1985); Timsit, op. cit.; Guy Peters, *The Politics of Bureaucracy* (New York, 1984).
21. See especially Peter Flora and Arnold J. Heidenheimer, eds., *The Development of Welfare States in Europe and America* (New Brunswick, 1981); and OECD Economic Studies, *The Role of the Public Sector, Causes and Consequences of the Growth of Government* (Paris, 1985).
22. See Robert O. Keohane and Joseph S. Nye, Jr., 'Power and Interdependence revisited', *International Organization*, 41/1987, p. 725.
23. See Robert O. Keohane, *After Hegemony, Cooperation and Discord in the World Political Economy* (Princeton, 1984); and Paul Kennedy, *The Rise and Fall of the Great Powers, Economic Change and Military Conflict from 1500 to 2000* (New York, 1987).
24. Wolfgang Wessels, *The growth of the EC System, A Product of the Dynamics of Modern European States? A Plea for a More Comprehensive Approach*, Paper XIVth World Congress of the International Political Science Association (Washington, DC, 1988).
25. See especially Karl W. Deutsch et al., *Political Community and the North Atlantic Area* (Princeton, 1957); Deutsch et al., *France, Germany and the Western Alliance, A Study of Elite Attitudes on European Integration and World Politics* (New York, 1967), p. 569.
26. Herbert A. Simon, 'Rationality as Process and Product of Thought', *The American Economic Review* (Vol. 68, 1978) p. 13.
27. See, for the latter approach, Roland Vaubel, 'A Public Choice Approach to International Organization' *Public Choice* (Vol. 59, 1986), pp. 39–57.
28. Pedro Sanchez da Costa Pereira, 'The Rise of a Secretariat', in Alfred Pijpers et al., eds, *European Political Cooperation in the 1980s* (Dordrecht, 1988), pp. 85–104;
29. See also, Gérard Blanc, 'L'Evolution quantitative des organisations internationales:

vers la croissance zero?' in Jéquier, ed., *Les Organisations Internationales entre l'Innovation et la Stagnation* (Lausanne, 1985), pp. 17–45.

30. Christophe Sasse, *The Council of Ministers, Governments, Parliaments, Decision-Making Processes in the EC* (Bonn, 1975); Colm Ó Nualláin, ed., op. cit.; Heinrich Siedentopf and Jacques Ziller, op. cit.

31. These data are estimates based on two independent approaches: focused interviews with civil servants in each of the West German ministries and 'demands' to participate in international organizations. The last method could only be applied to EC committees. Both estimates are quite consistent.

32. Putnam and Bayne, op. cit.

33. See, for a similar term, Harold K. Jacobson, op. cit., p. 200.

34. See, for the term, Aberbach, op. cit., p. 21.

35. See Helen Wallace in this volume.

36. See Simon Bulmer and Wolfgang Wessels, *The European Council, Decision-Making in European Politics* (London, 1987), pp. 80–102.

37. Marcell von Donat, *Das ist der Gipfel, Die EG-Regierungschefs unter sich* (Baden-Baden, 1987), p. 21.

38. See Wolfgang Wessels, 'Alternative strategies for Institutional Reforms', European University Institute Working Paper, No. 85/184 (Florence, 1984), p. 58; Simon Bulmer and Wolfgang Wessels, *The European Council, Decision-Making in European Policy* (London, 1987), p. 10 et seq.; Sabine Pag, 'The Relations between the Commission and National Bureaucracies', in Institut International des Sciences Administratives, Institut Européen d'Administration, *The European Administration*, (Maastricht, 1988), p. 446 et seq.

39. See Aberbach, op. cit.

40. See, for theories on cooperation in situations of interdependence, Keohane, op. cit.

41. Heinrich Schneider, *Rückblick für die Zukunft, Konzeptionelle Weichenstellung für die Europäische Einigung* (Bonn, 1986), p. 97.

42. Fritz W. Scharpf, 'Die Politikverflechtungsfalle, Europäische Integration und deutscher Föderalismus im Vergleich', *Politische Vierteljahresschrift*, 4/1985, pp. 323–57.

43. Delbrück, op. cit.

44. Eberhard Grabitz et al., *Direktwahl und Demokratisierung, Eine Funktionenbilanz des Europäischen Parlaments nach der ersten Wahlperiode* (Bonn, 1988).

14 The legal dimension
Renaud Dehousse and
Joseph H.H. Weiler

Relationships between the legal sphere – legal structures, institutions and norms – and the integration process at the economic or political level are both manifold and complex, sometimes even contradictory. A survey of the interactions between these different levels can certainly serve as a good basis for an overall reflection on the multi-faceted phenomenon of European integration. However, caution invites us to state at the outset the limits of our ambitions: we do not pretend to provide a global assessment of the relationships between legal, economic and political elements, nor even a comprehensive description of the changes that have taken place within the legal sphere. Rather, what we try to do is to present a somewhat impressionistic view of the integration phenomenon, stressing some aspects which appear to us to be unduly neglected and indicating certain paths which would, in our view, deserve a more careful exploration in the future.

Our main concerns are, therefore, twofold. First, we will explain briefly how integration manifests itself within the legal sphere and try to provide a series of legal parameters which can be of help in assessing the magnitude of the integration process in different institutional contexts. Secondly, we will outline the role legal and institutional elements play in the integration process and their relationship to the evolution currently taking place at other levels. To use the terminology developed in the introduction to this volume, we would say that the central thesis of this essay is that 'formal' factors of integration, although they are considerably influenced by external (non-legal) factors, also experience a dynamic of their own. Legal integration has made significant progress since the early 1960s. This dynamic accounts for a large part of the developments now taking place in Western Europe. Neither the nature of the European Community nor its role in the Europe of today can be understood without a reference to its legal and institutional structure. In other words, legal and institutional elements condition both the magnitude and the spatial scope of integration.

But before explaining the kind of contribution legal thinking can make to one's understanding of integration mechanisms, it is necessary to stress that legal factors should be approached from a series of viewpoints considerably broader than one generally imagines.

Functional and analytical approaches

The functional importance of law is well known: human beings have always felt the necessity to cast their relationships in a legal mould to both define and consolidate them. Likewise, for governments law is the instrument *par excellence*, the way to transform political discourse into political action. In spite of their apparent banality, these remarks are useful to understand the functional importance of legal elements in a complex process such as European integration, for they make clear a facet of the phenomenon which is not always clearly perceived by non-lawyers: more than a given sector with clear limits, law tends to be a necessary component of integration in most sectors. Indeed, legal elements play a double role; they are both the object and the agent of integration.

That law can be seen as one of the main objects of integration should come as a surprise to nobody, given our premises. It is a commonplace that nation-states are – probably by far – the main producers of norms in the twentieth century, even in spite of the emergence of a series of international actors. The crystallization of European societies in states and the general trend towards codification of national laws have given accrued importance to national borders. Already three centuries ago, Pascal noted in his *Pensées* that the very same situation can be legally regulated in a radically different manner on both sides of the same border: 'on ne voit rien de juste ou d'injuste qui ne change de qualité en changeant de climat. Trois degrés d'élévation du pôle renversent toute la jurisprudence; un méridien décide de la vérité . . . Plaisante justice qu'une rivière borne! Vérité au-decà des Pyrénées, erreur au-delà.' Clearly, the national character of the vast majority of legal norms can considerably hamper integration in a series of sectors. The mere fact that a problem has been given different legal answers in different countries may, at times, prevent exchanges or collaboration across national borders. In the legal realm, the principal meaning of integration is precisely the gradual removal of differentiated treatment. The main objective of the 1992 programme launched by the Commission's White Paper on the completion of the internal market is the elimination of barriers due to the existence of different (national) regulatory regimes within the European Community.

However, law is not a mere object of integration. Historically speaking at least, integration started as a law-making exercise, an attempt to establish – through the creation of institutions equipped with law-making and monitoring powers – conditions for an increase in exchanges and cooperation between European countries. Far from being market-driven, the creation of an ECSC was essentially a political response to a political problem. Law was then regarded as the central agent of integration: far from being market-driven, changes in the legal sphere were meant to transform production conditions. As time went by, this historical primacy of 'formal' integration was challenged by the growing importance of economic and technological developments. But one could argue that even today, integration remains largely a top-down process, although normal integration, when successful, can create bottom-up pressure for further integration.[1]

Very often,[2] legal integration takes the form of a replacement or an overlay of national norms by European ones. The extent to which this change is necessary and the means by which it can be ensured is an open question; some Member States of the EC have very strong views on this issue. The necessity of adopting European norms has also led to the creation of new institutions, with their own means of action, both legal and financial. This is certainly by far the most visible aspect of the entire process, although one could argue that it is only the tip of the iceberg: in the minds of many European citizens, the creation of Europe-wide institutions is the very definition of integration.

However, one should not consider the role of law exclusively along these functional lines, for one would miss important aspects of its role – actual or potential – by doing so. Not only are legal elements good indicators of the magnitude of the integration process but, more importantly, their actual impact can sometimes not be properly measured without taking into account their symbolic value.

At the analytical level, the language of law can sometimes be of great importance. Since law is often a translation of policies into operational terms, as we saw, the legal discourse sometimes demonstrates intentions which have not been explicitly formulated or confirms other signals. The choice between competing terms – for instance whether to use 'Member States' or 'High Contracting Parties' – is significant and will not escape the eye of a careful reader. The Single European Act provides a good example of this kind of hidden message. The silent shift from the intensive use of the term 'Member States' in Titles I and II, which deal with the European Community, to the less integrated concept of 'High Contracting Parties' in Title III, which deals with European Political Cooperation, summarizes the differences existing between these two systems. That this difference can be explained by the legislative origin of these two texts, which have been elaborated separately, does not alter the significance of the semantic shift, which emphasizes the existence of two distinct integration levels. Likewise, a shift from the status of 'foreigner' to that of 'national of another Member State' reveals a qualitative leap forward. Equally significant is the European Court of Justice's reference to the Treaty of Rome as the 'constitutional charter' of the Community in the case of *Les Verts*[3]: far from being mere lip service to the idea of integration, the Court's language is symptomatic of the line of teleological interpretation it has adopted from the outset.

Moreover, the symbolic value of law is not limited to language. Legal instruments carry signs of different sorts. The mere fact of 'going to law' (i.e., of giving legal value to certain arrangements) must sometimes be understood first and above all as a symbol, independently of the substance of the obligations thereby assumed. Seen in that light, the Member States' decision to give EPC a legal status by enshrining its basic principles in Title III of the Single Act can be viewed as a more significant change than a *prima facie* examination would suggest. Although it did not constitute a radical departure from existing practices – leaving aside, of course, the much awaited creation of a secretariat – the formal acceptance by the Twelve of a legal commitment to cooperate confirmed in a most symbolic way the importance they assigned to cooperation in this field.

The Franco-German Elysée Treaty of 1963 provides another instructive example. The outcry it provoked in Europe was completely out of proportion to the actual content of the agreement. What mattered most in this case was that, by stressing in solemn language the importance of their bilateral cooperation, France and the Federal Republic of Germany could appear – and indeed appeared to many – to give absolute preference to their mutual relationships over collaboration with other partners like the United States or the United Kingdom.[4] Significantly, to counterbalance this impression, the German Bundestag opted for an equally symbolic initiative and approved the Treaty with a preamble which stressed that it could not be used in a way that would be detrimental to the Atlantic Alliance or to British paticipation in European unification efforts. Although deprived of any legal value, this preambula was perceived by the French administration as undermining the political premisses on which the agreement rested.

The content of a legal instrument can also be of important symbolic value. The establishment of structures with a constitutional outlook – parliamentary assemblies, higher courts with a competence to control the compatibility of national provisions to 'integrated' rules – can also be more meaningful than their actual functional utility would suggest. The unlimited duration of a treaty is also a good clue of the value attached to it by its signatories. The EEC Treaty has been concluded 'for an unlimited period', which can be seen as an indication that it was conceived by its drafters not only as an instrument designed to foster their immediate interests, but also as a starting point for a broader venture.[5]

The above examples clearly suggest that any survey of legal patterns of integration ought not to neglect the symbolic dimension of law. One could even go further and argue that the symbolic dimension is also an essential factor for the functional efficiency of legal instruments. Every norm is first and above all a message, and the way this message is phrased and presented can be crucial. Let the norm be unclear, or simply unnoticed, and it will fail to achieve the objectives it was meant to reach.

Instruments which, *prima facie*, appear equally capable of attaining a given result can present important differences as far as their symbolic value is concerned. At first sight, for instance, both the harmonization of national regulations and the mutual recognition of their basic equivalence can be used, alternatively or together, to reach the same result: the free movement of factors of production envisaged by the Treaty of Rome. Technically speaking, however, they present great differences. Whereas harmonization tends towards the adoption of a Community-wide norm, mutual recognition is primarily a negative obligation imposed on the Member States to prevent them from applying their own regulations to imported goods. By way of consequence, their symbolic value will also differ considerably: harmonization will lead to a far more visible result than mutual recognition, which operates essentially *ex post*, as a conflict-solving device. This is no meagre advantage, if one keeps in mind that free movement is not an end in itself, but a way to promote a more efficient use of resources at Community level, *inter alia* through economies of scale. It is far from sure that mutual recognition will suffice to encourage economic operators to make the necessary adjustments. This is one of the principal difficulties in the new approach to technical harmonization adopted by the Community in 1985[6]: even if the emphasis laid on mutual recognition can be understood as a means of facilitating the decision-making process – it is much easier to impose negative obligations on Member States than to get them to define collectively the standards a given product must meet in order to circulate freely within the Community[7] – one must, nevertheless, realize that this stategy involves difficulties of a new type and that the relatively low profile of mutual recognition ought to be compensated by positive steps.[8]

To conclude on this point, it appears clear that the symbolic dimension of law must be seen not only as an analytical tool, which may help us to measure the political value of certain initiatives, but also as a crucial factor, able to condition the functional efficiency of legal norms. This is but one example of the necessity to adopt a broad conception of the impact of legal elements, in order to assess their true importance in the integration process.

Law and the dynamics of integration

It is generally accepted that integration must be regarded as a *process*, leading gradually, with the passage of time, to an increase in the exchanges between the various societies concerned and to a more centralized form of government. However, this evolving character renders any assessment of the role of legal elements within this process more difficult. By its nature, law tends to provide a fixed and relatively rigid image of the situations it takes into consideration. Thus, with the passage of time the legal system must often change to adapt to the emergence of new conditions.

It is probably for that reason that in many theories of integration legal and institutional elements are regarded more or less explicitly as dependent variables which reflect – more or less rapidly and accurately – the changes under way at the socio-economic or political level. The true impetus is often seen to originate in factors like technical progress, international trade, or changing political conditions. No doubt this analysis is essentially correct. However, legal factors can also play an important role in the integration process. The legal system is sometimes animated by a dynamic of its own, and one could argue that, even if law is not the main catalyst of change in the integration process, many changes are greatly conditioned by legal and institutional elements.

A legal dynamic can exist when autonomous organs are entrusted with judiciary competence. No matter how sensitive to their environment the persons sitting in those organs may be, their decisions cannot be regarded as a mere by-product of changes taking place at other levels: they rest essentially on the substantive rules the judges have to apply and on the way they conceive their institutional mission.

Although they are generally regarded as mere interpreters of the law, courts sometimes take on a truly creative role. In the EC context, for instance, the Court of Justice has been called on to develop a constructive interpretation of basic principles contained in the EEC Treaty, like the principle of non-discrimination and the broad concepts of customs union and of commercial policy, in order to fill lacunae caused by the inaction of Community legislative organs.[9] The Court of Justice has also opened many avenues which were not expressly envisaged by the drafters of the Treaties. By doing so, it has contributed greatly to the consolidation of the Community system, be it in terms of competence – in the field of external relations, for instance – or as regards the reach of Community law within Member States. Clearly, the possibility of a direct dialogue with national courts through the preliminary rulings procedure established by Article 177 of the EEC Treaty has contributed to this phenomenon of judicial law-making. This procedure has, *inter alia*, enabled the Court to help national courts to ensure the compatibility of national provisions with Community law – a rather uncommon feature in an international setting.[10] Likewise, the Council of Europe is almost always associated with the idea of protecting human rights – despite its activities in many other fields – essentially because it has established judicial organs to which private citizens can appeal in case of violation of the European Convention on Human Rights.[11]

The importance of these elements cannot be overestimated. For many years, the European Court of Justice has been the most active and creative Community organ – hence the protests which arose in some Member States against what was perceived to be a sort of 'gouvernement des juges'. The impact of the ECJ's case law often reaches well beyond the legal sphere. Had the Court been more shy in its handling of many questions, the Community would probably not have demonstrated the same resilience throughout the difficult 1970s. Most of the 1992 programme rests on the principle of mutual recognition first developed by the Court in its landmark *Cassis de Dijon* ruling.[12] It is, of course, impossible to say what would have happened if the Court had opted for another line. It seems clear, however, that the Commission would have faced many more obstacles in elaborating its internal market strategy. Moreover, it is not altogether clear that the Member States would have accepted the institutional reforms which were necessary to carry it out.

This provides a natural transition to our second point, which is that legal and institutional factors largely condition the evolution of the integration process. One of the reasons why this is not always clearly perceived is that the influence of these factors is often indirect. People generally accept that the institutional framework can directly affect the substance of the policies pursued by the various actors – or indeed be responsible for the fact that no policy whatsoever can be adopted. Much has been written, for example, on the difficulties arising in the EC as a result of the largely consensual character of the decision-making process.[13] Even so, the impact of rules on decision-making is often underestimated. Some tend to argue, for instance, that voting rules matter relatively little since even after the Single Act one votes relatively little – certainly less than treaty rules would allow – whether within the Council of Ministers or at committee level. This interpretation, however, neglects an element of great significance, namely the fact that the possibility of resorting to a vote is likely to influence the negotiating parties directly. When negotiations take place in the shadow of a veto, all parties know that the consent of each of them is necessary before action can be taken; when a vote is possible, a Member State knows that if isolated it can simply be outvoted. The pattern of negotiations will, therefore, differ considerably; no matter whether there is actually a vote or not, the flavour of consensus is, consequently, bound to be different. Thus, in order to assess the real impact of the shift to majority voting rendered possible by the Single Act, one should have regard not only to actual instances of a vote, but also to the time needed to achieve a consensus when no vote has been taken: in many fields where, for years, no decision had been possible, a compromise has now been reached within months. This change, it is submitted, owes much to the modification of voting rules.

This somewhat indirect influence of legal rules does not stop with procedural elements. To a large extent, the same could be said of rules governing the distribution of competences in the Community system. Throughout marathon sessions devoted to the fixing of agricultural prices, Member States must keep in mind that eventually a decision will have to be taken at Community level, since they have now granted the Community the exclusive competence to deal with that issue. Here again, the outcome of the negotiation is likely to be affected by the fact that certain policy options – a withdrawal from the negotiation table, for instance – are now either completely barred or rendered extremely costly.[14] In a similar way, although the legal structure of the Community cannot be seen as the catalyst which rendered possible the current explosion of contacts with Eastern countries, it seems clear that the current dialogue is conditioned by the fact that the Community, entrusted with an exclusive competence for commercial policy, is in many respects an unavoidable partner for Eastern countries.

Lastly, any overall assessment of the role of law in the integration process must take into account the inherent conservatism of any legal system. All policies have to be adjusted in response to economic and social change, and the mere fact that they are enshrined in a legal framework can render this adaptation more difficult.[15] As we said at the outset, this tends to be true in all legal systems, but there is in a transnational context an increased risk of legal obsolescence due to the largely consensual nature of the decision-making process. The adaptation of harmonization directives to technical progress, for instance, can prove extremely difficult, even if the political value of the problems is often minimal. In other words, there is a real danger that obsolete norms will remain in force for lack of an agreement either on their reform or their replacement. Such a deadlock can eventually lead to strong disintegrating pressures, and encourage violations of legal rules.

Packaging a given policy as a legal instrument can, therefore, be a double-edged sword. On the one hand, it can greatly contribute to the policy's consolidation and provide a guarantee of continuity. On the other hand, the very rigidity of the legal norm can prevent or make more difficult any further evolution. Seen in this light, the reference to economic aspects of security in Article 30 (6) of the Single Act represents both a success and a threat: a success because it has clearly established that cooperation in this field was possible and indeed desired, a threat because, in the future, cooperation between the Twelve in other branches of security policy is likely to be opposed on the grounds that it is not envisaged in this provision. The same could be said, actually, about the entire Title III of the Single Act, which has raised EPC (European Political Cooperation) procedures to the status of legal commitments.

To some extent at least, this danger of obsolescence can be avoided by legal techniques. If courts are willing to play a creative role, they can be in the position to compensate for the inherent conservatism of legal instruments.[16] Moreover, legal instruments themselves sometimes envisage the necessity of a change. Thus, Article 30 (12) of the Single Act provides for a review of the functioning of EPC five years after its entry into force, in order to determine whether any revision of Title III is necessary. More interestingly, flexible adaptation mechanisms, such as Article 235 of the EEC Treaty, can make it possible to achieve the necessary updating task without going through the lengthy and hazardous procedure of Treaty revision. This possibility has been used to launch Community policies which were not envisaged by the Treaty of Rome, like regional or environment policies. Thus, as serious as the problem of legal obsolescence can be, it can be resolved by the legal system itself.

Classifying integration parameters

Having reviewed some ways of thinking about the multifaceted relationships between the legal sphere and social, economic or political factors, we shall now turn to the parameters which can be used to assess the magnitude of the integration process within the legal sphere. We shall then try to sketch an overall picture of the entire process as it appears from the combined use of those various elements. At this level again, we do not pretend to be exhaustive: our principal ambition is still to suggest that the problem can be approached from many more ways than is generally thought.

The first thing to be said here is that any attempt at a review of legal patterns of integration should encompass the relationships between all actors interested by this phenomenon: public actors, of course, but also private ones. A greater integration of factors of production should, for instance, result in an increase in legal relationships at the European level among firms or between firms and other actors like, say, trade unions or consumer organizations. Moreover, private actors can play a semi-normative role in drafting integration instruments like standard contracts, standard or arbitration clauses, or in setting technical standards. Transnational bodies like the International Chamber of Commerce, the Economic Commission for Europe of the United Nations or the European normalization committees play an active role at this level. True, the use of these transnational bodies remains essentially voluntary, but public bodies can encourage it by attaching important legal effects to their decisions. One of the cornerstones of the Commission's strategy for completing the internal market lies precisely in the free circulation within the Community of goods conforming with the technical standards defined by private harmonization bodies.[17]

But since we defined integration as a top-down process, aiming at creating the conditions for a development of exchanges within Europe, we shall focus on public actors. Several types of legal variables can be of help in assessing both the depth and the magnitude of the integration process. Most of these concepts have been described at length in the literature dealing with legal aspects of European integration; we can therefore limit ourselves to a rapid synthesis.

The first set of variables covers the relationships between the various organizations which have been created on the European scene and their Member States, and deals with decision-making processes, the type of competences allocated to those various organizations, and the binding effect of the decisions taken in those fora. The most important of those variables, and by far the most widely used, relates to *decision-making*. The main distinction here is between supra-national decision-making and intergovernmentalism. Although there has been in the past a large debate between lawyers and political scientists on the use of these concepts, there seems to be a wide consensus to regard a series of features which depart from traditional diplomacy as supra-national. The most crucial of these features is the existence of organs autonomous from the Member States in their composition and their functioning, and the resort, in intergovernmental bodies, to decision-making processes which go beyond traditional diplomacy, such as the possibility of a vote and the giving up of the classical 'one state, one vote' principle. That the Commission and the Council of Ministers of the European Communities are regarded as the classical examples of these two types of organs should come as a surprise to no one since the concept of supranationalism was developed precisely to distinguish the Community from other organizations.[18]

The extent to which legal decisions of European organizations have *binding effect* can also vary considerably. Some organizations have retained a fairly traditional system, whereby their decisions take the form of an international agreement, which must then be ratified and, where necessary, incorporated into national law according to established procedures. In contrast, the Treaties establishing the European Communities envisaged from the beginning the possibility that Community institutions would adopt measures directly binding on those to whom they were addressed – thus disregarding the rules governing the relationship between international law and municipal law in the legal orders of the Member States. Equally important, the Treaty permitted certain international norms to enjoy an absolute supremacy over national provisions, even when the latter were subsequently enacted.

There may also be significant differences as regards the way the granting of *competences* to a given organization is conceived. Can those organizations be used at the discretion of their Member States, when they deem it more convenient than unilateral action, or are they vested with exclusive competences in the fields where some of these organizations are qualified to act?

As far as law-making is concerned, the range of *integration techniques* is even broader. Some instruments, like Title III of the Single European Act, only establish procedural obligations: information, consultation, concerted action, and so on. Others determine the national law applicable to a given situation, following a pattern often used in private international law.[19] Still others prescribe a uniform way of resolving a problem, by imposing, for instance, the mutual recognition of national norms or of judicial decisions.[20] Lastly, in the most accomplished form of integration, the interested states determine together in a uniform norm the legal consequences attached to a given situation: the approximation of national laws envisaged by Articles 100 and 100A of the EEC Treaty is the best example of this kind of legislative technique.

Another dimension to be considered is the *territorial scope* of integration instruments. As a rule, the territorial scope of a norm depends on the forum in which it is adopted: whether at the EC level, within one of the sub-systems of the Community or, by contrast, at a broader level like the Council of Europe

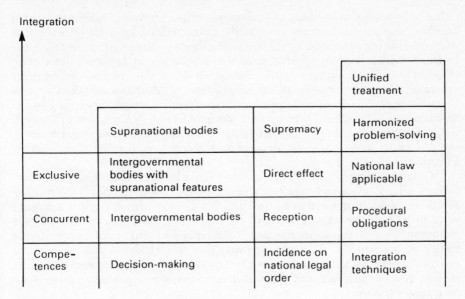

Integration

			Unified treatment
	Supranational bodies	Supremacy	Harmonized problem-solving
Exclusive	Intergovernmental bodies with supranational features	Direct effect	National law applicable
Concurrent	Intergovernmental bodies	Reception	Procedural obligations
Compe-tences	Decision-making	Incidence on national legal order	Integration techniques

Figure 14.1 Legal parameters of integration

will, of course, have a direct incidence on its territorial scope. But this variable is not exclusive: even within the framework of a given organization, there is also room for a certain flexibility, which can lead, as we shall see below, to the adoption of norms directed at some of its members only.

Figure 14.1 contains the main elements of this classification.[21] The interest of such a figure lies in the fact that it provides a comprehensive overview of the legal parameters of integration and of the interactions which can exist between them. Each European organization can be characterized by a different combination of those elements. Moreover, the combination can vary from one field to the other, even within a given organization. Legally speaking, the existence within western Europe of a multiplicity of decisional fora, each with its own specificity, is one of the most interesting aspects of the integration phenomenon. It is, of course, impossible to discuss here the main legal characteristics of the various bodies active on the European scene. Nevertheless, a number of points of a general nature are suggested by looking at figure 14.1.

One can note, for instance, that the existing constellations of legal parameters are not to be regarded as perennial: not only is the integration process in itself supposed to generate changes at the institutional level – leading, for instance, to the creation of more supranational bodies – but, more surprisingly, it appears that these changes will not necessarily be unidirectional. The 1992 programme, which is rightly regarded as the basis for the current relaunching of integration within the Community, is nonetheless characterized by a lesser emphasis on harmonization than in the past, and by a more intensive use of mutual recognition, which is, as we saw, a far less 'integrated' technique.

It also appears that 'smaller' organizations, those grouping together a limited number of partners, are not necessarily characterized by a more integrated decision-making system or by decisions of a more binding nature. Benelux, for instance, which is often referred to as the 'laboratory of Europe', has a quite classical decision-making system, dominated by a Committee of Ministers where all Member States stand on equal footing. All decisions taken by this Committee require their unanimous consent[22] and although, according to the wording of the Benelux Treaty,[23] they 'commit the High Contracting Parties', they are generally not regarded as having direct effect within the legal order of the Member States. *Mutatis mutandis*, the same is true of the Western European Union.

This latter point brings in turn another remark: in certain fields – defence, foreign affairs, monetary and (to a lesser extent) fiscal policies – only loose forms of cooperation seem to be possible. For lawyers this is hardly a surprise, since those fields constitute the hard core of sovereignty – a concept which is synonymous with resistance to outside influence and with a capacity to decide things autonomously. At the same time, this remark demonstrates a crucial difference between the European system(s), where sovereign powers remain in the purview of the states, and classical federations, where sovereign powers are (as a rule) centralized.

However, this difference should not be overemphasized, for it also appears that there is no absolute correlation between institutional and substantive integration: a more supranational structure will not necessarily end up producing more integrated norms. Assuredly, the American federal system is more centralized than the EC; yet sometimes Community norms impose more constraining obligations on the Member States than federal laws do on the States of the Union. Whereas it is quite acceptable for American state universities to charge higher fees to residents of another state, the European Court of Justice has held that this practice constitutes an unacceptable discrimination.[24] Likewise, the compromise reached on the second banking directive should allow, say, British banks to operate more freely in Greece than New York state banks would in neighbouring New Jersey.

Quite clearly, as we noted above, there is a strong link between institutions and the results which can be achieved at a substantive level: the former certainly condition the latter – which is why institutional reform is often sought by those who favour a more integrated Europe. But this link is far less one-sided than is often thought. Institutional reform may be easier to achieve when it is not expected to lead to significantly greater constraints. Thus, one of the main reasons why the Single Act could be regarded as an acceptable compromise by most Member States lies in the fact that they viewed the low profile adopted by the Commission in its White Paper on the internal market as providing a guarantee that there would be no excessive invasion of their sphere of autonomy.[25]

There appears to be an equally strong link between decisional structures and the binding effect of legal norms adopted in a given framework. In the EC context, for instance, the important progress achieved thanks to the twin concepts of direct effect and supremacy of Community law has been accompanied from the mid-1960s to the early 1980s by a clear erosion of the supranational features that characterized the decision-making system. Erosion of the initiative power of the Commission, reluctance to vote in the Council, creation of new intergovernmental organs like COREPER and the European Council: the phenomenon is well known and does not need to be described in detail.[26] What matters here is the fact that throughout this period there has been a striking contrast between the quasi-constitutional status gained by Community law and the institutional stagnation experienced by the EC.[27]

The relationships between these two levels of integration are undoubtedly manifold and complex. To a large extent, both can be due to endogenous factors: states have always demonstrated a clear reluctance to relinquish their powers to external bodies; the Court of Justice, on the other hand, has presented its legal constructs as direct corollaries of the old *pacta sunt servanda* principle and of the necessity of an uniform application of Community law. However, it is possible (and indeed likely) that there was some connection between the changes taking place at these two levels, even if there was no direct causal link between them. The Court, as guardian of the Community institutional system, may have deemed it necessary to prevent a drift towards a more intergovernmental model. Conversely, the considerable impact of EC law on national legal orders has given an even greater importance to the supranational features of the decision-making process: unlike what happens in most international organizations, a decision taken at Community level can have a strong impact on the legal order of the Member States – hence a greater need for Member States to make sure that no decision could be imposed upon them without their consent. The link between these elements was made apparent in the Single European Act: the new Article 100A of the EEC Treaty envisages an extension of majority voting, but this was compensated by several safeguard clauses which, in specific cases, authorize Member States not to apply provisions adopted against their wishes.[28] Thus, the interaction between decisional supranationalism and the 'constitutional' status of EC law appears to be one of the key elements of the 'acquis communautaire'.

The spatial dimension

The territorial boundaries of West European integration have always been a troublesome problem. The question is far from being merely academic: politically, it is impossible to dissociate it from the more general problem of defining the ultimate goal of the integration process. One cannot determine the institutional architecture of an integrated Western Europe without considering who is in and who is not. Failure to reach a consensus on these two issues has resulted in the creation of 'rival' organizations like the Council of Europe, the EC and EFTA. When the six founding states of the EC decided to reinforce the cohesion between their economies, they found it necessary to leave the door open to further enlargement. Now that most of the political energy of the Community is absorbed by an attempt to complete the internal market by 1992, there seems to be a consensus in favour of giving priority to this objective and postponing consideration of further enlargement until after that date. To make things even more complicated, the number of potential partners is far from being clear and stable. Countries which in the past were clearly ineligible for political reasons, like Spain, Portugal or Greece, are now fully fledged members. More recently, dramatic changes in Eastern Europe have resulted in a move eastward of the boundaries of possible collaboration, thereby giving rise to a mushrooming of ad hoc relations between the two sides of what used to be called the iron curtain.

Leaving aside future changes, it is submitted that law can provide some yardsticks in order to assess the current situation. Actually, all indicators contained in Figure 14.1 can be used for this purpose, since they measure the density of integration in different institutional settings. And the conclusion they suggest is fairly obvious: the core area of West European integration is the European Community. Thus, the most crucial variable in assessing the territorial scope of integration is where the external boundary of the Community is located.

In a way, this conclusion was quite foreseeable. Historically speaking, the Community was created to respond to the founding states' desire to establish closer ties among themselves than those which existed between most, if not all, West European states. Because that objective was not acceptable to all states, some opted against membership in the EC, favouring less constraining ties in the EFTA framework. But before commenting further on the implications of this choice, it is probably useful to explain briefly the reasons for the specificity of the EC vis-à-vis other European organizations.

Coming back to the integration parameters listed in Figure 14.1, one cannot but be struck by the fact that the EC ranks high on all levels. Enough has already been said on the elements of decisional supranationalism, which are without equivalent in other organizations, even those which group together only a few states.[29] What is generally less perceived is that as a rule Community law has – qualitatively speaking – a much more incisive impact on the legal order of the Member States than the decisions taken within other organizations. To take but one example, to be operational, conventions adopted in the framework of the Council of Europe, even when adopted by the Committee of Ministers, must be ratified by the Member States pursuant to their normal procedures; the vote expressed in the Committee by their representative is not even regarded as binding. By contrast, in the EC context, the limited wording of Article 189 has been considerably expanded by the Court of Justice, to the extent that much of Community law can now be regarded as having direct effect.[30] This case law was complemented by a series of rulings recognizing Community law – be it primary or secondary – as having an absolute supremacy over conflicting national provisions.[31] One can therefore speak in the Community context of a real *normative* supranationalism.[32]

True, unlike states, the Community does not have a power of coercive action to punish transgressors. But the possibility of a direct dialogue with national jurisdictions through the preliminary rulings procedure established by Article 177 of the EEC Treaty can be of considerable help in this respect. The results of the Florence Project on the working of Article 177 proceedings indicate that almost three-quarters of the preliminary rulings handed down by the Court until the end of 1985 involved a review of the compatibility of national provisions with Community law.[33] Legally speaking, the Court's competence ex Article 177 is limited to the interpretation of Community law, and the Court has often stated that the aim of the preliminary rulings procedure is not to monitor the implementation of Community provisions by Member States. What it can do, and often does, however, is to interpret Community law in such a way as to leave little, if any, discretion to the national Court which is to hand down the final verdict.[34] The final decision on compatibility will, therefore, be rendered by a *national* court, and it will enjoy all the authority a legal system attaches to its own decisions – including the ultimate power of coercion. Thus, the Court's limited competence ex Article 177, which could appear to be a source of weakness, has turned out to be a source of strength.

In terms of competence, too, there are significant differences between the EC and other European bodies. Like their counterparts at world level, many European organizations have been established as fora which can be used by Member States to carry out specific tasks as the need arises. This collaboration is, however, essentially voluntary: legally speaking, Member States are never constrained to act together in the framework of, say, the Western European Union or the Council of Europe; generally, they retain the full capacity to act on their own if they deem it preferable, provided of course that in doing so they abide by their substantive obligations. There is, in other words, no irreversible transfer of competence to those organizations. The situation is quite different in the European Community: in many fields of Community competence, the Member States are not only precluded from enacting measures contradictory to EC law (by virtue of the supremacy principle), but they are also forbidden to take any action at all, by virtue of a doctrine of exclusivity similar to the preemption doctrine applied in many federal states.[35] True, the Court of Justice has shown a great deal of flexibility in this field, admitting for instance the legitimacy of Member States' action to fill certain lacunae. But the idea of exclusive competences remains one of the cardinal principles in the Community's legal architecture. To use the Court's own language:

By creating a Community of unlimited duration, having its own institutions, its own personality, its own legal capacity and capacity of representation on the international plane and, more particularly, real powers stemming from a limitation of sovereignty or a transfer of powers from the States to the Community, the Member States have limited their sovereign rights, albeit within limited fields . . . The transfer by the States from their domestic legal system to the Community legal system of the rights and obligations arising under the Treaty carries with it *a permanent limitation of their sovereign rights* . . .[36]

Legally speaking, membership of the EC is bound to have a more decisive impact on Member States than does membership of any other organization, even if the Member States collectively retain ultimate control of the decision-making process. Not only are the Member States deprived of the capacity to act autonomously in certain fields but, on a substantive level, their mutual relations are considerably transformed by the bulk of obligations imposed upon them. Even their bilateral relationships are affected, as the recent *Matteucci* case demonstrated.[37] On the whole, the EC therefore appears better equipped than other international organizations to legislate and to see to it that its rule be duly implemented.

One could also argue that the EC's high degree of institutional integration is a key variable in the development of the relationships between the EC and its partners on the European scene. For all European organizations or all countries which want to strengthen their relationships with its members, the EC is likely to be an unavoidable partner, if only because it holds exclusive competences in the field of international trade. In contrast, the EC as an organization has less to gain from direct contacts with other European organizations, since their grip over their own members is far more limited.[38] In other words, there seems to be a sort of efficiency threshold – in terms both of decision-making and of implementation – beyond which the Community has moved and behind which the other European organizations remain stuck.

In East-West relations, for instance – a field whose current importance is beyond doubt – contact between the Community and the CMEA has been limited to the signature *pro forma* of a framework agreement in 1988; the most important decisions are, however, being made in bilateral dealings between the Community and East European states. To a large extent, the same could be said of what is often referred to as the EC-EFTA dialogue, which is hardly more than a dialogue between one organization, the EC, and a series of states. The free-trade agreements concluded after the British and Danish 'defections' were not treaties between the Community and EFTA, but separate agreements between the European Community and each of the countries concerned; the first multilateral conventions between the EC and EFTA countries as a group were signed only in 1987.[39]

This institutional imbalance often results in a political one. The Community is better equipped than any other European organization to take initiatives which will have a direct effect on non-member countries, a fact well illustrated by the recent upsurge of interest among EFTA countries for a dialogue with the EC in view of 1992. Moreover, the way this dialogue has developed gives the impression of a strong Community hegemony, be it at the level of agenda setting or in the discussion of the substantive content of the measures envisaged. Because of the weakness of EFTA's institutional structure compared to that of the EC, EFTA countries generally have little choice but to adopt an essentially *reactive* stance and to try to follow the tempo imposed on them by the Community; they do not appear to be in a position to dictate their own conditions.[40] This basic imbalance is largely reflected in the free trade agreements, the provisions of which are often based on concepts and rules derived from the Rome Treaty. As some of the EFTA countries have realized, the only way to rectify this power imbalance without seeking membership of the EC would be to strengthen the institutional structure of EFTA,[41] but for an organization based on a preference for a limited form of integration, this would appear as an intrinsic contradiction.

The specificity[42] of the institutional system of the European Community therefore appears to be the most important legal variable in the current spatial development of integration. Quite understandably, its influence is limited to the sphere of Community competences; in other fields, the level of integration between the 12 Member States is more limited. When examining the action of the Twelve in the Council of Europe, for instance, one is struck by the fact that they appear less eager to cooperate. Indeed, if one takes the number of signings or ratifications of Council of Europe conventions as evidence of the Member States' willingness to participate in the Council's legal integration programme, Member States of the EC as a group are no more integration-minded than are EFTA countries.[43] Likewise, as far as security and defence are concerned, other variables, like NATO membership, clearly have a much stronger impact than has EC membership. The voting pattern of the Twelve at the UN shows a clear division between fields of EC competence, where a common position tends to be the rule, and security matters, where the degree of cohesion displayed is far less impressive.[44]

On more than one occasion, Member States have also decided to leave certain aspects of their collaboration, such as EPC, the EMS, 'EUREKA', out of the EC context, partly in order to avoid the stricter Community discipline. Clearly, the insertion of those policies in a Community framework would prove difficult to reconcile with the maintenance of national sovereignty. Those are, however, exceptions that tend to prove the rule *a contrario*: had they not felt the strong grip of Community law, the Member States would probably not have deemed it necessary to try new forms of cooperation.

It must also be stressed that, in the Community context, membership is not the only variable. In a survey of the 'two-speeds' concept, Ehlerman has amply demonstrated that even in existing Community law there is considerable scope for differentiation, provided that certain key principles – non-discrimination, the prohibition of obstacles within the Community, and the need for time limits – are respected.[45] Safeguard clauses, minimum standards, optional rules, derogations, etc. can account for great variations in the level of integration between some Member States.

The same could be said about differences in their implementation records. Actual integration does not depend only on the number of provisions adopted, but also on their implementation. There is a certain shortage of information at this level. Although it has started to publish an annual report on the implementation of Community law, the Commission tends to focus on pathological cases, and does not provide an overall assessment of the Member States' diligence in putting Community provisions into practice. However, the Commission's Progress Reports on the completion of the internal market provide useful data in a sector of central importance. The latest one confirms the existence of wide disparities, and suggests that countries like Spain, Greece, Italy and Portugal find it difficult to keep in step with the rest of the Community. At the end of December 1988 these four countries had implemented less than half of the 45 directives adopted in the framework of the 1992 programme.[46] Thus, as far as implementation is concerned, a 'two-speeds' Europe is already part of today's problems.

Notwithstanding those important intra-Community differences, membership of the Community remains the most significant variable in any mapping of legal patterns of integration in Western Europe. As indicated at the outset, this derives largely from the dynamics experienced by the Community's legal order since the early 1960s. Had the Community not developed its specific features, it would not have been in a position to exert such a wide influence on today's European scene. One is inclined to believe that those elements are of such importance that their preservation should be given priority over other considerations. This, of course, does not prevent the establishment of manifold links of an *ad hoc* nature with external partners. All we wish to say here is that any enlargement attempt which would not pay enough attention to this concern is likely to be detrimental to the Community structure as a whole. To be sure, this question will be the object of intense debates in European capitals in the years to come.

Notes

1. For an economist's view on this phenomenon, see Dieter Helm and Stephen Smith, 'The Assessment: Economic Integration and the Role of the European Community', *Oxford Review of Economic Policy*, Vol. 5, No. 2 (1989), pp. 1–19.
2. But not always; legal techniques of integration are discussed further below.
3. Case 294/83 *Les Verts* of 23 April 1986, *E.C.R.* (1986) 1339, Recital 23.
4. Oddly enough, it seems that the solemn form of the treaty was first suggested by Adenauer and not by de Gaulle, as one might have thought. See M. Couve de Murville, *Une politique étrangère (1958–1969)*, (Paris, Plon, 1971) at p. 257.
5. Article 240 EEC. It is interesting to note in this respect that Article 97 of the ECSC Treaty stipulates that it is concluded for a period of 50 years from its entry into force. *A contrario*, the omission of any provision to this effect in the Rome Treaties can be regarded as particularly meaningful. For an analysis of these provisions, see J. Weiler, *Il Sistema Comunitario* (Bologna, Il Mulino, 1985), pp. 92–6.
6. Council Resolution of 7 May 1985, O.J. C136, 1.
7. For a full discussion of this issue, see R. Dehousse, 'Completing the Internal Market: Institutional Constraints and Challenges', in Roland Bieber, Renaud Dehousse, John Pinder and Joseph Weiler, eds, *1992: One European Market?* (Baden-Baden, Nomos, 1988), pp. 311–36.
8. This need has been perceived by the EC Commission, which has started to publish 'communications' on the current legal situation in several sectors. See, for instance, the Communication on the compatibility with Article 30 of the EEC Treaty of measures taken by the Member States relating to price controls and reimbursement of medical products, O.J. C310 of 4 December 1986.
9. See P. Pescatore, 'La carence du législateur communautaire et le devoir du juge', *Rechtsvergleichung, Europarecht und Staatenintegration-Gedächtnisschrift für Léontin-Jean Constantinesco* (Cologne, Carl-Heymans Verlag, 1983), pp. 559–80.
10. See below.
11. Significantly, the chapter on the Council of Europe in Roger Pinto's book on European organizations is entirely devoted to the protection of human rights. See *Organisations européennes* (Paris, Payot, 1963), pp. 79–201.
12. Case 120/78, (1979) *E.C.R.* 649.
13. The classical treatment of this question is Fritz Scharpf, 'The Joint-Decision Trap: Lessons of German Federalism and European Integration', *Public Administration* (1988), pp. 239–78.
14. See Weiler, op. cit. (above, n. 5), at pp. 95–6 on this 'all or nothing effect'.
15. For a remarkable discussion of this problem, see Guido Calabresi, 'Incentives, Regulation and the Problem of Legal Obsolescence', in Cappelletti, (ed.), *New Perspectives for a Common Law of Europe* (Brussels and Florence, Bruylant/Le Monnier, 1978), pp. 291–307.
16. See, for instance, the case *Les Verts*, cited above, where the European Court of Justice established that acts of the European Parliament, although not explicitly mentioned in Article 173 of the EEC Treaty, were susceptible to judicial review.
17. Like the Comité européen de la normalisation (CEN) or the Comité européen de la

normalisation électrique (CENELEC). Legally speaking, this must be regarded as a delegation of normative powers to private bodies, which has given rise to certain doubts as to the lawfulness of the strategy. See R. Lauwaars, 'The Model Directive on Technical Harmonization' in Bieber, Dehousse, Pinder & Weiler, op. cit. (above, n. 7), pp. 165–7.

18. For a review of these classification attempts, see J. Weiler, 'The Community System: The Dual Character of Supra-Nationalism', *Yearbook of European Law*, Vol. 1 (1981), pp. 268–73.

19. For a recent example, see the convention of Rome of 19 June 1980 on the law applicable to contractual obligations.

20. See, for instance, the Brussels convention of 27 September 1968 on jurisdiction and enforcement of judgments in civil and commercial matters.

21. One variable, the territorial scope, has been excluded because it does not lend itself easily to this kind of graphic representation.

22. Articles 16 and 18 of the Benelux Treaty.

23. Article 19,a.

24. *Gravier* v *City of Liège*, (1985) *E.C.R.* 593.

25. R. Dehousse, '1992 and Beyond: The Institutional Dimension of the Internal Market Challenge', *Legal Issues of European Integration*, 1989-I.

26. See for instance J.-L. Dewost, 'Les relations entre le conseil et la Commission dans le processus de décision communautaire', in *Nature et évolution des institutions de la Communauté européenne* (Paris, P.U.F., 1980), pp. 16–23.

27. See Weiler, op. cit. (above, n. 18), for detailed comment of these conflicting trends.

28. The link between majority voting and the possibility of escaping the application of Community law is explicit in paragraph 4 of Article 100A.

29. More than 20 years ago, in his classical treatise on European organizations, W.J. Ganshof Van der Meersch attributed the fact that a common agricultural policy had been agreed upon in the EEC and not in the Benelux to the existence within the EEC system of a dynamic element like the Commission. See *Organisations européennes* (Brussels and Paris, Bruylant/Sirey, 1966), Vol. I, p. 425.

30. The first step in this direction was the famous *Van Gend en Loos* case, (1963) *E.C.R.* 1.

31. *Costa* v *ENEL*, (1964) *E.C.R.* 585.

32. See Weiler, op. cit. (above, n. 17), p. 271.

33. The exact figure was 74.9%. This proportion, however, varied considerably from state to state: the maximum was 90.5% (in West Germany), with only 50.1% in France.

34. According to the Florence Project data, in 59.5% of the cases involving a review of national provisions, the Court left no discretion at all to national judges. As a rule the Court of Justice is even stricter in cases of mere interpretation of Community law.

35. Case 22/70, *ERTA*, (1971) *E.C.R.* 273.

36. Case 6/64 *Costa* v *E.N.E.L.*, (1964) *E.C.R.* 585.

37. See case 235/87, *Matteucci* v *Communauté francaise de Belgique*, judgment of 27 September 1988 (not yet reported) and the comments in B. De Witte's contribution.

38. Hence its apparent lack of interest for a counterpart like the Council of Europe.

39. Those were the Convention on the Simplification of Formalities in Trade in Goods, which introduced a single administrative document for all trade between the EC and EFTA countries, and the Convention on a Common Transit Procedure. Both were signed at a meeting between the Commission and EFTA ministers on 27 May 1987.

40. See, for instance, F. Laursen, *The EC-EFTA Dialogue: Agenda Setting, First Achievements, and Future Prospects*, paper presented at the conference on '40 Years

of Western Alliance – 40 Years of Western Cooperation; An Evaluation and a Perspective', University of Groningen, 20 April 1989, which gives several examples of this Community hegemony.

41. This is also the option suggested by the President of the Commission, Jacques Delors, in his programme speech before the European Parliament in January 1989. However, some EFTA members, such as Switzerland, do not seem willing to move in this direction. For a discussion of policy options facing EFTA countries, see Helen Wallace and Wolfgang Wessels, 'Towards a New Partnership: The EC and EFTA in the Wider Western Europe', *EFTA Occasional Paper* No. 28, March 1989.

42. It is worth stressing that the word specificity is used in a broader sense here than in works dealing with the specificity of Community law as opposed to international law. On this latter point, see Bruno De Witte, 'Retour à Costa: la spécificité du droit communautaire á la lumière du droit international', *Revue trimestrielle de droit européen*, 1984, pp. 425–54.

43. Of course, there are important variations within these two groups. See J. Steenbergen, 'The EFTA Countries and the EC Legal Systems: Is Integration Possible?', in Joseph Jamar and Helen Wallace, (eds), *The EC and EFTA: More than Just Good Friends?* (Bruges, De Tempel, 1988), pp. 290–9.

44. The votes of the Twelve in the UN are reported each year in the *EPC Bulletin*. See, for instance, issues 1985-2, pp. 245–53; 1986-2, pp. 249–57; 1987-2, pp. 319–27.

45. 'How Flexible is Community Law? An Unusual Approach to the "Two-Speeds" Principle', *Michigan Law Review*, Vol. 82 (1983–4), pp. 1274–93.

46. See the communication from the Commission on implementation of the legal acts required to build the single market, COM (89) 422 final of 7 December 1989.

15 The changing security framework
Reinhardt Rummel and *Peter Schmidt*

The field of security and defence differs from other sectors of West European cooperation and integration such as economy and technology in that all efforts since World War II to bring the West Europeans closer together have been embedded in an Atlantic framework. This embeddedness had the advantage that the European integration process was relieved of the heavy load of security and defence which is at the heart of the sovereignty of each nation-state. On the other hand, the Atlantic framework was both a demotivating factor and a convenient alibi for the European states to 'do their homework' in terms of substantial defence cooperation.

This framework explains most of the inability of the West European countries in the first half of the 1950s to establish a defence union. Prompted by the Americans, the Europeans had started to consider highly integrated defence and security structures (the Pleven Plan, the European Defence Community) in order to cope with a growing Soviet threat. Establishment of a West European union for defence was close, but due to rather high national sensitivities, above all in France, the Europeans failed to create a genuinely European security and defence system. The consequence for the European integration process was a change of strategy from a 'defence first' to a 'defence last' approach. An Atlantic-West European security system was created, within which the purely European part, the Western European Union (WEU), was of second rank and yielded a dominating position to the Americans. Efforts in Western Europe to improve security and defence cooperation did not have the aim of decoupling from the Americans. Some aimed to give more influence to the Europeans within the Atlantic structure; others, simply, to strengthen the political and military cohesion of NATO. Thus for 40 years the West European 'dynamics of integration' in security and the defence were inserted in an Atlantic context which invariably included the North Americans.

At the time of writing, the political landscape of the postwar European order is about to change dramatically. Due to the breakdown of communism in the former Eastern bloc and the demilitarization of Soviet foreign policy, the function of NATO to contain the Soviets is of less importance and thus, gives more leeway to the West European organizations (EC, WEU) to play an active part in the process of shaping a new security system for the European continent. However, NATO did not only have the task of containing the Soviets, it was also supposed to form a solid political (and military) framework which encloses German power. Today, this second function of the Alliance becomes more and more visible due to both the lessening of the threat which the Soviet Union used to impose on the West Europeans and the upcoming prospect of a united Germany. This is where the EC comes in. It seems obvious that a militarily devalued alliance of sovereign states cannot deal alone with German power, but has to be supplemented by the integrationist pressures of the Community.

The following analysis traces some characteristic patterns of political and military interaction of the West Europeans within the Atlantic context. It contrasts the traditional role played by security-related West European organizations (WEU, IEPG, EPC, Eurogroup; all discussed in detail later in this chapter) within the Atlantic setting with the most recent challenges and tasks for these organizations. Their original bulwark function against communism is about to be replaced by a new constructive function to build up a new type of all-European security. In this perspective, the EC and other West European organizations are taking over some of the former functions of NATO, recognizing new dynamics for regional integration in Western Europe as well as in Europe as a whole.

The traditional setting

Since the 1950s the countries in Western Europe and the Atlantic Alliance have been facing four outstanding challenges and threats, each of which had different weight at different times:

- *Defence, detente and the question of structural reform of the all-European security system:* The overriding problem during the entire existence of the Alliance has been how to cope with the threats and challenges arising out of the confrontation with the Soviet Union. While, at the beginning, attention in NATO was focused on providing and organizing an adequate Western defence to balance Soviet military power, later on elements of cooperative East-West relations were introduced and had to be handled, too. Today's task is more difficult: the Alliance has to find a stable framework not only for combining defence and detente but to enable structural changes to take place in Eastern Europe and the Soviet Union.
- *Intra-Alliance stability:* Each alliance has not only to face a threat by an opposing country or pact but also to find a way of stabilizing and harmonizing the relations among its members. Following this rule, the organizational structure and the pattern of interactions within the Alliance were influenced not only by the external Soviet threat, but also by the idea of managing some internal conflicts and security challenges. The most prominent internal problem to manage was West Germany's military role. The way it has been handled has had a significant effect upon the efficiency of the Alliance.

- *Economic and military-technological challenge:* To remain effective and to stabilize its internal relations, the Alliance has also to answer the question of how to organize economic and technological competition among its members. More specifically, under modern conditions, the question of how to organize the production and procurement of armaments has become more and more important. Part of this challenge has been the question of how far the members of the Alliance, and the Western industrialized world at large, should allow or encourage economic and technological exchanges with the opposing Warsaw Pact countries. Another part of the problem has been the question of how far the Americans should have access to the European defence equipment market and vice versa.
- *Legitimation and acceptance*: The fourth challenge has been how to find enough public support for the security and defence policy of the Alliance and for the Alliance itself. From the political struggles in West Germany at the time of the German rearmament in the 1950s to the beginning of the 1980s, with public demonstrations against the stationing of Pershing IIs and cruise missiles on West European soil, this problem was part and parcel of the problems the West Europeans and the Alliance as a whole had to solve. In the 1990s the challenge to acceptance is likely to stem from the reduction of the Soviet threat: the perceived need for collective defence is receding.

How did NATO and its Member States deal with these challenges during the last 40 years? What was the specific West-European contribution in meeting these challenges? Did regional and sectoral integration play a role?

The founding years of NATO

During the founding years of the Atlantic Alliance, the outstanding problem of these four challenges has been the threat to the West posed by the Soviet Union. There was a strong common threat perception which put pressure especially on the United Kingdom and France to comply with the conventional rearmament of West Germany, which could not easily be accepted by their European neighbours. It raised the big question of the multilateral framework in which the German army could be inserted in order to play a politically acceptable role, a question which is asked again at the beginning of the 1990s when models of German unification and the dissolving of military blocs are discussed. For several decades after World War II, the West Europeans were prepared and convinced to have to accept American and collective NATO protection vis-à-vis an aggressive Soviet Union. Common threat perception overwhelmed all attempts to separate out specific West European interests and identities. After the failure of the French proposal for a European Defence Community in 1954, because of the refusal of the Assemblée Nationale to endorse this integrationist concept, an Atlantic-European security system was established which obtained the function, as the first Secretary General of NATO, Lord Ismay described it, 'to keep the Americans in, the Germans down, and the Russians out'.[1] However, the function of controlling the Germans was more or less hidden behind NATO's dominant role to contain the Soviets. West European security cooperation was only mentioned as a goal in the WEU contract which – except for contributing to the control of West German rearmament – did not help much with pressing military and security challenges. The core defence-related decisions and the military command were transferred to NATO. While the Alliance, thanks to the existence of WEU, theoretically possessed an Atlantic-West European dual character, the West European element in it has had no practical relevance in balancing Soviet power.[2]

In those days the problem of legitimation and acceptance of the evolving security system and the question of how to cope with economic and techno-logical challenges played only a secondary role within the Western security system. Military-technological questions were largely handled on a national, bilateral, or flexible multilateral basis. Due to its overwhelming economic power, the United States played a major role within these relations. The WEU was also meant to be a first reaction to the economic and military-technological challenges. The member countries promised to cooperate not only in military and political, but also in economic matters. However, it was the intention of the WEU treaty that this task should very soon (1957) be taken over by the European Economic Community and other organizations.[3] Another objective of the WEU was to coordinate arms production, but the Standing Armaments Committee (SAC) never played a significant role in this respect. The WEU Council itself did not really try to meet such contractual goals and SAC was reduced to a committee for the exchange of research results and for the discussion of general questions.[4] Co-production and cooperation in the field of military technology developed, but in an unstructured bilateral and multilateral context rather than inside the WEU. Thus, from the beginning, it was not easy for West European countries to find a stable and effective framework for the coordination of their military-technological policy.

In most Member States the Alliance gained a positive image by virtue of the reputation of the United States as a strong, modern, and democratic leading power. Although there was considerable opposition to rearmament in West Germany during the 1950s, this was not a major problem from an Alliance point of view. The attractiveness of the United States (and the negative image of the Soviet Union) for the German people was such that it helped to overcome the protests: the American component of the Alliance system was decisive. One can assume that in France it was the European element in the Alliance which helped to legitimize the Atlantic-West European security system. Thus for its acceptance among all West European countries it was crucial to base the security system, formally at least, on an Atlantic *and* a European component.

From de Gaulle's opting out to the Harmel Report

At the end of the 1950s and during the 1960s a change in the perception of threats and challenges occurred and implied new ways for members of the security system to organize their responses. The ability to deter the Soviets remained at the top of NATO's agenda, but was not as widely supported as it had been. This was the reason for the allies to become preoccupied with problems of stability within the Alliance. Alliance stability was undermined by de Gaulle's questioning of the power structure within NATO, the consequent French withdrawal from the joint military command, the building up of a strategically separate French nuclear power, and the independent French approach to East-West relations that envisaged – in addition to the Atlantic Alliance – a new political structure from the Atlantic to the Urals transcending the ideological frontiers.[5]

De Gaulle aimed at a restructuring of the Alliance by strengthening its West European component. Moreover, his hope was that this kind of pluralization of the Alliance would stimulate a similar effect within the Warsaw Pact which, for de Gaulle, no longer looked as threatening in the 1960s. This process was designed in the long run to weaken the bilateralism of the superpowers and shift more influence to the middle powers, especially to France, which had special weight and power due to its nuclear force. However, de Gaulle was not successful in finding supporters for his ideas, not even in Western Europe. After the failure of the multilateral Fouchet framework[6] de Gaulle attempted to further his ideas on a bilateral Franco-German basis. However, after the Adenauer government signed the Elysée Treaty in 1963, which included provisions for Franco-German security cooperation, the Bundestag forced the government to introduce into the preamble all the basic elements of German security policy opposing de Gaulle's views: close partnership between Western Europe and the United States, integration of NATO forces, unification of Europe following the course of the EEC, admission of the United Kindgom to the EEC, self-determination for the German people.[7] Today, these preconditions for more West European self-assertiveness are partly fulfilled, partly still on the political agenda.

Despite its political crisis in the mid-1960s, the Alliance was able to return to stability:

– As expressed in the Bundestag's preamble to the Elysée Treaty the relationship between the Germans and the leading power within the Alliance, the United States, remained strong and turned out to be the central stabilizing factor. In a weaker form – indicating change – this German behaviour could also be observed during the ratifying of the protocol on the Franco-German Defence and Security Council in 1987–8. There was some resistance, not from inside the government but from the ranks of the opposition (SPD) that, while not strictly advocating an Atlantic orientation, expressed anti-nuclear feelings in West Germany. The SPD opposed the pro-nuclear wording in the protocol (strategy 'must be based on the appropriate combination of nuclear and conventional forces'). This time, the conflict could be ruled out by a memorandum on the protocols, which pointed out that no legal commitment to a particular defence strategy could be read into the wording of the protocol of the Elysée Treaty.[8]

– The French withdrawal from the military integration of NATO made room for a new consensus among the members of the alliance. This consensus was established, on the military level, by the acceptance of flexible response as the new military strategy opposed up to then especially by the French, on the political level, by the Harmel Report (1967) which assigned to the Alliance not only the task of deterrence and defence but also the management of detente and cooperative East-West relations. The cooperation function of the Alliance was primarily associated with East-West negotiations on Multilateral Balanced Force Reductions (MBFR) in Central Europe, which started in 1973 in Vienna.

Despite some American pressure to establish a full-scale politico-military European pillar, already expressed by President Kennedy at the beginning of the 1960s, WEU played almost no role during the crisis. According to Article IV of the WEU treaty, all military matters had been transferred to NATO and the original intention to use WEU to coordinate West European views on security and defence had lost its importance very quickly. The organization did play a kind of reserve role in Western Europe on the political level. From 1963 to 1970 – as long as the French opposed British membership of the EC – the WEU framework was useful for discussing economic and political questions beyond the EC with the United Kingdom.

Compared with the failure in the security field, West European countries were more active and more successful in collaborating in economic matters. Within the EC they increased their economic wealth and developed a considerable degree of economic and political cohesion. Security and defence remained areas which for most Europeans were best served in the Atlantic setting. The political environment, especially the Soviet invasion of Czechoslovakia in 1968, brought this message home even to de Gaulle. But the internal environment was also unfavourable to any identifiable, as well as useful, Europeanization of defence.

France's independent approach to national security, especially the withdrawal from NATO's military integration and the building up of a national nuclear force, had also something to do with French domestic policy. 'Grandeur nationale' was not only a matter of foreign policy but also a tool with which to gather and integrate the scattered political groupings in France. But this objective was only attained much later, not before the end of the 1970s when all relevant political parties in France supported, in principle, the basics of French security policy and, above all, the existence of a national nuclear deterrence force.[9] In West Germany the situation was different. An important part of the legitimation and the acceptance of Alliance policy was achieved via the double task of the Alliance as expressed in the Harmel Report: defence and detente. For the economic giant West Germany, the Community was the ideal homebase, while for the political dwarf as well as for the non-nuclear frontline state West Germany, the Atlantic Alliance provided the protected playground.

The detente period and its decline

The 1970s witnessed a period of detente in Europe and, more generally, between the Alliance and the Warsaw Pact. West European and American approaches to relations with the East were remarkably in tune in the first half of the 1970s, but developed growing dissonance during the second half of the decade. Even the deterioration of relations between the superpowers due to the

Soviet military intervention in Afghanistan (December 1979) and the suppression of Solidarity in Poland (1980)[10] did not cause the West Europeans to close ranks with their American ally. They felt that continuing the detente process was more urgent than keeping up with the Soviet military build-up. This attitude changed gradually in the case of the Soviet SS-20 missiles which increasingly became the symbol of a new strategically and politically threatening military Soviet power, creating the necessity for a cohesive Western military response combined with the readiness to negotiate. Concerning this subject NATO turned out, once again, to be the central framework for building Western consensus on crucial policies of deterrence, defence, and arms control: the Allies made the dual-track decision to respond in kind to the Soviet missiles by stationing intermediate range nuclear weapons in Western Europe and to negotiate with Moscow to reduce or scrap this category of arms. The Harmel concept served as a flexible and appropriate approach during this demanding period. NATO was able to accommodate and coordinate antagonistic as well as cooperative allied policies.[11] Yet, although the dual-track decision boosted the importance of NATO at the end of the 1970s and the beginning of the 1980s, a remarkable change had taken place concerning consensus-building among the members of the Alliance. The West Europeans had started, with their European Political Cooperation (EPC), to develop collective foreign-policy and security-policy positions of their own. The Conference on Security and Cooperation in Europe (CSCE) was a test ground to increase and to apply West European collectivity in practical East-West relations.[12] The scope and intensity of EPC had been gradually developed from its inception in 1970 to the Stuttgart Solemn Declaration in 1983 which officially included 'political and economic aspects of security' in policy coordination of the EC Member States.

Compared with the relative success of EPC, which was largely connected with the CSCE process, NATO policy, although also devoted to detente and cooperation, was perceived as less successful in East-West relations. This negative image was largely due to the long, tedious, and unsuccessful negotiations on troop reductions in Europe (MBFR) which, besides an East-West dimension, had the function of countering a certain political current in the US to cut down American forces on European soil (the Mansfield initiatives). This assessment reveals an important underlying trend: as they coordinated their policies for East-West relations, West European countries focused on detente and cooperative elements of the overall Western security policy, whereas the effort to coordinate decisions in defence and deterrence remained the domain of NATO.[13] WEU, which theoretically has capabilities in defence questions, did not exercise them very actively. Even the opportunity to coordinate European views in response to certain policies and developments in the United States was not successfully seized, as is shown by the poor effort to reach agreement on SDI.[14] On the other hand, NATO also failed to enrich its functions in the detente sphere and in other areas, although it tried to reach for new tasks by creating committees on the 'Challenges of Modern Societies', on 'Science', and the like.[15]

An exception to this rough pattern of division of labour (defence in NATO, detente in EPC) was Eurogroup, which brought together the European members of NATO's military integrated structure. The subject of this grouping of West European defence ministers has been defence policy and military cooperation, but primarily limited to a specific purpose within the West: to ensure that the contribution which the European members make to Alliance defence is presented in as strong and cohesive a way as possible to the United States. This has been tailored to meet American demands for a more balanced burden-sharing and to counter attempts at American troop withdrawals from Western Europe first advocated by the Mansfield amendments at the end of the 1960s and the beginning of the 1970s. Although Eurogroup also laid special stress on promoting practical cooperation and established technical sub-groups working on battlefield communications, logistical cooperation, long-term planning, army structures, medical services, and training,[16] the organization did not attract much political attention as a West European actor. There were probably two reasons for this. First, the group did not include the foreign ministers and therefore could not treat and implement security decisions, such as those on arms control, in a comprehensive manner. Secondly, it clearly subordinated its policy to that of the Alliance – without France the development of a distinctive West European profile in addition to NATO was muted.

In respect of the economic-technological challenge, European-American competition was intensified and – as demonstrated by the creation of the Independent European Programme Group (IEPG) – carried into the armament sector,[17] a decision which transferred activities from the national armament directors of Eurogroup. IEPG was established in 1975–6 to promote European research, development, and production of defence equipment among West European NATO allies including France. It was meant to help maintain a healthy European industrial and technological defence base and to counter American competition. This attempt to coordinate arms production among West European governments and industries was more than a symbolic gesture of European self-assertiveness, but less than the determination to achieve a concertation of military industrial policies of all West European NATO members.

Taken together, West European defence and security cooperation from the early 1950s to the late 1970s was characterized more by halfhearted attempts and fully fledged failures than by serious progress or the promotion of first moves towards a genuine collective West European defence capacity. Despite some national intransigeance (France) and some European foreign policy cooperation (EPC), the traditional setting prevailed.

Change in the traditional setting

In the 1980s, West European security and defence cooperation has been characterized by four developments: contractual extended consultations, further concentration on the cooperative aspects of East-West relations which led to some conflicts with the US on economic exchange issues, embryonic institutional structures in the defence sector, and a very cautious step concerning West European power projection in the Gulf region (a mine-sweeping operation).[18]

These developments were prompted by the particular threats and security challenges which dominated this period. At the beginning of the decade the

Alliance had to solve two problems: to ensure the nuclear strategic coupling of the United States to Western Europe and to counter the Soviet Euro-strategic threat potential, the SS-20 missiles. Both the stationing of the Intermediate Range Nuclear Forces (INF) in Western Europe in 1983 and the 'double-zero decision'[19] in 1987 to dismantle them and other nuclear systems put major strains on the NATO consensus and increased demands for more European influence in the Western Alliance. It also prepared the ground for various attempts among West European nations to intensify their security cooperation.

At the beginning of the 1980s, during the period of the INF stationing debate, questions of legitimation and acceptance as well as Alliance stability were in the foreground. France, though not directly involved in the decisions, participated actively in meeting the challenge.[20] During the discussion on the double-zero solution the legitimation question became less prominent in West Germany, while the problem of stability in the Alliance continued to exist – at least, from a French point of view, due to a perceived danger that the West Germans might trade a German-German rapprochement or even unification for a drifting apart of Western Europe and the US.

Conflict and cooperation

During the INF stationing period, which was a time of severe conflicts between East and West, the intensification of West European security cooperation was intended to help meet two challenges. First, there was the question of acceptance in the sense of a 'political-psychological strategy' to influence public opinion.[21] Given the increasing public criticism of the American leadership, it was obvious that the NATO framework was regarded less and less as a vehicle for the legitimation of major decisions on defence and security. Secondly, the traditional French interest in keeping West Germany as a reliable partner in the Alliance led France to enhance Franco-German as well as West European security cooperation. Thus, the 'West Europeanization' of Western security policy served to legitimize and stabilize the Alliance.

It was WEU and bilateral relations and not EC-EPC or Eurogroup which helped to fulfil these functions. Since 1982 a progressive increase in consultation mechanisms among the West Europeans has occurred. Already in February 1982, German Chancellor Helmut Schmidt and French President François Mitterrand decided to upgrade Franco-German defence and security consultations and to establish a committee for defence and security with several working groups and subgroups.[22] In the following years Chancellor Helmut Kohl and President Mitterrand gradually extended Franco-German defence cooperation. WEU was formally reactivated as a security framework in October 1984. It underwent several institutional changes which are not yet finalized.[23] The new focus of WEU is on conceptual innovation and discussion of West European defence and disarmament policy.

The activation of both the West European Union and the security cooperation clause in the Franco-German Treaty enhanced the pattern of division of labour within the Atlantic-West European security system. Neither WEU nor the Franco-German security tandem had a direct impact on Alliance decisions as such; rather, they aimed at making NATO decisions acceptable to the West European public and thus stabilized the Alliance at large.

That EC-EPC was not considered a suitable consultation forum for questions connected with the stationing of INF may be explained by the fact that a small group of countries (Ireland, Denmark, Greece), were reluctant to add a security and defence dimension to the Community. EC and EPC did play an important role in the cooperative part of East-West relations, mainly in the context of CSCE follow-on meetings. Much against American will, the West Europeans managed to keep alive part of the East-West dialogue. On the other hand, the special status of France in NATO excluded any subgrouping of the Alliance to take on the role of a vehicle for Europeanization.

Summing up, it seems fair to conclude that the new military challenges at the beginning of the 1980s led to Western responses which, on balance, were equally distributed among NATO and West European cooperation bodies.

Detente and cooperation

In the second half of the 1980s the zero option and, later, the double-zero option for INF were considered and finally decided upon in an American-Soviet treaty in December 1987. The strategic community in Western Europe, mainly in Bonn and Paris, perceived these developments as a political-strategic challenge because they seemed to imply a tendency towards the so-called denuclearization of Western Europe. France was particularly worried about the minor role which the Europeans played in the INF negotiations and about the domestic pressure in West Germany for a denuclearization of Mitteleuropa with all its disastrous consequences for the Alliance as well as for France's position. The Bonn government tried to dampen French concern by strengthening its West European ties.[24] Germany had a self-interest in a more active participation in West European security cooperation: because of the remaining tactical-nuclear systems on German soil, parts of the German security community to both right and left of the political spectrum perceived the Federal Republic to be in a singular position of nuclear threat. They looked for a West European solution to that problem,[25] but neither WEU nor Franco-German institutions nor the EC-EPC framework were helpful in this regard.

As far as decisions for closer security cooperation in Western Europe were taken, in the second half of the 1980s, they addressed mainly issues of intra-Alliance stabilization and technological cooperation. It remained unclear, however, what kind of new structures for Western defence they were aimed at. Several initiatives deserve mention.

First, since 1984 the chairman of the IEPG defence ministers may speak 'on behalf of Europe' to the United States.[26] Thus, the discussion of the 1970s on the so-called two-way-street in transatlantic weapons trade was partly taken account of. Also during the 1980s, a new and more adequate approach to arms cooperation has been created, starting with the definition of operational requirements in order to find a solid basis for the development of joint projects. In 1988 the decision was taken to establish a small secretariat for IEPG in order to support the country holding the chair. When, at the same time, the transatlantic arms trade balance turned positive for the European side, and the Europeans, in addition, tried to push a 'buy European' attitude, this looked like a double 'defeat' of the Americans.[27] Moreover, a strong European policy in technology and trade was also underlined in the Single European Act (Article 30), which states that the signatories are determined to maintain the technological and industrial conditions necessary for their security. The West Europeans thus seem to have prepared legal and institutional groundwork for a more identifiable European stance in crucial sectors of defence. Yet, all these efforts appeared to serve a fallback position in case of major changes in the US commitment in Europe rather than to develop a defence union alongside the economic and monetary union of Western Europe.

Secondly, the so-called 'platform' of the WEU of October 1987 is – despite its plea for a European Union including security and defence – rather oriented towards the status quo.[28] Nevertheless, the recent adherence of Spain and Portugal to the WEU widens the group of West European countries which seeks consultations on major security questions such as a European position on the conventional force reduction (CFE) talks in Vienna.

Thirdly, via their new Defence Council, created in January 1988 by an amendment to the Elysée Treaty of 1963,[29] France and Germany have reached a degree of density of consultation which is certainly unique in Europe, and this despite – or maybe because of – both countries traditionally holding widely differing views on major security and defence questions. The establishment of a common brigade points towards a new defence structure without, however, questioning NATO's military integration in its present form. Nevertheless, this step created some political turmoil among the Allies which criticized Franco-German bilateralism.[30] In a fundamental sense and in terms of a genuinely autonomous West European defence union the Franco-German institutions can be regarded as the only, albeit tiny, nucleus for a multilateral European army.

However, in practical terms, the crucial decision in 1989 on a follow-on to the Lance missile showed the limited reach of the Franco-German axis as well as that of West European cooperation in defence and disarmament at large. The US pressure to go ahead with NATO's earlier decision to modernize Lance, a short-range nuclear missile (120 km) to be based on West German soil, was strongly supported by London and opposed by Bonn. France, given its nuclear interests and its special status in NATO, was not in a position to ease this dispute. The Franco-German Defence Council and WEU were not helpful either. In the end, the United States again played the good old role of a pacifier among the allies: President Bush's proposal to postpone the implementation of the decision on Lance modernization was collectively accepted during a NATO summit meeting in May 1989.

Assessing the characteristics of change

In summarizing the developments of the last decade one has to note, first of all, the increasing complexities involved in meeting the dual challenges of defence and detente. NATO continued to be decisive as far as defence questions were concerned, but Western Europe, as a political actor, was increasingly represented when it came to the shaping of cooperative East-West relations.[31]

In *defence* matters Western Europe had not become a competent actor, except for a timid beginning in the bilateral Franco-German framework. This raised the challenge of *intra-Alliance stability*. For how long could the Alliance count on the support of the member countries, if it were predominantly identified with defence questions? The increasingly dual nature of the Atlantic-West European Alliance with, on the one hand, a Western Europe specializing in economic, foreign policy, and cooperative aspects of East-West relations and, on the other hand, an Alliance which is perceived to limit its activity increasingly to military defence questions, was likely to conjure up major tensions between the Atlantic and the West European bodies of cooperation which in the long run might well have been to the detriment of NATO as well as of European integration.

Moreover, the analysis shows a functional and geographical differentiation of the security-related frameworks in Western Europe. This differentiation certainly had the advantage of a highly flexible system, but it complicated the concertation processes among the allies and hardly permitted a sufficiently consistent and comprehensive strategy.

Conflicts have increased in the linked sectors of civil and military technology. The high-tech research programme 'Eureka' was launched as a very flexible structure.[32] This example stresses the tendency which seems to exist in this field: the preference for sectoral solutions with a varying number of cooperating countries (as in the case of the European Space Agency). 'Eureka' also illustrates the West Europeans' difficulty in going beyond bilateral and multi-lateral ad hoc cooperation and developing military-technological cooperation in a more systematic way. Reasons for this inability are numerous, including the 'civilian power Europe' philosophy, the dominance of strong national interests in arms production, and the intra-European difference in cooperation strategy: West Germany favoured the civil character of the 'Eureka' programme while France put the emphasis on militarily useable programmes.[33] The recent decision of IEPG to develop a West European armaments market may help to overcome some of the obstacles.[34]

In relation to the *legitimation and acceptance* problem, European bodies have had a growing role alongside NATO. In public declarations in Western Europe, more and more the formula has been used that its security is based on 'integration and cooperation in Western Europe and the Atlantic Alliance', reversing the old order of mentioning the Alliance first. The idea of the necessity of a European pillar within NATO indicates in this regard not only a politically desirable goal but also a politico-psychological strategy to generate more public support for the West European/Atlantic security set-up by underlining European self-determination.

Beyond the traditional setting

The Atlantic framework which has dominated West European cooperation in defence and security for the past forty years rested upon the German problem and the Soviet threat. The context for the gradual shift in the balance between the Atlantic and West European dimensions over the past decade, noted above, has been shaped partly by declining perceptions of a Soviet military threat in Western Europe, and partly by rising awareness of common West European security interests – including West Germany – distinct from the security priorities of the United States. This gradual evolution was, however, overtaken in the winter of 1989–90 by the apparently fundamental transformation of European security which followed the transition away from Socialist regimes in Eastern Europe and the demolition of the Berlin Wall.

At the time of writing it is far too soon to assess the implications of these changes for West European integration. Given the importance of the 'high politics' of American-led security policy for the 'low politics' of West European economic integration, they seem likely to affect not only the defence and security sector but also many other crucial areas of the West European integration process and, indeed, the pursuit of 'European Union' as such. As the dynamics of disintegration in Eastern Europe interact with those of the West European community-building process, the balance is likely to tip further from NATO to West European structures – whether the EC/EPC, or WEU.

As long as the Soviet Union exists as a European and Asian superpower, and as long as Western Europe disposes of no developed structure for integrated common defence, the basic framework of the Alliance is likely to be maintained. Nevertheless, the process whereby West European cooperation has slowly evolved from underneath the American umbrella is already evidently quickening. The roles of both Britain and France in a reformed system of nuclear deterrence are unavoidably on the West European agenda, as well as the issue of Anglo-French nuclear cooperation – hesitantly raised on several occasions over the past thirty years, but allowed to drop between the reality of American nuclear dominance and the principle of national sovereignty. Old ideas for strengthening the West European role within the Atlantic Allaince have been revived, against the high probability that US forces in Europe will be substantially reduced: proposals to replace the American hold on the Saceur position with a European, or to modify Saceur's jurisdiction. Military integration through multinational forces, beyond the existing NATO standing forces and the Franco-German brigade, is under consideration.

The result of these changes would be a more discernible West European defence identity, and closer defence cooperation among West European countries. Questions of defence burden-sharing, debated for so long primarily within a transatlantic context, may well emerge as an intra-West European issue, thus pushing bargaining over asymmetries in military spending closer to bargaining over the Community budget and the allocation of contributions to the costs of transition in Eastern Europe. Financial pressures may thus operate to bring defence and security issues into the same framework as civil technology and economic issues, in spite of the political arguments for maintaining a formal separation – between WEU and EC obligations, as some governments would prefer.

The separation of defence – as an exceptional sector in which American leadership was essential and the Atlantic framework therefore dominant – from other areas of *European* integration may well thus be breaking down.

Transatlantic bargaining over the terms and conditions of a continued American military commitment to Europe might indeed bring defence and economic issues still closer together, as West European governments calculate the advantages of maintaining a US presence and Washington bargains over the implications of the 1992 programme and the European technological cooperation for American interest. The evolution of West European integration, as we argued at the beginning of this chapter, was eased by the embedding of the sensitive and heavy issues of security and defence within the broader Atlantic framework. The dissolution of the East-West antagonism which embedded these issues within the Atlantic Alliance will force West European governments to confront a difficult set of choices about the broad scope of European Union which they have managed largely to avoid until now.

Notes

1. Quoted in Michael Howard, 'Peace: The Vital Factors', in *The Times*, 13 January 1983, p. 10.
2. For the political functions of the WEU see Peter Schmidt, 'The WEU – A Union Without Perspective?', in *Aussenpolitik* (English edn), no. 6 (1986), pp. 388–99.
3. Article I of the WEU treaty says that the work of the WEU in economic cooperation 'shall not involve any duplication of, or prejudice to, the work of other economic organizations in which the High Contracting Parties are or may be represented but on the contrary assist the work of those organizations'.
4. For details see Assembly of the West European Union (ed.), The West European Union, document 928, Paris, 29 October 1982.
5. See Alfred Grosser, *Frankreich und seine Außenpolitik 1944 bis heute* (Munich and Vienna, Hanser Verlag, 1986).
6. See Robert Bloes, *Le 'Plan Fouchet' et le problème de l'Europe politique* (Bruges, Collège d'Europe, 1970).
7. See Alfred Grosser, *Frankreich und seine Außenpolitik* (above, n. 5), p. 229.
8. See memorandum on the protocols, German Bundestag, 11th legislative period, Drucksache 11/3258, pp. 11–14 (at p. 12).
9. See Michael M. Harrison, *The Reluctant Ally. France and Atlantic Security* (Baltimore, Md., Johns Hopkins University Press, 1981).
10. For a description of the European reactions see Corinne Covillers, *Y a-t-il une politique extérieure des Communautés Européennes?* (Paris, Presses universitaires de France, 1987), pp. 95–107.
11. See Lothar Rühl, *Mittelstreckenwaffen in Europa: Ihre Bedeutung in Strategie, Rüstungskontrolle und Bündnispolitik* (Baden-Baden, Nomos, Internationale Politik und Sicherheit, vol. 12, 1989).
12. See Corinne Covillers, *Y a-t-il politique extérieure des Communautés Européennes?* (above, n. 10), pp. 55–8.
13. See Peter Schmidt, 'Die Westeuropäische Union und ihr Verhältnis zur NATO', in Lothar Brock and Mathias Jopp, (eds), *Sicherheitspolitische Zusammenarbeit und Kooperation der Rüstungswirtschaft in Westeuropa* (Baden-Baden, Nomos, 1986), pp. 95–104.
14. See the contributions of Philippe Chapal, Daniel Hiester and Walter Schütze in J.-F. Guilhaudis and J. Fontanel, (eds), *Course aux armement et désarmement, arès*, no. 1 (1988).
15. For a description of the work see *The North Atlantic Treaty Organization. Facts and Figures* (NATO Information Service, Brussels, 1984).

16. See Der Bundesminister der Verteidigung. Informations- und Pressestab (ed.), *Der europäische Beitrag zur atlantischen Verteidigung – Die Eurogroup* (Bonn, 1983).
17. See Johan Jörgen Holst, 'The Independent European Programme Group', *NATO-Brief*, vol. 29, no. 2 (April 1981), pp. 8–11.
18. During the Gulf crisis the WEU arranged meetings of all WEU members at a politico-military level. This way the image of a European presence in the Gulf region could be created, while some of their members helped with mine-sweeping operations in the Red Sea and the Persian Gulf. (See Joseph Coffey and Gianni Bonvicini, *The Atlantic Alliance and the Middle East* (Basingstoke, Macmillan, 1989), pp. 96–9.
19. This expression refers to the reductions of all land-based nuclear missiles in Europe with a range between 500 and 5,500 km.
20. See Mitterrand's address in the Bundestag, 20 January 1983.
21. See Konrad Seitz, 'Deutsch-französische sicherheitspolitische Zusammenarbeit' in *Europa-Archiv*, vol. 37, no. 22 (1982), pp. 657–64.
22. Political-strategic working group, subgroup: SDI; military cooperation, subgroup: logistical support for the French Force d'Action Rapide (FAR) in the Federal Republic; Franco-German military unit, problems of extended air defence, armament cooperation. See Peter Schmidt, 'The Franco-German Council on Defence and Security', in *Aussenpolitik* (English version), Fall 1989, pp. 388–99.
23. Recently, the Agencies have been replaced by a research institute.
24. See Peter Schmidt, 'Die deutschen Interessen an Zusammenarbeit', in André Brigot, Peter Schmidt and Walter Schütze, (eds.), *Sicherheits- und Ostpolitik: Deutsch-französische Perspektiven* (Baden-Baden, Nomos, 1989), pp. 77–94. (The book is also published in French under the title *Défense, désarmement et politiques à l'Est* (Paris, Fondation pour les études de défense nationale, 1989).)
25. See Alfred Dregger, *Entwurf für eine Sicherheitspolitik, Deutsches Strategieforum* (Bonn, Pro Pace, 1987) and Horst Ehmke, 'Eine Politik zur Selbstbehauptung Europas. Überlegungen angesichts der Entfremdung zwischen Alter und Neuer Welt', in *Europa Archiv*, vol. 39, no. 7 (April 1984), pp. 195–204.
26. See the results of the ministerial meeting of the IEPG, The Hague, 23 November 1984.
27. See Terrell G. Covington, Keith W. Brendley and Mary E. Chenoweth, 'A Review of European Arms Collaboration and Prospects for its Expansion under the Independent European Programme Group', A Rand Note, N-2638-ACQ, July 1987.
28. See *Europa-Archiv*, vol. 42, no. 22 (November 1987), pp. D613–16.
29. See the documentation: Presse- und Informationsamt der Bundesregierung (ed.), *25 Jahre Elysée-Vertrag. Dokumente zur sicherheitspolitischen Zusammenarbeit* (Bonn and Paris, 1988).
30. See Reinhardt Rummel, 'Reaktion der Bündnispartner auf die jüngsten Entwicklungen der deutsch-französischen Sicherheitskooperation – Gewöhnung an ein Novum oder Anregung zu neuer Dynamik?', in André Brigot, Peter Schmidt and Walter Schütze, (eds.), *Sicherheits- und Ostpolitik* (above, n. 24), pp. 35–50.
31. The NATO declaration of May 1989 is not an exception in this respect, although there is much to read about the political functions of NATO.
32. See Christian Deubner, *Kritische Überlegungen zu 'Eureka'* (Ebenhausen, 1985).
33. See the interview with the Secretary of State for Defence, Gérard Renon, in *La Tribune de l'expansion*, 8 June 1989, p. 11.
34. See *Towards a Stronger Europe, a Report by an Independent Study Team established by Defence Ministers of Nations of the Independent European Programme Group to Make Proposals to Improve the Competitiveness of Europe's Defence Equipment Industry*, vol. 1 (Brussels, December 1986).

16 Conclusions: Community politics and institutional change
Robert O. Keohane and Stanley Hoffmann

As William Wallace indicates in his introduction, this project seeks to outline an economic, social and political 'map' of Western Europe and to provide a basis for a new conceptual debate on European integration. European experts in a variety of fields have sketched, in their chapters, particular details of that map; but little attention has been paid by most contributors to major conceptual and theoretical issues, such as those raised by the integration literature of the 1950s and 1960s. In particular, the chapters devote relatively little attention to discussing the overall nature of the political system of the Community, or to exploring the conditions for, and causes of, the dramatic changes that we have observed in Community institutions. On the whole, the contributions to this volume are longer on detailed description than on analysis.

We write as students of world politics based in North America, whose primary research interests have not been in the subject of European integration. As a result, our grasp of the detailed institutional history of the European Community is not as firm as that of the authors of the other chapters here. If our contribution has value, it lies in our sweeping, 'bird's-eye' view of the contemporary political system of Europe, and in our attempt to explore how theories and concepts of political integration, developed much earlier but then largely discarded, could help us understand the contemporary dynamics of European integration.

Even a sweeping view of European integration must have a clear focus; otherwise complexity would simply overwhelm analysis. Our emphasis throughout this chapter will be on the Community, rather than on Europe as a whole; and we will specifically stress the political institutions of the Community and their evolution.

Both Europe and the world political economy have been transformed, economically, socially and politically, since 1945. The major trends are familiar to us all: trade and finance are much more highly internationalized; international regimes for management of the world political economy more complex; environmental dangers more severe; Europe less central to political and economic decisions; the United States less powerful in relative terms. The

European Community has displayed a magnetic attraction for countries on its periphery, leading both to expansion of the EC itself and to the development of institutional ties with EFTA countries and other West European non-members. Recently, the sharp boundaries between Western and Eastern Europe have begun to blur, as the EC's magnetism and Gorbachev's Perestroika create major changes in what used to be known as the 'Soviet bloc'.

We accept the assumption of this project that the politics of European integration can only be understood within the context of these changing economic and social dynamics. The Community is part of a larger complex of activities, including those, such as Western European Union, which are outside the Community structure. A number of contributions to this project describe these activities, as well as the Community's relations with its neighbours and associated states. Nevertheless, to make an analytical contribution to such a vast field in the compass of a short chapter, it is necessary to be selective in what one wishes to describe, interpret or attempt to explain. Our focus here is on decision-making and institutional change in the European Community.

We seek first to characterize observed patterns of decision-making. The European Community, we argue, is an experiment in pooling sovereignty, not in transferring it from states to supranational institutions. Nevertheless, the concept of 'supranationality' that Ernst Haas developed 20 years ago remains relevant, although it has so often been stereotyped, misinterpreted or ignored. The European Community can best be viewed as a set of complex overlapping networks, in which a supranational style of decision-making, characterized by compromises upgrading common interests, can under favourable conditions lead to the pooling of sovereignty.

Next, we move from statics to dynamics, seeking to provide some clues to the dramatic and unexpected extension of Community policies and strengthening of Community institutions that has occurred in the 1980s. In particular, we investigate whether 'spillover' has taken place as posited by neofunctionalist theory. We contend that the expansion of Community tasks depends ultimately on the bargains between major governments; but that after such a bargain has been made, Community tasks can be further expanded as a result of linkages among sectors, as envisaged in the theory. However, such an expansion is by no means automatic; there are limits on spillover. More unexpectedly, a sort of *institutional spillover* has occurred: enlargement of the Community to 12 members set in motion a process that *strengthened* Community decision-making institutions.

Finally, in our conclusion we speculate about the future of the Community in the light of changes taking place in world politics, particularly in relations between West and East Germany, and between Western and Eastern Europe in general. The crucial question that we briefly address, but do not pretend to resolve, is that of the degree to which the European Community can meet the aspirations of West Germany, its strongest member, while making those aspirations acceptable to its neighbours, both within the Community and to the east. Europe proved that it could create institutions to promote cooperation, even without a hegemon in its midst; now it must test whether this system of cooperation can adapt effectively to rapid changes in world politics, especially within Europe itself.

Supranationality

As students of world politics and political economy, we are struck by the distinctiveness of the Community among contemporary international organizations. Most evident, perhaps, is the Commission, a coherent executive body which is able to take initiatives and whose president plays a role at summit meetings of heads of government of industrialized countries. Another distinction is its legal status: no other international organization enjoys such reliably effective supremacy of its law over the laws of member governments, with a recognized Court of Justice to adjudicate in disputes. As Dehousse and Weiler argue in Chapter 14, the Community legal process has a dynamic of its own. Despite a number of cases of non-implementation of Community law, by the standards of international organizations implementation has been extraordinary. A recent study concludes that national administrations implement Community law about as effectively as they apply national law, and in its own analysis of issues of implementation, the Commission has concluded that most national courts 'are collaborating effectively in the implementation of Community law'.[1] Indeed, of the Community institutions it is the Court that has gone farthest in limiting national autonomy, by asserting the principle of superiority of Community law, and that of the obligation of Member States to implement binding national acts consistent with Community directives.

In addition to its executive capacity and legal powers, the Community has financial resources at its disposal. Furthermore, unlike any other organization in the world political economy, it makes trade policies for 12 states, constituting the largest market in the world. The contrast with the new North American Free Trade Area is instructive: the latter constitutes an agreement between two sovereign countries, with arrangements for dispute settlement between the United States and Canada but without common policy-making institutions which would have authority to negotiate on behalf of both countries with the rest of the world.

Boundaries are difficult to draw in a world of complex interdependence – since relationships cross boundaries and patterns of coalition vary from issue to issue, it is never possible to classify all actors neatly into mutually exclusive categories. Europe is no exception. But institutional boundaries are clearer than those of trade or loyalty. The 12 EC states make decisions jointly, whereas EFTA members, no matter how important they are to the European economy (as Per Wijkman shows in Chapter 5), do not participate in that decision-making process. As Philippe de Schoutheete has commented (in Chapter 6), there is a 'Community-centred network' which includes 'peripheral influences' and 'non-Community activities', but Europe has an institutional core, which is the European Community; and the Community clearly has a political system.

The kind of entity that is emerging does not, however, much resemble the sort of entity that the most enthusiastic functionalists and federalists had in mind. For they envisaged a transfer of power to institutions whose authority would not derive from the governments of the Member States, and a transfer of political loyalty to the centre. According to the most optimistic scenarios, a 'United States of Europe' would have come into being – a state, with the key attributes of internal and external sovereignty: 'supremacy over all other authorities within that territory and population', and 'independence of outside authorities'.[2]

Portrayals of the state are often bedevilled by the image of an ideal-typical 'state' whose authority is unquestioned and whose institutions work smoothly. No such state has ever existed; viewed close-up, all modern states appear riddled with inefficiencies and contradictions. Nevertheless, the European Community by no means approximates a realistic image of a modern state, much less an idealized one. If, in comparison with the authority of contemporary international organizations, the Community looks strong, in comparison with highly institutionalized modern states, it appears weak indeed. This weakness is not only legal but political: as discussed elsewhere in this volume and later in this chapter, the Community depends inordinately on one state – Germany. The European Community political system rests on national political systems, especially that of the Federal Republic.

The anomalous situation of the Community – stronger than a mere international organization, weaker than a state – is made evident by looking once again at the problem of compliance with Community law. Although by international organizational standards compliance has been extraordinary, the Community suffers a significant degree of non-compliance.[3] Governments may deliberately fail to comply with Community law, rationalizing their non-compliance or blaming their legislatures.[4] More pervasive is faulty compliance, as a result of a collapse of enforcement at the bureaucratic or judicial levels, or due to enforcement in a manner that distorts or conflicts with Community norms.[5] Faulty compliance can generally be corrected through diligent detective work by the Commission and action, when necessary, by the European Court of Justice; but deliberate non-compliance, however camouflaged or rationalized, is more difficult to correct.

The originality of the Community is also evident in foreign affairs. Traditionally, confederations, federations and unitary states confer on their central institutions what Locke had called the 'federative power' – the power to act for the state in international affairs, or, to use the correct legal term, external sovereignty. This is not the case in the EC, whose central institutions have full jurisdiction over external trade alone, with no more than a power of coordination over the rest of foreign policy and no power yet over defence. In international meetings other than those of the GATT, the Community is not yet a distinctive actor; at best it is represented along with its members (as at the G7 meetings); usually the Member States are the actors, in world monetary, diplomatic and military affairs.

Thus, the Community is not a state in the classsic sense. What are we to call it?

If any traditional model were to be applied, it would be that of a confederation rather than a federation, since the central institutions are (a) largely intergovernmental, (b) more concerned with establishing a common framework than with networks of detailed regulations, and (c) apparently willing to tolerate a vast amount of national diversity in standards and practices, through 'mutual recognition', to create a kind of free market of competing national norms, and to allow for a multiplicity of exceptions, delays and derogations. Popular loyalty has not been transferred to the centre from the Member States. And the intergovernmental bargains that were essential to the development of a single market are consistent with the confederal model.

However, confederalism alone fails to capture the complexity of the interest-based bargaining that now prevails in the Community, among representatives of interests, between them and committees of bureaucrats, and among bureaucracies (with the formation of transnational coalitions of functional bureaucrats). For this process, the most appropriate label, perhaps surprisingly, is Ernst Haas's notion of 'supranationality'. The conception of supranationality, rarely referred to in the recent literature on Europe except with disdain, has suffered grievous misinterpretation and stereotyping over the years. For Haas, supranationality did not mean that Community institutions exercise authority over national governments: 'General de Gaulle equates supranationality with a federalism which he detests; Jean Monnet identifies it with a federalism of which he is a leading partisan. Both gentlemen mistake the essence of the phenomenon.' Supranationality is not at the end of a continuum, whose other end is occupied by strict intergovernmentalism. Instead, supranationality refers to a process or style of decision-making, 'a cumulative pattern of accommodation in which the participants refrain from unconditionally vetoing proposals and instead seek to attain agreement by means of compromises upgrading common interests'.[6] Haas saw this process as implying, structurally, 'the existence of governmental authorities closer to the archetype of federation than any past international organization, but not yet identical with it'.[7]

Haas viewed supranationality as a style of political behaviour through which political interests would be realized, not as a depoliticized form of technical decision-making. What Haas called the 'three core assumptions' on which theories of regional integration were based can be seen more accurately as the institutional results of the supranational decision-making style: '(1) that a definable institutional pattern must mark the outcome of the process of integration, (2) that conflicts of interests involving trade-offs between ties with regional partners and ties with non-members should be resolved in favour of regional partners, and (3) that decisions be made on the basis of disjointed incrementalism'.[8] Haas emphasized that 'learning is based on the perceptions of self-interest displayed by the actors', and that lessons will only be generalized 'if the actors, on the basis of their interest-inspired perceptions, desire to adapt integrative lessons learned in one context to a new situation'.[9]

It can be argued that precisely what the Single European Act and the abandonment of the Luxembourg Compromise accomplish, in institutional terms, has been the dramatic revival of a largely supranational decision-making sytle that was lost after 1966, frequently lamented in the years thereafter, and only partially restored with the reforms after the Paris Summit of 1974.[10] Yet what we observe is supranationality with only limited progress towards political integration. 'Progressive regional centralization of decision-making' has taken place. But we do not observe political integration in the more demanding sense of Haas's formulation in *The Uniting of Europe*: 'the process whereby political actors in several distinct national settings are persuaded to shift their loyalties, expectations and political activities towards a new centre, whose institutions possess or demand jurisdiction over the pre-existing national states'.[11]

Unlike international organizations, the European Community as a whole has gained some share of states' sovereignty: the Member States no longer have supremacy over all other authorities within their traditional territory, nor are they independent of outside authorities. Its institutions have some of the authority that we associate with institutions of sovereign governments: on certain issues individual states can no longer veto proposals before the Council; members of the Commission are independent figures rather than instructed agents. Especially when it is led by a statesman with a vision and a method, such as Jacques Delors, the Commission is an indispensable fount of proposals and prodding; under the complex provisions of the Single European Act, futhermore, its recommendations can only with great difficulty be amended by the Council.

Yet national governments continue to play a dominant role in the decision-making process. As Siedentopf and Ziller point out, 'Community institutions and national government bodies involved do not act autonomously, but in common'.[12] Policy is fragmented by sector, although within sectors a great deal of informal coordination, among national bureaucrats and interest groups, takes place. There are innumerable committees of national experts and bureaucrats, preparing the Commission's proposals and the Council's decisions.[13] The Council has recently asked one such committee, rather than the Commission, to supervise the granting of licences to banks, although at the time of writing the method of supervision is not yet settled and follow-up supervisory arrangements are an open question. The execution of the Council's directives by the Commission is closely supervised by committees of national bureaucrats, some of which can overrule the Commission's moves.

The European Community operates neither as a political 'market' – characterized by arms-length transactions among independent entities – nor as a 'hierarchy', in which the dominant mode of regulation is authoritative rule. Rather, the EC exemplifies what sociologists refer to as a 'network form of organization', in which individual units are defined not by themselves but in relation to other units.[14] Actors in a network have a preference for interaction with one another, rather than with outsiders, in part because intense interactions create incentives for self-interested cooperation and for the maintenance of reputations for reliability. Bressand and Nicolaïdis (in Chapter 2), and Sharp (in Chapter 3), analyse the rapid growth of intercorporate networks in Europe during the 1980s, especially in high-technology industries such as telecommunications and biotechnology. In these industries, as well as in the Community itself, authority remains dispersed but joint benefits can be gained by the exchange of reliable information – which long-term partners have more incentives to provide than have rivals.[15] Wessels (in Chapter 13) shows how the complex system of committees, working groups and expert groups creates networks of European bureaucrats and of national administrators who play a dual role – as representatives of their states and as European agents. There are also networks in which bureaucrats and representatives of private interests cooperate in the preparation of public policy – as in the various theories of 'neo-corporatism', derived from the diverse practices of the modern West European states.

The notion of a network is more a metaphor than a theory. It helps to emphasize the horizontal ties that exist among actors and the complexity of their relationships, but it does not elaborate clear hypotheses about behaviour. In 1975 Ernst Haas sought to take related notions a step further by characterizing the European Community as a 'semi-lattice' form of organization, something between a hierarchy and a simple matrix: 'There is a clear centre of authority for some activities and decisions, but not for all. Lines of authority duplicate and overlap; tasks are performed in fragments by many sub-systems; sometimes authority flows sideways and upwards, at other times the flow is downward.'

Haas went on to predict that in a semi-lattice form of organization, actors would first react to increased complexity and interdependence by incremental, piecemeal approaches – seeking to 'decompose' issues. In the longer run, he speculated, these actors might realize that they were sacrificing potential benefits with such a response, and might devise new policies.[16]

As Haas recognized, the networks of the European Community constitute neither a hierarchy nor a *Gemeinschaft*, despite the Community rhetoric. Reciprocity in Europe is often quite specific – demanding 'tit for tat' exchanges of equivalent value. Yet as in the Community's 'North-South bargain', actors in the EC sometimes practice 'diffuse reciprocity', transferring resources to others in the expectation that doing so will increase the legitimacy of the Community and its long-term stability, as well as providing the donors with political influence in the interim.[17]

The inappropriateness of statist, strictly inter-governmental or even confederal models of how European politics operates stems from the inconsistency of these images with the network metaphor or the semi-lattice model, which serve as the best approximation to the evolving reality. 'Supranationality', despite the unfortunate connotations of federalism encrusted onto the term, is compatible with these notions. The Community political system can best be visualized as an elaborate set of networks, closely linked in some ways, partially decomposed in others, whose results depend on the political style in the ascendant at the moment. When conditions are propitious and leadership strategies appropriate, as they have been since 1985, the political style of supranationality enables connections to be made between points in the network, and allows an expanded conception of tasks. When conditions are less benign or strategies inappropriate, the results are policy stagnation and separation of policy spheres.

To explore how benign or malign conditions develop, we now turn to the dynamic side of our analysis. How should we understand the institutional changes in the Community that have taken place during the last five years?

Institutional change and 'spillover'

Political scientists interested in theory development thrive on puzzles – contradictions between what we should expect from conventional theory and what we actually observe. During the past two decades, such contradictions have appeared between the realist state-centric view of world politics and the spread of transnational relations; and between the view that hegemony is essential to cooperation and the reality of extensive cooperation after the waning of American dominance.[18] Now the sudden and unexpected success, so far, of the Single European Act (SEA) similarly confronts us with a puzzle.

In the years immediately before the signing of the SEA in February 1986, few observers anticipated more than halting progress, and many expected stagnation or even decay of the European movement towards regional centralization of decision-making. In his sceptical analysis of European decision-making during the 1970s, published in 1983, Paul Taylor stressed the limits imposed by states on European integration, arguing that 'the challenges to sovereignty were successfully resisted and the central institutions failed to obtain the qualities of supranationalism.'[19] His academic analysis echoed the cover of the *Economist* on 20 March 1982, showing a tombstone with the words, 'EEC born March 25th, 1957, moribund March 25th, 1982, *capax imperii nisi imperasset*'. (It seemed capable of power until it tried to wield it.)[20] Even after agreement on the Single European Act, as Albert Bressand points out, its significance was underestimated both by sceptics and by federalists. Margaret Thatcher referred to it as a 'modest decision', and Altiero Spinelli predicted that it 'will almost certainly have proven its ineffectiveness within two years'.[21] The *Economist* commented that 'Europe has laboured long to produce a mouse'.[22]

The reality since 1985 has, of course, belied these predictions. Most publicized has been the movement towards completion of the internal market mandated by the Single European Act. Of the original 300 directives proposed in the Commission White Paper, 39% had by mid-1989 undergone final adoption by the Council and 5% had received some degree of assent from that body. The new doctrine of mutual recognition – that each member country must accept products made under the others' product laws, subject to Europe-wide standards – has been especially important in facilitating action to remove technical barriers to free trade: 'Half the directives to stop national product regulations and safety rules blocking the free flow of goods' had gone through the Council by mid-1989.[23]

The scope of the Single European Act is not exhausted by its provisions for completion of the internal market. The Act represents a bargain about other issues as well, including limited foreign policy cooperation. Decision-making procedures have also changed dramatically. As Helen Wallace points out in Chapter 12, the Council has instituted qualified majority voting not only on issues related to the internal market as mandated by the SEA, but also on issues related to the Common Agricultural Policy and the external trade policy of the EC. In December 1986 the Council amended its procedures on voting to require the president to call for a vote on such issues, at the request of a member of the Council or the Commission, whenever a majority of the members of the Council favour a measure. The Commission recently reported that 'the now fully accepted possibility of adopting a decision by a qualified majority forces the delegations to display flexibility throughout the debate, thus making decision-making easier'.[24]

As surprising as these changes have been to observers of Europe, continuity as well as discontinuity can be discerned. In particular, as Philippe de Schoutheete pointed out in commenting on a draft of this chapter, four major actions were taken during the frustrating years after 1973 which have played a major role in the European revival that we now observe: the creation of the

European Council in 1974, the decision to have the European Parliament elected directly, the establishment of the European Monetary System, and the enlargement negotiations that added six new members to the original six. Nevertheless, although institutional changes between 1974 and 1985 prepared the way for the dramatic events of the last five years, there is little doubt that European decision-making has quite suddenly become more decisive, expeditious, and effective.

Since none of us anticipated such a dramatic and coherent revival of Community policy-making, any attempts to explain it should be viewed with scepticism. What was unpredicted by analysts working with established theories cannot, in general, be adequately explained, post hoc, through the use of such theories.[25] Indeed, perhaps a new theory of joint European decision-making should be invented, discarding loaded terms such as 'supranationality' and 'spillover', and drawing instead on contemporary theories of strategic choice in collective situations, or recent attempts to understand institutional innovation.[26] Yet without attempting such an ambitious task here, it may be useful to recall some of the insights of neofunctionalist theories of change, ambiguous and insufficient as they may have been. It seems unfortunate to us that many of the accounts of European Community politics have discarded older theories, such as neofunctionalism, without putting anything theoretical in their place: recourse is had to mere description of processes and events. Attempts to avoid theory, however, not only miss interesting questions but rely implicitly on a framework for analysis that remains unexamined precisely because it is implicit.

State decisions and the world political economy

Any attempt to understand the institutional changes of the Single European Act must begin with a recognition that *governments* took the final crucial steps leading to its negotiation and ratification.[27] Franco-German relations, based on a series of mutually beneficial bargains, have always been at the core of the politics of the European Community. The revival of a supranational style of decision-making, and the strengthening of European institutions in the Single Act, resulted most immediately from decisions by governments to press, in their own interests, for a removal of internal economic barriers and for institutional changes that would permit such a policy to be carried out.

To say this is not to declare that a state-centric perspective will provide a satisfactory explanation of the Single European Act, only that such an explanation must *begin* with governmental actions, since these actions are what we observe leading directly to the Act. At the same time, we must recognize that governmental decisions were made in the context of a political economy of the 1980s that was greatly changed from that of the previous decade. American policy had facilitated European integration in the 1950s and early 1960s, but the economic turbulence of the 1970s had created incentives for competitive extra-European affiliations (especially with oil-producing states). In the 1980s, oligopolistic competition intensified, but for European industry, it appeared increasingly necessary to merge or collaborate to attain sufficient economies of scale, and technological capability, to cope with American and Japanese competitors.

The 'conversion' of the French government in 1983 and the enthusiasm of the British after 1979 for deregulation opened the way for elites from big business and the Commission, concerned about the 'waning competitiveness' of the EC vis-à-vis the United States and Japan and the perception that 'international business seemed to turn its back on the EC'. The 'national champion' strategy of the 1970s, which had increased the perceived diversity of national situations and competition among European states, was now perceived as a failure; European firms could only compete on an international scale if their home market became united rather than fragmented.[28] Thus, events in the world political economy were important influences on the governmental decisions associated with the Community's revival.

'Spillover, and the Single Act

At the core of the dynamic theory of political integration devised by Ernst Haas and the neofunctionalist school was the concept of 'spillover'. Haas was interested in what he called the 'expansive logic of sector integration', which followed an initial bargain, such as that between the French desire for a common agricultural policy and Germany's search for a common market in industrial goods.

Spillover for the neofunctionalists was not a manifestation of enthusiasm for the ideology of Europe, but a more prosaic result of 'swapping concessions from a variety of sectors':

Lack of agreement among governments can give rise to increased delegated powers on the part of these [supranational] institutions. Dissatisfaction with the results of partial economic steps may lead labour and industry to demand new central action. Supranational institutions and national groups may create situations which can be dealt with only through central action, unless the nations are willing to suffer deprivations in welfare . . . No statesman, even if he deeply dislikes the process, can permanently isolate his nation from a commitment to unity which is only partially implemented, unless he is willing to pay the price in diminished welfare.[29]

Haas was sophisticated about the politics of spillover – in contrast to the distortions of his views common in the contemporary literature. 'The spillover process', as he said, 'is far from automatic.' It depends on the continued division of Germany and 'the tacit recognition of that status in the minds of West German leaders'. Furthermore, spillover does not presume continued enthusiasm on the part of elites; indeed, its significance is most evident in the continuation of regional integration even as *élan* declines.[30]

'Spillover' is an ambiguous word. It can be used simply descriptively, to refer to the enlargement of 'an authoritative and legitimate international task'.[31] But its theoretical interest derives from a causal conceptualization. Joseph S. Nye, for instance, defines spillover as referring to a situation in which 'imbalances created by the functional interdependence or inherent linkages of tasks can press political actors to redefine their common tasks'.[32] This latter definition can be used either to characterize changing incentives facing *states*, or to a more complex pattern of transnational activity in which national actors 'appear as *differentiated* actors, a plurality of negotiating units (classes, status groups, subregions, clientèles, bureaucratic agencies, ideological clusters, etc.)'.[33]

Whether the changing incentives posited by the causal conception of spillover provided an explanation for task expansion was a point of controversy among neofunctionalists. Nye argued that 'the functional linkage of tasks has been a less powerful mechanism than was originally believed to be the case', and sought to construct a 'revised neofunctionalist process model' in which deliberate linkages, actions of exernal actors, elite socialization, and other factors played comparable roles. Leon N. Lindberg and Stuart A. Scheingold even sought to refute Haas's conception that spillover led to the Common Market: 'The successful transformation that gave birth to the Common Market was not a result of functional spillover'.[34]

The neofunctionalist literature on political integration therefore yields three competing hypotheses about task expansion in the Community:

1. Task expansion occurs as a result of the impact of new policies on the incentives facing *differentiated* actors, including multinational enterprises, transnational interest groups, Commission technocrats, and semi-autonomous elements of national bureaucracies. These actors form coalitions to increase the extent of Community decision-making in new sectors, in order to protect gains from policy integration in sectors on which agreements have already been reached.
2. Task expansion occurs as a result of the impact of new policies on the incentives facing *states*, which remain relatively coherent actors with functioning hierarchies of authority, and which continue to make the crucial policy decisions in the Community.
3. Task expansion occurs as a result of *intergovernmental bargains*, which are not generated by previous decisions to expand Community prerogatives or devise joint policies.

The first of these hypotheses is purely neofunctionalist; the third is statist; and the second represents a synthesis of the two perspectives: states remain the crucial actors but they respond to conditions created by their past actions and may therefore be to some extent prisoners of those actions. Which of these hypotheses is best supported by the evidence of the late 1980s will not be clear before much empirical research has been carried out. Nevertheless, the neofunctionalist hypothesis, and the state-centred variant of it, should be on the research agenda. As Helen Wallace observes in Chapter 12, the internal market programme, agreed upon in intergovernmental bargains, 'has provoked a more thorough coverage of the freedom of movement of all four factors of production and the reactivation of a previously stalled debate on a common transport policy. It could even be argued that the neo-functionalists' concept of "spillover" is now being vindicated'.[35]

Indeed it could be so argued – although this contention has not yet been meaningfully proven, and will surely have to be qualified. In particular, it appears to us that spillover does not account adequately for the major decisions, such as those of the Milan summit in 1985 and subsequently that led to the Single Act. If spillover and pressure from the European institutions had been sufficient to create such a step-level change, it would have occurred much earlier. After all, the members had repeatedly committed themselves to full economic union, but it had been accomplished neither through spillover from the earlier bargains nor through mere pledges. A large part of the explanation for these major changes must, we think, be found elsewhere. For these events, an emphasis on intergovernmental bargains will probably be more fruitful. It is much more plausible to conjecture that spillover leads to task-expansion in the wake of a major intergovernmental bargain, than to hold that such bargains are themselves explained by the changing incentives coming from past policy change. As we have seen, the 1992 programme was much more strongly affected by events in the world political economy outside Europe – especially by concern about international competitiveness – than it was driven by the internal logic of spillover.

Our hypothesis is that successful spillover requires prior programmatic agreement among governments, expressed in an intergovernmental bargain. Such a bargain is clearly important in accounting for the Single European Act. Without the turnaround of French economic policy in 1983, and the decision by the British government to accept treaty amendment in order to institution-alize deregulation, no consensus could have been reached on a programme to dismantle barriers within Europe. The British government was very clear that it was entering into a bargain, and not acting on the basis of an ideology of unity or solidarity with Europe. When Margaret Thatcher was asked in May 1989 why she had agreed to ratify the Single European Act, she replied simply that 'we wished to have many of the directives under majority voting because things which we wanted were being stopped by others using a single vote. For instance, we have not yet got insurance freely in Germany as we wished.'[36]

Focusing on intergovernmental bargains, i.e. on governmental decisions, leaves out one actor: the Commission. The role of the Commission in preparing the White Paper on the creation of a single market by 1992, presented to the European Council in Milan in June 1985, was crucial in defining the agenda which governments had to decide. The Milan summit endorsed that programme, and also decided on the institutional reform that led to the Single Act. Still, it can be argued that Delors and his fellow Commissioners did no more than focus the states' attention on the one issue – the single market – that was acceptable to the three major actors, Britain, West Germany and France.

In one sense, attributing major changes to an intergovernmental bargain only begs the question of accounting for such an agreement. In seeking to answer this question, we could benefit from recalling some neofunctionalist arguments; in particular Haas's own warning that incrementalist strategies, which are necessary for spillover, depend on shared objectives. In the 1950s and early 1960s, Europe thrived on what Haas called 'a pragmatic synthesis of capitalism and socialism in the form of democratic planning'. With such shared objectives, tactics and means can vary, as interests and alignments change; furthermore, the specific objectives of the participants can be quite diverse as long as, with respect to proposed Europe-wide policies, they are complementary. Haas explained the ratification of the European Coal and Steel Community Treaty in the early 1950s not as the result of idealistic enthusiasm but as

'the convergence, not of six separate national interests, but of a sufficiently large number of separate national party positions to push the Treaty over the top . . . The very ambiguity of the Treaty, of course, made this pattern of convergence possible. Something seemed to be "in it" for everybody and a large enough body of other-wise quarrelling politicians was persuaded to launch the first experiment in deliberate integration.' [37]

There is much in this description that could be applied to the Single European Act. Like the Treaty of Rome, its ratification resulted less from a coherent burst of idealism than from a convergence of national interests around a new pattern of economic policy-making: not the Keynesian synthesis of the 1950s and 1960s but the neo-liberal, deregulatory programme of the 1980s. Reliance on 'mutual recognition' rather than harmonization reflected the decision to focus Community attention on removal of barriers rather than on means of economic intervention.[38] This particular bargain illustrates the general point that the members of a regional organization must regard themselves as having a great deal in common, distinguishing themselves from outsiders. It is, as one of us wrote during the earlier debates, 'not that the units be in "objectively" similar situations but that there be "subjective" similarity – a conviction on the part of the policy-makers that the similarity exists'.[39] It was only after the shift in French economic policy in 1983, and the general turn towards deregulatory preferences, that such subjective similarity reappeared in Europe.

Yet these underpinnings for the intergovernmental bargain of the Single European Act had little to do with spillover, which explains neither mutual recognition nor deregulation. We are left, therefore, with the task of trying to explain why the interests of the major actors became convergent after having failed to be 'subjectively similar' for so long – despite many earlier attempts at creating a single market. In the case of Britain the decisive factor was the resolution of the dispute over budgetary contributions in 1984. This made it possible for Mrs Thatcher to move on to the task she deemed important – deregulation – and to overcome her own objections to the abandonment of the rule of unanimity, since qualified majority rule was necessary to the adoption of the single market programme.

The decisive concession to her had been made possible by a change in French policy. In order to account for the new definition of France's interest, we have to examine both international and domestic factors. The fiasco of the socialist policy of 1981–3 did not require a turn to the EC. Many socialist leaders and businessmen, as well as the communists, advocated autarchy and the removal of the French franc from the EMS. But such a choice would have (a) put Mitterrand at the mercy of his communist allies and of the Left of his party; (b) cut France off from West Germany and the US, to which Mitterrand, at that time, wanted France to cling, and (c) most probably undercut even further France's competitiveness. Thus we end with a tentative conclusion congruent with regime theory: the existence of a 'regime' – in this case, the EC – affected these states' calculations of incentives, and made it possible for them to see a policy of European *relance* as advantageous.

Spillover is an important concept, but it can only be usefully employed within a carefully delimited sphere. Before it is used effectively in research, different meanings of the concept of spillover will need to be distinguished, as above, and the *conditions* under which spillover can be expected to operate must be kept in mind.[40] The 'theory of spillover' has, therefore, not been discredited: in the wake of an intergovernmental bargain based on subjective similarity and a common policy orientation, actors can have incentives to promote task expansion into new sectors in order to protect gains already achieved. But it remains to be seen, from empirical research, how much this theory will explain of the institutional developments under way in the European Community at the end of the 1980s.

Bargains that cover only certain sectors, omitting to provide for sectors linked to those, can stimulate a spillover process either on an interstate basis (as incentives facing states change) or on a transnational one. This core idea of the neofunctionalists is consistent with much of what we know about how changes in the international political economy affect incentives for states. It leaves open for investigation, however, the question of *how fast and how far* spillover from an initial bargain will extend.

Spillover and geographical expansion

Any explanation of the institutional changes in the Single European Act must take into account the Community's long preoccupation with the expansion from nine to twelve member governments. For the better part of a decade the Commission had declared, as in 1978, that 'with twelve members, the institutions and decision-making procedures will be under considerable strain and the Community will be exposed to possible stalemate and dilution unless its practical *modus operandi* is improved'.[41] As William Wallace put the issue in 1978:

The fundamental question is . . . can one at the same time enlarge the Community and strengthen it? M. Calvo-Sotelo insisted that we could and would; many interventions in the Working Group discussions implied that we couldn't and wouldn't. My own conclusion is that we can – but that we are unlikely to, unless the current members accept the full responsibilities of enlargement and act towards each other and towards the Communities in approaching enlargement in a more positive spirit.[42]

Despite prevailing expectations, enlargement did contribute to strengthening of Community institutions, not because of idealism or governments' senses of obligation but because governments sought to use Europe to promote deregulation, and because decision-making was becoming virtually impossible under the practice of unanimity. By the mid-1980s, it appeared even to the British government that it could not attain expected large benefits from deregulation without some way to ensure that its partners would open up their markets; and the most credible guarantee that this would occur was treaty amendment, institutionalizing the deregulatory process and instituting qualified majority rule over it. With 12 members, the unit-veto system of the European Council would, in the absence of complex package deals, lead to stalemate on increasing numbers of issues. For a major advance in policy integration to take place, these package deals would have had to be so complex that the costs of negotiating them would have become prohibitive.

The contrast with the French position in 1965–6 is quite instructive. The Common Agricultural Policy had been agreed upon, as had the customs union. Both could and did continue without implementation of the EEC Treaty provisions for qualified majority voting. De Gaulle could therefore block qualified majority voting, as well as increases in the power of the Commission, without jeopardizing France's economic policy goals. Britain, in 1985, could not do this: changes in the voting procedures, and indeed treaty amendments, were the price to be paid for the 1992 programme to complete the internal market, since to achieve this objective, recalcitrant governments had to be outvoted.

Ultimate British willingness to accept majority voting reflected its acceptance of the argument that enlargement made effective use of unanimity impossible. In June 1985, the Minister of State at the Foreign and Commonwealth Office, Malcolm Rifkind, declared: 'We believe that enlargement of the Community to 12 will make the existing procedures more unlikely to be capable of reaching early agreement on matters of importance.' Similarly, in the French Senate debates on ratification of the Single Act, the French Minister of Foreign Affairs, Jean-Bernard Raimond, stated that 'l'Europe des douze ne pouvait être gérée comme l'était la Communauté à six et devait adapter des mécanismes de décision à ce nouvel élargissement'.[43]

Part of the story of the Single European Act, therefore, is that governments decided to strike a bargain on deregulation, which seemed to them to require reform of the decision-making system. The Single European Act can even be seen, as Helen Wallace has argued, as a consequence of the bargain for the enlargement of the community to twelve members.[44] A new form of spillover, not from one economic sector to another but from one institutional dimension to another, took place. Expansion of the Community led to anticipation of institutional stalemate, and (since the key actors sought policy changes) created incentives for formal institutional change.

Thus in a dialectical manner, the enlargement of the Six to the Twelve, first appearing as an antithesis to effective decision-making, became a decisive element in decision-making reform. Spillover took place, not as a functional expansion of tasks, but rather in the form of the creation, as a result of enlargement, of incentives for institutional change.

Spillover in contemporary Europe: insights and limits

Jacques Delors explicitly refers to imbalances, or spillover, as the most likely motor of further integration. As in Haas's theory, spillover for Delors (and also for Monnet) does not take place automatically but through pragmatic political strategies. Economic integration and political cooperation are two parallel roads that will merge some day. Economic integration must precede social policy, but will lead to a demand for such a policy, just as within the realm of economic integration, deregulation (on which all members agree) must precede joint programmes and policies, but will create a need for them:

History is knocking at the door. Are we going to pretend that we cannot hear? . . . It will not be enough to create a large frontier-free market, nor, as implied by the Single European Act, a vast economic and social area. It is for us, in advance of 1993, to put some flesh on the Community's bones and give it a little more soul.[45]

How realistic is this expectation? There is little doubt that the realization of the single market will create demands for further measures. The 'Delors package' adopted by the Council in February 1988 – an agreement to increase the resources of the Community and the funds for the poorer countries – is an example of such demands being met. But it is equally important to be aware of the limitations on spillover (one of which is the legal requirement of unanimity in areas other than the internal market, and even in the tax and social dimensions of the latter).

The controversy over monetary union in 1989–90 provided an example of both the existence and the limits on spillover in contemporary Europe. The very success of the European Monetary System had generated concern in Italy and France that their monetary policies were being controlled by the Bundesbank. At the same time the agreement to abolish capital controls by 1 July 1990 led to fears that the parity grid system of the EMS would not hold up under the pressure.[46] Thus the logic of spillover from the internal market suggested to many – although by no means all – informed observers the necessity of monetary union, defined as 'an area of permanently fixed exchange rates, with no exchange controls or other barriers to the free movement of capital or the circulation of currencies'.[47] Perceptions of functional linkages between the single market and exchange rate arrangements led to a process that was both supranational – the report of April 1989 prepared by the Delors Committee – and intergovernmental – the adoption of its first phase by the Council in Madrid two months later.

Yet nothing in the functional logic of spillover requires a European central bank. Without a radical change of policy in London, its partners would have to choose between a compromise with Britain, which would probably mean no European central bank, and a break with Britain, creating a system in which the central bank would be a superficially Europeanized Bundesbank – a bank independent of governmental direction and provided with a committee of central bank governors whose role would be more consultative than directive. It is far from certain that the French and Italians will ultimately prefer the second outcome to the first. The German government might also prefer the first to a continental EMU in which the de facto hegemony of the Bundesbank would be seriously reduced.

On social policy and taxation, the same combination of pressure for, and resistance to, spillover was evident. The Commission's proposals met such opposition that a relatively loose scheme of regulation – under which each member would be left free to set its own course within broad limits – seemed likely to emerge, in which the principles of mutual recognition and subsidiarity may provide a clever 'European' camouflaging of different national practices, eliminating the conflict between national regulation and community rules by giving a European label to the former.

The strong demand for closer European political cooperation (EPC) predated the single market programme. Behind EPC lies the changing position of

Western Europe in the fading cold war and the impossibility, in the long run, of keeping negotiations on economic issues, entrusted to European institutions, separate from the definition of a common foreign policy. Increasingly in coming years, international politics will be played on the chessboard of economic interdependence, where Community authority is predominant: association agreements, applications for membership, deals with EFTA countries, bargains in GATT and the OECD, and the like. But these issues will be closely linked to traditional diplomatic concerns, as both relations with Eastern Europe and the occasional impingement of economic issues on alliance politics (in both the US-European and US-Japanese relationship) make clear. As economic and diplomatic issues become entangled, a common European identity, and desire for a more coherent foreign policy, based both on multiple bargains among members and empathy for one another's positions, may emerge. And, in the case of relations with Eastern Europe, a common West European policy may well be (as in the monetary realm) a way for Bonn to obtain broader legitimacy for its *Ostpolitik*, and for Bonn's partners to try to exert some control over it.

Yet for political cooperation as well as monetary and social policies, there are manifest limits on spillover. There was little evidence during the 1980s of any spillover into defence policy. And even in a period of expanding political cooperation, the common function under the Single Act (unlike foreign economic policy under the Treaty of Rome) leads to pooled powers rather than to power for a central authority distinct from the states.

Thus we must distinguish between the preservation of the Community and its further development, both in scope and institutional autonomy. Preservation appears reasonably secure – not because there is a single purpose, but because the Community, as it has evolved, not only serves the multiple purposes of its members, but can also accommodate changes of purpose and of policies, within certain limits. Thus, today, it serves the French strategy of reaching through 'Europe' national goals that can no longer be achieved at a purely national level, the Spanish strategy of economic modernization and political return to Europe, the British ideology of deregulation and realization of economies of scale, the West German desire for a zone of monetary stability, a broad market for German goods, and an anchor in the West. The lesson of the 1970s is probably vivid enough to prevent destruction of the Community even in the event of a recession. An economic slump might put a temporary halt to the dismantling of barriers, to the opening of public procurement, to the tightening of monetary and fiscal cooperation required by the Madrid Council. It might lead members to use the various safeguards and provisions for temporary restrictions (articles 36 and 100). But – as in the 1970s – the Community would survive, not only because of its capacity to accommodate different views, but because of the habits of cooperation created by its many networks of private and public bargaining, which characterize the European mode of governance.

On the other hand, a further development of the Community in what might be called, in short, the Delors direction, is more problematic. It might be stopped not only by a world recession, but also by a set of domestic backlashes against the economic hardships the single market might impose on certain sectors, professions or regions. If the disadvantaged turn to Brussels for relief and find that Brussels simply doesn't have either the financial means to provide it or the political clout to force significant redistribution, such revolts may become more serious.

This review of spillover in the contemporary Community supports the generalizations offered above. Spillover depends on prior intergovernmental bargains. When those bargains are fresh and viable, pressures appear for intensified cooperation in sectors where the bargains were made, and for extended cooperation in related sectors. But these pressures by no means automatically lead to common policies, and they certainly do not necessarily create new centralized institutions. Indeed, for the latter to happen, a new set of intergovernmental bargains – perhaps generated in part by prior spillover pressures but by no means preordained by them – must be consummated. Until the end of 1992 spillover pressures are likely to be evident in the European community, as the bargain of the Single European Act works itself out. What happens afterwards will depend on the vagaries of domestic politics, the diverse pressures of the external environment, and the health of the economies of Western Europe, as well as on the individuals leading European governments, and the Commission, at that time.

Conclusions

As we have seen, the Community political system can be viewed as a network. But networks can be curses or blessings. Their proponents regard them as particularly adaptive and well-suited to coping with changes in complex, information-rich environments. Critics of networks, by contrast, question whether such forms of organization can act decisively at all: if sovereignty corrupts, loss of sovereignty may corrupt absolutely![48]

To what extent has the sovereignty wrested from individual Member States been acquired by identifiable Community institutions, and to what extent lost in what often appears as a vortex of competing forces – or perhaps even a 'black hole' from which coherent authority can never emerge? The Community has its share both of centrifugal and centripetal forces: the former are not only national but sectoral, characterized by bureaucratic coalitions, poorly coordinated with one another; the latter are centred on the Commission, the Court, and to some extent the Council of Ministers. From this perspective, the relative power of Commission and Council may be a less important issue, despite the decades of debate about supranationalism, than their joint ability, along with the Court, to keep the decentralized coalitions of bureaucrats and interest groups – Europe's parallel to America's 'iron triangles' (bureaucrats, interest groups, and congressional committees or subcommittees) – in line. Indeed, to ask whether sovereignty is being 'transferred' from nation-states to a community may be quite misleading; more relevant may be the question of whether the sovereignty being lost by individual states can be focused at all – or whether Europe will become simply a network without a decisive or accountable centre of authority.

The issue we raise here is often called the democratic deficit. It has several aspects. The first is that the Court often behaves, in the words of one commentator, as a 'substitute legislator', which has moved into areas the Council had not reached and gone beyond the Council's intentions in some cases.[49] It is, indeed, the Court that has gone farthest in limiting national autonomy, not only by asserting the principle of superiority of Community law, but by insisting on the direct applicability of directives, when specified conditions are met. The Court has also ruled consistently in favour of freedom of movement within the internal market when that objective has conflicted with national policies. Ever since John Marshall, the US Supreme Court has often sought to expand national powers at the expense of the states. But the Supreme Court derives its legitimacy from the US Constitution – the very foundation of American citizenship. The legitimacy established by the Treaty of Rome is of a flimsier nature.[50]

To be sure, the judges of the Court would argue that they have a far better reason to be a 'substitute legislator' than the Supreme Court; the Council is a confederal body only, and the parliament has just a limited power of amendment. Here we reach the second dimension of the democratic deficit. In modern democracies, the elected legislature has – usually – the final say on bills within its jurisdiction, and the important power of checking the activities of the executive. The European Parliament has neither. Moreover, whereas enforcement is left to the states, this usually means the states' bureaucracies, not the national parliaments. One of the most frequent complaints concerns their declining role as integration progresses. The supremacy of Community law diminishes the role of national parliaments, and the direct applicability of Community regulations, and of some directives, often eliminates them altogether. What the Community's political process does is to dispossess them of their power in a whole series of realms, and to transfer it to the Council and, indirectly, to the ECJ. Jacques Delors has expressed his fear of a nationalist reaction in these parliaments.[51] Precisely because enforcement is the states' business, Delors believes that the re-enforcement of the national parliaments' role is more important than an extension of the European parliament's powers.

To be sure, national parliaments have seen their role diminish in all parliamentary democracies, either because the bills they vote are usually initiated by the cabinet, or because – in countries where the parliamentary majority, and therefore the cabinet, is a weak coalition – the legislature is less important than the directorates of the parties in power. However, the national parliament remains the foundation of the whole government's legitimacy, both because it is elected by the people and because the executive emanates from it. The Community's executive most assuredly does not issue from the European Parliament, and its popular election since 1979 has not provided the Parliament with an authority comparable with that of national assemblies, both because of its limited powers and because of the absence of party or popular politics on a European scale, which is the most fundamental aspect of the democratic deficit.

The process characterizing the European Community in its most dynamic periods, the early 1960s and the late 1980s, is probably the only one that allows for integration despite the opposition of the states to outright transfers of power and loyalty to supranational institutions. The Single Act was both a *relance* and a way of sidestepping the Federalist political union treaty advocated by Spinelli with the support of the European Parliament. But a heavy price has to be paid for this: the paradox of integrated economies and separate politics, the paradox of an elaborate process of multinational bargaining coexisting with an obstinately 'national' process of political life and elections, the paradox of the emergence of a European identity on the world scene coexisting with continuing national loyalties.

This identity remains hindered by the weakness of the Community in world affairs. Foreign policy and defence are activities that often require great domestic sacrifices, if only in the form of resources taken away from internal welfare and development, for such tasks as national defence and aid to other countries. In democracies, these sacrifices can be obtained by institutions that claim popular legitimacy and support. European Community institutions, dominated by bureaucrats and national ministers, with a parliament that has very narrow budgetary powers and a procedure of foreign policy cooperation that is intergovernmental, can draw on no such legitimacy.

Our analysis of the dynamics of the Community and of spillover suggests that despite the revival of supranationality and the emergence of a Community-wide political system in which state sovereignty is both pooled and shrunk, what matters most are the bargains among the major players. The two indispensable ones remain France and West Germany, whose alliance continues to provide the political motor of the enterprise. Suspicion of 'Europe', even of supranationality, has dramatically declined in France, especially in the present generation of elites. But some fear that the resurgence of the economic and financial power of the Federal Republic, its new eminence in East-West relations, and the economic and, above all, national opportunities provided to it by the breakdown of communism in Eastern Europe, and by reunification, may make Bonn less committed to the Community. Competing demands and interests may make its government less willing to pay large sums to the Community budget, its industrialists and bankers less open to cooperation or alliances with others, its diplomats less eager to seek a European legitimation, once the single market – a major opportunity for the German economy – is achieved: a situation comparable to that of de Gaulle as we described him in 1965. Will France and the other continental members be willing to pay a price in order to make a further development of the Community – in effect, of controls and limits on German autonomy – more attractive to a German government preoccupied with managing reunification and its consequences?

At a concrete level of analysis, what is raised here is the centrality of Germany to the Community – which, as many chapters in this volume demonstrate, is already impressive and becoming more so all the time. The future of the Community depends, above all, on the stability of German politics and the steadiness of German policy. At a more abstract level the issue is the degree to which even the European Community (which was established without a hegemon and which is stronger than ordinary international regimes) can adapt to a newly fluid pattern of European politics in which its strongest member plays a strategically pivotal role – and in which that power's national identity is involved. Especially in a set-up where the power in question does not provide military security to its partners in exchange for economic preponderance, can the Community's existence and policies help to dampen a rising hegemon's national aspirations so that they remain acceptable to the less powerful states, without at the same time appearing too burdensome to the hegemon? This is, obviously, a very different case from those which recent arguments about American hegemony, and cooperation 'after hegemony', have considered.[52]

At present, one can only note that the evolution of world politics still favours the strengthening of ties among the partners of the Community. In such an environment, ties of European networks will deepen as habits of pooling sovereignty develop. Spillover will lead to incremental deepening of joint decision-making, and European organizations will – like all organizations – seek to extend their authority. Thus, barring a major slump in the world economy, or catastrophic events in Eastern Europe and the Soviet Union whose international fall-out cannot be predicted, there are reasons to be at least moderately optimistic about the Community's future prospects.[53]

Notes

1. It must quickly be added, however, that the 1992 legislation will test the Community's implementation and compliance procedures. Signs of stress are already evident: Between the end of 1985 and the end of 1987, the number of cases of Court of Justice judgments not yet complied with, listed by the Commission, had risen from 33 to 53. Compare the *Third Annual Report to the European Parliament on Commission Monitoring of the Application of Community Law* (1985), *Official Journal of the European Communities*, 1986 (86/C 220), with the *Fifth Annual Report to the European Parliament on Commission Monitoring of the Application of Community Law* (1987), *Official Journal of the European Communities, 1988* (88/C 310), p. 43. For a good review of implementation, see Heinrich Siedentopf and Jacques Ziller, (eds), *Making European Policies Work. Vol. I, The Implementation of Community Legislation in the Member States: Comparative Synthesis.* European Institute of Public Administration, published by Sage Publications (London and Beverly Hills, CA, 1988), p. 58.
2. Hedley Bull, *The Anarchical Society* (NY, Columbia University Press, 1977), p. 8.
3. In addition to the volume cited in n. 1, see its companion vol. II, *National Reports*, and the much less guarded article by Hjalte Rasmussen, 'Les Etats membres et l'inexécution des obligations communautaires', in *Pouvoirs*, no. 48 (1989), pp. 39–56.
4. Rasmussen mentions health, the environment and legislative overload as frequent rationalizations or excuses.
5. Ibid., p. 54.
6. Haas, 'Technocracy, Pluralism and the New Europe', in *A New Europe?* ed. Stephen R. Graubard (Boston, Houghton Mifflin, 1964), pp. 64, 66.
7. Ernst B. Haas, *The Uniting of Europe: Political, Economic and Social Forces, 1950–57* (Stanford, Stanford University Press, 1958), p. 59.
8. Ernst B. Haas, 'Turbulent Fields and the Theory of Regional Integration', *International Organization*, vol. 30, no. 2 (Spring 1976), p. 173.
9. Ernst B. Haas, *Beyond the Nation-State: Functionalism and International Organization* (Stanford, Stanford University Press, 1964), p. 48.
10. Europe's paper trail is littered with complaints about the Luxembourg Compromise and proposals for a return to what the Commission in 1969 called 'normal functioning of the institutions as laid down in the Treaties' (*Bulletin of the European Communities*, vol. 3, January 1970). See also the Tindemans Report

(*Bulletin of the EC, Supplement*, January 1976), the Conclusions of the 'Three Wise Men' who reported to the Council on institutional arrangements in 1979 (*Bulletin of the EC*, 11-1979, pp. 25–8), and, of course, the report of the ad hoc Committee on Institutional Affairs (Dooge Report) in March 1985 (*Bulletin of the EC*, 3-1985, pp. 102–11).

11. Haas, *The Uniting of Europe* (Stanford, Stanford University Press, 1958), p. 16.
12. Siedentopf and Ziller, vol. I, p. 30. On the dominance of national governments in the process, see ibid., p. 71.
13. See Dusan Sidjanski, 'Communauté européenne 1992: gouvernement de comité?' in *Pouvoirs*, issue on Europe 1993, no. 48 (1989), pp. 71–80.
14. Walter W. Powell, 'Neither Market Nor Hierarchy: Network Forms of Organization', draft (July 1988) prepared for Barry M. Shaw and Larry L. Cummings, (eds), *Research in Organizational Behaviour*, vol. 12 (New York: JAI Press, 1989).
15. Networks may eventually extend beyond the limits set by farsighted self-interest: 'entangling strings of reputation, friendship, interdependence and altruism [may] become integral parts of the relationship.' That is, in networks that William Wallace refers to in his introduction as 'values, loyalties, shared identities' can become important: a sense of solidarity may develop among elites even though a sense of community, in the sense used by Karl Deutsch, may never come into being. See Deutsch et al., *Political Community in the North Atlantic Area* (Princeton, Princeton University Press, 1957).
16. Ernst B. Haas, 'Is There a Hole in the Whole? Knowledge, Technology, Interdependence and the Construction of International Regimes', *International Organization*, vol. 29, no. 3 (Summer 1975), pp. 827–76.
17. See Robert O. Keohane, 'Reciprocity in International Relations', *International Organization*, vol. 40, no. 1 (Winter 1986), pp. 1–27.
18. Robert O. Keohane and Joseph S. Nye, Jr, *Transnational Relations and World Politics* (Harvard University Press, 1972); Robert O. Keohane, *After Hegemony* (Princeton University Press, 1984).
19. Paul Taylor, *The Limits of European Integration* (NY, Columbia University Press, 1983), p. 56. Writing in the mid-1970s, the editor of this volume perceptively pointed out the continuing strength of the Commission and the extent to which Community institutions facilitated coordination of national policy-making; and he anticipated the possibility of the Communities having by the mid-1980s 'widened and strengthened their ability to formulate and implement policies in concert or in common'. However, he argued that if this occurred, 'it is unlikely to have been the result of any overall strategy'. William Wallace, 'Walking Backwards Towards Unity', in *Policy-Making in the European Communities* (London and NY, Wiley, 1977), eds Helen Wallace, William Wallace and Carole Webb, p. 322.
20. Taylor, *Limits of European Integration*, p. 231.
21. Albert Bressand, 'Beyond Interdependence: 1992 as a Global Challenge', *International Affairs*, January 1990, p. 54.
22. *The Economist*, 7 December 1985, cited in *Project Prométhée, Perspectives No. 9* (March, 1989), p. 5.
23. *The Economist*, 8 July 1989, 'Survey on Europe's Internal Market', p. 12.
24. *22nd General Report on the Activities of the European Communities* (1988), pp. 31–2. *20th General Report* (1986), pp. 28–36. The dramatic effect of the Single European Act on voting practices was not universally anticipated: for instance, former French Foreign Minister Maurice Couve de Murville, speaking in the French Senate's ratification debate on 10 December 1986, claimed that with respect to the Luxembourg Compromise, 'le nouveau traité n'y changera rien'. French Senate *Debates*, session of 10 December 1986, p. 5969.
25. The present authors doubt whether any theory that can perfectly predict strategic

behaviour of states will ever be devised. Unconstrained strategic behaviour is inherently unpredictable insofar as optimal action changes depending on each party's perception of the expectations of others. Theory, if widely known and accepted, creates expectations, which provide incentives for actors to devise strategies exploiting those who have those (now conventional) expectations – thus invalidating the theory. This conundrum applies to theories about much market behaviour, insofar as it depends on inter-actor strategies, and also to politics. However, to the extent that rules and practices structure incentives and constrain behaviour, *patterns* of action may become understandable, although surprises will, in the nature of politics, continue to occur.

26. One source of insight would come from the 'new economic history', exploring institutional change with theories of transactions costs, as in Douglass C. North, *Structure and Change in Economic History* (NY, Norton, 1981). Work on international regimes using similar concepts could also be helpful, as in Robet O. Keohane, *After Hegemony: Cooperation and Discord in the World Political Economy* (Princeton: Princeton University Press, 1984). Another promising line of analysis would be to investigate the impact of increased trade on domestic political institutions, as done by Peter Gourevitch, *Politics in Hard Times* (Ithaca, Cornell University Press, 1986), and by Ronald Rogowski, *Commerce and Coalitions* (Princeton, Princeton University Press, 1989). We are indebted to Leon Lindberg for raising this set of issues at the Florence conference.

27. Intergovernmental 'bargains' are emphasized by Wayne Sandholtz and John Zysman, '1992: Recasting the European Bargain', *World Politics*, vol. 42, no. 1 (October 1989), pp. 1–30. For an excellent detailed account, dealing with institutional as well as policy change, see Andrew Moravcsik, 'Negotiating the Single European Act: National Interests and Conventional Statecraft in the European Community', Department of Government and Centre for International Affairs, Harvard University, July 1989.

28. Sandholtz and Zysman emphasize the role of international competition, particularly from Japan, in prompting action on Europe's internal market. See also Jacques Pelkmans and Alan Winters, *Europe's Domestic Market* (London: Royal Institute of International Affairs, Chatham House Paper no. 43, 1988); and Paolo Ceccini, *The European Challenge, 1992: The Benefits of a Single Market* (Aldershot, Wildwood House, 1988).

29. Haas, *The Uniting of Europe*, p. 243; chapter 8, pp. 283–317.

30. Taylor, *Limits of Integration*, cited, p. 299.

31. Ernst B. Haas, *Beyond the Nation-State: Functionalism and International Organization* (Stanford: Stanford University Press, 1964), p. 407. This is similar to his usage in *The Uniting of Europe*, in which he talks about 'spill-over' (in quotation marks) to describe the movement of policy integration into 'new economic and political sectors' (p. 292). Haas uses the term similarly, to describe *task expansion*, in 'The Study of Regional Integration: Reflections on the Joy and Anguish of Pretheorizing', in Leon N. Lindberg and Stuart A. Scheingold, (eds), *Regional Integration: Theory and Research* (Cambridge, Harvard University Press, 1971), pp. 3–44.

32. Joseph N. Nye, Jr, 'Comparing Common Markets: A Revised Neofunctional Model', in Leon N. Lindberg and Stuart A. Scheingold, (eds), *Regional Integration: Theory and Research* (Cambridge, Harvard University Press, 1971), p. 200. This is a restatement in propositional terms of a formulation by Haas, which indicates imperatives (or incentives): 'policies made in carrying out an initial task and grant of power can be made real only if the task itself is expanded.' *Beyond the Nation-State*, cited, p. 111. Philippe Schmitter defines the 'spillover hypothesis' ('the basic functionalist proposition') as follows: 'Tensions from the global environment and/

or contradictions generated by past performance give rise to unexpected performance in the pursuit of agreed-upon common objectives. These frustrations and/or dissatisfactions are likely to result in the search for alternative means for reaching the same goals, i.e., to induce actions to revise their respective strategies vis-à-vis the scope and level of regional decision-making.' 'A Revised Theory of Regional Integration', in Leon N. Lindberg and Stuart A. Scheingold, (eds), *Regional Integration: Theory and Research* (Cambridge: Harvard University Press, 1971), p. 243.

33. Schmitter, cited, p. 260; his italics.
34. Joseph S. Nye, *Peace in Parts: Integration and Conflict in Regional Organization* (Boston, Little, Brown, 1971), pp. 65, 76; Leon N. Lindberg and Stuart A. Scheingold, *Europe's Would-Be Polity: Patterns of Change in the European Community* (Englewood Cliffs, NJ, Prentice-Hall, 1970), p. 242.
35. Helen Wallace, 'Making Multilateralism Work', p. 19.
36. *Financial Times*, 19 May 1989, editorial page.
37. Haas, 'Technocracy', p. 68; Haas, 'Turbulent Fields', p. 183; Haas, *Uniting of Europe*, pp. 154–5.
38. In his 1983 volume, *The Limits to European Integration*, cited above, Paul Taylor distinguished 'negative integration' – the removal of barriers – from 'positive integration', which he defined as the establishment of common ways of intervening in economies. He characterized the former, in Europe, as generally successful and the latter as unsuccessful. The revival of European integration after 1985 can be seen as a validation of this insight: the strategy chosen by European elites was successful, in this interpretation, because it relied on negative rather than positive intervention. The Commission White Paper of June 1985, 'Completing the Internal Market', classifies all proposed measures under three categories: 'the removal of physical barriers, the removal of technical barriers, and the removal of fiscal barriers'.
39. Hoffmann, 'Obstinate or Obsolete: France, European Integration and the Fate of the Nation-State', in *Decline or Renewal? France Since the 1930s* (NY, Viking Press, 1974), p. 395. Adapted from Hoffmann, 'Obstinate or Obsolete: The Fate of the Nation-State and the Case of Western Europe', *Daedalus*, Summer 1966. Hoffmann added: 'Integration means a common choice of a common future, but that requires certain attitudes about the past and the present.' It is worth noting that imperfect scholarly memories have stereotyped the debate of the late 1960s between neofunctionalists and statists. As we have seen, Haas never believed that spillover was automatic. Nor did the critics see a resurgence of integration as impossible. Hoffmann argued in 1966 that 'one can conceive of a set of circumstances in which a speedy forward march could succeed.' ('Obstinate or Obsolete?', p. 393.) The question is not so much, 'will European integration succeed?' but 'under what conditions can integration progress?' Haas recognized this in his *International Organization* article of 1976, which characterized integration theory as 'obsolescent but not obsolete'. 'Theories of regional integration', he declared, 'retain a good deal of relevance wherever and whenever the setting they were designed to describe and explain continues to exist' ('Turbulent Fields', p. 177). It is our contention here that the conditions for the relevance of neofunctionalist theory are stronger in Europe now than they have been since the 1960s.
40. The predictions of a theory can fail to be borne out by events for one of two distinct reasons: (1) because the propositions of the theory were false, so that even if the preconditions specified in the theory apply, anticipated results do not occur; or (2) because the conditions for the operation of the theory are simply not met. In the latter case, the theory is not falsified, but just appears irrelevant to the situation.
41. 'Report of the Commission on Enlargement of the European Community: General Considerations', *Bulletin of the European Communities*, Supplement 1/78, p. 15.

42. William Wallace, 'Conclusions, Working Groups A and C', in W. Wallace and I. Herreman, (eds), *A Community of Twelve? The Impact of Further Enlargement on the European Communities* (Bruges, College of Europe, 1978), p. 412. The usual view in the late 1970s was that the enlargement of the Community would make it more like a free trade area. However, when President Valéry Giscard d'Estaing was asked by *Le Monde* in July 1978 if a Community of twelve could function normally, he replied that 'enlargement provides a golden opportunity to look into ways of improving' [Community institutions] and proposed a committee of 'three wise men', subsequently appointed, to examine desirable institutional reforms. See Emanuelle Gazzo, 'Enlargement of the Community: Attitudes of Member States', in J.W. Schneider, (ed), *From Nine to Twelve: Europe's Destiny?* (Alphen aan de Rijn, Netherlands, Sijthoff & Noordhoff, 1980). The quotation from Giscard d'Estaing appears on p. 13.

43. *United Kingdom House of Commons Parliamentary Debates*, 26 June 1985, vol. 81, c. 900; French Senate *Debates*, 10 December 1986, p. 5956. Helen Wallace, *Widening and Deepening: The European Community and the New European Agenda* (London: Royal Institute of International Affairs, December 1989).

44. *Inter alia*, in her contribution to this volume.

45. Quoted in *The Economist*, 8 July 1989, 'Survey: Europe's Internal Market', p. 38.

46. *Financial Times*, 10 July 1989, p. 10.

47. Samuel Brittain, 'Don't Sell Madrid Short', *Financial Times*, 29 June 1989, editorial page.

48. For an enthusiastic view of networks, see Powell, cited, p. 58. By contrast, Karel van Wolferen describes the Japanese body politics as a 'system without a core', an overlapping network of relationships among bureaucracies and businesses: 'a set of relationships, with reasonably predictable effects, between those engaged in socio-economic pursuits'. In his view, no one is able to direct this system, not even the Japanese Prime Minister; and it is correspondingly not accountable to the public. In some ways this concept may be as applicable to the emerging European Community as it is to Japan. See Karel van Wolferen, *The Enigma of Japanese Power: People and Politics in a Stateless Nation* (NY, Knopf, 1989), pp. 43–9.

49. Mario Bettati, 'Le *Law-making power* de la Cour', *Pouvoirs* no. 48 (1989), pp. 57–70.

50. And, one might add, it required a civil war in the United States to establish the principle of national supremacy. Before the Civil War the Supreme Court was by no means consistent in its predilection towards national power.

51. *Le Monde*, 15 June 1989, 'Le Parlement européen en mutation', p. 7.

52. Keohane, *After Hegemony* (cited, above, no. 20).

53. Compare our conclusions with William Wallace's in 1982: 'Europe as a Confederation: the Community and the Nation-State', *Journal of Common Market Studies*, vol. XXI, nos. 1 and 2, September and December 1982.

Index

Internal Market Programme, x,
    27, 59, 78, 117, 137–8,
    220–2, 249
investment, 50–1, 78, 137
Ireland, 72, 77, 79, 176, 184, 223,
    270
Islamic nations, 155
Ismay, Lord, 263
Israel, 156, 159
IT companies, 228
Italy, 2
    balance of current account, 77
    and CAP, 33
    and the EMS, 72–3, 75, 79
    government of, 219
    industrial revolution, 14
    inflation in, 76
    links with other EC countries,
        97, 111, 112
    lira, 77
    migration, 183, 184, 187
    R&D in, 54
    Schengen agreement, 118
    students in, 176, 180
    tourism, 171–6, 189

Japan
    agreements with US firms, 62
    competition from, 38, 57, 285
    creditor of US, 80
    migrants, 187
    negotiations with EC, 221
    political leaders in, 8
    students in, 179
    technological strength, 27, 30,
        55, 65
    and USSR, 90
Jenkins, President Roy, 110, 123n
Joffe, Josef, 12
Jordan, 159

Kennedy, John F., US President,
    266
Keohane, Robert O, 28, 29, 45,
    276–300
Keynesianism, 69, 288
Kissinger, Henry, 23n
Kjellén, Rudolf, 135
Kohl, Helmut, 109, 110
Kola peninsula, 129
krona, 138

labour market, 136, 160, 182–3,
    184, 189
Lance missile, 271
languages
    Dutch, 199, 207n
    English, 6
    Estonian, 127
    Finnish, 126
    French, 6, 207n
    German, 6, 199
    Igrian, 127
    Inuit, 126
    Latvian, 138
    teaching foreign, 194

law
    Community, 205n, 221, 224,
        252, 278, 294
    and the dynamics of
        integration, 246–9
    functional importance of the,
        243–4
    Roman, 126
Lebanon, 159, 161
Leningrad, 130
Les Verts, case of, 244, 258n
Libya, 159
Liechtenstein, 104
Lindberg, Leon, 8, 19, 286
'Lingua' programme, 204, 210n
lira (Italian), 77
Livi Bacci, Massimo, 161
Locke, 279
London, 81–2, 109, 114, 115, 116,
    271, 291
Louvre accords, 77
Low Countries, 15
Lower Saxony, 152
Ludlow, Peter, 109, 114, 123n
Luxembourg, 42, 82, 116, 185,
    207–8n, 220, 221, 226
Luxembourg Compromise, 280,
    296n

M&As (mergers and acquisitions),
    35, 41
MacDougall Report (1978), 33
Madrid, 74, 84, 85, 114, 291,
    292
Maghreb countries, 157, 159–61,
    163, 164, 221
Malta, 90, 101, 103, 159, 164, 165,
    227n
management cultures, 35
Mansfield initiatives, 267–8
Marjolin, Robert, 10
Marshall, John, 294
Marshall Plan, 2
Marx, Karl, 8
Matteucci case, the, 204, 255
MBFR see Multilateral Balanced
    Force Reductions
media regulation, 200, 201–2
Mediterranean countries, 155–67,
    187, 188–9, 225
merger/takeover, 61, 63–4,
    136–7
migration, 136, 161, 177,
    188–90
Milan, 109, 110, 113, 114, 220,
    287
Minc, Alain, 46
Ministry for Inner German
    Relations, 148
Minitel, 42
MITI, 67n
Mitrany, David, 8
Mitterrand, François, 73, 109,
    110, 202, 219, 288
models
    confederal, 280

European, 18
    of an integrated European
        Community, 9
    of the international system, 19
    of meta-bureaucracy, 235
    of the modern nation-state, 19
    traditional, 279
    network, 45
    of transnational collaboration,
        213
    Weberian, 229
monetary
    Compensatory Amounts
        (MCAs), 34
    and fiscal policy, 76–7
    integration, 83–6
    interdependence, changing
        patterns of, 69–86
    Union, 3, 29, 31, 291 see also
        Economic and Monetary
        Union
Monnet, Jean, 3, 10, 29, 108, 109,
    110, 280, 290
Morocco, 159, 163, 164
Multilateral Balanced Force
    Reductions (MBFR), 266,
    267
multilateral negotiations, 213–28
multinational companies, 52, 53,
    58, 59, 64, 66, 208n
Murmansk, 129, 130

nation-state, 1, 5, 7, 17, 19, 22n,
    30, 155, 243
national
    borders, 243
    bureaucracies, 29
    champions, 37–8
    currencies, 80
    economies, 40
    sovereignty, 10
nationalist movement, 16–17,
    132, 150, 152, 200
NATO (North Atlantic Treaty
    Organization), 12, 20, 119,
    120, 128, 162, 165–6, 231,
    232, 235, 245, 257, 261–75
    passim
neo-corporatism, 281
Netherlands, 42, 61, 78, 82, 97,
    116, 175, 180, 184–5, 188
Nicolaïdis, Kalypso, 4, 27–49,
    281
Nordic
    cooperation, 125–40
    Council, 133–4, 138, 199
    countries, 92, 96, 100, 125–40,
        172
normalization committees, 249
Northern Periphery, 92–7
Norway, 72, 85, 128, 130, 136,
    137
nuclear missiles, 275n
Nyborg, 75
Nye, Joseph, S., 285–6